The Shock of the Global

THE 1970S IN PERSPECTIVE

EDITED BY

Niall Ferguson

Charles S. Maier

Erez Manela

Daniel J. Sargent

THE BELKNAP PRESS OF HARVARD UNIVERSITY PRESS

Cambridge, Massachusetts

London, England

2010

Library of Congress Cataloging-in-Publication Data

The shock of the global : the 1970s in perspective / edited by Niall Ferguson . . . [et al.].
p.   cm.
Includes bibliographical references and index.
ISBN 978-0-674-04904-8 (cloth : alk. paper)
1. Nineteen seventies.   2. History, Modern—1945–1989.   3. Globalization—History—
20th century.   4. Globalization—Social aspects—History—20th century.   5. Globalization—
Political aspects—History—20th century.   6. Social change—History—20th century.   7. Culture
shock—History—20th century.   8. Economic history—1971–1990.   9. Social history—1970–
10. World politics—1945–1989.   I. Ferguson, Niall.
D848.S53 2010
909.82′7—dc22   2009035935

To

Ernest R. May

1928–2009

Teacher, mentor, friend

Contents

Acknowledgments

PREPARATION OF THIS BOOK and organization of the conference "The Global 1970s" from which it emerged benefited from the extraordinary goodwill and cooperation of many institutions and individuals.

Thanks are due, first and foremost, to the Weatherhead Center for International Affairs at Harvard University, its director, Beth Simmons, and executive director, Steven Bloomfield, for sponsoring and hosting an intense and lively scholarly gathering, "The Global 1970s." Emmanuel Roman of GLG Partners provided indispensable financial assistance. Harvard's Charles Warren Center for American History, under Joyce Chaplin's leadership, also gave enthusiastic backing.

We owe a special thanks to the friends and colleagues who chaired panels and commented on individual papers. David Armitage, Akira Iriye, Paul Kennedy, Lawrence Summers, Bruce Mazlish, and Thomas Schwartz served in these roles and contributed much to our discussion. Lien-Hang Nguyen and Tim Borstelmann commented on papers in addition to contributing essays. Odd Arne Westad participated in the plenary session that concluded the Global 1970s conference. Our colleague Lizabeth Cohen found time in her first months as Chair of the Harvard History Department to join us for the plenary discussion. Others who traveled to Cambridge to take part in what one participant dubbed our "Seventies Show" included Patrick Cohrs, Garret Martin, Greg Mitrovich, Brad Simpson, Sarah Snyder, and Louise Woodruff.

We were particularly fortunate to have Zbigniew Brzezinski, national security adviser to President Carter (1977–1981) and a former faculty associate at Harvard's Center for International Affairs, present a keynote address and enter into a frank discussion of the era.

All who took part will no doubt join our chorus of appreciation for Adelaide Shalhope, who coordinated and managed the Global 1970s conference on our behalf. Without her hard work, initiative, and organizational skills, this endeavor would not have proceeded so effectively—and deceptively effortlessly—as it did. Other staff members of the Harvard History Department and the Weatherhead Center extended help throughout. Colleagues who shared their insights at early stages in this project's gestation included Rawi Abdelal, Sam Abrams, Jorge Domínguez, Bill Kirby, Noel Mauer, and Kenneth Weisbrode.

Particular gratitude is owed to all who helped bring this book project to completion: to our literary agent, Andrew Wylie; to the staff at the Wylie Agency, especially Rebecca Nagel and Nadia Wilson; and to Harvard University Press and our editor, Kathleen McDermott, for her close engagement with the project and for the patience that a volume of this scope must have demanded. Two anonymous readers devoted particular attention to the essays and offered a series of useful suggestions. We are grateful for their combination of overall enthusiasm and trenchant questions.

We completed this volume in melancholy circumstances, as we mourned the unexpected passing of Ernest R. May. Charles Maier had first studied with Ernest May as an undergraduate in 1960; across a generation he was a mentor to two of us in our graduate studies and friend and colleague to us all. For half a century his name was synonymous with international history at Harvard and beyond. He was a giant of the field and a man of disarming humility, unusual decency, and great generosity.

More than most scholars, Ernest gave freely of himself—to public service, to his students, and to intellectual camaraderie. His bibliography includes a surprising number of coauthored projects, from his book with Richard Neustadt on the uses of history, to his (unpublished) history of the strategic arms race, to his more recent collaborations with Philip Zelikow, including their work on the 9/11 Commission Report.

While Ernest resisted our entreaties to join this project as an editor, he participated fully in our planning meetings and contributed much to this enterprise. With his commitment to scholarly collaboration very much in mind, we hope that he would approve of what *The Shock of the Global* has become. We dedicate the volume to his memory.

The Shock of the Global

Crisis, What Crisis?

The 1970s and the Shock of the Global

NIALL FERGUSON

ON JANUARY 10, 1979, on his return from an economic summit held on the sunny Caribbean island of Guadeloupe, the British prime minister, James Callaghan, was asked by a journalist: "What is your general approach, in view of the mounting chaos in the country at the moment?" Callaghan replied: "Well, that's a judgment that you are making, and I promise you that if you look at it from outside, and perhaps you're taking rather a parochial view at the moment, I don't think that other people in the world would share the view that there is mounting chaos. . . . Please don't run down your country by talking about mounting chaos." At the end of the conference Callaghan joked that he doubted he could "even find a cup of coffee" if there were such mounting chaos. This show of insouciance did not go down well with the British press. The front page of the following day's *Sun* newspaper bore the headline "CRISIS, WHAT CRISIS?"[1]

The seventies are indeed still popularly remembered—in the English-speaking world at least—as a time of crisis. The crisis was economic, as inflation rates rose into double digits and growth rates slumped. It was political, with one head of state famously driven to resign to avoid impeachment. It was social, as abortion, crime, class conflict, marital breakdown, and racial tension all increased. It was a crisis of popular culture, too: the Beatles split up; Elvis died; ABBA was scarcely a substitute. For all these and many other reasons, as Bruce Shulman has said, the decade is often represented as "the sickly, neglected, disappointing stepsister to that brash, bruising blockbuster" which had preceded it.[2]

1

In one memorable formulation, however, the crisis of the seventies was primarily a *personal* crisis. For Tom Wolfe, the "Me" Decade was a time of rampant solipsism.

> The trainer had said, "Take your finger off the repress button!" Let it gush up and pour out!
>
> And now, as she lies here on the floor of the banquet hall of the Ambassador Hotel with 249 other souls, she knows exactly what he meant. She can feel it *all,* all of the pain, and on top of the pain all the humiliation, and for the first time in her life she has permission from the Management, from herself, and from everyone around her to let the feeling gush forth. So she starts moaning.
>
> "Oooooooooooooooohhhhhh!"

The woman in question is in fact preoccupied with the physical and emotional crisis caused by her hemorrhoids. But with the trainer's encouragement, everyone in the room is able to focus on—and moan about—his or her very own crisis: "My husband! my wife! my homosexuality! my inability to communicate, my self-hatred, self-destruction, craven fears, puling weaknesses, primordial horrors, premature ejaculation, impotence, frigidity, rigidity, subservience, laziness, alcoholism, major vices, minor vices, grim habits, twisted psyches, tortured souls . . ." While other journalists preferred to "interpret all new political phenomena in terms of recent disasters, frustration, protest, the decline of civilization[,] . . . the Grim Slide," Wolfe suggested that the real crisis of the 1970s was an inner crisis. The spirit of the age was introspective. It was also transformative: the dream of "changing one's personality—remaking, remodeling, elevating, and polishing one's very *self* . . . and observing, studying, and doting on it. (Me!)" Indeed, "the appeal was simple enough. It is summed up in the notion 'Let's talk about *Me.*' No matter whether you managed to renovate your personality . . . or not, you had finally focused your attention and your energies on the most fascinating subject on earth: *Me.*"[3] This narcissistic quest for self-renewal, Wolfe argued, was the foundation of that eclectic religious reawakening which he saw as the most important American trend of the period, from Primal Scream to the Jesus People, from Uri Geller to Sun Myung Moon. It explained other seventies trends, too: the rise of divorce, wife-swapping, even pornographic magazines.

Wolfe's was the view from within. Yet viewed from without—viewed, as it were, from the final frontier so recently opened up for exploration by the spacemen—the crisis of the seventies was as much global as it was personal. Solipsism played little if any part, after all, in the expulsion of the Palestinians from Jordan in 1970, the secession of East Pakistan (Bangladesh) in 1971, the killings of Israeli athletes at the Munich Olympics in 1972, the military coup in Chile in September 1973, the Middle Eastern crisis of the following month, the Iranian Revolution of 1979, or the Soviet invasion of Afghanistan that same year. Pol Pot's murderous regime in Cambodia was scarcely to be understood in Wolfe's terms. Nor was Lebanon's civil war. Nor were Ethiopia's famine and revolution. Richard Nixon's resignation over Watergate will long remain the best known of the political crises of the 1970s, and perhaps the self-destructive paranoia that lay at the heart of the scandal was to some degree emblematic of the "Me" Decade. But around the world no fewer than eleven other heads of state were assassinated during the 1970s, more than in any other decade in modern history. Terrorism, a negligible phenomenon before 1968, became a recurrent problem from the Falls Road to Entebbe Airport. Any attempt to write a global history of the 1970s must make sense of this kind of crisis. Were the seventies characterized by exceptional levels or distinctive kinds of political violence around the world? And if so, why?

There is of course the obvious objection that the years 1970 to 1979 no more form a significant chronological sub-period than the years 1969 to 1978 or the years 1971 to 1980. Why *those* ten years? And why ten years rather than five or twenty-five? The answer is, of course, that there is always a degree of arbitrariness about historical periodization. Scholars generally work with the units of time to which potential readers are already accustomed; if enough people have a sense of "the seventies" as a distinctive era, then the exercise of reexamination is probably worthwhile. And if, on closer inspection, the supposedly distinctive features of the seventies first appeared in 1968 and continued until 1981 or even 1989, we may speak without too much apology of the "long 1970s," in the spirit of Eric Hobsbawm's "long nineteenth century," beginning in 1789 and continuing until 1914.

Crisis, what crisis? The 1970s were certainly "years of upheaval," in Henry Kissinger's phrase. But were they really more crisis-ridden than previous or subsequent decades? According to the Correlates of War project, there were seven interstate wars fought during the 1970s, three colonial

Table I.1. Violence in the Cold War, by decade

| | Number of wars | | | | Estimated deaths | | | | World population | |
	Interstate	Extrastate	Intrastate	Total	Interstate	Extrastate	Intrastate	Total	At mid-decade	War deaths
1950s	3	6	11	20	917,056	68,000	98,900	1,083,956	2,757,399,000	0.04%
1960s	6	3	16	25	1,057,224	14,500	1,018,857	2,090,581	3,337,974,000	0.06%
1970s	7	3	25	35	66,901	19,000	2,621,254	2,707,155	4,073,740,000	0.07%
1980s	4	0	19	23	1,256,145	—	1,742,132	2,998,277	4,843,947,000	0.06%

Source: Meredith Reid Sarkees, "The Correlates of War Data on War: An Update to 1997," *Conflict Management and Peace Science* 18, no. 1 (2000): 123–144.

Note: Wars are allocated to the decade in which they began.

(extrastate) wars, and no fewer than twenty-five civil (intrastate) wars, giving a total of thirty-five. For the 1950s the total number of wars was lower—twenty—and for the 1960s it was also twenty-five. For the 1980s the total was twenty-three. By this simple measure, then, the 1970s were a time of crisis. As Table I.1 shows, however, when account is taken of estimated war-induced mortality, the differences between the decades are much less pronounced. In absolute terms, the wars that began in the 1970s killed more people than the wars that began in the 1950s and the 1960s; but the wars of the 1980s killed even more. And relative to world population, the death toll attributable to war in the 1970s was not especially remarkable. Likewise, we should beware of exaggerating the importance of terrorism in the seventies. According to what is probably the most comprehensive dataset, there were just over 5,000 fatalities and injuries due to international terrorism in the 1970s. But the figure for the 1980s was 13,206, and the figure for the 1990s was 23,205. The figure for the first decade of the present century may very well end up being higher still.[4]

Because of the attention that has been paid to the military coups that occurred in countries such as Chile, the seventies also have the reputation as a bad decade for democracy. Yet as Table I.2 shows, this reputation is not especially warranted. In 28 percent of countries there was an improvement in terms of political rights, compared with 24 percent where there was a deterioration. For civil liberties, 24 percent of countries saw improvements; in 30 percent things got worse. In just under half the world's countries there was no change. When the total sample of countries is weighted by population size, a similar picture emerges. Whereas the percentage of the world's population living under democracy declined from around 41 percent to around 35 percent between 1960 and 1970, it rose slightly between 1970 and 1980.[5] In other words, while democracy did not

Table I.2. Democracy in the 1970s

	Better	Worse
Political rights	28	24
Civil liberties	24	30

Source: Freedom House, http://www.freedomhouse.org/template.cfm?page=439.

Note: The table shows the percentage of countries whose Freedom House scores improved or deteriorated between 1972 (when the surveys began) and 1979.

stride forward as it certainly did in the 1980s and 1990s, it did not retreat in the way that it had in the 1930s. As for coups d'état, the best available dataset from the Center for Systemic Peace indicates that there were 119 coups around the world in the 1960s, 135 in the 1970s, but 140 in the 1980s.[6]

In economic terms, too, we should beware of exaggerating the scale of the 1970s crisis. This author has clear memories of the "great inflation" of the period: his first ever publication was a letter to the *Glasgow Herald*, published in 1974, complaining about the rising price of children's shoes. With average consumer price inflation running at just under 13 percent, the United Kingdom unquestionably had a more serious problem with inflation in the 1970s than in the 1960s or the 1980s. Indeed, when the annual inflation rate peaked at 27 percent in August 1975, it was the worst inflation the country experienced in the entire twentieth century—worse than in either of the world wars. Yet not all developed countries, as Table I.3 shows, suffered double-digit inflation for the decade as a whole, although most experienced it for at least some months (Germany being the sole exception in the sample). Out of a larger sample of seventy-one countries for which inflation data are available, only one (Indonesia) had higher inflation in the 1960s than in the 1970s. But 48 out of 105—just under half—had higher inflation in the 1980s than in the 1970s. Roughly the same proportion (52 out of 106) succeeded in keeping average inflation below 10 percent between 1970 and 1979. Of the countries with the highest average inflation rate during the seventies—Argentina (133 percent) and Chile (175 percent)—the former had even higher inflation in the eighties (566 percent), while the latter reduced inflation to 21 percent, which was lower than in the sixties.[7]

The picture is no less equivocal when we turn to economic growth. As Tom Wolfe put it, the postwar decades had "pumped money into every class level of the [American] population on a scale without parallel in any country in history. . . . One can't even call workingmen *blue collar* any longer. . . . They all have on $35 Superstar Qiana sport shirts with elephant collars and 1940s Airbrush Wallpaper Flowers Buncha Grapes and Seashell designs all over them."[8] The early 1970s brought this postwar boom to a painful end. There were at least six quarters of negative growth. According to the National Bureau of Economic Research, the decade saw two recessions: one that lasted from December 1969 to November 1970, the other from November 1973 to March 1975.[9] The U.S. economy con-

Table 1.3. Consumer price inflation (%) in the 1960s, 1970s, and 1980s

	Belgium	France	Germany	Greece	Italy	Netherlands	Portugal	Spain	UK	USA
1960s	2.9	3.8	2.5	2.0	3.9	4.2	4.3	6.1	3.8	2.4
1970s	7.1	8.8	4.9	12.4	12.3	7.0	18.3	14.4	12.6	7.1
1980s	4.9	7.4	2.9	19.5	11.2	2.9	17.7	10.3	7.5	5.6

Source: OECD.

tracted by −0.5 percent in 1974 and −0.2 percent the following year. Nevertheless, this poor performance needs to be set in context. There had been recessions in 1948–49, 1953–54, 1957–58, and 1960–61, and the output losses had in fact been greater in the recessions of the fondly remembered fifties. Moreover, the recessions of January to July 1980 and July 1981 to November 1982 were in a number of respects more painful than those of the previous decade. The economy contracted by −1.9 percent in 1982. On average, it is true, growth was lower in the 1970s than in the 1960s: real gross domestic product increased at an average annual rate of 3.6 percent compared with 4.6 percent between 1960 and 1969. But the figure for the 1980s, usually portrayed as a decade of economic success, was actually worse: just 3.4 percent.[10] The British experience was not so different. The recession of 1980–81 was deeper than the recession of 1974–75. Only by comparison with the recent past—the Swinging Sixties—were the 1970s a time of crisis; the future had worse in store, as governments and central banks on both sides of the Atlantic engineered sharp contractions in order to bring down inflation (and, some would say, to break the power of organized labor). This becomes even more apparent when we turn to the data on unemployment. It seemed very shocking when the seasonally adjusted U.S. unemployment rate rose from 4.6 percent in October 1973 to 9 percent in May 1975. But at its peak in November 1982 it was just under 11 percent. When the Conservative Party launched its "Labour Isn't Working" poster in late 1978—showing a long queue of jobless benefit claimants—the unemployment rate in Britain was just above 4 percent. At its peak in late 1986 it reached 10.9 percent.[11] Only Arthur Okun's "misery index"—the sum of the inflation rate and the unemployment rate—makes the seventies look worse than the eighties, though the difference is more striking for Britain than for the United States.

The value of the global perspective becomes clear when we consider economic performance in the world as a whole. According to the World Bank's data on real per capita gross domestic product, 61 percent of the world's countries grew more slowly in the 1970s than in the 1960s, while 69 percent grew more slowly in the 1980s than in the 1970s. As Table I.4 shows, the seventies were better than the sixties for both the East Asia–Pacific region and Latin America including the Caribbean, while the eighties were worse than the seventies for every region except East Asia. It is true that the estimated growth rate for the world economy very nearly

Table I.4. Real per capita gross domestic product, average annual growth
by decade

	1960–1970	1970–1980	1980–1990
Worldwide	3.5	1.8	1.3
High income: OECD	4.4	2.6	2.5
East Asia and Pacific	2.4	4.6	5.6
Latin America and Caribbean	2.4	3.5	−0.8
Sub-Saharan Africa	2.6	0.7	−1.2

Source: World Bank, World Development Indicators.

halved between the 1960s and the 1970s. But if global growth was even lower in the subsequent decade, it becomes difficult to represent the seventies as especially crisis-prone. Moreover, recent surveys of macroeconomic and financial crises confirm that the period between 1970 and 1979 was not exceptional. Indeed it emerges from Robert Barro's recent work as having suffered markedly fewer severe economic shocks (declines in output greater than 10 percent) than most other decades of the twentieth century. Only Chile (in 1975) and Peru (in 1979) suffered a contraction of this magnitude, whereas in the subsequent decade no fewer than eight countries did (Argentina, Chile, Mexico, Peru, the Philippines, South Africa, Uruguay, and Venezuela).[12] Similarly, the 1970s saw very few sovereign defaults compared with the 1980s and 1990s, and far fewer than in the 1930s. The rare exceptions include Chile (1972 and 1974), India (1972), Peru (1976), Turkey (1978), and Nicaragua (1979). The same is true of banking crises, currency crises, and extreme bouts of high or hyperinflation. The only banking crises to occur in the 1970s were in Uruguay (1971); Britain (1974); Chile and the Central African Republic (1976); Germany, Israel, and Spain (1977); Venezuela (1978); and Thailand (1979). Of these the most dramatic was probably Spain's, which brought nearly half the country's banks to the brink of insolvency. By comparison, during the 1980s such crises afflicted more than a quarter of the world economy (weighting countries by their share of global income).[13]

Why, then, has the reputation for economic crisis stuck so adhesively to the seventies? Part of the answer may be the dominance of the literature on the period by Anglophone academics. Professors have typically lacked the capacity for collective action which is necessary to raise nominal salaries in response to inflation. British university lecturers were particularly

vulnerable to inflation in the 1970s because of the existence of a national age-related pay scale. The combination of double-digit inflation and
public sector pay freezes seemed to threaten a generation of dons with
proletarianization. Moreover, because of their social background, academics were also more likely than average citizens to own financial assets. In
both America and Britain the 1970s saw negative inflation-adjusted returns on both stocks and bonds—the first time that had happened since
the First World War. So professors could not even rely on their investments to compensate them for sharp declines in their real pay. As for the
money to be made from writing books and other extracurricular activities,
this was substantially reduced by very high marginal tax rates. The lamen-
tations recorded in A. J. P. Taylor's diary of the period summed up the
mood of a generation of dons.[14] Like most of his generation, Taylor was a
man of the Left, though he was also proud of his ability to earn money
from his prolific writing and broadcasting (a consolation after the disap-
pointment of being passed over for the Regius Chair at Oxford). He
worked hard, lived modestly (spending much of his life in Magdalen College housing), and managed his own finances meticulously. Divorce was
his sole extravagance. But this Victorian thriftiness was the worst possible
strategy for surviving the seventies. As Kathleen Burk has demonstrated,
Taylor's income from books, broadcasting, and journalism collapsed in real
terms after 1969.[15] His wealth was also severely depleted because, as
he told his mistress and future third wife, the Hungarian historian Éva
Haraszti, "all [his] resources were in stocks and shares" in November
1973—the eve of one of the greatest stock market crashes in British history, which saw the Financial Times All Share Index decline by more than
half.[16] "The economic situation here is terrible," he told Haraszti in May
1974. "Prices go up every day, and soon the pound will be almost worth-
less. It is all right for workers and such-like who can push up their wages,
but it is ruin for those with fixed incomes. I can't see at all what is going to
happen to me, and I am too old to discover new ways of earning a living.
The only consolation is that there are many thousands in the same position."[17] Two months later he was even more despondent:

> You can't realize how near we are to catastrophe. Many serious judges
> think that all our banks may close their doors in a few months' time. Prices
> have doubled within the year and are going up faster than ever. My income
> does not go up. Indeed, it gradually goes down as I write less. . . . My pen-

sion and my insurance policies which will start in two years' time are calculated according to the pounds I paid in the past, and these are now worth only a few shillings. You must remember a time in Hungary when all pensioners, including even professors, were starving or very near it, and we may come to that soon.[18]

Taylor was right to speculate that he was not alone. As Table I.5 makes clear, the inflation-adjusted returns on both stocks and bonds were negative in the 1970s. Not just for aging professors but for a large proportion of the Anglophone middle class, accustomed to deriving a significant portion of their income from investments, the seventies were the worst decade of the twentieth century aside from 1910 to 1919, when bourgeois portfolios had been hit even harder by world war and the first serious inflation in a hundred years. That experience had also triggered a bout of cultural pessimism.

For someone Taylor's age, the trauma of financial crisis was in some measure compounded by the strained relations with students (not to mention teenage sons) that characterized the period after 1968. Not everyone would agree with Jeremi Suri that a "global revolution" began in that year.[19] The student protests at Berkeley, Columbia, and Nanterre had relatively little in common with the Prague Spring, much less the Cultural Revolution in China, at least as far as their stated goals were concerned.

Table I.5. Real returns on stocks and bonds, United States and United Kingdom

	United States		United Kingdom	
	Stocks	Bonds	Stocks	Bonds
1900–1909	7.1	0.0	4.2	0.0
1910–1919	−2.5	−4.9	−4.5	−9.3
1920–1929	14.9	6.9	13.9	12.1
1930–1939	1.9	6.3	4.4	4.1
1940–1949	4.0	−3.1	6.2	0.2
1950–1959	15.7	−1.8	13.6	−3.6
1960–1969	5.5	−0.7	4.9	−1.1
1970–1979	−0.6	−3.0	−1.3	−4.1
1980–1989	11.0	7.6	15.5	7.1

Source: Global Financial Data, Barclays Capital, *Equity Gilt Study* (London: Barclays, 2008).

But what these different upheavals did have in common was youth. The *soixante-huitards* really were "talkin' 'bout their generation": the postwar baby boom generation, more numerous and more prosperous than the young had been for many years. The change was especially pronounced in the United States, where the proportion of the population aged between sixteen and twenty-four surged from 11.5 percent in 1957 to a peak of 17.2 percent in 1978. Elsewhere the increase was smaller, but the peak share of the young in population was even higher. In South America by the end of the 1970s more than a fifth of the population were aged between fifteen and twenty-four.[20] The effects of the postwar baby boom were amplified by the expansion of higher education. Before the Second World War, only a tiny elite of young people had attended university, even in the United States, where students in higher education accounted for just under 1 percent of the entire population. In Europe the shares ranged downward from 0.29 percent in Austria to just 0.07 percent in Portugal. By 1968 these proportions had increased by factors of between 2.5 and 12.8. In the United States there were now nearly 6.7 million college and university students, equivalent to 3.3 percent of the population. The expansion of higher education significantly increased the presence at American universities of two groups who had previously been discriminated against in various ways: African Americans and women (whose share in the U.S. student population had been significantly reduced by the 1944 GI Bill, which guaranteed veterans a college or vocational education). Already by 1968 the female proportion of the student body had risen back to 40 percent (compared with 29 percent twenty years before). By 1979 the women's share had risen above half. Perhaps all this also helps to explain the mood of crisis that afflicted so many senior academics in the 1970s. Not only were their own material circumstances getting worse, but also they found themselves accorded significantly less respect than they had been accustomed to in the classrooms and lecture halls—to say nothing of the senior common rooms, now invaded by the trendy leftist lecturers personified by Malcolm Bradbury's "History Man" Howard Kirk.[21]

Even at home there was no respite. For surely nothing changed more radically in Western (and especially Anglophone) societies in the 1970s than the role of women. Economic discrimination was reduced, divorce was made more equitable, contraception and abortion were made (in most countries) legal. Today these changes are conventionally celebrated as milestones on the great progressive pathway. But even to a liberal-minded professor there was much here that was unnerving—especially as elderly academics were precisely the people radical feminists most enjoyed taunting. Published in 1970, Germaine Greer's book *The Female Eunuch* remains one of the indispensable documents of the era, not least for its memorably fierce denunciation of the "enemies" of "the revolutionary woman": "the doctors, psychiatrists, health visitors, priests, marriage counsellors, policemen, magistrates and genteel reformers." Women, Greer urged, must "stop loving the victors in violent encounters. . . . Women must not marry. . . . Women must reject their role as the principal consumers in the capitalist state. . . . They should form household cooperatives . . . and use cosmetics strictly for fun." Characteristically for the times, she also held out the hope that feminism would make it possible to skip the less appealing coercive phases in the Marxist model of revolutionary progress. "Women's liberation, if it abolishes the patriarchal family," she argued, "will abolish a necessary substructure of the authoritarian state, and once that withers away Marx will have come true willy-nilly." Greer's "fantasy" was that "it may be possible to leap the steps of revolution and arrive somehow at liberty and communism without strategy or revolutionary discipline."[22] That one sentence says it all about the seventies. Small wonder Greer makes a cameo appearance in Wolfe's "Me" Decade, setting fire to her own hair in a London restaurant.

Crisis, what crisis? Charles Maier—himself an academic during the seventies—argues in this volume that the period constituted, along with the decade before World War I and the 1930s, one of three systemic crises of the twentieth century, though unlike the others it did not produce a major war. If the crisis that had brought about the First World War was a "crisis of political representation" and the crisis that had produced the Second was a "crisis within capitalism," then the crisis that (perhaps narrowly) failed to produce the Third World War was a "crisis of industrial society." On both sides of the Iron Curtain industrialized economies had to attempt the transition to what the sociologist Daniel Bell called the "post-industrial society," one that would be characterized by a structural shift from manufacturing to services, the increasing importance of science and technology, and the dominance of technical elites expert in these fields.[23] Western societies ultimately achieved this transition but passed through a purgatory of stagflation on the way. Eastern (in the sense of Soviet bloc) countries failed to do so, experiencing little more than straight stagnation, with physical shortages in place of rising prices, dearth instead of dearness. The political consequences revealed themselves in the 1980s. While the English-speaking world tilted away from the postwar institutions and policies that had so expanded the role of the state in economic life, the Communist system failed to reform itself and then, in 1989, collapsed. Yet no one was to know that in the 1970s. From the vantage of 1979, indeed, it seemed to some observers equally likely that the Soviet system would endure and the Western system decline and fall.

The metanarrative of a Western "slide," satirized by Wolfe, was indeed remarkably pervasive and persistent. "I think of what happened to Greece and Rome," Nixon mused to media executives in 1971. "What is left—only the pillars." Like his national security adviser Henry Kissinger, who detected on unruly college campuses the sinister scent of Weimar, Nixon was haunted by discouraging historical parallels. Yet history was only one of many bases for pessimism. For Alvin Toffler, the postindustrial society would subject people to "shattering stress and disorientation": "future shock" was as much to be feared as the repetition of declines past.[24] For the Club of Rome, the crisis would be demographic: the world was heading for a Malthusian reckoning as a result of overpopulation. The 1975 report of the Trilateral Commission, by contrast, fretted about a "crisis of democracy" due in part to the "growing multinationalization of formerly domestic issues." With the nuclear arsenals of the superpowers reaching their peaks (and with the Soviet Union now ahead by many measures), there also seemed ample reason to fear a Third World War, which General Sir John Hackett imagined breaking out in August 1985. As Matthew Connelly shows, these were only the most respectable of a host of millenarian visions that haunted the human imagination in the 1970s. While American evangelicals looked forward with a strange enthusiasm to "seeing Armageddon," some Muslims also detected an imminent apocalypse. With somewhat stronger evidence, as J. R. McNeill demonstrates, environmentalists and ecologists fretted about man's "crimes against the biosphere," from the algal blooms in Chesapeake Bay to the shrinking of the Aral Sea. The unintended consequences of the "Green Revolution" combined with highly publicized oil spills and accidents at nuclear power stations and chemical plants to raise public concern about the negative externalities of economic growth.

There was, in short, a widespread *perception* of crisis in the 1970s—and very often a crisis that was global in scale. Although American involvement in the Vietnam War ended ignominiously in 1975, as Lien-Hang Nguyen shows, the ramifications of that defeat extended far beyond Indochina, fundamentally changing American domestic politics, helping shatter the unity of the Communist bloc, and inspiring Third World revolutionaries from Central America to the Middle East. A key preoccupation of this volume is the extent to which political leaders, particularly in the United States, correctly analyzed and responded to this "shock of the global." For Daniel Sargent, it was the 1973 oil crisis that made Henry Kissinger first feel what he called the "birth pains of interdependence." For Francis Gavin it was the achievement of nuclear parity—at a terrifyingly high level—that forced not only Kissinger but many other strategic thinkers as well to question the centrality of nuclear deterrence to U.S. foreign policy. Jeremi Suri argues that even before Kissinger became national security adviser, he had already mapped out a new concept of international order based on some kind of polycentric federalism.

Some of the contributors assembled here are highly critical of the way in which these and other insights were applied (or not). For Mark Lawrence, Kissinger never successfully reoriented American policy beyond an "axis of history" that he saw stretching from Moscow through Bonn to Washington and on to Tokyo. Despite his repeated allusions to the new phenomenon of interdependence, he was in practice indifferent to the fates of countries in the Southern Hemisphere, regarding their internal affairs as mere subplots in the great superpower struggle. Not until the Carter administration was policy even slightly influenced by the intergovernmental and nongovernmental organizations that proliferated during the decade. Ayesha Jalal is even more scathing about American foreign policy: from the Bangladesh crisis to the invasion of Afghanistan, policy toward the Islamic world was, in her view, a succession of unmitigated blunders. Indeed the fateful growth of Islamic fundamentalism in Pakistan and Afghanistan was a direct if largely unintended result of an American policy that continued to treat the Cold War as a two-player zero-sum game. Other contributors, however, make it clear that there were in fact significant changes to the international order in the 1970s, and that these were at least partly American in inspiration. Michael Morgan's "explosion of international civil society" made human rights an increasingly important preoccupation of American lawmakers such as Donald Fraser, Henry "Scoop" Jackson, and Charles Vanik. Kissinger was certainly irked by what he saw as their counterproductive intrusions into his domain. Yet the Helsinki Final Act, complete with its provisions on human rights, was negotiated and signed when he was secretary of state. Like the joint program to eradicate smallpox discussed by Erez Manela, Helsinki represented a fundamental change in the character of relations between the superpowers. In the same vein Glenda Sluga delineates the simultaneous transformation of the United Nations that followed from decolonization and the admission of newly independent states—though how far the increasingly assertive General Assembly represented the "truly global society" of which Kissinger had spoken in 1975 was open to debate. The succession of international environmental accords detailed by J. R. McNeill provides a good illustration of interdependence in action. (It is again noteworthy that nearly all were signed before Carter entered the White House.) From the Christian organizations studied by Andrew Preston to the feminists who participated in the International Woman's Year (1975), myriad new influences were indeed being brought to bear on international relations. When Kissinger appointed a man to lead the U.S. delegation to the IWY conference in Mexico City, as Jocelyn Olcott notes, there were indignant protests. But the significant thing is surely that these were heeded, and a female co-chair was hastily added.

In no field was the shock of the global more palpable than in the economic realm. Traditionally, as we have seen, historians have viewed inflation as the principal problem of the period, and the explanations they have offered have ranged from the laxity of Western central banks to the excessive power of organized labor. The contributors to this volume offer an alternative view. Alan Taylor argues that the continued liberalization of trade was the essential precursor for that "great retransformation" which would do away with the postwar restrictions on international capital flows. Though earlier writers have paid little attention to the phenomenon, the decline in tax burdens on trade was one of the most important underlying trends of the seventies; as Taylor shows, countries went down this road of liberalization more or less readily according to the severity of their sufferings forty years before, in the Great Depression. Moreover, as Daniel Sargent points out, the seventies also saw the first phase of financial liberalization. Arising from the Eurodollar market of offshore dollar deposits, the Eurobond market was born in the late 1960s and flourished in the 1970s, a harbinger as much of global as of European financial integration.[25] It was the resulting strains on the American capital account, not the current account, that undermined the Bretton Woods system, severing the dollar's link to gold in 1971 and finally breaking up the entire system of transatlantic fixed exchange rates two years later. As Sargent shows, perhaps the biggest of all the global shocks in the period was the oil export embargo and price hike imposed by the Arab members of the Organization of Petroleum Exporting Countries (OPEC) in 1973. Though taken by surprise, Western policymakers were not slow to make institutional adjustments in response. The creation of the International Energy Agency (IEA) in 1974 and the first Group of Six (G-6) summit at Rambouillet in 1975 were important and enduring additions to the international system. Yet perhaps the most striking thing was an act of omission: the successful American opposition to any expansion of the role of the International Monetary Fund. The U.S. Treasury's view prevailed that the recycling of petrodollars (the dollar surpluses rapidly accumulated by the oil exporters) should be left to the private sector—in other words, the banks of Wall Street and the City of London. The IMF was henceforth confined to crisis management, bailing out the desperate (such as Britain in 1976), but with only limited influence over the big players. As became increasingly clear after the Bonn Summit of 1978, a world without fixed exchange rates, in which capital was increasingly free to move across borders, and in which national governments pursued monetary policies with at least one eye to the "political business cycle," was bound to be a world of currency volatility.

It was not merely "hot" money—portfolio investment—that began to cross borders more easily in the 1970s. With the rise of the multinational corporation, foreign direct investment also grew. Vernie Oliveiro shows how big a change this made to the international system. Within the United States, business organizations such as the National Foreign Trade Council and the National Association of Manufacturers became powerful lobbyists against protectionism. Abroad, anxieties about the power and practices of multinationals resulted in the OECD's Guidelines on Multinational Enterprises, released in June 1976. The real significance of these lay in the fact that they were only guidelines. Aside from the Foreign Corrupt Practices Act of 1977, remarkably little was done to circumscribe the operations of the multinationals. Meanwhile, as Louis Hyman demonstrates, the first important steps were taken to liberalize and galvanize the U.S. mortgage market, with the privatization of the Federal National Mortgage Association ("Fannie Mae"), the creation of the Federal Home Loan Mortgage Corporation, and the launch of the first mortgage-backed securities (MBS) in February 1970. These regulatory changes, too, had global implications. Within a short space of time, as Hyman shows, foreign purchases accounted for between 5 and 10 percent of the total MBS market.

This, more than the problem of inflation, was what made the seventies significant. For capital market liberalization, especially in the United States, pointed the way to what I have called the "Age of Leverage." The rise of international debts was not, as Jeremy Adelman points out, by any means inevitable. Indeed the bout of price and exchange rate volatility that followed the breakdown of Bretton Woods strongly inclined some politicians—for example, the French Socialists—to turn back the clock and reimpose capital controls and other financial regulations. But the temptation to tap international pools of capital was simply too great, especially when the real interest rates that sovereign debtors had to pay were so low. No one in Latin America foresaw the disastrous effects of the monetary tightening in the United States that began after Paul Volcker became Federal Reserve chairman in August 1979. Nor did the politburos of Eastern Europe anticipate that borrowing from Western banks might be a primrose path to perdition, though the ghosts of Marx and Lenin surely ought to have warned them. As Stephen Kotkin observes, the difference turned out to be, ironically, that while Latin American countries defaulted on their debts—beginning with Mexico in 1982—the Poles and Hungarians soldiered grimly on toward the year of reckoning, 1989. By that time the swelling torrent of international capital had moved on to East Asia, where there were rather better uses for foreign money.

Crisis, what crisis? Perhaps Jim Callaghan was right after all. Perhaps there really was no crisis in the 1970s, beyond the perceived crisis of economically distressed Anglophone intellectuals of a certain age. It was more that the seeds of future crises were sown at that time. The real shock of the global turned out to be this: that liberalizing international capital markets would raise the growth rate of the world economy, but retaining national sovereignty in the realm of monetary policy would raise the frequency of financial crises. This was the paradox of globalization: the more the world economy was "optimized," the more complex and therefore crisis prone the system became.[26] Those who led the political backlash in the West against the perceived crisis of the 1970s underestimated this, believing—as they had been taught by Friedrich von Hayek or Milton Friedman—that so long as market forces were given free play, Adam Smith's Invisible Hand could never develop a tremor. When tight monetary policies plus deregulation combined to cause a bigger economic crisis than anything seen in the seventies, the neoliberals were unapologetic. Only such a painful "regime change" could break the vicious circle of inflationary expectations. Perhaps the remarkable thing, with the benefit of hindsight, is that this "regime change" was achieved in so many countries without the overthrow of democratic institutions. Those who had read Michael Crozier, Samuel Huntington, and Joji Watanuki's *Crisis of Democracy* might well have anticipated many Chiles. In fact the overwhelming majority of governments that adopted policies such as monetarism, privatization, and financial deregulation did so while retaining—and in many cases actually acquiring—democratic institutions.[27] Less than fifteen years separated the ominous "crisis of democracy" from the euphoric "end of history," when the institutions of the free market and representative government supposedly stood poised to take over the whole world.

As this volume makes clear, nevertheless, the seventies are probably better not understood as some kind of prelude to the rise of the New Right in the eighties. As Andrew Preston shows, the evangelical movement that was the dominant force in the Third Great Awakening contained within it at least two political contradictions. It was ultrapatriotic yet deeply suspicious of the federal government. And it was economically individualistic yet also wary of what one "born again" pastor called "this monolithic commercial system which has controlled the world and today controls our lives." Although the evangelicals ended up being successfully yoked to the Reagan Republican bandwagon by the Moral Majority, they were not talking remotely the same language as the devotees of the Laffer curve—not to mention the neoconservative critics of détente—who were already on board and holding the reins. Indeed, Rebecca Sheehan suggests that the evangelical movement is better understood as a product *of* the seventies rather than a reaction against it. Tom Wolfe would surely agree that "Operation Penetration"—a recruitment drive by the Campus Crusade for Christ after its "Christian Woodstock" held in Dallas in 1972—nicely epitomized, with its surely unintended double entendre, the zeitgeist of the "Me" Decade. In 1966 John Lennon had claimed that the Beatles were "more popular than Jesus," but just five years later it was Jesus Christ who was the superstar, thanks to the eponymous rock opera by Tim Rice and Andrew Lloyd Webber.

Perhaps, then, we should think of the 1970s as having generated multiple backlashes: not only the backlash that produced Reagan and Thatcher, but also the backlash within the Soviet Communist Party that produced Gorbachev and his fatal reforms (a far more lethal solvent of the system, according to Stephen Kotkin, than the few and far between dissidents) and the backlash within the Chinese Communist Party that produced Deng Xiaoping and his much more successful reforms. Odd Arne Westad's chapter makes one wonder if the single most portentous event of the 1970s was in fact Deng's visit in 1979 to the United States, which so astonished him with its technological superiority that he could not sleep for several days. What Deng saw was not a country debilitated by crises of stagflation and democratic distemper but the world's economic superpower. Alongside the crisis from which China was emerging—the one caused by the lunacies of the Cultural Revolution—America's much-debated "malaise" paled into invisibility. The other great backlash of the era was, of course, the fundamentalism that swept the Islamic world. This too was in some measure a backlash against socialism, though the "Great Satan" of capitalist America and its ally Israel were the Islamists' principal bêtes noires. But it was also, as Jalal argues, a product of calculation by elites from Riyadh to Islamabad, as well as—needless to add—miscalculation by American policymakers.

The Soviet collapse, the Chinese miracle, the Islamist terror: all these huge shocks lay ahead. The essays gathered here therefore tend to recast the 1970s more as the seedbed of future crises than as the crisis conjuncture itself—the decade when autarky yielded to interdependence, but before the full implications of interdependence became clear. In terms of political violence and economic instability, the seventies were in truth an unexceptional decade. Indeed, as I have suggested, the period's dire reputation may owe more to the bad experiences of Anglo-American academics, caught between inflation and student radicalism, than to any measurable increases in global disorder. A. J. P. Taylor was much too gloomy about the West's prospects; it was Deng who got it right. Stagflation or no stagflation, after all, there was a major technological advance in virtually every year of the 1970s:

1970   bar codes
1971   the microprocessor, computer floppy disks, computerized axial
         tomography (CAT scanning), and the gamma electric cell
1972   e-mail

1973   the catalytic converter
1974   the pocket calculator
1975   Altair, the first home computer
1976   Betamax and VHS videocassette recorders
1977   magnetic resonance imaging (MRI)
1978   in vitro fertilization and ultrasound
1979   the Sony Walkman

Nor were these the only indicators of progress. Lyme disease and Legionnaire's disease were discovered and treatments for them devised. Microsoft was founded in 1975, followed a year later by Apple. Democracy returned to Greece, Spain, and Portugal, all of which applied to join the European Community. Women served as the presidents or prime ministers of eight countries (Argentina, Bolivia, the Central African Republic, India, Israel, Portugal, Sri Lanka, and of course the United Kingdom). A black man (Arthur Ashe) won Wimbledon and a black woman appeared on the cover of *Vogue*. In 1971 David Reuben's book *Everything You Always Wanted to Know About Sex but Were Afraid to Ask* outsold the New English Bible. American cinema audiences were frightened by evil spirits *(The Exorcist)* and great white sharks *(Jaws)* but heartened by the sight of a beleaguered republic beating an evil empire in *Star Wars* (1977). In the realm of popular music, the decade began with Simon and Garfunkel's doleful "Bridge over Troubled Water" and Don McLean's sardonic "American Pie" (the top-selling U.S. singles of 1970 and 1972 respectively), but it ended with the unfettered hedonism of the Bee Gees' "Saturday Night Fever" (1978) and the Knack's "My Sharona" (1979).

No doubt Callaghan committed a blunder in challenging the thesis of "mounting chaos." But the very fact that the question was posed in terms of *mounting* chaos as late as January 1979 is itself revealing. Even in the depths of Britain's "Winter of Discontent," it still seemed to many people that the real crisis was yet to come. And so it was. Now that the "sickly, neglected, disappointing" decade has receded sufficiently to admit of historical reassessment, we can see that the shock of the global had only just begun.

PART I

Into an Emerging Order

CHAPTER 1

"Malaise"

The Crisis of Capitalism in the 1970s

CHARLES S. MAIER

"MALAISE." Although he never actually used it, the term stubbornly clings to Jimmy Carter's remarkable speech of July 15, 1979. What he actually said was: "The threat [to America] is nearly invisible in ordinary ways. It is a crisis of confidence. It is a crisis that strikes at the very heart and soul and spirit of our national will. . . . The erosion of our confidence in the future is threatening to destroy the social and political fabric of America."[1] What brought Carter and many other leaders, not just in the United States but in the Western alliance and capitalist economies more generally, to perceive so dangerous a mood?

"Crisis," of course, is an overused word—not French, like "malaise," but Greek in origin—taken by analogy from the course of a serious illness to describe the point at which the patient either dies or recovers. Applied to a society or a regime, it refers to a situation in which institutional arrangements no longer deliver the results expected of them—whether public order, economic transfers and social justice, or economic growth—and where normal corrective actions seem only to make the situation worse. Societies and regimes appear caught in vicious circles: policy responses produce only more disorder, less justice, and more stagnation. Crises also differ from isolated political turmoil or conflicts because they afflict different social mechanisms simultaneously. The economy falters, politics stagnates, families fall apart, crime and violence rise. In a crisis all regulative institutions seem to disappoint at the same time; there is a sense of profound interconnection. The normal arrangements for mediating social demands seem to fail, and the dissatisfied take to the streets and sometimes take up arms.

Crises do not always destroy regimes or economic systems, but they do significantly recast institutions. The arrangements that emerge will have different principles or ground rules from those that prevailed earlier, whether for holding power or distributing wealth and honors. The institutions and values that are under stress seem clear enough; but those that may emerge in their stead are usually indistinct. As the Italian Marxist Antonio Gramsci aptly wrote of earlier turmoil, the crisis consists in the fact that the past is dying but the future is not yet born. The turmoil of the 1970s provoked a fundamental rethinking of the economic and political axioms that had been taken for granted since the Second World War. It closed the "postwar" era and its policy premises. What might replace them would be in dispute. This chapter suggests that while the economic debates of the era focused on the familiar variables of monetary and fiscal policy or the role of exchange rates and labor unions—aggravated to be sure by the awareness of "interdependence"—the difficulties experienced rose from the still murky and certainly painful transition to what has been described as post-Fordist production and postindustrial values.

After a crisis passes, its severity or uniqueness often seems to fade. Given the apparent buoyancy of the 1980s, it makes sense to ask whether there really was a general crisis of the 1970s, even the long 1970s, extending from the late sixties to the early eighties. If crisis requires revolution or war, perhaps the word serves us badly. In the economic sphere, symptoms of inflation and international financial turmoil were present in the 1980s. Conversely, Niall Ferguson's introduction to this volume correctly demonstrates that many of the economic and political indicators we associate with underperformance got worse in the 1980s. But the seventies brought visible breaks in the trend lines and shattered some of the complacent or naïve assumptions that had taken hold in the preceding decade.

This chapter focuses on economics, but economic difficulties were only part of a general sense of meltdown, whether measured in family stability, criminal statistics, or Western military capacity. Authoritative commentators felt that major attributes of Western society—its capacity for self-discipline, for a return to stability, for ensuring its internal and external security—were eroding rapidly. Admittedly critics chalked up much of what seemed so disquieting in the "seventies" to the turmoil of the preceding decade, which culminated in 1968, with all the turbulence that date represented. But the 1970s, certainly in the West, added economic difficulties and political incapacity to the youth revolts of the previous decade.

If "crisis" describes a painful transition that compels new assumptions about how societies are best governed or how they progress, then the "West" did experience a decade of crisis, comparable to the earlier period of twentieth-century economic hammering in the 1930s and to the geopolitical meltdown that preceded World War I. Unlike those two earlier turbulent eras, 1905–1914 and 1929–1939, events in the 1970s did not lead to a major world conflict. Nuclear arsenals apparently compelled restraint, although the success of deterrence was never foreordained. Indeed the calculus of stable deterrence tended to unravel in the late 1970s and early 1980s as arms control faltered and what Spencer Weart has labeled "nuclear fear" surged anew and intensified the ambiance of insecurity.[2] Add to the arms race a surge in domestic violence, not just in the Third World but also in hitherto orderly democracies. Terrorist squads murdered or wounded several hundred West German and Italian officials and businessmen, culminating in the murder of the reformist ex–prime minister Aldo Moro. Seemingly intractable violent conflicts seethed in Northern Ireland and the Basque lands of Spain. As inflation and violence surged, a reverse alchemy turned memories of gold into years of lead.

"Stagflation": Economic Difficulties in the 1970s

Where there was "malaise," there was "stagflation," a new term for simultaneous inflation and unemployment. Without attributing causal priority to the material aspects of the crisis, in the United States, at least, economic difficulties seemed most preoccupying to many policymakers and ordinary citizens. The pollster Daniel Yankelovich wrote in 1979: "For the [American] public today, inflation has the kind of dominance that no other issue has had since World War II. . . . It would be necessary to go back to the 1930s and the Great Depression to find a peacetime issue that had the country so concerned and so distraught." In the years from 1973 to 1981 "the high cost of living" topped the menu of national worries offered to respondents by the Gallup poll.[3] By the end of the 1970s all the favorable indices of a decade earlier seemed to have eroded, as shown in Table 1.1.

Conventional accounts at the time did not reveal much about causation. They traced the deteriorating indices quarter by quarter, incrementally explaining one disappointing outcome as a consequence of an earlier one.

Table 1.1. Economic indices, 1960–1980

Average annual:	GDP growth		CPI change				Unemployment	
Years averaged:	1960–69	1970–79	1960–69	1973–75	1970–79	1979–81	1967–73	1974–80
France	5.5%	3.9%	3.8%	11.9%	8.8%	12.7%	2.4%	4.8%
FRG	4.6%	2.9%	2.5%	6.2%	4.9%	5.7%	1.0%	3.2%
Italy	5.8%	3.0%	3.8%	16.5%	12.2%	17.8%	5.7%	6.7%
Japan	11.1%	5.4%	5.4%	16.5%	8.7%	6.2%	1.2%	1.9%
UK	2.9%	2.3%	3.6%	18.2%	12.4%	13.9%	3.5%	5.6%
USA	4.4%	3.4%	2.4%	9.6%	7.0%	11.3%	4.5%	6.7%

Sources: For growth rates: *World Business Cycles, 1950–1980* (London, 1982); for inflation rates: IMF, *International Financial Statistics*, vol. 37 (1984), and diverse previous issues; for unemployment: *OECD Economic Outlook* 34 (December 1983): 163.

For many commentators, the oil crisis of late 1973 and early 1974 constituted the turning point from a remarkable twenty-five years or even *les trente glorieuses* of unprecedented European economic growth since the late 1940s. In fact there were significant earlier points of inflection in the record of untroubled growth from the mid-1960s on, including a growing impatience on the part of labor unions and a worsening American current account balance that was unsettling the structure of international trade and payments.[4]

Early warning signs of difficulty in the 1960s can be understood as a reaction to the relative consensus of the 1950s around the need to rebuild the stock of European capital after the destruction of World War II. The ideological discipline nurtured by the Cold War also contributed a powerful if intangible role. Marshall Plan aid allowed the governments of Western Europe to finance reconstruction, colonial wars, and an emergent welfare state without rigorous deflationary measures or consumer austerity. This helped to secure the cooperation not of Marxists and their sympathizers but at least of pivotal social democratic leaders with new Christian Democratic mass parties, thus precluding a dangerous descent into class politics. Neofascism and its variants were not a serious option for governance after 1945. Under American leadership, West European societies thus avoided the worst of the polarizing disputes of the 1930s. They secured a minimal consensus around aspirations for long-term economic growth ("the politics of productivity"), in which divergent class interests moved beyond their earlier conflicts over distribution.[5] By the end of the 1950s political sociologist Daniel Bell noted the "end of ideology" and the "exhaustion" of world-transforming political ideas in the postwar decade and a half. Five years later Otto Kirchheimer similarly commented on the absence of fundamental opposition to European centrist politics.[6]

But the solutions for the 1950s contributed to the reactions of the 1960s, while the policies of the 1960s would call forth the difficulties for the 1970s. After a decade of successful reconstruction and centrist politics in the fifties, including the German and Japanese "miracles," there were signs that a significant change in public orientation might be under way. The late 1950s suggested that intellectuals and publics were seeking more open societies, with more scope for private relationships, personal fulfillment, or social spending. Eisenhower and Soviet leaders alike sought to explore a less confrontational coexistence. Although historians tend to attach major political and social trends to decades, the breaks in trend for both the "sixties" and then the "seventies" took place in the last couple of years of the preceding decennia and then gathered momentum.

By the 1960s social theorists talked of "convergence" between Communist and Western systems. Center-left governments or their ideological equivalents came to power in Italy and the United States, then in Britain, and in West Germany. Under the reformist Pope John XXIII, the Roman Catholic Church began to career through a period of liturgical and political transformation. New coalitions turned from private capital accumulation to social investment and spending (university expansion, welfare spending) and increased private consumption (of television sets, automobiles, vacations). Labor unions argued that workers had patiently demonstrated wage restraint while postwar economies were recuperating and now pressed for higher wage settlements. They called out the first serious strikes in the Netherlands and West Germany after 1966. Major wage increases would be sought and conceded during the crisis of May 1968 in France (the Grenelle Accords) and the Hot Autumn of 1969 in Italy.[7] Industry and labor could blame the resulting wage-price spirals, whether offset by devaluation or not, on each other or, in the case of conservative economists, on government social spending. The stage was set for a long debate over the impact of "cost-push" or "demand-pull" inflation.

Two other major sources of inflation also intervened. First, the United States slipped into a current account deficit by the end of the 1950s, in part because of government spending abroad, and in part because of the growth of American foreign investment. The dollars America spent abroad were accepted (until 1965 in France) as central bank reserves according to the Bretton Woods agreements. Daniel Sargent's chapter in this volume outlines the tumultuous breakdown of those agreements as Europeans increasingly protested the inflationary pressures originating from the United States, but Washington resisted tamping down until the Nixon administration ceased to accept foreign dollar holdings for gold in August 1971.

Economists argued that eliminating a fixed rate among currencies would prevent the transmission of inflation, but very shortly thereafter a new series of shocks hit the Western monetary systems.[8] Following the oil embargo at the time of the Yom Kippur War, the OPEC countries effectively quadrupled the price of oil in early 1974, thus ending the era of cheap energy imports. Importing countries reacted differently—some treating the new price increase as an inflationary surcharge that had to be counteracted by higher interest payments at home; others viewing it as an ultimately deflationary tax that had to be counteracted by easing interest rates to sustain employment. In the United States, the anti-inflationary campaign (Whip Inflation Now, or WIN) of 1975 was followed by a stimulus program a year later but was not sufficient to reelect President Ford. In any case, the combined results of American deficits, the ending of the Bretton Woods system, the labor pressure on wages, the OPEC price increases—and a renewed OPEC increase in 1979—led to sustained inflationary pressure that lasted into 1980–1982, only to be followed by sharp recessions.

Economists have tended to attribute this buffeting to proximate policy decisions made at the time. But a long-term perspective suggests that the economic difficulties were not just exaggerations of the normal business cycle and not just, as during the 1930s, a failure of collective consumption or other parameters.[9] The prosperity of the postwar years benefited from special circumstances. Charles Kindleberger pointed early on to the relatively inexpensive labor costs as the one-time transformation of agriculture (fertilizers, mechanization, and the like) released farm workers for urban employment. The extraordinary economic growth of the 1950s and 1960s was also facilitated by the prolonged stretch of relatively cheap energy prices. U.S. oil production grew through the 1960s; the Anglo-Americans retained control of Iranian petroleum after the crisis of 1950–51; and OPEC remained ineffective until the 1970s.[10]

The difficulties that ensued did not represent just the usual exhaustion of the business cycles that were familiar from before the war. Indeed the period of growth had already broken the rules. For the first time since the nineteenth century, moreover, prosperity continued through a second decade, as private American investment increased in the late 1950s and Europeans returned to convertible currencies and launched the European Economic Community. But by the late 1960s the phenomenon of stagflation likewise sprang from a longer-term transition in the Western world as basic heavy industries (iron and steel, coal mining) were shut down, eventually to be replaced by an economy oriented more toward services, leisure, and the postindustrial, post-Fordist array of products. But the transition was not smooth or easy, and Keynesian remedies of increasing demand could not really stimulate employment, which depended rather on the advent of increased services employment and new industries. The "rust belt" of the American Great Lakes, the coal mines shut down in the Ruhr, or Charleroi, or northern Britain, provided the long-term dismal signs of such "creative destruction."

The Fugitive Phillips Curve

What lessons were drawn for economic theory? Start with the fate of the Phillips curve—the tantalizing smile, as it were, on the fading neo-Keynesian Cheshire cat. In 1958 A. W. Phillips had claimed to establish a simple inverse correlation between any period's unemployment and rate of wage inflation. The original tradeoff was favorable—low unemployment to coexist with low inflation—such that neo-Keynesian governments believed they could stimulate even fuller employment with an inconsequential dosage of spending and inflation. By the mid-seventies, after countless studies, the curve was no longer so benign. It was skidding toward the vertical and to the right so that it seemed to take greater increments of inflation to achieve any reduction of unemployment. By the end of the seventies the whole notion of a stable tradeoff lay in tatters.

Persistent neo-Keynesians increasingly tried to separate out an underlying long-term Phillips correlation, which allegedly remained robust, from the unfortunate short-term deviations. Perhaps the trend of the mid-seventies was merely a contingent one. This was the conclusion of the so-called McCracken report commissioned by the OECD and published in 1977: "The immediate causes of the severe problems" could "largely be understood in terms of conventional economic analysis. There have been underlying changes in behavior patterns and in power relationships internationally and within countries. *But our reading of recent history is that the most important feature was an unusual bunching of unfortunate disturbances unlikely to be repeated on the same scale, the impact of which was compounded by some avoidable errors in economic policy.*"[11]

For both the Left and the Right, this was whistling past the graveyard. Inflation, to cite the monetarists, is indeed always a monetary phenomenon, but it has political and social roots. The Phillips curve embodied an implicit sociology: the fact that there must always be some cost to lowering unemployment suggested that the atomistic labor market no longer existed after the Second World War. Powerful purchasers of mass labor power faced collective sellers. The pre-Keynesian model of the labor market had yielded to one in which unions were key players. Keynes had explained that unions could not successfully bargain for real wages, but obviously they could drive hard bargains over nominal wages. Still, the tradeoff seemed to remain benign into the mid-1960s, and then it had gotten out of control. "Who threw the ratchet into the soup?" asked Arthur Okun, representative of what might be thought of as a Brookings consensus on the value of neo-Keynesian prescriptions.[12]

Monetarist theoreticians were quick to insist that the Phillips curve had always been a myth. Policymakers could not purchase higher employment with a measured dose of inflation. In the long run one could not push unemployment below what Milton Friedman termed its natural rate, dependent on deep-seated technological and societal factors. To attempt such a policy would only generate ever greater inflation. For hard-nosed theorists, unemployment above this level was in fact "voluntary," in large measure the consequence of workers' taking time out to search for better jobs. Societies must learn to live with what would soon be known to the policy world, after a bit more jiggering, as NAIRU, or the non-accelerating inflation rate of unemployment.[13]

The economists who had opposed the effort at inflationary stimulus were sometimes defined as monetarist, although strictly speaking they were far more diverse. Monetarists believed that the inflation problem derived from the timidity of policymakers and central bankers, who had provided monetary accommodation of inflationary wage settlements or welfare increases. They did not usually inquire into the sociopolitical pressures that central bankers responded to. There were paradoxes to their position. Monetarists argued that unions could not really produce wage inflation in the marketplace, but as collective political actors they could pressure policymakers into inflationary monetary policies. Other market-oriented advocates argued that high state budgets "crowded out" private sector spending—a variable frequently cited by *The Economist*. In fact, states governed by social democrats did not show significantly higher rates of inflation as long as they imposed the taxation or funded the debt needed to cover social spending.[14]

Market-oriented economists also discovered—or at least christened—the idea of "interdependence." No economy had complete freedom of action: the economic policies carried out within one's own nation would always provoke countervailing pressures from abroad such that Keynesianism in one country, or detachment from the international economy, was impossible. Stimulate the economy by lowering interest rates at home in a world of free-floating currencies and capital mobility (which increased in the 1970s as the United States and United Kingdom removed remaining controls), and the only result would be a fall in the exchange rate and domestic price inflation.[15]

Left, Center, and Right in the profession might agree on these mechanisms, but they drew different lessons. They learned a lot, but as Okun again wrote, "different people learned widely different things."[16] Economists on the Left insisted that the underlying contest over economic shares was a political one and had to be controlled politically. Labor unions and industry representatives were locked in a standoff of imperfect competition; each party had become too collectivized to let market mechanisms work, but they were not controlled enough, at least in the West, to find a healthy balance between consumption and investment. Workers who drew a society's wage bill remained opposed to investors who lived off assets but also invested in future productivity. Periodically, so the Left suggested, capitalism was forced to provoke a recession just to weaken trade union power.[17]

Other theorists advanced ideas with the same underlying lesson. The French "regulation" school suggested that economic systems tended to function by working to control one key parameter. Western societies had gone silently from a gold standard that until 1931 had subordinated all variables to the objective of fixed currency values to a labor standard that as a consequence of social democratic and trade union recovery after World War II had set full employment as its objective.[18] And finally the newly fashionable political economists looked at state budgetary issues. National economies had to balance the "accumulation" needs of capitalism against its "legitimation" requirements. James O'Connor's *Fiscal Crisis of the State*, published in book form in 1973, recycled the concepts of Austrian fiscal sociology from the early twentieth century, which Josef Schumpeter had himself embraced. The state had, on the one hand, to create the conditions for capital accumulation, but also had, on the other, to provide enough social welfare and ensure sufficient high consumption to retain legitimacy. These contradictory requirements came into inevitable conflict.[19]

Although use of the term "accumulation" usually tipped the reader off that the analysis came from the Left, Marxists tended to agree with spokesmen for industry that the working classes would inevitably exert enough pressure on entrepreneurs or overload the state budget with welfare provisions so that savings and investment and thus productivity must lag. Ultimately the crisis had to be resolved by state supervision of the economy. Neo-Keynesian economists and businessmen loosely grouped in the center of the policy spectrum were referring to the same phenomenon when they lamented a profit squeeze and pointed to a decline in long-term productivity growth in the 1970s that they saw as pervasive but puzzling.[20] They looked to such solutions as political wage bargaining in tripartite boards representing unions, business associations, and the state. Attempts to control inflation by concerted action or neocorporatist union-management agreements supervised by the state (in the United States, Britain, and Sweden) consumed vast amounts of public effort but did not work effectively.[21] The United States went through Phase I, II, and III of the Wage-Price Board. The Swedes tried Haga I and II (Haga Castle being the site of the negotiations). The Callaghan government limped from its own Phase I to Phase IV. Other societies—notably Italy, Israel, Brazil, and Argentina—relied on wage indexation so that workers allegedly would not feel that they continually had to wrest higher nominal salaries from their employers. By the mid-1970s social democrats similarly proposed to key pensions to inflation rates (so called COLAs), or to provide tax rebates if inflation caused so-called "bracket creep," provided that labor accepted wage restraint.

By the end of the 1970s some Western observers were implying that democracy and a noninflationary economy were incompatible objectives. In a "political business cycle," officials facing election contests, for example, Richard Nixon in the run-up to 1972, would always be tempted to stimulate the economy and generate inflation.[22] A decade earlier Keynesian economists had argued that public goods would always be undersupplied, since their diffuse benefits could not compensate the public for the assignable costs. By the 1970s conservative social scientists claimed the reverse. Since constituents easily perceived the targeted benefits of spending, but did not really feel the diffuse costs of legislating them, there was an inbuilt bias toward excess spending. A major school of social choice theory elaborated these assumptions, winning one of its principal exponents, James Buchanan, the Nobel in economics by 1986.

Their arguments were based in a broader social theory, often implicit, but increasingly argued explicitly—and shared remarkably across the political spectrum. Many economists and political observers came to fear that democratically elected governments would never turn off the printing press. Alfred Kahn, one of the champions of deregulation and a Carter adviser, speculated that "this time is different—that we really have entered a new era of chronic, permanent inflation, at least so long as democracy and welfare state capitalism survive."[23] Conservatives felt that democracy precluded individual and social saving: essentially the masses wanted to spend what they earned. But liberals did not argue very differently: Daniel Bell and John Goldthorpe, the British sociologist of the new working class, talked about the vanishing moral basis of capitalism. The Protestant ethic had followed the Phillips curve out the window. The age of affluence tended to erode the fear of lean times that led the masses to save. The only democratically effective way to restrain wage earners was to make them stakeholders (a term that emerged only later) in capitalism, whether through socialized firms or the use of parity commissions to set wages and profits in a process of political bargaining. "Anyone whose primary commitment is to the market," Brian Barry wrote in a critique of much of this economic argumentation, "must, therefore, look on the democratic state, with its inevitable tendency to regulate, make collective provision, and redistribute, with antipathy. . . . The beauty of inflation is that it can be used as a rallying cry to sweep up people who might otherwise be chary of plans to cripple the ability of governments to make economic policy. . . . Anti-inflationary hysteria is an opportunity to mobilize behind proposals that would, in calmer times, be widely recognized as reactionary twaddle."[24]

But the times were hardly calm. By the end of the 1970s the efforts at running an economy by negotiating a consensus among its powerful producer groups seemed to have failed. What resulted, of course, was not the collapse of capitalism or parliamentary and party governance but rather a rejection of the neo-Keynesian and neocorporatist prescriptions and a surprisingly successful turn to market solutions. The defeat of the Swedish socialists in 1976 after over forty years in power, the election of Margaret Thatcher in 1979 and of Ronald Reagan in 1980, the 1982 defeat of the Social-Liberal coalition in the German Federal Republic, and the abandonment of a traditionally Popular Front spending program in favor of market measures by the Mitterrand government in 1983 all revealed the swing of public opinion. By 1980 the Communists in Italy had declined from their 1976 highpoint and had abandoned their unsuccessful search to conclude a *compromesso storico*. Indeed in the fall of 1980 workers forced an end to a party-led strike at Fiat, while within a year the Bank of Italy had won the right not to finance government debt.

Political regimes everywhere moved to insulate their central banks from governmental supplication to monetize deficits. In 1979 President Carter appointed Paul Volcker, Gibraltar-like in appearance and policies, as head of the Federal Reserve. Just as liberal democracies had learned to protect civil rights against democratic passions, so now they moved to make stable currencies a basic right shielded from majority pressures. At the same time, the political climate did change. Again, in Italy—which in fact was a bellwether for so many social trends in the West in the 1970s, whether terrorism or the defense of abortion and divorce rights—the Christian Democratic electorate was reduced, and "lay" or Republican and Socialist Party ministers could take control of the ministries. Before the Italian Socialists yielded to the temptations of municipal corruption later in the decade, they inaugurated a remarkable series of reforms. Unions, too, were beginning to understand that they were not really winning welfare gains by constant labor turmoil and inflationary settlements. Indexation would be wound down in Italy, Argentina, and Israel in the coming years.

Perhaps we can take the presidential debate of October 28, 1980, when Ronald Reagan persuasively asked, "Are you better off than you were four years ago?" as the moment when the regime changed. By the early 1980s one would live without the Phillips curve, and in fact the apparently impossible was under way in the West. The Keynesian settlement was being significantly amended. Welfare states were hardly dismantled, but trade unions were reduced in power. The right side of the political spectrum had learned to call in the international market to redress the balance of the Keynesian domestic arena. Market liberalism was back—Keynes was out of fashion—at least until 2008.

But to return to the realm of economic theory, monetarism as such was hardly an uncontested paradigm. By 1980 the most fashionable of the newly influential doctrines stressed less the monetary aggregates than the signals sent by policymakers, as Thomas Sargent's influential article on the end of hyperinflation claimed to demonstrate.[25] Such a view quickly became a well-developed school of rational expectations. The institutional issue was how to send such unambiguous signals. The answer usually suggested was to remove central banks from the control of legislatures and finance ministers. Breaking unions was a corollary test of manhood.

Sargent himself claimed that what counted was the learning process on the part of policymakers and agents. Learning was indeed crucial, but learning involved psychological signaling based on a resolute political coalition.[26] During the decade the key to the inflation problem had evolved from curbing union behavior to finding leaders with the political steel needed to accomplish this. In the mid-1970s such a condition seemed almost utopian, confined to the Reaganite fringes of the GOP or to Keith Joseph and the Thatcherite conventicler of the British Conservative Party. Mainstream Republicanism was still associated with the Nixon-Shultz effort to seek interest group consensus. So, too, the British Conservatives seemed to have settled into the benevolent Toryism of Harold Macmillan and Edward Heath. There was a curious and unavowed meeting of minds among the restorationist Right and the neo-Marxist Left: what counted was politics. And the politics, while no longer authoritarian, had to be tough.

"Overloaded Democracy"

"Can a democracy discipline itself?" Alfred Kahn asked with reference to the interest group struggle to preserve constant income shares.[27] The crisis of the 1970s was not just economic; it encompassed a collision of older and newer values, as exemplified by the university insurrections, the emergence of a distinctive youth culture and feminist agenda—all that we understand under the notion of "1968," which epitomized so many of the discontents. But the crisis of the 1970s differed from the direct challenges of popular protest in the preceding decade. Then the United States had witnessed the civil rights movement, the formation of Students for a Democratic Society to agitate for "participatory democracy," increasing numbers of antiwar protests, and finally efforts to transform the universities into centers of radical change. Students in Mexico and Western Europe likewise mobilized, creating in Germany, for example, an "extra-parliamentary" opposition, taking to the streets, and everywhere increasing the violence of their confrontations with police. What was taking place by the 1970s was the transformation of spontaneity into institutional challenge and durable organizations—whether African American movements, women's networks, or the small hard core of increasingly terrorist cells in Italy and Germany.[28] The question was whether pluralist states of parties and interests might accommodate these new actors. The U.S. Democratic Party conventions of 1968 and 1972 epitomized the transformed challenge: the first one, in Chicago, provided the setting for a quasi-insurrection by outside assailants, which was harshly suppressed by the local police. The second, in Miami four years later, was presented by the media as an overstretched and somewhat chaotic "tent" thrown over a crowd of political claimants, including gays, seeking recognition of their own "identity politics."

Liberals were unprepared for the mobilization of society that had taken place. Where now was Daniel Bell's famous "end of ideology"? Social theorists had expected a de-ideologization of politics, a "convergence" between post-Stalinist communism and welfare state capitalism. Increasing numbers of issues would be settled by bureaucratic administrators and experts: society was becoming less adventurous and conflictual, routinized and rational. The chancellor of Berkeley and labor economist Clark Kerr had envisaged a "multiversity" that would open higher education for all but summoned young people to take up the role of experts in this new society rather than to become versed in humanistic knowledge. Of course, not all students accepted this functional a view of their future; they returned to Marx's 1844 manuscripts or read Paul Goodman's *Growing Up Absurd* and decided not to become faceless participants in the new Leviathan. In effect the 1960s revealed that ideology was not dead; students were not content to be young technocrats; workers were not always satisfied with productivity-keyed wages; and all were ready to take to the streets even at the risk of being seen as spoiled children by mature adults.[29] The year 1968 involved many impulses, but everywhere it signaled the unwillingness of a generation largely born without experience of World War II's collective discipline to accept the social roles prescribed by those who had reconstructed postwar societies. The virtues of sacrificing for the future, the assumption of an identity as producers, the acceptance of the metanarratives of modernization all came under scrutiny, sometimes utopian, sometimes intolerant, sometimes violent.

For conservatives and some liberals as well, the sixties had been an era of moral declension. "The 1960s witnessed a dramatic renewal of the democratic spirit in America," Samuel Huntington wrote in 1975. With admirable frankness he stated that this was not necessarily a good thing. There had been "a marked upswing" in "marches, demonstrations, protest movements, and 'cause' organizations." Blacks, Indians, Chicanos, white ethnic groups, students, and women all mobilized. This testified to the ability of the system to respond to and assimilate newly active groups, but it had its dangers. Public spending had tipped from national defense to social welfare (see Figure 1.1). The primacy of equality had been reasserted as a goal in social, economic, and political life.

Governmental activity had increased, but the authority of government had diminished. "Input institutions"—parties and the presidency—had weakened. "Output institutions"—bureaucracies and regulators—had grown stronger. The vigor of democracy had contributed to a "democratic distemper," according to Samuel Huntington in *The Crisis of Democracy*, written with Michel Crozier and Joji Watanki.[30] Crozier tended to agree. He offered a complex sociological analysis of France and suggested that bureaucratization had led social passions to spill out of control. Moreover, the Communist Party—no longer revolutionary, perhaps, but prepared for hardboiled machine politics—stood ready to take control.

The Huntington-Crozier-Watanki lament appeared in perhaps the most celebrated publication of the Trilateral Commission, organized in 1973. Trilateralism had a dual thrust. On the one hand, it represented an effort to coordinate policy responses to dilemmas that could no longer be resolved at the national level. Wise experts had to step in because the

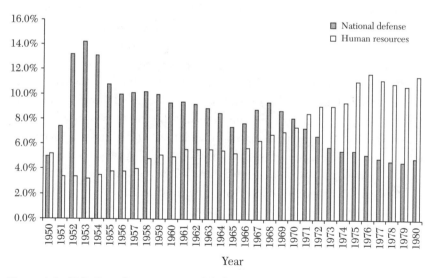

Figure 1.1. U.S. Spending on national defense and human resources, 1950–1980 (as percent of GDP). *Source:* Office of Management and the Budget, Historical Tables (2006).

challenges were broader than democratic regimes might individually address. On the other hand, commission members were prompted by what they perceived as a crisis of democratic overload within their respective societies. Trilateral members thus spoke not with the voice of a nationalist Right but with the tones of self-conscious and somewhat sententious adulthood: the reassertion of the grownups, the calm stewards of social and political rationality, who sought to rein in a society that celebrated infantile urges under the guise of an infatuation with youth. The dominant theme of the very elite network that the Trilateralists co-opted seemed to be that the popular world was slipping out of control and that it required an international effort by men in responsible positions to call the establishments to order.[31] Not surprisingly, the Trilateral Commission became the easy target of a whole undergrowth of conspiracy theorists who were certain that, along with David Rockefeller and the Council on Foreign Relations, it controlled global finance and politics.

The term "overloaded democracy," after all, was a normative one. It was not that democracy merely carried heavy burdens in the age of the welfare state; its burdens needed to be reduced. Government by qualified experts had to work on a transnational level to preclude destructive outbursts of populism. Conservatives in the 1970s denounced these trends—so dramatically symbolized by the student explosions of 1968—as the advent of hedonism and shortsighted pursuit of today's consumption at the expense of tomorrow's capital. But the turmoil testified to a new generation's shedding of the older social roles assigned by industrial society—those which stressed work, production, and family formation—and their complex trying on of successive protean identities.

Ironically the Trilateralist analysis of overloaded democracy converged with critiques of liberal politics raised by some on the Left. Western critics of capitalism also argued that the liberal state as managed by its political parties no longer possessed adequate "steering" or "control" mechanisms. The crisis of liberal capitalism, Jürgen Habermas and Claus Offe, among others, suggested, lay in its inability to impose an overriding "rationality" on the divergent interests of its powerful economic actors. In the 1960s these theorists might have hoped for a democratic socialist resolution of the resulting contradictions. By the 1970s they tended more just to take note of the West's continuing crises. The political parties of the liberal state had called interest groups into being, or at least had given them public functions in an effort to solve social problems. Sometimes this yielded stable corporatism, but increasingly it had gotten out of control. The corporatist regime was a potential Frankenstein monster.[32]

From Interdependence to Globalization

"Malaise" was a transnational phenomenon. At one level it represented the collective uneasiness generated within the Western political economies of the 1970s. It was also the response of the great, the good, and, by all means, the grownups to what they beheld as a breakdown in social discipline and deference since the 1960s, as the public commitments of the postwar years allegedly gave way to inflationary wage spirals, leftist political coalitions, and spineless monetary accommodation on the part of central bankers, to the protests of peace activists, and to the continuing Dionysian claims of youth culture.

So far this account has followed these tensions within individual societies. What rendered them particularly menacing, however, was their transnational power. The Left of the 1960s included a powerful international dimension, and the difficulties of global capitalism that emerged between the late 1960s and late 1970s likewise represented a global phenomenon. Both those who cheered the new societal actors and those disquieted by their success recognized that global space, a domain in its own right, was changing the rules of political economy. The question was whether the same realm of transnational interactions might be appealed to for the sake of stabilization. Political and economic stabilization (just like radical agendas) might be more easily achieved by transcending the fiercely contested arenas of the local and the national, already so permeated by interest groups and democratic pressures. Might not the new global "there there" serve as a domain where market regulation could claim renewed viability? Could a beleaguered capitalism be reinforced at the global level?

It was politically expedient, therefore, that "interdependence" was invoked so persuasively and with increasing frequency. Richard Cooper perhaps most notably placed the term on the marquee of international economics in 1968.[33] Interdependence demonstrated that there could be no successful Keynesianism in any single country, that workers could not demand a share of wages greater than productivity increases without job loss. Indicative of the lesson learned was the fact that the Swedish Social Democrats were voted out of power in 1976 for the first time since 1932. Interdependence was fully certified when the French Socialists abandoned their neo–Popular Front program of income distribution in 1983 to opt for the *franc fort* and monetary linkage with Frankfurt. Interdependence functioned as a reality check on utopianism, in much the same way that globalization has served to justify capitalist economic "reforms" in more recent years.

The Marxists had a point, but it was the same point that market advocates also made: capitalism—the production and distribution of goods by decentralized price signals and market transactions and non-state control of assets—depends on accumulation, or as Adam Smith would have said, on parsimony. And the key question capitalism poses over and over is: Who is to defer from consumption? Keynes wrote in 1919 that the pre–world war international economy depended on a double bluff: workers accepted vast inequality in return for the capitalist nonconsumption of the cake that was cut so inequitably.[34] The 1970s were a decade in which that bluff was called and the question of redistribution was reopened. Interdependence supposedly provided a demonstration that no radical change in the ground rules was feasible without major sacrifices in society's aggregate welfare. Cut the cake significantly differently, and no cake would be baked! Interdependence thus carried a one-two punch: It meant that capitalist societies were linked such that any domestic policy must provoke international ramifications. But it also implied that international economic society could be stubbornly neo-mercantilist and zero-sum. Competition for capital and for jobs remained its underlying premise.

Interdependence, as invoked at the end of the 1970s, then, taught that governments must tax less and contain welfare spending just as globalization now teaches that jobs are at stake if entitlements remain high. Of course, globalization involves far greater degrees of capital flows and of migration. Theorists of interdependence focused on the impact on particular societies; theorists of globalization stress global balances as a whole. Globalization is far more rhetorically expansive than interdependence: it promises great benefits, whereas interdependence tended to threaten them. Still, as pedagogical devices for teaching the rules of accumulation, they both operate in the same way. In both cases a well-functioning capitalism seeks to enlarge the scope of economic activity to a worldwide system of production and exchange taking place across borders—not merely by intensifying trade or international banking and investment, but by postulating a nonterritorial domain for economic activity. Precisely through the crises it faced, the capitalism of the 1970s sought to expand the notions of international economic space. Political economy fled toward the global.

Crisis as Norm?

Let me suggest in conclusion another long-term framework for thinking about the transformations of the 1970s. The turmoil of the 1970s, I have argued elsewhere, formed what I believe was one of three systemic crises of the twentieth century.[35] The first of these overarching crises lasted from about 1905 through the First World War. It involved the well-known international rivalry between alliance systems and a sustained conflict over political representation, indeed over which groups might claim (or be denied) the status of political actors—whether identified by ethnicity (as in Ireland, the Dual Monarchy, and the American South), or by socioeconomic markers (for example, the industrial working classes or a dependent peasantry). Political systems thus faced demands for greater inclusion, which they sought to resolve by partial suffrage reforms and co-optation of the moderates among the claimants.

As a widespread crisis of political representation, the pre–World War I decade witnessed such disparate events as the Russian Revolution of 1905; the controversies over universal male suffrage in Austria-Hungary, Italy, and Prussia; and the conflict over reform of the House of Lords in Great Britain; not to mention the vast revolutionary upheavals in Mexico and China.[36] In many countries the characteristic procedure created by nineteenth-century liberalism, that is, parliamentary discussion and legislation, seemed paralyzed. The Right drew the lesson that parliamentary institutions should be curtailed and power restored to strong executives, based if necessary on military authority.

The second of these systemic major crises was the world economic depression of the 1930s and involved the collapse of employment and national incomes after an effort to reestablish prewar economic exchange under vastly more difficult postwar circumstances. It was a *crisis within capitalism* and was resolved by de facto Keynesian programs of government spending including rearmament and wartime expenditure and ultimately by the postwar welfare state. It did not destroy capitalism, but it brought down the German democratic regime and undermined many others. Eventually, across the course of the Second World War, it changed the balance of the interest groups within Western societies, enhanced the role of industrial labor and eventually stabilized the role of a vastly reduced agrarian sector, and brought about a commitment to social spending, but not before incurring the advent of National Socialism and a second world war.[37]

The third of the century's crises, and the one treated in this chapter, was less a collapse within a system of political economy than *a crisis of industrial society* and thus of two rival sets of institutions: postwar Fordist capitalism and Fordist state socialism. The political economies developed to revive capitalism after the Great Depression and to sustain the military efforts of the 1940s through the 1960s—the Second World War, colonial wars, and the Cold War—seemed to fail in their turn as unemployment deepened and inflation persisted during the 1970s. The measures that for a quarter-century after World War II had helped to secure sustained growth proved unable to solve the troubles of the 1970s. Although misguided policies, heightened class conflict, and the oil price increases all played a role, so too did the difficult transition from one set of economic activities to another. Daniel Bell invented the term "post-industrial society" to describe a transformation whose scope in the mid-sixties was only becoming apparent.[38] The transition was based on the electronic revolution brought about, above all, by transistors, computation, and information processing, which in turn helped generate a vast and painful shift in occupational structure. The epochal change resulted, too, from the industrialization of previous Third World countries that could now produce many of the basic products earlier reserved to the West.

Three questions virtually impose themselves in turn. The first is what relationship the crisis that so lethally afflicted the European Communist regimes in the 1980s had to the crisis that Western economies had undergone from the late 1960s to the end of the 1970s. Most narratives make no connection between the two, but I would urge that they represented, in fact, two phases of one epoch of unrest confronting the industrial world—capitalist and Communist. The difficulties of the post-Fordist transition gripped first the Western countries that sought to shut down some of their old industrial and mining sectors, and eventually the East European societies that sought to preserve them. It was only logical that the socialist and nonsocialist worlds should face systemic changes that had an impact on both. Throughout the entire postwar period the two systems had helped shape each other's politics, military strategies, and economic choices. While Western capitalism survived, many of its underlying assumptions that had marked what might be called the Keynesian age from World War II to the mid-1970s were powerfully transformed. Political democracy survived, but its economic reach was cut back. Labor unions lost members and became notably weaker (even in Great Britain and Italy). Monetary policy had to be taken out of the reach of political parties and placed in the hands of central bankers, who were granted increasing degrees of autonomy—a process completed a decade later by the creation of a European Central Bank.

Arduous as these changes were, the Communist world faced even more challenging ones, which the successive decade revealed it could not surmount. It could not institute a functioning price system while simultaneously protecting party control of regimes that claimed to master economic allocation as well as political decision making. It could not satisfy the consumer demands that its constant comparisons with the West required while also maintaining the heavy defense budgets it thought necessary. And it could not make the adjustments to a post-Fordist economy in which decentralized innovation in the computer sector had become so important. Indeed it could not even make the adjustments needed for an adequate reduction of its agricultural sector. By the 1980s the European state socialist regimes faced their own shock of the global—namely the painful realization that they could no longer function as a closed system of exchange, but had to rely on imports from the nonsocialist world furnished on credit.

The "short" twentieth century effectively came to an end between 1973 and 1989. What tended to emerge as disruptive forces at the end of the century were no longer just the tensions of political economy but grave issues of identity and citizenship—not just the recurrent issue of which social groups were entitled to shares of national output, but the question who in fact constituted a group or collective claimant. The stake of politics was evolving from what you got to who you were. The role of minority rights and group affiliations, including new claims to nationhood, had also emerged in the 1960s and 1970s. Sometimes the claims were territorially based, as in Quebec, Biafra, or later in Yugoslavia. These issues raised again questions of representation and identity that had constituted the first twentieth-century crisis. In that respect the twentieth century had come full circle. Sometimes the claims were based on nonterritorial identity, whether rooted in race or gender or age. Market procedures and rational expectations did not easily assuage these claims, but this discussion cannot follow their passionate history.

Rather, in the midst of a renewed episode of economic difficulty—one reminiscent in some ways of the world economic crisis of the 1930s—a second question intrudes: whether the forces of recuperation that seemed to revive market economies by the 1980s did not harbor sources of future vulnerability. Since the 1970s the advanced and transitional capitalist economies have faced significant recessions and crises: for the West in the early 1980s, briefly after 1987, during the "dot-com" failures after 2001, and most severely in the contraction of 2008 and beyond. Severe debt and currency crises with heavy costs on real output and employment gripped the Russian transitional economy, Mexico, Southeast Asia, and Argentina in the 1990s—not to take into account a decade of Japanese stagnation or the long systemic immiseration of much of sub-Saharan Africa.

To each arena of poverty can be attributed local causes and local policy failures. Still, such widespread difficulties require us to give thought to overarching causes. For all the excellent researches into economic history, its underlying currents—the differential pace of development, the persistence of cycles, the inequality of rewards—often remain obscure. The great technological and financial transitions among the most developed "players," we can say, radiate outward to embroil more precarious systems on the perimeter, just as opportunities for markets, surpluses, and investments found at the perimeter accelerate changes at the core. Indeed the capitalist countries at the core can at least for a period offload or devolve the consequences of their own excesses onto the emerging economies. The difficulties as well as the opportunities of globalization are a two-way street. The 1970s intensified such a spatial circulation, and the argument can be made that we are still caught up in its wash.

The third question, which arises from this recurrence of difficulty, concerns not economics but the concept of crisis. It is the question posed by Niall Ferguson's introduction to this volume—"Crisis? What Crisis?"—but generalized. James Callaghan was credited with the original question and rejoinder—but he apparently no more uttered it than Jimmy Carter used the term "malaise." If what historians and commentators label as crises recur with so insistent a rhythm, might they not be better construed as the normal condition of complex societies, and the periods of apparent stability or equilibrium as exceptional moments? Perhaps a final lesson for social scientists and historians is not that crises are exceptional but that periods of relative equilibrium are. "Non-crisis, what non-crisis?" What allows us to believe that we have come to rest or have reached safe harbor or the end of history? What conditions or policies allow societies to resolve their issues of distribution, identity, and belonging without recourse to more or less violent conflict? And can we ever expect more than a decade's respite from painful outcomes? Rightly examined, the 1970s force open all these inquiries.

CHAPTER 2

The United States and
Globalization in the 1970s

DANIEL J. SARGENT

IN FEBRUARY 1974 representatives of thirteen Western countries gathered in Washington, D.C., for an emergency summit. Three months earlier, Arab petroleum exporters had declared an embargo—an oil "jihad"—on petroleum exports to the United States in an effort to curtail U.S. support for Israel's war with Egypt.[1] Coinciding with a 70 percent hike in the price of oil, which would have occurred even without the October War, the embargo menaced the industrial world economy. The price of crude oil quadrupled in a matter of weeks. Now, in the winter of 1973–74, Americans waited in gasoline lines. While exempt from the formal embargo, Western Europe and Japan suffered near identical increases in the price of energy, with similarly debilitating consequences.[2]

Costly and divisive, the 1973–74 oil crisis threatened the unity and prosperity of the West. One of the seventies' seismic events, it shifted the balance of power in the world economy away from the importing nations and toward oil exporters. "We are now living in a never-never land," exclaimed Secretary of State Henry Kissinger, "in which tiny, poor, and weak nations can hold up for ransom some of the industrialized world."[3]

Yet the crisis had sneaked up quietly on American leaders, who, until proclamation of the embargo, had failed to perceive their own vulnerability—despite the warnings of oil economists who analyzed the rise of "oil power" and warned of its consequences.[4]

Believing that fear of the Soviet Union would keep the Arab states in line, Kissinger had assumed that the United States could aid Israel without jeopardizing its own access to oil. Slow to comprehend how the global energy economy had changed since the mid-1960s, Kissinger presumed that Cold War politics could induce Saudi Arabia to play the role of America's "good little boy" in the region.[5] Despite clear warnings, the Nixon administration failed to anticipate the power of petroleum as a political weapon.

Having contributed to the crisis by his reluctance to countenance an embargo, Kissinger proved more adept at dealing with its consequences. Strikingly, the oil crisis forced him to acknowledge—for perhaps the first time—that global problems demanded global solutions. At the Washington Energy Conference in February 1974, Kissinger roused U.S. allies to deal with a crisis that revealed "the birth pains of interdependence." Exchanging Machiavelli's insights for Pareto's, the prince of American *Realpolitik* declared that nations would fare best by subordinating their selfish interests to the common good. "The realities of interdependence," Kissinger proclaimed, made the diplomacy of "nationalistic rivalry" almost "suicidal."[6] Should the West fail to cooperate in a quest for energy conservation and alternative fuels, the result would be the breakdown of the international energy market and a desperate rush for bilateral barter deals with the oil exporters. That scenario would only benefit the petro-states and (he did not publicly add) imperil American economic leadership of the West.[7]

The 1973–74 crisis thus marked the point at which Kissinger began to wrestle with the imperatives of economic order in a shrinking world. Before long this journey would lead him to embrace a vocabulary (if not yet substantive policies) incongruous with his image as a hardnosed practitioner of geopolitics. "Old international patterns are crumbling," Kissinger noted in 1975; "the world has become interdependent in economics, in communications, and in human aspirations." In private he began to contemplate how the United States could lead in a world in which the soft power of economics and ideas was speaking louder than military force. "The trick," he suggested in 1974, might be "to use economics to build a world political structure."[8]

Historians of Kissinger's career tend to focus on the grand diplomacy of 1969–1973, the so-called Nixinger years. They have paid less attention to the phase of his career that began with the oil crisis. From 1974 to 1977 Henry Kissinger began to formulate a response to the challenge of rising interdependence. He did so because circumstances required it. While Kissinger continued to exalt the nation-state as the building block of international order and to resist developments, notably the politics of human rights, that threatened its sovereignty, he recognized that the United States could not resist the reality of its own diminished autonomy in an integrating world.

The 1973–74 oil crisis was thus the pivot of interdependence for the United States: the point at which acknowledgment of new limits became unavoidable. Having exalted the diplomacy of maneuver and élan, Nixon and Kissinger were taken aback in the winter of 1973–74 to discover just how vulnerable to external economic shocks the United States had become. Only in the moment of crisis did they begin to acknowledge the reality of an interdependence in which the autonomy of nations was becoming limited by transnational flows of energy and goods, of money and ideas, and even—as contributors to this volume show—of pollution and diseases.

But what was this new "interdependence," as contemporaries dubbed it? The term implies more than just the proliferation of transnational flows, although sharp increases in levels of international exchange were undoubtedly crucial. Interdependence meant that this greater level of international economic activity turned out to restrict the capacity for autonomous national policies, political as well as economic. What made interdependence a striking phenomenon in the 1970s was that it compelled policymakers to take account of what the political scientists Joseph Nye and Robert Keohane called "reciprocal effects among countries."[9] Statesmen had always had to envisage what political or military responses their foreign policies might arouse, but they were less attuned to the economic impacts that might follow—and less capable of insulating themselves. U.S. commitments to Israel's survival helped provoke, for instance, Saudi Arabia's embargo on oil exports to the United States and then the OPEC price hike, which contributed to adverse pressures on price stability and employment. Smaller economies could be buffeted even further. Any single country's possible responses to these effects could provoke further new pressures on its economy or currency, including responses from investment communities and labor unions. Interdependence, as Zbigniew Brzezinski wrote in 1973, blurred "the distinctions between foreign and domestic policy and between economics and politics."[10] Caught in a mesh of intensifying interdependence, American leaders—much like the heads of other advanced industrial nations—acknowledged that they had entered an era of new limits.

For readers in the early twenty-first century, "globalization" is a more familiar term than "interdependence." It is in some respects a better word—and the term that I favor in this chapter. Whereas "interdependence" implies a condition of vulnerability or state of being, "globalization" suggests a process. Even if we have experienced it as an onrushing tendency, it is a process that can retreat as well as advance, as it had in the 1930s. "Interdependence" highlights the impact on individual states that perceived restricted policy choices; "globalization" suggests a trend that grips them collectively. Moreover, we can acknowledge that international relations are being globalized without defining the elusive threshold at which they become interdependent. A long-term and sinuous process, globalization is by no means a recent phenomenon; some historians have proposed dividing it into archaic, premodern, and modern phases.[11] But "globalization" is an appropriate word for the 1970s. As we shall see, the decade brought a resurgence of long-term globalizing patterns among the nations of the advanced capitalist world. This came after a forty-year hiatus, from the late 1920s to the late 1960s, during which nation-states had appeared, especially in their political-economic lives, to be moving toward increasingly autonomous and self-determining futures. The birth pangs of a new era of globalization in the 1970s bequeathed a new order of challenge for the United States—and this was a reality that even Kissinger could not avoid.

At the same time, the position of the United States as the international system's leading power imposed on it special responsibilities for managing globalization. From the mid-1970s American policymakers struggled to master the implications of the decade's integrative upheaval. To say that they sought to manage structural change is not, however, to argue that they were architects of it. On the contrary, the coming of complex interdependence caught most of them unaware, and the United States struggled in the 1970s to reconcile its desire for leadership with its own diminishing autonomy.

Addressing the relationship between the United States and globalization in the 1970s, my argument in this chapter has three objectives. First, it describes the extent, scope, and nature of globalization as the republic experienced it during the 1970s. I propose that the seventies witnessed a historic passage from an era of relative autonomy for American society to one of growing interdependence. Second, I consider the extent of U.S. agency in the decade's globalizing integration. I contend that U.S. officials did not pursue interdependence as a coherent objective. Globalization in this view appears more as the consequence of exogenous structural changes than as the achievement of specific policy choices. Finally, I consider the United States as an object of globalization in the 1970s. I argue that national policy autonomy, especially in the political-economic realm but in public policy more generally, became circumscribed by global integration during these years. This constitutes a shift toward interdependence that few historians of domestic politics and policy have grasped. While American leaders embraced the language of globalization most fully after 1991, it was in the 1970s that the imperatives of an integrating world came to weigh decisively on national policies.

As an alternative interpretative concept to Cold War détente, globalization offers a useful lens through which to view American relations with the larger world in the 1970s. Like any interpretive prism, it is not all-encompassing, but it yields insights into the larger forces that lay behind this pivotal decade.

Globalization has a long history. But only in 1974 did the word first appeared in the pages of the *New York Times,* in a quotation from a wary economist, Ronald Müller. It entered common parlance in the early 1980s, by which time it would be glimmering with the promise of an orgiastic future. Popularizing the term in the *Harvard Business Review,* Theodore Levitt in 1983 christened globalization a technology-driven force that was integrating markets, pushing the world toward "converging commonality," and leading humanity to a common desire "for modernity's allure."[12]

Globalization, as Levitt used the word, involved the integration of markets, but it also implied the convergence of cultures, societies, and aspirations. While some of these phenomena lend themselves more readily to quantification than others, global aggregates give a sense of the changes that the seventies brought. Worldwide exports increased from 18 percent of global gross domestic product in 1973 to 23.1 percent in 1985. More dramatic, the size of the international banking market (as a percentage of world GDP) grew from just 1.2 percent of global output in 1964 to 16.2 percent in 1980.[13] To take an index of political globalization, the number of nongovernmental organizations (NGOs) worldwide more than doubled between 1968 and 1981.[14]

While cross-border flows and the proliferation of non-state actors are symptoms of globalization, they are not the full story. Globalization implies convergence and interdependence; it involves politics and governance; it surmounts territory, integrates space, and scrapes away at the autonomy of heretofore self-reliant communities. Yet globalization does not necessarily corrode the form of the sovereign state—despite the avowals of globalizers such as IBM vice president Jacques Maisonrouge that interdependence rendered "the world's political structures . . . completely obsolete."[15]

Any nuanced understanding of the march of globalization will have to come to terms with the nation-state and its relations to globally integrative processes. As the sociologist Saskia Sassen has proposed, globalization does not necessarily lead to the withering of the state, but it does involve changes "deep inside territories and institutional domains" as national institutions, processes, and policies are "oriented towards global agendas and systems."[16] The territorial state, in Richard Rosecrance's formulation, is displaced by the virtual state; the nation-state, in Philip Bobbitt's, by the market state.[17] If planetary aggregates give us a measure of the changing landscape, we may also approach the history of globalization from the experience of the state—in this instance the United States.

For the United States, an enduring theme of the 1970s was the jolting reintegration of economy and society with the larger world after a forty-year interlude of relative autonomy. While resistance to integration remained a durable trope of domestic politics, Americans could not avoid the reality that, as Richard Nixon envisioned in 1969, "the world is going to get much smaller."[18] What would be the implications for governance, politics, and diplomacy? In many areas of national life—from macroeconomic management to the conduct of foreign policy—the integrative 1970s would be a time of coming to terms with the realities of diminished autonomy as well as the demands of leadership in a globalizing arena.

The integrative 1970s followed a four-decade phase in which U.S. relations with the external world had been characterized by the paradox of political engagement and economic disengagement. As Figure 2.1 illustrates, Americans conducted less international economic exchange, in relative terms, in the decades between the New Deal and the late 1960s than at any other point in their post–Civil War history. Like other industrial societies, the United States turned inward in the 1930s. FDR suspended dollar convertibility and erected exchange controls. With the support of the U.S. Treasury (if not of the State Department), the Bretton Woods settlement of 1944 legitimated economic controls that gave governments throughout

the industrialized world the autonomy necessary to manage their economies and to sustain growth through national monetary and fiscal policies.[19]

While presidents from Truman on pursued trade reform as an article of
faith and national interest, it was not until 1958—when Western European
countries returned to currency convertibility—that the postwar economy
began to shift decisively toward openness. With the encouragement of the
1964–1967 Kennedy Round of tariff reductions, international trade increased. At the same time, the growth of multinational business accelerated. When the resurgence of cross-border trade and finance began to
destabilize Bretton Woods from the mid-1960s, policymakers on both
sides of the Atlantic resorted to economic controls, especially capital controls, in an effort to sustain the Bretton Woods system of compartmental-
ized capitalism.

The Johnson administration made ready recourse to capital controls,
but the reintegration of the United States with the international economy
could not be prevented by fiat. With domestic productivity declining at
what Nixon's economic adviser Arthur Burns called "startling" rates from

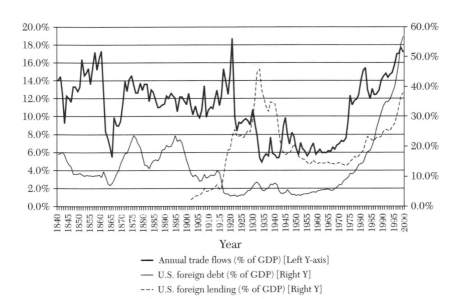

Year

— Annual trade flows (% of GDP) [Left Y-axis]
— U.S. foreign debt (% of GDP) [Right Y]
--- U.S. foreign lending (% of GDP) [Right Y]

Figure 2.1. The U.S. and the global economy, 1840–2000. *Sources:* Historical
Statistics of the United States, http://hsus.cambridge.org, and Office of Management and the Budget, Historical Tables, http://www.whitehouse.gov/omb.

the late 1960s, American consumers continued to import from overseas.[20] The year 1971 was the first since 1893 in which the United States ran a trade deficit, a grim landmark that gave rise to much consternation about the future of American industry.[21] With economic decline foremost among his concerns, Nixon compared America's slippage to the ends of empires past: "I think of what happened to Greece and Rome," he pondered; "what is left—only the pillars."[22]

Financial globalization in the early 1970s exacerbated the consequences of relative economic decline. From the late 1960s, the rise of the "Euro-markets"—offshore markets for dollars—created new uncertainties. By 1973 the total value of the transnational financial markets amounted "to more than twice the total of . . . reserves held in all central banks and all international money institutions."[23] In tandem with trade deficits, the speculative movement of these footloose funds exacerbated a series of currency crises. For strong currencies such as the Deutschmark, influxes of short-term capital brought inflationary pressures; for weak currencies such as the dollar and the British pound, movements of short-term funds could trigger runs on reserve assets. Speculation on the offshore capital markets was a crucial element in the crises that forced the United States to suspend dollar convertibility in 1971 and to abandon fixed exchange rates in 1973. Less disposed than LBJ to favor economic controls and mul-tilateral surveillance, the Nixon administration ignored the issue for as long as it could before succumbing to new economic realities by embrac-ing floating exchange rates in 1973 and abolishing capital controls in 1974.

Nixon might have favored "benign neglect," but by the mid-1970s for-eign policy intellectuals were advocating more active engagement with the challenges that globalization brought. Spurred by Brzezinski, David Rockefeller in 1972 envisaged an assembly of experts from the industrial-ized nations that would address "the problems of the future," such as the "accelerating" impact of "technological and social change on policy-making."[24] Constituted as the Trilateral Commission in 1973, Rockefeller's initiative brought together experts from North America, Japan, and Eu-rope to address a range of subjects, from the management of monetary re-lations to energy interdependence. These efforts bespoke a conviction that government in its classically territorial form was no longer competent to address economic, social, and political problems of transnational scale.

While Trilateralists disavowed interest in "setting up a supergovernment," their elitism rankled many Americans, making the commission an object of enduring suspicion.[25] They did not assuage their critics when a 1975 report on "the crisis of democracy" concluded that democracies were prone to "provincialism" and "parochialism"—that they were ill-suited to manage an incipient world society.[26] Such diagnoses revealed a discomforting tension between what elites saw as the imperatives of global governance and the stubbornly territorial nature of electoral processes.[27]

If Trilateralism was an activist response, interdependence became a prominent theme for academic reflection in the 1970s, as scholars asked how transnational relations might subvert old assumptions about the primacy of sovereign states in international relations. Some, like Raymond Vernon, paid particular attention to multinational corporations, transnational leviathans that, in Vernon's words, "threaten the concept of the nation as an integral unit."[28] The proliferation of interdependence studies, notably at Harvard's Center for International Affairs, suggested that the state was becoming more porous than classical models of Westphalian international relations allowed.

Concern over the world's interdependence transcended the academy in the 1970s. Ecological issues gained prominence, and a 1968 photograph of the planet taken from space—"Earthrise"—symbolized the dawning reality of a borderless world. The panorama was not necessarily comforting. Environmental degradation and ecological strain were the ultimate transnational issues; their consequences were inescapable. In 1972 the Club of Rome warned of an imminent world population crisis, sounding an alarm that reverberated in public debate. Even Kissinger's National Security Council worried that global population growth posed a tangible threat to U.S. national security.[29]

Whether spectators perceived interdependence as an opportunity or as a threat, the seventies saw broad agreement on the integrative direction of the international system's evolution. "Our interdependence on this planet," Henry Kissinger announced, "is becoming the central fact of our diplomacy."[30] This reflected the view, as Gerald Ford told his cabinet, that "there is an interdependence among the industrial powers in the economic, political, and security spheres."[31] Significantly for our understanding of the 1970s, the contemporary perception that the United States was becoming more entwined with a larger global community is, as we have seen, corroborated by statistics that reveal sharp increases in levels of international exchange. How the U.S. government contributed to these integrative changes—the question of agency—remains an urgent historical problem.

Some authors have interpreted globalization as the purposeful recasting of American hegemony: a "radical restructuring of international capitalism" through which the United States has imposed "neo-liberal practices on much of the world."[32] But there is little historical evidence to suggest that American officials in the 1970s anticipated the transformative potential of globalization. Occasional government analysts perceived that "the scope of American commercial, technical, and cultural influence" might transcend the ebbing of U.S. military and political power, but it was geopolitical decline that preoccupied the architects of U.S. foreign policy, especially in the early 1970s.[33] The advent of Soviet-American bipolarity and the Vietnamese morass were their overriding concerns. Sensing that the United States was "going down the tube" as a great power, Kissinger and Nixon worked to sustain American strength and influence in the world through an intricate diplomatic triangle with Moscow and Beijing.[34]

Tellingly, critics at the time lambasted the Nixon administration not for promoting interdependence but for neglecting it. Brzezinski, for example, had in 1970 perceived "the beginnings of a global community" in which a "global reality" was supplanting the Cold War's "era of certainty."[35] From his position as director of the Trilateral Commission, he would be a leading voice among the foreign policy intellectuals who criticized Nixon's lackluster response to interdependence and sought to devise alternatives.

Finding the Democrats more attuned to the politics of world order, Brzezinski attached himself to Jimmy Carter, a former Georgia governor who Brzezinski hoped might pursue a more creative approach to global leadership than had Nixon. Carter's presidential campaign became a rallying point for proponents of trilateral cooperation. The task ahead, the economist and Carter adviser Richard Gardner wrote in 1975, was "to make the world safe for interdependence."[36] Even Henry Kissinger joked in 1976 that his State Department might enhance its commitment to the politics of interdependence by taking "something out of the Democratic platform."[37]

Kissinger's humor notwithstanding, the Ford administration did in fact make strides toward the management of economic interdependence. The

1973–74 oil crisis was, as this essay has noted, a turning point. The 1974 energy conference led to the creation of the International Energy Agency (IEA), which preserved a modicum of unity among the oil-importing nations and prevented a generalized resort to bilateral deals with the producers. At home Ford worked to develop the United States' first energy policy. While Kissinger's energy strategy hinged on Saudi moderation, Ford accepted the need, in principle, to abolish domestic controls that kept U.S. oil prices below world market prices. Only when prices rose to world levels, he acknowledged, would Americans rein in their energy consumption—thereby reducing the world's demand for oil.

Without having been set in motion by American leaders, globalization transformed the context for public policy in the 1970s. At the same time, U.S. choices helped to define the terms of global integration. After the oil crisis, for example, American leadership ensured the triumph of market-based financial globalization over regulated alternatives. The cost of the energy shocks, the Organization for Economic Cooperation and Development (OECD) estimated, amounted to $87 billion in 1974 alone, a sum larger than the U.S. defense budget.[38] The question of how to finance these deficits became an urgent concern. The only solution, of course, was for the exporters to lend money to the importers. But whether "petro-dollar recycling" would proceed within an official International Monetary Fund facility or be conducted by private financial intermediaries (banks) remained a contentious issue. Exhibiting a preference for market-based solutions, U.S. delegates blocked the IMF plan, which the Saudis and a majority of the West Europeans favored, ensuring that the oil crisis spurred the further growth of offshore financial markets.[39]

While we might interpret Washington's preferences for market-based solutions as evidence of a creeping neoliberal influence, the United States in the mid-1970s found itself as bereft of long-range strategic vision as any other country. While some West European countries had became accustomed in the 1960s to conducting domestic policy with a view to external limits, the United States was facing up to such constraints for the first time since the Second World War. Seeking to regain control, some policymakers began to argue, as Treasury Secretary Michael Blumenthal did in 1978, that "increased economic interdependency" demanded a "degree of [international] cooperation unparalleled in history."[40]

The Group of Eight (G-8) summits began during the 1970s as an effort to achieve multilateral cooperation commensurate with the realities of an integrating world economy. The United States, France, and West Germany pioneered these annual summits, which began with a colloquium in the White House Library and developed in 1975 into the first G-6 summit, at Rambouillet. Ford's accession and the coming to power of Valéry Giscard d'Estaing, Helmut Schmidt, and James Callaghan facilitated cooperation, for this group of leaders shared a bonhomie that their predecessors had lacked. But it was the integration of national economies that—as Kissinger argued—made "isolated solutions impossible" and mandated cooperation.[41] While Rambouillet did not, in Giscard's view, produce "far-reaching concrete results," it "sensitized the major industrial powers to a greater degree than in the past to their profound interdependence."[42] Within a few years successive summits—London, Bonn, and Tokyo—would achieve more tangible ends.

Novel as the summits might have been, the efforts that American leaders made in the 1970s to develop collaborative responses to common challenges were reactive rather than prescriptive. The nature of American agency in the making of a globalizing world was unintentional and ironic far more than it was deliberate and coherent—and it far predated the 1970s. Paradoxically, it is to the Cold War of the 1950s and 1960s that we should turn to understand how the United States promoted the cause of globalization.

In its pursuit of anti-Soviet containment, the U.S. government pioneered many of the technologies on which globalization has depended. Satellite communications, which have facilitated the globalization of production and the integration of financial markets, were an offshoot of the Cold War's ballistic arms race. "Earthrise" might have symbolized a one-world future, but the exploration of lunar space was a function of a deadly two-world struggle. The Internet developed out of a Department of Defense initiative to create a decentered computer network able to survive a nuclear strike. The U.S. government, in key respects, promoted the infrastructure of globalization after 1945, but it did so because of Cold War security imperatives. Yet the rise of globalization in the 1970s proved both corrosive and transformative for the international security system that the United States had constructed in the name of the Cold War.

From the mid-1940s to the mid-1960s the United States was the benefactor of a Western international system; dollars, guns, and butter flowed outwards from North America and sustained the frontiers of anti-Soviet containment in Europe and East Asia. This was a system, dominated by U.S. power, that Charles Maier has aptly characterized as an American "empire of production."[43] With the rebirth of globalization from the 1970s, however, the system was transformed. The United States became an importer of foreign capital, no longer a net exporter. No more would American factories satiate the world's demand for consumer goods and capital machinery; the shelves of Wal-Mart are now stocked by China. And no longer could American leaders pursue visions of the good society at home with little regard to the world outside. Americans have been losing control since the 1960s; while globalization has in some respects reinvigorated the republic's influence and affluence, it has also been a discombobulating experience.

Not to belabor the point, external factors came to weigh decisively on the making of U.S. domestic policy during the 1970s as they had not done since the Great Depression. While Gerald Ford acknowledged the imperatives of cooperation in the context of what Helmut Schmidt called the world's "first global business cycle," it was Jimmy Carter who took the first substantial steps.[44] From the late 1970s, as the political scientist Michael Webb concludes, macroeconomic policymaking became "internationalized."[45]

Recognizing that interdependence was altering the landscape, the Carter administration worked to develop a multilateral solution to the "stagflation" crisis that wracked the transatlantic world from the mid-1970s. Trying to project Keynesian solutions on a transnational scale, Carter sought to persuade U.S. allies to implement fiscal stimuli. Implicit in his "locomotive strategy" was the belief that foreign growth was an essential counterpart to domestic growth.[46] Without West German and Japanese expansion, any domestic stimulus, Carter's team believed, would be ineffective and would cause the beleaguered dollar to deteriorate further. While Japan and especially Germany were reluctant to accept this logic, fearing that it would stir inflation, the United States offered to dismantle controls on oil imports as a "quid pro quo."[47] By allowing domestic energy prices to rise to world levels, decontrol promised to diminish U.S. energy consumption and reduce worldwide oil demand—and prices. This quid pro quo, which was achieved at the 1978 Bonn Summit, secured German and Japanese support for a coordinated stimulus. It constituted a bold effort to deal with what Blumenthal called "a new and totally interdependent world economic structure."[48]

Yet multilateral Keynesianism failed to stem the dollar's decline, and in the fall of 1978 the currency plunged to new lows. In an effort to prop it up, the Carter administration embraced a complex rescue package. Besides drawing on IMF funds, the Federal Reserve ratcheted up the interest rate to 9.5 percent and jumped into foreign exchange markets to defend the dollar. The Treasury also issued $10 billion worth of bonds denominated in foreign currencies. Soon 1979 brought one of the great historic shifts in U.S. economic policy, with the appointment of Paul Volcker as chairman of the Federal Reserve Bank of the United States. Volcker declared his determination to subdue the seventies' Great Inflation and ratcheted up interest rates accordingly. After nearly a decade of monetary turmoil, American officials had resolved to get the dollar under control. The contrast with 1971, when Nixon ordered the Fed to loosen monetary policy in order to produce a quick stimulus for the 1972 election, was striking.[49] As interest rates rose into the teens and the U.S. economy ground into recession, Carter refrained from publicly criticizing Volcker or lobbying him to reverse course—in effect privileging the international stability of the dollar over his own political survival.[50]

Carter fell to defeat in the election of 1980, but his acceptance of Volcker's belief that "issues of monetary stability cannot be shrugged away" marked a coming to terms with the realities of diminished autonomy in an integrating world—a recognition that domestic policy had to be conducted with a view to larger circumstances and that reckless autonomy reaped international consequences.[51] That said, the United States would expect the same—if not more—discipline from others. As the majority shareholder in the IMF, the United States took a "hard line" and aggressively supported the attachment of "policy conditionality" (expectations that borrowers balance budgets and trim social spending) to IMF loans, even when the beneficiaries were close allies—as with the British in the late fall of 1976.[52] Such power was not used simply to achieve economic ends. The Carter administration supported congressional efforts to tether U.S. votes on IMF assistance to the human rights records of recipient regimes and even opted, in some cases, to deny export financing to U.S. firms trading with human rights violators.[53]

While the United States would from the 1980s on benefit from what the political economist Susan Strange has called its "embedded power" in a liberalizing international system, it is too simplistic to see the process of globalization itself as merely the projection of American influence.[54] That the Congress, for example, sought to link IMF lending to human rights attested to the ways in which even the objectives of U.S. diplomacy were shaped by the erosion of barriers between domestic and foreign realms. Much as foreign capital washed over the American economy, so did the transnational politics of human rights bore from the outside in to reshape national priorities. Amnesty International, a British-based NGO that blossomed during the 1970s, worked with liberals in the U.S. Congress to enshrine human rights conditions within the legal framework of American diplomacy for the first time. The politics of human rights in the seventies depended, as Michael Morgan explains in his chapter, on both cross-border activism and technological innovation that made formerly "domestic" abuses more visible in the international arena.

The United States' coming to terms with globalization had consequences not only for its autonomy but also for its role as a superpower among nations. Interdependence might, over the long term, have enhanced American structural power in the international system, but it also increased the permeability and vulnerability of the United States to the exterior world. Globalization enabled Washington to draw on global capital markets to sustain its deficits; it helped preserve the dollar as the world's dominant currency, allowing the United States to borrow without currency premiums; and it affirmed liberal ideals—freedom, human rights, and consumer choice—that informed a wave of democratic revolutions in the Eastern bloc and global South. To a certain extent these sources of structural power compensated for the dwindling of traditional power assets—money, industrial output, and military force—that had been declining, in relative terms, since August 1945.[55]

Yet if the seventies appear to have launched a "second wind" for the United States in its career as global superpower, as the historian Charles Maier proposes, we ought to recall that the republic has paid for its reinvigorated primacy with new kinds of vulnerability.[56] Globalization has eroded public authority over the economy and has encouraged the outsourcing of industrial labor, devastating the manufacturing heartland; it has subjected U.S. actions at home and abroad to the oversight of global opinion (Abu Ghraib being an exception that demonstrates the rule); and it has facilitated the violence of transnational terrorists, as we learned on 9/11. Historically, to return to the question of agency, globalization has been anything but an imperial project imposed on weak nations by the United States. As the experience of the 1970s implies, the United States has been an object as much as an agent of globalization. Its autonomy in an integrating world has been diminished, while its leadership role, the nature of its power among nations, and the character of its influence in the world have been transformed.

CHAPTER 3

The Great Transformation

China in the Long 1970s

ODD ARNE WESTAD

CHINA PLAYS A MAJOR ROLE in the great two-acter of 1970s global transformation. In Act 1 she is the estranged divorcee of the International System (a village known for its ferocious feuding), where she lives in self-imposed isolation in a run-down shack until successfully wooed by a nouveau riche squire from across the river and his cunning consigliere and brought into a marriage of convenience directed against the belligerent heirs of her former husband. In Act 2 her role is, well, *transformed.* No longer the passive left-behind of former times, and buoyed by her new *alliance*, China drops the obsession with her previous husband, sheds her old dresses, and puts on new and glamorous ones (presents from her rich paramour), repairs the shack herself, and plans a new and prosperous existence as the village shopkeeper. The storyline shows the marks of grand opera. The score could have been by Berlioz.[1]

As with all stories about transformation, operatic or not, there are many twists, subplots, and misunderstandings connected to this tale, but its basic elements reflect reasonably well what we know happened: during the long 1970s—from 1969 to 1982 or thereabouts—China went from being an outcast of international affairs to a very central position, in which it could finally turn the Cold War to its advantage (only a pity, as some smart Chinese writers observe nowadays, that it ended too soon). Taking advantage of what became a de facto alliance with the United States, China embarked on its long transformation from the chaos of the Cultural Revolution to a blossoming market. Meanwhile, it kept its national integrity, preserved its security, and stabilized its authoritarian political system.

All great performances need to have critical light shed on them. This chapter is part of a project that may, a few years from now, force a somewhat different interpretation of these events than the ones that exist today.[2] I argue here that China's transformation to a market economy has its origins within the 1960s Cultural Revolution (CR), an era when the socialist planned economy was gradually destroyed. The chapter claims that the destruction of Chinese cultural values was as important for change as the destruction of the planned economy; the campaigns of the 1950s and 1960s, which deliberately pitted son against father, pupil against teacher, young against old, while—in part by accident—dramatically furthering the emancipation of women as well as general social and spatial mobility, meant the completion of the collapse of the Confucian value system, a necessary ingredient for transformational change. I maintain that political change in China came out of the conflicts within the Chinese Communist Party (CCP), and that both the content and outcome of these conflicts were, in historical terms, more than usually contingent, haphazard, or accidental. Finally, I claim that in international affairs China's siding with the United States and with the market system was a key element, possibly *the* key element, in bringing the Cold War to an end.

Destruction and Transformation: Economy and Society

From a socialist perspective China's economy performed rather well in the 1950s, with growth rates in both agriculture and industry during the first five-year plan (1953–1958) well exceeding what was seen in Eastern Europe at the same time (though of course starting from a much weaker position). This growth is particularly significant because it came after the dual disasters of the Korean War and the Communists' violent campaign against real or imagined enemies that together set China's growth potential back even further from where it had been at the end of the Civil War. Although massive Soviet assistance helped the Chinese economy to a great degree, it is clear that there was real domestic growth in all sectors during the first five-year plan. The planning system, which was well entrenched by the late 1950s, may not have held the potential for the hyper-growth of China's most recent era, but it did set the country on the road to recovery after a half-century of war.

All of the advances made during the Sino-Soviet alliance were wiped out starting with the Great Leap Forward (GLF) of 1958–1961. That campaign left China's economy in tatters, with some sectors—according to recent Chinese figures—in worse shape than in 1950. When the campaign petered out in 1961–62, those whom Mao Zedong entrusted to clear up the mess—at the central level first and foremost Liu Shaoqi, Zhou Enlai, and Deng Xiaoping—were willing to reach for desperate measures in order to get the economy going again. For most of them this meant returning as quickly as possible to the basic elements of planning. But for some, especially in the party secretariat and in the southern provinces, there was also a need to go further than the first five-year plan had promised to do. Experimentation was encouraged in order to increase production. In some areas the party accepted an element of private production in agriculture. Bonuses and material rewards for increased productivity were accepted in some industrial sectors. While this period of reform was limited both in duration and in extent (by the summer of 1962 Mao had turned on the reformers with a vengeance), it still held some of the seeds of the reforms that were accepted after Mao's death in 1976. Also some of the key people involved in the aborted reforms of the early 1960s reappeared in the late 1970s, if they had been lucky enough to survive the Cultural Revolution.

There is an increasing amount of evidence that at least for parts of China the Cultural Revolution, in spite of its violence and destructiveness, was somewhat less disastrous for the country's economic development than was earlier believed. While it limited growth through the chaos it initiated and led to structural problems in terms of the breakdown of administration and education, the CR affected production to a more limited extent than the GLF or even the antibourgeois campaigns of the early 1950s had done. As I will show, one of its key effects was probably to kill off Marxism as a credible framework for China's development. In this narrower sense the CR was itself an interruption of China's road to reform from the early 1960s to the early 1970s.

What the new evidence shows is that already by late 1972 (and possibly earlier in Guangdong) reform was back on the agenda. With the ideological frenzy of the CR behind them, local leaders turned to new measures in order to get the economy going, in spite of the official prohibition on any such initiatives. There were several reasons for the timing of the new trends. First and foremost, as we shall see, the purge and death of Mao's designated successor, Marshal Lin Biao, in 1971 weakened the party center and signaled the ideological bankruptcy of the regime. In early 1972 the Chairman suffered a severe heart attack, indicating to others that he

might not have much longer to live. And finally, the first opening to the
United States promised not only a more clement international climate for
China but also the potential for obtaining U.S. technology and for increased foreign trade. In sum, while CCP politics on the surface seemed
fully dominated by Mao, the Cultural Revolutionaries (first and foremost
the Chairman's wife, Jiang Qing), and the many who had benefited from
the CR, during the last four years of Mao's life an extraordinary reversal
was taking place in parts of Chinese society, which broke not only with the
radical trend in the CCP but with the Communist orthodoxies of planning
as well.

There were five different kinds of economic experimentation going on
in China in the last phase of the Maoist era: marketable agricultural production outside the plan (mostly by communes or parts of communes);
workshops and small factories operating their own accounts; a credit system between units; larger factories engaging in import of technology; and
units setting up their own contacts abroad (legal and extralegal) for export.
All of these trends should be regarded only as small seeds prior to 1978,
and for each of their individual manifestations that survived, hundreds
were wiped out. They were greatly helped by Mao's emphasis on devolv-
ing authority to the provincial, county, and commune level that came out
of his mistrust of the central party apparatus. They were also assisted by
the chaos of the CR and the uncertainty—even at the highest levels—
of what the political line was at any given time, especially after Deng
Xiaoping's return to the party leadership in 1973. But each of them contained aspects of what was to come; whoever today gazes in amazement at
the high-tech factories in Shenzhen or the office buildings in Pudong
should consider these early seeds of reform and the risks some people
took in carrying them out.[3]

A return to marketable production for small plots within the agricultural communes started in the South—especially in Guangdong, Guangxi,
Jiangxi, and Hunan—sometime before 1973, in response to distribution
difficulties created by the Cultural Revolution. In most cases the plots
were cultivated by members of the same family or clan, and the income
was shared among them, though in technical terms it constituted a form of
bonus from the commune. By far the most significant aspect of this production was how it was distributed: in quite a few cases peasants reconstituted small local markets that had existed in the prerevolutionary period. In some cases intermediaries of various kinds—people who knew

something about market practices from abroad or from the early 1950s—helped out. But most significantly, the idea of selling produce in a market was reconstituted, even though traditional terms for buying and selling had to be avoided. (In one case the sign for a cabbage seller read, "Superfluous people's produce redistributed here.")

As simple machinery made in the 1950s and 1960s started to wear out—and replacements were hard to get hold of—enterprising units set up their own repair shops, which sometimes also did work for other units or for individuals. The fees they charged for these services were set by themselves and in some areas—for instance in sections of Guangdong province—did form part of their own accounts (meaning that the unit could profit from improving service and productivity). The profit could be reinvested or spent on the needs of the workers and their families (or kept in accounts controlled by the unit's bosses). The repair shop could use its key role as intermediary to function—at least in part—outside the official economic system for some of its activities, thereby pointing the way to the village enterprises that played such a key role in Chinese capitalism in the 1980s and 1990s.

Some of the most remarkable examples of "marketization" pre-1978 that I have come across are the systems of credit that existed between units of production in parts of the South. The model probably came from local credit arrangements during the Qing and early Republican eras, when "letters of credit" often noted both a nominal monetary value and a value in terms of production: two eighteen-inch steel pipes equaled fifty railway rails or 200 yuan. When the allocations according to the plan were not enough to keep production going, factory bosses could draw on any surplus they had achieved from bartering with other units to get what they needed, either by using its nominal value (debited to the factory that had a deficit) or by providing the railway rails or whatever they had been storing. The central party condemned such practices, of course, and in a few cases managers were purged or arrested, but in most instances the local bosses got away with it because it helped keep production going.

Some larger factories—my favorite example is the aircraft factory in Jiangxi, constructed by the Soviets in the 1950s and expanded in the 1960s as part of China's "Third Line Defense"—were directly involved in getting hard currency credit to import technology and parts (legally or illegally) through the international market. There were different ways of getting such credit. One was through trade agreements with foreign—mostly overseas Chinese—companies. Another was through the Ministry of International Trade or provincial trade bureaus that were sanctioned to handle income from foreign sources. In a couple of cases factories got indirect loans from Hong Kong or Singapore banks, which they would have to pay back through skimming off some of their foreign income (a very difficult process, since factories were in principle not allowed to handle any of the foreign income from their products themselves).

Finally, in a few places, such as along the Fujian coast and in parts of Guangxi and Guangdong, illegal buying and selling through foreign markets (meaning mostly Hong Kong and Southeast Asia) had begun in the first half of the 1970s and increased after 1978. These activities—what we would call smuggling and illegal export—of course reconstituted, in microformat, what had been one of China's economic lifelines before 1949 and especially before the collapse of the Qing. (They could even be compared in form with the so-called tribute trade of the eighteenth and early nineteenth centuries, since most of them went through official contacts established through the Chinese state.) Even more than the market practices outlined earlier, this contact with foreign markets was of course in direct contravention of the planning system, and was cracked down on by the central government on the few occasions when it was capable of seeing beyond the factional battles in Beijing. But the persistence of these kinds of contacts tells us something about the weaknesses of the socialist economy as well as the distractedness of the central government. They point back to a China that had been and would come again.

The main point of this story is not the inventiveness of Chinese managers in circumventing a bankrupt planning system. It is that all of this was going on, especially in China's southern provinces, while Mao Zedong was still alive, while the most radical revolutionary propaganda was coming out of Beijing, and while the battles between Politburo factions seemed to ebb and flow (including quite a few times when the radicals, supported by Chairman Mao, were on top). By the early 1970s the collapse of the planning system in China—under the weight of its own insufficiencies, but first and foremost because of the politically induced chaos of the Great Leap and the Cultural Revolution—was already far advanced. People in the southern provinces, who had felt the brunt of this collapse because they were further from the center, but who for the same reason were freer to take their own drastic initiatives to counter it, began a process that would eventually engulf the whole country. "Reform" in China was not just a product of central decision making after the end of the Maoist era; in some parts of the country it came from below and as a necessary consequence of the self-destruction of the planning system that the Communists had put in place after 1949.

Destruction and Transformation: Ideas and Policies

In the Chinese Communist Party, Marxism as a political theory has always been a thin veneer over a modernizing developmentalism aimed at transforming China into a strong state and highly productive society along Western lines. In spite of what many in the West believed at the time and believe today, the CR was a product of this developmentalism: its primary aim was to remove the last vestiges of Chinese thinking from the prerevolutionary period. In this sense the party got more than it bargained for. The attacks on Communist cadres in many cases not only implied the removal of "old" thinking and Soviet-style development but also destroyed the belief that any Westernization of a socialist kind would work for China. The search for new and more flexible forms of thinking was already under way in the early 1970s, even though it took strange and contorted forms because of the terror and chaos that still remained as legacies of the CR.

In this chapter I briefly survey the ideological transformation that Chinese elites went through from the late 1960s to the early 1980s, emphasizing the extraordinary and unforeseen consequences of some of the late CR debates. But first it is necessary to note what the CR did to the beliefs and worldviews that had sustained the Communist elite and its allies since the late 1930s.

Intended as a political campaign to purge the party of Mao Zedong's real or imagined enemies—much in the style of Stalin's purges of the 1930s—the Great Proletarian Cultural Revolution had already got out of hand by the winter of 1966–67, because it released many of the grievances of young people against the strongly regimented society that they lived in. In 1949 the CCP had taken over a society that still retained much of the Confucian authoritarianism of former years and had reversed the liberalizing trends of the early twentieth century. By the 1960s many of those who had grown up under Communist rule—irrespective of their "class background"—felt alienated from their own society. The Korean War and the GLF had fed their nationalism, as had the relentless propaganda about the infallibility of Mao Zedong Thought and how it was superior to any other political ideology. But they did not feel that China was making rapid progress toward the lofty goals of communism, which would establish the country as the paragon of the world.

After the CR got under way, many aspiring leaders among China's youth—especially in the cities—were emboldened by Mao's own radicalism to take matters into their own hands, forming Red Guard groups that attacked the party's senior leaders at all levels and demanded more of a role for themselves. Mao and the new party leadership that had formed around him by 1967 could always in principle intervene to save someone from being attacked, purged, or killed, but they soon got lost in the factional infighting at the central and local levels. As China descended into chaos, many of the youth leaders themselves began to lose faith in the process they had helped ignite.

By the autumn of 1969, as the Soviet war scare peaked and as it became clear that the Ninth Party Congress of the CCP had not led to any plan for renewed stability after the frenzied period since 1966, an increasing cynicism began to spread among those who had survived the political infighting. The army—the only institution capable of doing so—had quelled the unrest in China's cities with the Chairman's implicit blessing, but without a clear result emerging from the CR. Instead of moving China forward, the CR seemed to be moving it backward. Both CR beneficiaries and the old cadres who slowly began returning to positions of power viewed the campaign as a failure, even though they disagreed on what had gone wrong. In both cases, though, the belief in Marxist solutions was at an all-time low. New answers to China's difficulties would have to be found, especially after the Lin Biao affair brought the level of cynicism to an all-time high.

The debates and conflicts over China's future between 1971 and 1978 saw a number of very different trends develop, with only one of them having much to do with the party's Marxist background. That trend—let us call it "the Plan"—saw the ideal as a return to the situation of the 1950s, with Soviet-style socialist planning as the key to China's development. While popular among some of the senior party leaders who came back to Beijing after the peak of the CR, it was obvious to the leaders at the provincial level that a return to planning was not enough to make up for China's mounting difficulties. It also indicated to them an unwanted return to the much-criticized Soviet experience.[4]

Most immediately opposed to the planners were the party radicals, who saw the CR as the key achievement of the CCP in power. Though in no way a unified group, people such as Mao's wife (the former actress Jiang Qing) and the Shanghai intellectual Zhang Chunqiao believed that the CR was the beginning of a radical transformation of Chinese culture, which was what had held the country back. They and their allies thought China was breaking through to a new form of civilization whereby man could realize his true potential; they wanted, in a utopian sense, to help create a "new man." This Chinese ultra-Left, which Mao Zedong had encouraged but rarely given concrete power, had more than a few things in common with the radical Left in Europe and the Americas in terms of their focus on the need to form a revolutionary vanguard and to cleanse the working class of its ills. A small but influential minority in the party, the radicals as a trend survived the 1976 coup against their main leaders, and even the purges that accompanied the trials of the so-called Gang of Four, but played a diminishing role during the 1980s.

The leaders who owed their promotions to the upheavals of the CR, but who—having arrived at the pinnacle of power—were afraid of further chaos that could threaten their position, are usually referred to as the CR beneficiaries. Best symbolized by Hua Guofeng—the obscure party official from Hunan who joined the Politburo in 1973, became Chinese premier in February 1976 after Zhou Enlai's death, and eight months later succeeded Mao—the CR beneficiaries combined an intense nationalism with boundless faith in the "scientific" aspects of Mao Zedong Thought. Lacking in both education and general political experience—and vague on even the most basic tenets of Marxism—the beneficiaries wanted to lead China toward a unique form of specifically Chinese modernity in which technology and mass mobilization joined hands.

The CR democrats represented two small trends that, in different ways, were going to have a major influence on China in the 1980s, until they joined forces in 1989. One consisted mostly of disaffected Red Guards from the 1960s, often student leaders who had participated in the CR with enthusiasm but had been purged at various stages of its history. Having been able to read freely and to think in different directions from what the party ordained, quite a few such leaders went from Maoism to some form of democratic thinking, in some cases harking back to China's history in the early twentieth century to find examples of where they wanted to go politically. Another group were younger party leaders who had been purged at the outset of the CR and who had concluded that only through a democratization of the state and of Chinese society would it be possible to avoid disasters like the outcome of the CR in the future. People such as Hu Yaobang, who became general secretary of the CCP in 1981, belong to this group, just as the dissident Wei Jingsheng belonged to the former group of democrats.

Finally there were the modernizers, the group that came to be symbolized by Deng Xiaoping, the most powerful party leader from 1977 on. Consisting mostly of party leaders who had participated in politics before 1949 and therefore knew a different kind of CCP, or military leaders who had tried to keep their distance from the inner party upheavals of the PRC period, the modernizers were desperate to fulfill the hopes and dreams that had caused them to join the revolution in the first place: to make China rich and strong, and to make Chinese society a better environment for its people. Even though they had been willing to follow Mao into the CR, they had seen their hopes for China dashed and their own political careers in ruins. In the aftermath of the CR they were willing to experiment with almost any method that would jump-start China's economy without causing major social upheaval. While keenly observing the progress made in other Chinese states—Singapore, Taiwan—they wanted to "restore party norms" as they had existed prior to 1958 and keep the party dictatorship in place.

As could be imagined from this overview of the main groupings in the confused and chaotic Chinese politics of the 1970s, the outcome of the struggle for power was largely contingent and accidental. That Deng's modernizers came out on top was the result of Deng's own skill in forging political alliances (initially, not least with the beneficiaries and some of the party democrats), but also perhaps first and foremost because of his alliance with military leaders in different parts of China. All the way up to the early 1980s Deng's reform plans could have been derailed and China could have taken a very different political route, with the most likely outcome being a Brezhnevite slow decline of a reinstated and strengthened planning system. Also, one should in no way rule out a resurgence of the party radicals, not in power in Beijing but possibly as a terrorist element that could have led to a much more delicate balance of power at the center and weaker links to provinces where the radicals were strong, such as in Shanghai and areas of the Northeast.

The outcomes of key events were likewise unpredictable. The October 1976 coup against the radicals in Beijing (later referred to as the "Gang of Four" in CCP propaganda), which we now know was carried out mostly by Hua Guofeng and his beneficiary ally Wang Dongxing (the head of Mao's bodyguard), succeeded mostly because it came as a complete surprise to almost all the party leaders. The 1979 crushing of the dissident democrats prevented an open split in the party, at least for a while. The uneasy and contradictory relationship between modernizers, beneficiaries, and planners in the party leadership held together because of their joint fear of the radicals, of the democrats, and of a return to open warfare within the party. There was also a real fear that the country could disintegrate along the lines of its various military districts. At the same time, however, the remainder of other groupings within the leadership forced a radicalization of the modernizers. If Deng and his allies were to get their reform plans through, they would need to show immediate and direct production results in areas that fell within their brief, such as agriculture. And in order to achieve that, they would have to experiment, in some cases well beyond what they felt politically comfortable with. They also had to ally themselves with local leaders and with leading officers in the regional commands, and thereby gradually came to fuse their reforms with the economic experimentation that had been under way at the local level since the early 1970s.

As Deng Xiaoping also admitted over and over again, realizing just how weak China was after the CR took time even for him after he returned to the core leadership. What Deng was willing to do out of desperation, at least from 1978 on, was to use the iconoclasm, the mobility, and the readiness to criticize that the CR had produced, particularly in many younger people, in order to serve the purposes of economic development away from the plan and along market-oriented lines. Part of this trend was conviction, part was necessity, and part was pure chance. Deng had, for instance, grown up with an intense hatred for nepotism and corruption, but he came to accept massive amounts of both in the name of economic progress. And all the while—in what is possibly the biggest difference between China's reform at the end of the 1970s and what Gorbachev attempted north of the border ten years later—many reform initiatives, and the transformation in beliefs that accompanied them, came as the result of already ongoing processes in the provinces.

China in International Affairs

The CCP modernizers' control of the country's foreign affairs was a big advantage in the struggle for power after 1976. Granted, working in the foreign affairs field had been something of a poisoned chalice in China since

1949 (or even in earlier CCP history), and very few of the country's top foreign affairs specialists had survived the CR. But in the reform plans that came into being in the late 1970s, control over the relationship with the United States (and to a lesser degree Japan and Southeast Asia) was of critical importance. From 1978 at the latest, the Dengists felt convinced that they could develop Mao's tenuous opening to the United States into a de facto alliance that would, at least for a while, both improve China's security and provide access to the technology China needed to develop. By piggybacking onto one of the superpowers of the international system, the CCP modernizers could get what they needed to secure their position in the hothouse of Beijing politics.

China's foreign policy in the 1970s originated in one of the great geopolitical misunderstandings of the twentieth century: that the Soviet Union was the ascending superpower and the United States was a power in decline. For Mao Zedong it had become almost an article of faith by the late 1960s that at some point during the coming decade Soviet power would dominate the world, and at that moment, or soon after, the Soviet Union would attack China. After 1969 Mao's entire foreign policy was based on this premise. His strategic thinking (or what remained thereof as he gradually succumbed to mental and physical illness) paralleled his experience from years back. Just as he had sought an alliance with all comers, including the United States, against Japan in the 1940s, he would now seek a new alliance with the Americans against the rise of Soviet power. The United States could give China the breathing space it needed to complete the CR and strengthen itself for future war.

Mao never imagined the double use that Deng Xiaoping found for China's American alliance. One of the main reasons why the Chairman had brought Deng back into the leadership in 1973 was the diminutive statesman's anti-Soviet credentials: in the early 1960s Leonid Brezhnev had referred to Deng as an "anti-Soviet dwarf." There is every reason to believe that Deng's dislike of the Soviet Union was personal as well as political. But what Deng had learned—unlike many of the other CCP leaders of his generation who had survived the CR—was a dislike not only of the way the Soviets had lorded it over Chinese Communists in the past but also of the inefficiencies and sloth of the Soviet planning system. While the planning faction in the post-Mao Politburo, to which a majority of Deng's surviving contemporaries belonged, believed that China needed *more* of the original socialist plan, Deng's (belated) conclusion was that it needed *less*. Ironically, it is quite possible that Deng's support for Mao's anti-Sovietism had led him away not just from the Soviet planning experience but from excessive planning altogether, and toward making use of market-driven modes of development.

Upon solidifying his control of the party's foreign affairs in 1978, Deng had begun to seek ways in which the strategic relationship with the United States could be expanded into a more active aid to his country's development efforts. Deng and most of his assistants continued to believe—in some cases against their better knowledge—that Mao's predictions for future world politics would hold up, and that the primary purpose of the strategic closeness to the United States was the country's short-term security. But if the United States was willing to assist the modernization of China within, or even beyond, the context of a military and strategic alliance, then a double advantage could be had for Beijing. As the Carter administration's conflict with the Soviet Union intensified, and Washington—in part in consequence—prepared a full recognition of the PRC, Deng began to outline detailed plans for how the United States could assist the ambitious development aims Beijing was setting up.

In order to understand Chinese foreign policy, it is important to realize how poor the Chinese leaders' grasp of the outside world was in the 1970s. Contrary to Henry Kissinger's belief that his Beijing visits brought him into the presence of strategic geniuses, Mao (in his later years), Hua Guofeng, and Deng Xiaoping would have had trouble placing even midsized countries on the map and had only the most hazy concepts of actual American strategies abroad. As more unbiased information about the outside world started to filter through to the CCP leadership toward the end of the decade, this deficiency slowly started to change. But in Deng's case, crucially, it was his own visit to the United States in early 1979 that marked a turning point. According to his reports, Deng's tours of U.S. farms and factories bowled him over; he was so taken by the technology and the productivity levels he saw in the United States that he, according to his own testimony, could not sleep for several days—not surprising, perhaps, since Deng himself had recently spent three years working as a fitter in a rather basic tractor factory in Jiangxi. What he saw in the United States was what he wanted for China in the future; his U.S. trip radicalized him and made him more determined to experiment in order to secure China's rapid development.

It was the combination of the deterioration in the Soviet-American relationship and China's development needs that created the high point of the informal Sino-American alliance between 1979 and 1982–83. During these years the United States and China engaged in an unprecedented (and never repeated) level of cooperation on matters from ranging from intelligence to technology which was of crucial importance to China's development efforts. What marked a change in Sino-American relations after that was not so much the election of Ronald Reagan as Deng's growing worry—as more information became available to him—that he had misinterpreted the international situation. If the Soviets were *not* advancing but rather retreating as a result of U.S. pressure, then the world of the late 1980s—a world China had helped create through its anti-Sovietism— could, because of its unipolarity, become a more dangerous place for China than the world of the 1970s had been. Deng wanted U.S. assistance and U.S. technology, but he feared any influence from Washington on Chinese politics, especially if the United States were to be the dominant power of the future. After the planners were defeated in Chinese politics in 1982–83, the room for the democrats to maneuver within the party became ever smaller toward the mid- and late 1980s.

The transformation of China's domestic politics and the beginning of the transformation of its economy during the long 1970s were key parts of the fundamental global changes that were taking place during the decade. As the Chinese scholar Yang Kuisong has pointed out, in the longer run these internal changes—which mainly took place for domestic reasons—had a more profound effect internationally than even the process of Sino-American diplomatic normalization. By delegitimizing dependence on state planning as an instrument of economic growth, China's reforms implied to many countries that the Soviet road to modernity had reached a dead end. If China, the most intense admirer and defender of the original Soviet Communist road, had concluded that it had to be deviated from in order to reach high levels of modern development, the significance if you happened to live in South Yemen, or in Mozambique, or even in East Germany was quite obvious and stark. China's defection from socialist planning helps explain why so many other regimes, especially in the Third World, prepared to ditch their Soviet-style economic systems well before Gorbachev came to power in Moscow.

While there is no doubt that the early 1970s diplomatic opening to the

United States presented a framework within which foreign trade and investments in later years could help spawn a breakthrough for capitalism in China, it would be entirely wrong to say that any of this was Mao's original intention from 1969 on. Mao's opening to the West was almost an act of panic as confrontation with the Soviet Union seemed to draw nearer. While Mao was pleasantly surprised with the willingness of the United States to work with his regime for strategic reasons, he never intended to let his U.S. connection influence the character of his rule. On the contrary, there is some evidence that Mao—buoyed by his new sense of strategic security—was planning a further round of radicalization of his revolution as his life came to an end.

The initiatives and impulses that were to transform China after 1978 originally emerged from below and from the (political) periphery, and were a result of the mismanagement of the economy that Mao's regime had led to. A large number of Chinese in influential positions, especially in the South (a region of more than 400 million people), had decided that they did not want to go on living the way they were doing, and they were setting up ways to get themselves out of their predicament. After the coup against the radicals in Beijing in 1976, central leaders began picking up some of these signals, and started a cautious reform policy that turned into a flood of economic experimentation toward the end of the decade. While the experiments that had been going on locally and the attitudes of some senior party leaders made the change possible, it was in no way a given result; China could have gone in many different directions after Mao's death. The two extremes would have been democratization (the Jiang Jingguo option, to use the Taiwan example) or collectivist utopianism (the Pol Pot option, if you will). But the policy the party arrived at through Deng's modernizers was also fairly extreme, given China's immediate past. China's change of role to become the shopkeeper of the international system may have normalized the country, as seen by a foreign audience. But for those who had lived out China's previous decade, it was a radical departure from all that they had once believed in and a step toward a world that was largely unknown to them but that they knew they wanted to be part of.

CHAPTER 4

The Kiss of Debt

The East Bloc Goes Borrowing

STEPHEN KOTKIN

WHAT TOOK PLACE in the East bloc in the 1970s was scarcely appreciated at the time, but it proved to be momentous. Edward Gierek, the Communist Party boss in Poland, and Walter Ulbricht, the East German Communist leader, each hit upon a bold new development strategy: borrow from the West in convertible currency in order to effect a great economic leap. The ostensible goal was to use the money to buy technology and expand industry in order to export goods to . . . pay back the loans. But the regimes also felt a deep need to mollify their populations by importing Western consumer goods. The immediate upshot was that the production of goods such as cars and television sets grew appreciably, while foodstuffs, clothing, and other daily items became more readily available. In the early 1970s, at least, economic times were good in Eastern Europe.[1]

Before the decade was out, however, the borrowing gamble turned into a bust. Both Poland and East Germany found themselves stuck with huge loans in currencies other than their own that they could not readily pay: the increased hard currency revenues from exports never materialized. A major part of the problem was the 1973 oil shock, or the pan-Arab refusal to sell oil to the West against the background of the Arab-Israeli War. The price of crude spiked 400 percent in a matter of months, and energy costs shot up substantially for East European industry. But the deeper problem was the fact that communism locked in low productivity while also doling out living standard subsidies. The dangers of the failed borrowing strategy were remarked in internal discussions. Yet the regimes lacked the political legitimacy to take the necessary hard measures of a structural adjustment, such as cutting off subsidies (that is, raising prices) and throwing people out of work in the worst-performing sectors. The bloc was not merely on the verge of economic bankruptcy; more consequentially, it was politically bankrupt.

The capitalist West, meanwhile, in many ways had the exact opposite experience in the 1970s. The crippling oil shock sparked the formation by 1975 of the Group of Six, or G-6, a forum consisting of the United States, Japan, West Germany, Great Britain, Italy, and France (Canada would be added the next year), in an attempt to coordinate policy. All these countries underwent stock market swoons, grueling recessions, rises in unemployment, and declines in living standards. Times were tough in the first half of the 1970s. Still, the longer-term consequence of the oil shock and the market-induced structural adjustment in the leading capitalist countries was more robust economies. The postwar capitalist world in the 1950s and 1960s was extraordinarily different from its interwar incarnation: no more Great Depression and fascist militarism, but instead democracy and consumer boom. Furthermore, despite the economic difficulties of the early 1970s, and another recession in the 1980s, capitalism would manage renewed high performance. This was game changing for socialism. Either socialism was the antidote to capitalism, or it had no reason to exist.

The Polish Disease

Consider the crucial case of East Germany. In building socialism, the Soviets had radically suppressed consumption, but that was back when the capitalist world had been mired in 1930s mass unemployment. In the 1950s West Germany's growth rates were *in the double digits,* yearly. In July 1960 Ulbricht wrote to Soviet leader Nikita Khrushchev: "You can be sure that we are doing everything in our powers. But West Germany has turned out to be economically powerful." The upshot: the German Democratic Republic was being subverted by "hostile-negative forces," that is, by Western daily life. "In the final analysis, we cannot choose against whom we would like to compete," concluded Ulbricht, the son of a tailor. "We are simply forced to square off against West Germany. However, the GDR does not have enough economic power to do this alone." Ulbricht begged for more hard currency. Moscow said no. In January 1961 Ulbricht wrote again: "The booming economy in West Germany, which is visible to every citizen of the GDR, is the main reason that over ten years about two million people have left our republic."[2] Those runaways included entrepreneurs and skilled professionals (one day the entire mathematics department of the University of Leipzig defected). Small wonder Moscow consented later that year to Ulbricht's requests to wall in East Germans. But the living standard differential could not be walled out.[3]

Under Ulbricht, supplication before the Soviets never ceased, but he also turned to the enemy. In 1970, the year before his ouster, he told the chairman of the USSR Council of Ministers that because the Soviets would not underwrite the GDR to the extent necessary, the GDR would have to borrow from the capitalist West. "We know the plan will be upset by it," Ulbricht admitted.[4] But the GDR needed hard currency to make an industrial leap and, in theory, pay the debt back with a range of new manufactured goods. This, however, presupposed Western demand for GDR goods—as well as no competition from other low-price exporters. It also required expensive imports of components and raw materials, on top of the consumer imports necessary to placate a populace aware of West German lifestyles. And unless the GDR's export earnings kept ahead of these import expenditures, the country would suffer a trade imbalance and be unable to pay back the hard currency loans. Brezhnev and the comrades in Moscow suspected that in turning westward for loans, Ulbricht was signaling his readiness to sell out the Soviet Union in a deal to resolve the German question. Ulbricht, though, remained a dreamer. The same year he told the Soviets about his need to go cap in hand to the imperialists, he assured his chief planner that within five years the GDR would be selling computers to the West.

Erich Honecker elbowed Ulbricht aside and redoubled the efforts to build up a socially oriented consumer society under the banner of socialist orthodoxy. As late as 1971 the GDR's semiprivate and private sectors still employed nearly half a million people and accounted for 11.3 percent of output, but Honecker nationalized these mostly small, flexible private enterprises, whose profits were deemed politically anathema. Ironically, they had manufactured specialty machines and other goods for Western export (one GDR efficiency expert had dubbed them the country's "secret weapon").[5] Reducing revenues, Honecker also ratcheted up outlays for consumer and housing subsidies, which leapt nearly sevenfold between the onset of his rule and 1989. "The people need cheap bread, a dry flat and a job," the former roofer remarked. "If these three things are in order, nothing can happen to socialism."[6] The subsidies, however, came on top of pensions, hospitals, schools; the GDR regime could not raise productivity to pay for the lifestyle that it promised and the populace had come to expect. The almighty rulers walked on eggshells for fear of triggering a repeat of the June 1953 Uprising, when only Soviet military assistance had prevented a regime collapse. Communism's locked-in low productivity also derived from the inherent nature of planning, which through the unlimited demand for labor gave workers the power to shirk (even in an emigration-depleted GDR). East Germany's supposed ace in the hole was the big bet on high technology, which Honecker increased—right when the limits of the GDR's Fordist production model were being felt globally, thanks to rising energy costs. In the international political economy, socialist East Germany was not capitalist East Asia, as would soon be poignantly demonstrated when East Asian goods produced by market discipline economies trounced East German goods on global export markets.

The Kremlin, which had egged Honecker on in his palace coup against Ulbricht and in his total eradication of private enterprise, balked at underwriting his rule. Not long after the first oil shock hit in 1973, the Soviets announced price rises for their oil, and the GDR found itself needing to export 20 percent more goods to the West just to stay even in hard currency. GDR economic growth began to taper off (either from more than 7 percent on average to around 4 percent, or from around 4 percent to not much more than 1 percent, depending on how one assesses East European data). Honecker had also been re-exporting some of the cheap Soviet oil (at world prices), but in August 1981 Brezhnev informed his pal that after three consecutive poor harvests in the Soviet Union, Moscow would have to shrink oil deliveries to the GDR. State Planning Chairman Gerhard Schürer implored his Soviet counterpart, Nikolai Baibakov: "I assume that a healthy, stable, socialist GDR plays an important role in the strategic thinking of the USSR. Imperialism stands right at the door of our house with its hate on three television channels." In addition, said Schürer, complaining of the independent trade union Solidarity, "now we have counterrevolution in Poland at our backs." He begged for 3.1 million tons more fuel. "Should I cut back on oil to Poland?" Baibakov asked rhetorically. "Vietnam is starving . . . should we just give away South East Asia? Angola, Mozambique, Ethiopia, Yemen . . . we carry them all. And our standard of living is extraordinarily low."[7] (This was in 1981: so much for the oil-fueled uplift experienced by the Soviets in the 1970s.)

And so Honecker, too, found himself going to the imperialists, worker's cap in hand. He had blasted Ulbricht for running up the foreign debt, then he himself ballooned it beyond anything previously seen. The GDR's increasing dependency on the imperialists, especially West Germany, struck a psychological blow among the leadership. It was embarrassing enough that GDR schoolbooks taught that the goods of the West—which the regime doled out as rewards, and for which the GDR was sinking into debt—were produced by exploitation. But Honecker forbade even internal debate about the debt issue. When in November 1973 the regime's chief finance expert had warned the party chief that by 1980 the GDR's foreign debt would soar by a factor of ten, from DM 2 billion to DM 20 billion, Honecker instructed him to cease making the calculations. (The debt in 1980 turned out to be DM 25 billion.) Schürer, the chief planner, strove again and again to put across the dangerousness of the situation, but he was told to avoid taking any actions, lest they magnify the troubles. By 1989 GDR foreign debt had reached DM 46 billion, or $26.5 billion. The cost of servicing those obligations was $4.5 billion, nearly 60 percent of export earnings. And there was no end in sight to more hard currency borrowing. Finally, in October 1989, Schürer disclosed the extent of the debt to the rest of the GDR leadership. By then there was no way out, except for Western debt forgiveness. Living well beyond its means, the GDR had essentially lost its sovereignty.[8]

The Polish case—though extremely different in many ways—nonetheless bears some striking similarities to that of East Germany. Gierek, a former miner, had been in charge of a heavily industrialized coal mining region, Silesia, prided himself on being a manager, and, unusually, had lived abroad (in Belgium) and spoke French. Upon taking power as supreme party boss in 1970, he installed his "Silesian mafia" in Warsaw and broke up the country's seventeen voivodeships (the largest administrative units) into forty-nine smaller ones, eliminating any chance that someone could accumulate the power to challenge the authority of the first secretary (the way he had done as an overlord in Silesia). Besides centralizing power as well as expanding party membership—which rose from 2 million to 3 million over the decade of the 1970s—Gierek implemented the same strategy as Ulbricht: borrowing hard currency from the West to fatten consumption in Poland and turbocharge the economy. Poland's GDP grew at a stunning annual clip of nearly 10 percent during the first half of the decade, and salaries leapt accordingly.

Whereas in 1970 there had been 450,000 private cars in Poland, by the end of the decade, thanks to local production of the "small Fiat" from 1974, more than 2 million private cars were on the roads. But Polish production mostly failed to find buyers in the West, and the hard currency loans were eaten up; by 1979 up to one half of the raw materials and basic inputs necessary to keep production going in Polish factories had to be imported for hard currency. Foreign debt, nearly $4 billion in 1974, doubled the next year and reached $20 billion by decade's end. Gierek had loosened the autarky, exposing the system far more than ever before to the world economy.[9] Gierek also entered into long-term agreements linking Poland to Soviet-sponsored projects through Comecon. This guaranteed better access to cheap Soviet raw materials, particularly oil and natural gas, but in the second half of the 1970s Poland experienced shortages of capital goods (such as locomotives) because Comecon obligations required exports of such products out of Poland.

Above all, though, the 1973 oil shock, on top of the inherent wastefulness and nonmarket rigidity of planning, bludgeoned the borrowing strategy, leading Gierek again to try to lower the costly subsidies for food. In June 1976 price hikes—69 percent for meat and fish, 100 percent for sugar, 60 percent for butter—provoked strikes at 130 factories. (The atmosphere had been inflamed the preceding year by attempts to insert the "leading role" of the party as well as the "special friendship" with the USSR into the country's constitution.) The workers humiliated the establishment; an ashen prime minister went on television and revoked the "price adjustment" for meat products *one day* after having introduced them and belatedly promised consultations with unspecified "representatives of society." Imagine a state with monopoly control over everything—economy, education, the media, cultural institutions, unions, police, the military, entertainment—which could not raise the price of sausage without risking mass social protests.

By the late 1970s Gierek's consumption-led "boom" strategy had stalled in "growth fatigue," and Poland's current accounts balance had sunk to $25 billion in the red. The price for the compensatory foreign loans, moreover, was not just economic dependence on the West but, as would become evident, a certain independence of maneuver for Poland's opposition. It was now that in combination with workers' strikes, some members of a self-styled opposition formed KOR, or the Committee for Workers' Defense, offering recourse to beaten and incarcerated workers and their families—efforts that were supported by Poland's strengthened post-1968 political emigration. Suddenly every provincial party secretary had to reckon with the likelihood that if anything untoward happened to a member of the opposition, this fact would be publicized on Radio Free Europe and might affect Poland's standing with Western creditors.

Western banks, meanwhile, had the money to lend because of the selfsame oil shock: they recycled gushing Middle East petrodollars that had been placed on deposit with them to the bloc (as well as to Latin America). Although it was Tito's Yugoslavia that had first opened to Western funding, receiving around $2.7 billion between 1951 and 1960 from the United States alone (nominally in exchange for good behavior vis-à-vis Greece and Italy), East bloc borrowing became known as the "Polish disease." It could also have been called the East German disease. But even Ceauşescu's Romania, which had long prided itself on its near self-sufficiency, eventually succumbed to the temptation of Western borrowing.

Loss of Élan

In the late 1940s across Eastern Europe the Communist establishments were small minorities, yet their members seemed completely assured. They had resisted and defeated fascism; they were part of the movement of history; therefore their theories and actions were right, even if majorities of their compatriots did not immediately appreciate it; so they could lie at will. By the 1980s these Communist establishments had become enormous and possessed massive force, well-developed censorship mechanisms, and tight border controls. But the much bigger Communist establishments of the 1980s displayed the opposite sense of what the minuscule Communist establishments had known in 1948, namely that history was moving in the wrong direction, that defections could not be ignored, that the pervasive lying was sapping the will of the system's own functionaries. "All it will take," remarked one anxious Soviet general in the world's biggest armed force, "to bring the entire house down is just one spark."[10] In other words, sometime between the late 1940s and the 1980s the establishment suffered a psychological blow, a loss of its arrogance. That shift occurred not primarily because of the Hungarian events of 1956 or the Czechoslovak events of 1968, as important as those episodes were, but because the bloc's economic performance fell short against the backdrop of extraordinary Western capitalist successes.

Eastern European elites who had come to power with Communist systems viewed the latter as an instrument to force a modernization leap (of a particular nonmarket kind) on their "backward" countries. That is precisely what happened, with great violence, but all the same this had failed to close the gap with the West.[11] Between 1913 and 1950 per capita GDP growth in Eastern Europe had been an anemic 1 percent annually, slower than world averages, but from 1950 to 1973 it jumped to 3.9 percent annually, above world averages. For those twenty years, Eastern Europe's growth per capita was even slightly above Asia's (3.7 percent). To put the matter another way, having been entirely within the Axis wartime orbit, which culminated in vast destruction, Eastern Europe underwent an impressive postwar recovery led by heavy industry. But then the Communist tree ceased leafing. For example, Hungary's annual average growth rate of around 6 percent dropped to 1.6 in 1979, and to zero in 1980. The precipitating cause, again, was the 1973 oil shock. The Soviet Union, a major oil exporter, was buoyed by rising revenues. But despite some initial Soviet energy cushioning of the East European satellites, the oil shock worsened intrasocialist terms of trade. In 1974 the Soviets accepted eight hundred units of Hungary's Ikarus bus in exchange for 1 million tons of oil, but by 1981 that same quantity of oil required 2,300 buses, and by the mid-1980s 4,000 buses.[12]

Soviet-style economies mostly grew not by gains in productivity but by ever greater inputs of capital and labor (so-called extensive growth) and had notorious problems innovating. They could not even manage to assimilate the innovations their spy agencies succeeded in stealing from abroad. Most fundamentally, the systems invested in but misused (and abused) their human capital. Shortages (and queues) were endemic to the planned economy's normal operation, while the mania for heavy industry, the collectivization of agriculture (in most cases), and the suppression of the service sector (as capitalist) combined to ensure that even during the high growth spurt, rises in consumption lagged. True, after Stalin's death the regimes made concessions to the consumer across the bloc. But that only compounded the challenge: subsidies for housing, food, clothing, and other consumer items became ever more costly to maintain, while the least price hikes (when tried) sparked revolts that sometimes shook the regimes to their foundations. East European economies could not grow fast enough to meet the living standards challenge, on top of outsized expenses for military security and elite perquisites (which violated the ethos of social justice the regimes promoted). And yet the costly daily life subsidies seemed ever more necessary, because unlike the Soviet Union in the 1930s, the Eastern European satellites faced a capitalist world—in many cases right across the border—that had undergone its greatest-ever consumer boom in the 1950s and 1960s.

And nearly everyone knew it. They learned from the media—foreign but also official—and, partly thanks to détente, increasingly from direct contacts with visiting foreign tourists, and sometimes even from their own travels. Despite massive security police apparatuses, and despite monopolies on property and the public sphere, the East bloc establishments turned out to be paralyzed. None had much political capital. On the contrary, the regimes doled out the subsidies, and yet they still labored to burnish their legitimacy. They could not—again, unlike the Soviet Union—draw on a World War II victory to compensate for their relative failings. So predictably they fell back on cultivating nationalism. With some irony, Communist regimes promoted national feeling partly on the basis of anti-Russian sentiment. Be that as it may, whatever the straining of credulity on carrying the nationalist banner, each bloc country's "national communism" was linked to promises of economic and technical modernization, perhaps the core of the regimes' claims to legitimacy. And that was the killer: after all the exertions, violence, and sacrifice, far from outdueling the West, the East had fallen into dependency on it.

The East Europeans used the Soviet Union as a dumping ground for the inferior goods that they simply could not sell in hard currency export markets (low-quality, outdated clothes, footwear, fabrics, leather goods, furniture). But even Eastern Europe's supposedly Western-export-grade goods left a lot to be desired. And then came a market surprise. When Gierek, the Polish party chief, exhorted, "Build a Second Poland!" he meant doubling GDP in a decade. Such a great leap forward proved an utter fantasy—except in the capitalist world, especially East Asia. Japan's export-led boom inspired, and funded, the "tigers" of South Korea, Taiwan, Hong Kong, and Singapore. In the 1980s East Asian manufacturers blindsided the East Europeans. Lower-cost exports turned out to be a game others in the global economy could play, and better, with far cheaper labor and higher quality.

The East European borrowing strategy also depended on affordable interest rates and on foreign bankers' willingness to roll over the loans—something that the bankers began to rethink around 1979, the time of the second oil shock. By then Poland's convertible currency debt had reached around $20 billion; servicing that debt ate up 80 percent of the country's export earnings. (The neglect of agriculture, meanwhile, meant that food accounted for nearly a quarter of Polish imports in 1978, costing valuable hard currency.) Hungary's convertible currency debt ballooned from around $1 billion in 1972 to $9 billion by 1979, a burden that could be serviced only by taking on more debt. By 1989 Hungary's debt hit $18 billion, meaning that the country needed a surplus in hard currency from exports of more than $1 billion annually *just to pay the interest.* (The corresponding figure for Poland was $2 billion.) Across the bloc, total hard currency debt shot up from $6 billion in 1970 to $21 billion by 1975, $56 billion by 1980, and $90 billion by 1989, with no end of escalation in sight.[13]

To paraphrase Lenin, the capitalists had sold the bloc the rope with which to hang itself. Perhaps East European regimes could have united to default simultaneously, seeking to deal a blow to the global financial system that held them in a vise, or at least to gain leverage in a write-down. But they were Communists, not global casino players. Anyway they now needed continued access to Western capital markets (to say nothing of Western consumer goods) for their survival. Only Ceauşescu's dictatorship in Romania imposed a brutal austerity program (from 1982), demonstrating the ruinous cost of paying off the debt: blackouts, freezing interiors, severe rationing of food. This was a price the East German and Polish establishments could not pay. Staring at Romania's debt-reduction despair on one side and, on the other, at West Germany's relentless cornucopia, East Germany and Poland, as well as Hungary, took out ever more foreign currency loans to pay back their old foreign currency loans. "Most of Eastern Europe's economies had plunged head-first into the swimming pool of Western capitalism," two scholars have written, "and instead of emerging refreshed and revitalized had surfaced gasping for air and saddled with unsustainable debt."[14] The bloc had become a Ponzi scheme.

Geopolitics and Ideology

The profound structural changes after World War II, and especially during the 1970s, radically altered the global geopolitical context for Eastern Europe and demanded a response from its establishments. Over the years the responses generally boiled down to two opposed versions of trying to make socialism better. One involved the old reformers' dream—socialism with a human face—which, however, had shown itself to be not a renewal of socialism but its unwitting liquidation. Party conservatives were properly wary of Gorbachev's revival of socialism with a human face in the 1980s. But their alternative, conservative modernization—meaning a further tightening of "discipline" as well as profligate investment in technological panaceas—also failed to reenergize the systems, seemingly leaving them only with trying to muddle through by borrowing. Muddling through (albeit on capitalist money) held a certain appeal. After all, the system had raised up the members of establishments, and most hoped that if necessary, the system would somehow save them, especially if capitalism finally descended into the second Great Depression that Communists had long predicted for it. But someone forgot to tell the post–World War II capitalist world to go into a death spiral.

The compromises with capitalism made by the East bloc in the 1970s forced a severe reckoning in the following decade. Borrowing from the West had amounted, consciously or not, to a substitute for conceding the establishment's monopoly on power. But the bill came due. Predictably the bloc's establishments upped their pleas to the Soviets, but the Soviets could not bear the extra burden. From the 1970s—after having long paid below world market prices for imports from East Europe while extracting higher prices for Soviet exports—Moscow found itself needing to provide its satellites with raw materials at below world prices, while importing shoddy goods in return.[15] Then, after the world price of oil tumbled precipitously in 1985–86, thanks partly to deliberate Saudi overproduction, the Soviet Union—which could not implore *itself* for more money—eventually also became contaminated with the "Polish disease," borrowing from the capitalists to satisfy the consumer desires in a socialist country.

Meanwhile, Moscow fumed that the satellites were living better than their Soviet "friends," yet these "shameless" peoples were not even satisfied. Rank-and-file East European dissatisfaction, however, could not be directed at abstractions such as "the market" or "globalization"; the regimes themselves were held responsible. Many members of the Communist establishments voiced outrage at the "petty-bourgeois" hankering for dachas and cars, washing machines and refrigerators (as did many dissidents, including Vaclav Havel). Of course the elites, with their wives and children, enjoyed the best access to Western goods and services. In any case, those who decried "refrigerator socialism" were spitting into the wind. That said, even the dimwitted comprehended the depth of the trap.

If socialism was merely aiming to placate consumers just like capitalism, only not as well, was socialism's existence even justified? To put the matter in its starkest terms, how long could muddling through and borrowing continue if Western bankers refused to roll over the loans?

What to do?[16] Communist rulers in China—who endure as of this writing—discovered a solution for the party: a police state market economy. On June 4, 1989, when the multicandidate elections took place in Poland that would culminate in the formation of a Solidarity government, the tanks rolled into China's Tiananmen Square, cracking down on the demonstrators. It was a coincidence, but an extraordinary one. One Communist establishment found itself, unexpectedly, in a process of capitulation and went along; the other stood firm. But in bloodying its people who were demonstrating against corruption and for socialism to open up politically (and live up to its promises), the Chinese leadership also deepened the country's turn toward economic openness. Who would have guessed it would be the Chinese Communists, rather than the East Europeans, who would embrace the market? The East Europeans (Albania excepted) had not railed against the USSR for being in bed with imperialism (in détente) and abandoning world revolution.[17] Unlike Mao and his homicidal Cultural Revolution of 1966–1976 (which, unintentionally, destroyed China's economic planning capacities), the East European establishments had ceased to be militant. Rather, they turned out to be conservative, which derived from their long terms in power, and which had seemed vindicated by events in Prague in 1968; indeed 1968 helped formalize their conservative identities across the bloc as the resolute "healthy forces." They branded their nemeses—reformers—as counterrevolutionaries even though the latter also fought *to defend socialism.* In other words, members of the establishments of Eastern Europe, whether conservative or reformist, remained largely bound by ideology, especially in the economy, unlike the Leninist-type copycat single party in Taiwan or the post-Mao recovering Communist Party in mainland China.[18]

For the East European systems, the reformers such as those of the Prague Spring were the more immediately dangerous, since reform of the system invariably amounted to unintentional self-liquidation. But the conservatives bear the greater responsibility for the happy circumstance of the implosion. The mundane fact about the Communist establishments in Eastern Europe was that they were full of . . . Communists. And the single most important fact about the formerly secret Communist archives is this:

behind closed doors the Communists spoke with the same vocabulary and worldview that they used in public. Although the idea of permitting some market mechanisms had come under discussion early in the revolutionary regimes, it was always only as a way to have profit-and-loss calculations assist administrative methods, not as a displacement of planning. Even Hungary's János Kádár, considered one of the more flexible leaders on economic experimentation, pointedly remarked during a visit to a large factory in 1986: "It must be understood that the foundation of Hungary's people's economy is socialist, that the means of production are 96–97 percent in social property and that our future will be decided in the socialist factories. Everything else can be a useful supplement to this, but nothing else."[19]

The June 1989 crackdown in Tiananmen Square resounded throughout the bloc that summer and into the fall, but the incipient market success of the Chinese Communists mostly escaped the East Europeans. Károly Grósz—the fifty-seven-year-old who had emerged as Kádár's prime minister in 1987 on a platform of a "reform dictatorship" and then shunted Kádár aside as party chief in 1988—supported many long-contemplated economic reforms (capitalist-style banking, majority foreign private ownership). Grósz also showed intransigence over the party's monopoly (and explored the possibility of martial law). This desperate, crisis-ridden groping appears to have been inspired not by Communist China's example, however, but by the high-growth authoritarianism of 1980s South Korea. Be that as it may, in October 1989 Grósz was definitively eclipsed by Hungary's Communist Party political reformers, who sought survival in a Western-style multiparty system.[20] The possible exception of Grósz aside—the evidence is ambiguous and the time period short—the East European ruling circles that were insistent on retaining one-party rule ruled out embrace of the market. For them it was tantamount to treason.

For East Germany—which faced a hugely successful market economy Germany right across the barbed wire—"capitulation" to the market appeared to mean the end of the country. Would the East German establishment risk suicide? Would the Soviets accept the "loss" of East Germany, paid for with 27 million Soviet lives? Here ideology meshed with geopolitics. A reversion to capitalism under Communist rule—something like China's market Leninism—seemed out of the question. Socialism had been a promise to transcend all problems, but the accumulated entrenched interests of socialism, its establishments, would not countenance an attempted transcendence of socialism's problems, only "more social-ism." The Soviets, in other words, were not alone in keeping Eastern Europe locked on its fatal trajectory, in the teeth of the radically altered world circumstances of the postwar era. But the Soviets upset the apple cart even further with Gorbachev's repeal of the Brezhnev Doctrine of using force to retain socialism in Eastern Europe, and with his socialism-with-a-human-face insistence that the bloc regimes themselves not use force to try to hold on.

PART II

Stagflation and the Economic Origins of Globalization

CHAPTER 5

The Global 1970s and the Echo
of the Great Depression

ALAN M. TAYLOR

THE DECADE OF THE 1970s sits on a delicate cusp: receding from conversations on the contemporary world, detaching from pressing policy debates, and sliding imperceptibly into the arena of historical scholarship. A tumultuous time in many respects, the era that began circa 1970 appears to offer the richest seams for students of social history, geopolitics, and culture; but in this chapter I argue that in the sphere of economic history the 1970s may yet emerge as one of the most important turning points of the modern era.

Twenty years ago, when some of the contributors to this volume were beginning graduate school, new research on the economic history of the Great Depression, which is now indisputably a part of the standard syllabus, was at the cutting edge. The view that World War I demarcated the endpoint of history had been left behind. The new interwar scholarship has been a vital area of research ever since, and has helped us understand the first great economic turning point of the world economy in the twentieth century: the great deglobalization of the interwar period.

Time has now rolled on; from where we stand that Great Reversal is surely long over, and it is the postwar process of reglobalization that now looms in the economic historian's rearview mirror. Understanding, documenting, and explaining that process is only just beginning—but as with the scholarship of the Great Depression a generation ago, the postwar period will form the new frontier for researchers. Where that exploration will take us remains to be seen, but I think we can already start to discern some important terrain.

In this chapter I sketch how enduring questions about globalization, of both markets and society, can be seen to link the 1970s back in time to the Great Depression. Moreover, these very same concerns still resonate today in what many are starting to perceive as a moment when globalization, and the consensus behind it, is at risk of reversal yet again.

Economic historians discussing these topics are naturally drawn to an enduring account of the last Great Reversal, still one of the most controversial and influential theses in the social sciences, Karl Polanyi's study *The Great Transformation*.[1] I do not discuss, much less endorse, many of the claims of that wide-ranging book—its much-disputed characterization of the premodern natural state of markets embedded in society, and its plainly incorrect expectation that developed economies operating as social democracies would henceforth be inimical to trade and financial openness. But as a description of the Great Reversal as it happened, the book has much to commend it.

After World War I, policymakers understood that the global economy had been damaged by the suspension of the gold standard, restrictions on trade, and exchange controls. Adverse policies were coincident with, and amplified by, the spillovers from, and the elevated levels of, distrust and belligerence between nations. But everyone fully expected the situation to normalize, albeit after some effort, with a return to something like the largely laissez-faire pre-1914 global economy.

Following the Great Depression (and another war), the political economy equilibrium shifted dramatically against this vision. Polanyi, if not the first to note this shock to economic structures and their supporting ideology, grasped its ramifications and deeper meaning. A global economy built along anything resembling the lines of the pre-1914 model was unlikely to return anytime soon (or ever, in Polanyi's view). The puzzle, then, is to understand what happened next, and how globalization was in many ways rebuilt after that time of massive retrenchment—what might be called a Polanyi Moment.

My first task is to present a set of facts: what actually happened in terms of globalization from the 1940s through the 1970s and up to today. As we shall see, the 1970s were notable for the persistence of controls on international capital flows, but at the same time saw a loosening of exchange rates and growing world trade supported by major—but very uneven—steps toward trade liberalization.

This focuses my question. Why was reglobalization so slow and so uneven? We can discuss various forces that may have coalesced fortuitously in the 1970s to spark the engines of globalization into life, despite some other pressures that worked in the opposite direction. But to move from a descriptive narrative to an analytic one, we need some theory and a testable hypothesis.

As we now know, most countries, once stuck in the Great Reversal, eventually shifted policy gears and liberalized. Some trade-oriented countries liberalized very quickly in the 1970s or before; others oriented inward and clung to protectionist barriers up to the 1990s and beyond. But why were some so quick to liberalize and others much slower? That is the question.

Empirical variation naturally invites closer quantitative scrutiny. On the basis of preliminary evidence—and there is much more work to be done—I argue that it was here that the Great Depression had its lasting effect, not (*pace* Polanyi) by preventing countries from ever globalizing again, but by conditioning the speed at which they ultimately re-embraced globalization in the postwar period. The destination was the same, but the many routes taken diverged remarkably—and in some respects predictably. Especially among the developing countries—economies outside the advanced core, with a limited role in the General Agreement on Tariffs and Trade (GATT), and no role in the European Union project—those that suffered more of a downturn in the 1930s were more "reactive" in policymaking afterwards, to use Carlos Díaz-Alejandro's term, and they were more inclined to resist globalization the second time around.

If this argument withstands scrutiny, it becomes an important link in our historical and institutional narrative, a bridge from the interwar calamity to more recent events, part of the making of the modern world economy. We could then argue that the global capitalist economy was not subject to a "hard reset" in 1946, starting from scratch under the new Bretton Woods order. Rather, there was a legacy from the 1930s, an institutional memory. Path dependence meant that the experience of the 1930s hung like a shadow over each country—its policymaking institutions, its interest groups, its politics and ideology. And it was a long shadow: policy persistence was shaped by this history for decades, carrying some countries forward into the vanguard of reglobalization while holding others back.

Against this backdrop the lessons for the present are drawn into sharp focus in the conclusion to this chapter. Policymakers have cautioned that the world stands on the brink of its worst financial crisis since the 1930s.

For example, just before the August 2008 Jackson Hole Symposium, most of the policymaking elite attending this conference revealed that they had no clear idea how bad conditions were or might yet become. But history suggests that an exclusive focus on resolving the immediate credit crunch risks confusing the trees and the forest.

If a policymaker took a short-run view, one that could take globalization for granted, the response to the crisis might focus on how to contain periods of financial panic, fear, and distrust, which destabilize and disrupt financial markets in the manner explained by Hyman Minsky.[2] Such a Minsky Moment was certainly witnessed in the 1930s, and fear of a replay has haunted, and motivated, policymakers as a similar collapse in asset prices, credit, and liquidity erupted in 2008–09. But if we pause to take the longer view, then the example of the 1930s also shows that there can be more serious and longer-lasting downsides to any major crisis of capitalism. The worse the downturn, the greater the surge in anti-globalization and anti-market sentiments, reactions that can endure for decades once embedded in policy. On past form, a Minsky Moment may pass relatively quickly, but a Polanyi Moment will not.

Facts: What Do the Data Show?

Today "globalization" is everywhere; in the 1970s it was mostly latent. As of August 2008 the word appeared in 3,840 book titles in the Library of Congress catalog; of those, 3,839 were published after 1987, the other one in 1983. Narrowing the focus simply to the scholarly literature in economics would also expose a profession forced to grapple more and more with problems in international economics from the 1980s onward: trade and wages, currency crises, global imbalances, and so on, shifts that have mirrored the reality of a rapidly changing economic environment.

Prior to the 1970s, with the exception of occasional cracks in the Bretton Woods fixed exchange rate regime, international economic relations were conducted under conditions of limited freedom for trade and almost total prohibition for finance.

The evolution of trade policy from 1945 until the 1970s was constrained in terms of speed and scope. Unilateral liberalizations were few (but not unimportant for the countries in question), and with one notable exception (the European Economic Community) preferential free trade areas did not amount to much. That left GATT as the main locus for progress on trade liberalization. Yet the number of goods whose tariffs were cut was always very limited in this era, and the list of countries meaningfully participating in this bargaining process was very small—essentially just the developed countries. Until the GATT Tokyo Round (1973–1979), developing countries played little effective role; they would not have a major say until the Uruguay Round (1986–1993).

Trade liberalization may have been slow prior to 1970, but financial liberalization was virtually nonexistent. This was by design, of course, the goal of the Bretton Woods architecture being to make a world safe for international trade, not for international finance. After the 1930s the latter was seen as destabilizing and was clearly inimical to the new desire for macroeconomic policy autonomy in a world still wedded to fixed exchange rates. Thus by the 1960s only current account transactions were liberalized (though not rapidly), even as capital account transactions were still outlawed. But it did not take long for investors to find ways around these restrictions, and the porous controls led with increasing frequency to larger financial drains, reserve leakage, and currency crises as the system lurched, with all its contradictions, toward collapse.

After 1970 the reglobalization trend intensified, but this tendency was at first much stronger in the sphere of trade transactions than financial transactions. Figure 5.1 shows the evolution of trade policy since 1970, using the longest-span dataset we have based on a trade-tax proxy for protectionism. (Note: it is only a proxy, and excludes many other important distortions such as quotas and exchange rate premia which might have been at least as large in their own right; but it is the only measure with adequate temporal and spatial coverage for our purpose.)

The decline in trade taxes was dramatic but occurred more rapidly in the developed countries. The developing countries, on average, liberalized trade later, with major moves occurring at the time of the Uruguay Round in the late 1980s and early 1990s. Nonetheless, some developing countries did liberalize much sooner: well-known examples include the more export-oriented economies of East Asia. Meanwhile, other countries maintained a more protectionist stance. It is this variety of trade liberalization experiences in the 1970s that deserves a closer look.

Why focus on trade policies in this discussion? Simply because financial liberalization in the 1970s was almost nonexistent. Most developed countries—even fast movers such as Britain in 1979 and Germany in 1981—delayed their financial liberalization until long after they had started to liberalize trade. They even waited until many years after the end of the Bretton Woods system had obviated the need for capital controls to protect fixed exchange rates in a world of nascent monetary activism. In the EU as a whole, financial liberalization was a slow process in the 1980s, with even some setbacks (as in France under Mitterand); and it would not be until the end of that decade, with the Maastricht Treaty looming, that capital market integration would be consolidated as part of the single market goal. Outside the advanced economies, progress was slower still. In the emerging markets and developing countries, financial liberalization was a rare event before the 1990s.[3]

Since the focus of this study is the 1970s as a turning point, and since the wave of financial liberalization came so much later, I turn my attention now exclusively to questions surrounding the advance of free trade policies. Why did it take so long for free trade policies to be reestablished?

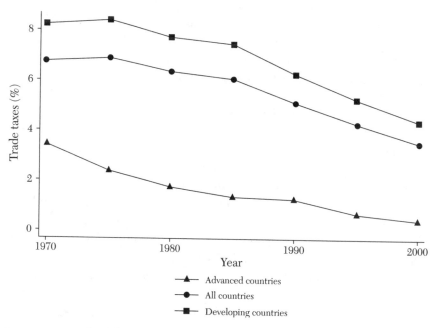

Figure 5.1. Trade liberalization, 1970–2000. To present a proxy for trade liberalization across many countries and years, this figure shows average levels of trade taxes as a percentage of exports plus imports for the full sample of countries in the Economic Freedom in the World 2005 dataset. Also shown are average levels for advanced and developing countries.

Why did some countries liberalize much more rapidly than others? How did this matter for economic outcomes in the longer run? And what lessons does this episode carry for today? These are large enough questions to more than occupy the remainder of this chapter.

Puzzles: Why Was Reglobalization So Slow?

This discussion treats the 1970s as a key turning point, when the first major postwar moves toward globalization emerged in the sphere of trade policy.

Why the 1970s? Despite the attempts after 1945 to forge a new international economic order around a consensus for prosperity through trade, the greater part of the trade liberalization that we now take for granted was delayed at least twenty-five years. The period 1945–1970 saw only modest progress, but the period 1970–1995 witnessed much more rapid opening, albeit only in selected countries. Why did this rebuilding process take so long? Certainly the structures of GATT did not prevent a slow pace, and may even have encouraged it. Admittedly GATT was off to a flying start when the first agreement in Geneva (1947) achieved big results, slashing 45,000 tariffs on $10 billion of trade among the twenty-three founding members. But subsequent rounds expanded the membership only slowly and achieved fewer cuts on ever-smaller tranches of an ever-expanding volume of world trade. The second round (Annecy, 1949) covered only 5,000 tariffs and admitted ten more countries. The third (Torquay, 1950–51) cut 8,700 tariffs and admitted four new countries. The fourth round (Geneva II, 1956) covered just $2.5 billion of trade—one-quarter the level of the first round a decade before. The Dillon Round (1960–61) achieved more (4,400 cuts on $5 billion of trade). Little in this record would have led one to predict an imminent acceleration in openness in the developed countries, or any expansion of these trends to the developing countries.[4]

The 1970s were also an inauspicious moment for globalization in other respects. An oil shock and global stagflation led many countries into recessions that were deeper than anything seen since the 1930s. Downturns have generally encouraged protectionist sentiments, and not just since the 1930s: Polanyi saw similar mechanisms at work, albeit with less destructive results, in the protectionist backlash during and after the recession of the 1870s, when the free trade treaties worked out in the 1860s by Richard

Cobden and others gave way to rising tariffs, especially in Continental Europe.

All that said, some opposing forces were present in the 1970s that could encourage, or at least sustain, trade opening. Most notable of these was the absence of the "golden fetters"—fixed exchange rates such as the gold standard system that had amplified previous slumps. But the breakdown of the Bretton Woods system released monetary policy and exchange rates, giving countries other levers to control aggregate demand: as a tool to stimulate expenditure switching toward home goods, a devaluation could be as effective as a tariff, at least in the short run. And indeed the larger trade flows are, the more powerful that tool becomes.

In addition, in the 1970s the success, actual or potential, of some pro–free trade projects was starting to become apparent. The EEC was attracting new applicants, and the growth accelerations of the East Asian newly industrializing countries (NICs) were just starting to register qualitative significance, if not yet statistical significance—although the latter would build over time. Meanwhile the limitations of import-substituting industrialization in the more inward-looking countries were becoming clearer.

There had also been signs within trade negotiations of an increased desire for openness. Many more developing countries had joined GATT in the 1960s. The Kennedy Round (1964–1967) was the biggest advance in twenty years, with fifty countries using across-the-board negotiations to achieve concessions on $40 billion of world trade. Even so, these agreements still covered mostly manufacturing trade and the developed countries. But by the early seventies, ninety-nine countries were present for GATT's Tokyo Round, and some success was achieved in reducing tariffs for tropical goods as well as manufactured goods, with agreements covering $300 billion in world trade. (These figures are not adjusted for inflation.)

Still at some level these explanations lack a deeper explanatory power, and in some cases they suffer from a serious simultaneity problem. Macroeconomic policies may have been reconfigured after the 1970s, and GATT may have been reinvigorated—all encouraging events for trade liberalization—but are these events causes or symptoms? And why did steps toward liberalization occur at different times in different countries?

We need to look back and explore the causal connections that bridge the gap from the historical crisis of globalization circa 1930 and the reconstruction that began in earnest circa 1970.

Hypotheses: A Legacy of the Great Depression?

A familiar yet unquantified narrative bridge is often used to link the policy shocks of the 1930s, the reaction against laissez-faire orthodoxy, with the endurance of these policies into the postwar era. It is central to Polanyi's thesis, although he saw the shock as more permanent. It is present in the narratives of economic history and the history of economic thought. For example: Carlos Díaz-Alejandro explaining the "reactive" trade isolationism of South America; Deepak Lal exploring the rise of "dirigiste" economic thinking more broadly; or Peter Temin describing the legacy of the Great Depression as "socialism in many countries." In these and other accounts the crisis of the 1930s demanded a response; but it was not to be temporary, and after wartime autarky there were strong political economy constraints that ensured the long-run persistence of the new policies, as political inertia and the rise of new interests set policy on a path-dependent course.[5] While this narrative is true at a general level, it was obviously by no means a uniform trend in all countries. Thus we can potentially learn much more by looking closely at the variation among them. Some countries experienced deep economic pain in the Great Depression; and by the same logic, if this deep pain were translated into policy responses, we ought to have seen more "reactive" policies imprinted in countries that had the deepest slumps. Conversely, in countries where the slump was mild, or almost nonexistent, the political dynamic ought to have been very different, with less of a reaction against economic orthodoxy.

To sum up, where the standard narrative focuses on a representative experience common to many countries—Great Depression then policy reaction—I think we can make further progress by thinking about the extent to which there was a heterogeneous shock in the 1930s. We can then use that variation in the data and subsequent policy responses to understand why the Great Depression echoed so loudly in some countries that were clinging to inward-looking policies in the 1970s and reglobalizing slowly, while in other cases reactive policies were more temporary and policy reform pushed ahead more rapidly.

The key problem is to explain *policy persistence.* If this idea has empirical content, then we can make advances on other fronts; we can cease thinking of the policy choices of the postwar period as purely exogenous random variations, or as simply problematic endogenous responses to economic growth. Instead we can confront and put to further analytical use their origins as historically contingent, or as path-dependent outcomes possessing some regularity.[6]

Empirics: Evidence of the Echo?

Given the space available, I will show some preliminary evidence that the depth of the Great Depression did carry over, through the subsequent decades, into policymaking responses in the latter part of the twentieth century. I also show that this path dependence was more strongly evident in direct measures of policy reform than in measures of participation in the liberalization process under GATT.

More than any other institution GATT was supposed to be the venue for countries to work together and repair the damage to international trade wrought by the interwar crisis. Thus, one might think, one useful measure of policy persistence, of attitudes toward a return to free trade, might be gleaned from the point in time when countries actually signed up to GATT. For example, as I noted earlier, few developing countries were involved in the early GATT rounds, but by the time of the Tokyo and, especially, Uruguay rounds, dozens had signed up.

Can we detect any impact of Great Depression experiences in this process? Did the countries that were hurt most by the Great Depression spend a longer period of time on the sidelines outside of GATT, thus manifesting their greater reaction against orthodoxy and resistance to open trade? The answer is no, but this is by no means damaging to my hypothesis.

As column 1 of Table 5.1 shows, there is absolutely no correlation between the date of entry into GATT and the depth of the Great Depression, where the latter is measured by the standardized cumulative GDP losses in the years 1930 to 1934 relative to the 1929 level in each country. In fact the correlation is slightly negative but not statistically significant. (Data for former Soviet Union and Eastern bloc countries are excluded.)[7]

But this is not damning evidence for the policy persistence hypothesis. After all, being a member of GATT has never been the same thing as being an active and effective participant in GATT. Many developing countries joined GATT and yet participated little at first, and offered few tariff concessions until the later rounds. Therefore their GATT membership date tells us nothing about the point at which they seriously moved to lower trade barriers and promote trade.

Table 5.1. Postwar liberalization and the Great Depression

	1	2	3	4
Dependent variable	Year country joined GATT	Year country went open	Average change in trade taxes in the 1970s	Average change in trade taxes in the 1970s
Sample	All	All	All	Above-median trade taxes in 1970
1930–1934 output loss (standardized)	−3.843 (2.89)	1.334 (2.86)	0.171° (0.084)	0.264°° (0.090)
Constant	1961°° (2.60)	1974°° (2.49)	−0.0362 (0.075)	0.0661 (0.080)
Observations	41	35	41	21
R-squared	0.04	0.01	0.10	0.31

Notes: The table shows cross-country OLS regressions of various measures of postwar trade openness on the depth of the Great Depression, measured by cumulative real GDP loss in Maddison's data in the years 1930–1934 relative to the 1929 level (standardized to a mean of 0 and an s.d. of 1). Angus Maddison, *The World Economy: Historical Statistics* (Paris, 2001). Column 1 uses as a dependent variable the year when a country joined GATT according to Andrew K. Rose, "Do We Really Know That the WTO Increases Trade?" *American Economic Review* 94, no. 1 (March 2004): 98–114. Column 2 uses as a dependent variable the year when a country became open using the Sachs-Warner criteria according to Romain Wacziarg and Karen Horn Welch, "Trade Liberalization and Growth: New Evidence," *World Bank Economic Review* 22, no. 2 (June 2008): 187–231. Column 3 uses the proportional change in the 1970s in the ratio of trade taxes to total trade. Column 4 is the same as (3) but restricted to countries that initially had high (above-median) trade taxes in 1970, mostly the developing countries. The Great Depression output loss measure is statistically significant in columns (3) and (4) at the 5 percent and 1 percent levels respectively. Standard errors are shown in parentheses. Asterisks denote statistical significance at the 5 percent (°) and 1 percent (°°) levels.

This finding is therefore consistent with recent influential research by Andrew Rose which shows that there is no correlation between joining GATT (or the World Trade Organization) and an increase in trade. Actions speak louder than words: GATT membership is neither necessary nor sufficient to ensure liberalization at any given moment.

Thus we should look more carefully to find more accurate measures of changes in trade policy. But this task is not so simple, given the broad span of time I wish to investigate. Hence the next natural candidate I examine is the widely used index of openness created by Jeffrey D. Sachs and Andrew Warner, updated by Romain Wacziarg and Karen Horn Welch.[8] This is a binary (0–1) indicator, where 1 is openness as judged by multiple criteria, including tariff levels, quotas, exchange rate distortions, and market structures (socialist planning and export monopolies). In contrast to the GATT entry date, the Sachs-Warner openness variable, as a policy proxy, is a measure better suited to gauging when liberalization actually happened.

As column 2 of the table shows, using this indicator, we find that there is a positive correlation of dates of opening with the intensity of the Great Depression. Economies damaged more by the Great Depression waited longer to liberalize in the postwar period, as my working hypothesis would suggest. Nevertheless, the statistical significance of this relationship is weak (though it is higher if the sample is restricted to developing countries).

Can we do better? And to address the question posed earlier, can we focus specifically on that critical period of the 1970s, when some countries took the lead in opening their economies for the first time since the 1930s while others lagged behind? In search of a more precise measure of trade policy alone, I finally turn to direct estimates of trade taxes as a fraction of total trade (exports plus imports), based on the Economic Freedom in the World database.[9] These narrowly defined and continuous data might be preferred by some to the Sachs-Warner dummy indicator as a measure of trade reform, since the latter includes some components that are not connected to trade policy per se (such as exchange rate distortions and export marketing boards). I consider the percentage change in the level of the trade tax ratio in the 1970s. Note that this variable is used only as a proxy for trade barriers; many other policies (such as quotas) are not captured by this measure.

As column 3 demonstrates, in the 1970s there appears to have been a very clear echo of the Great Depression. The near-zero intercept shows that there was barely any trend toward policy liberalization on average in these data, which is not that surprising in the context of a decade of global slowdown and the first deep recessions in many countries since the 1930s. Still, heterogeneous outcomes stand out when we look across countries. The countries that suffered relatively mild downturns in the 1930s were still more likely to lower trade barriers in the 1970s. Countries that suffered the worst slumps in the 1930s were much more standoffish when the prospect of reglobalization appeared on the horizon, and their trade taxes tended to stay high or even rise. A country with a 1 standard deviation lower level of output loss in the early 1930s was likely to cut trade taxes by an additional factor of 17 percent in the 1970s. Moreover, these results are statistically significant, despite the small sample.

In column 4 I consider the problem that some early liberalizers (most EEC and OECD countries and some open developing countries such as South Korea) had already lowered their trade barriers before 1970. These countries might bias the results toward a null finding or a low correlation, since they would have little to gain from further trade liberalization and would have completed their own reversal.

I therefore exclude from the sample the countries that already had below-median trade taxes in 1970. I find that in the sample that is left, the "more protected" group (mostly developing countries, as one might guess), the echo of the Great Depression is even more pronounced, as might also be expected. Here a country with a 1 standard deviation (s.d.) lower level of output loss in the early 1930s was likely to cut trade taxes by an additional factor of 26 percent in the 1970s.

To put it another way, if we take seriously the argument of an "echo effect" from the Great Depression, these results say that during the 1970s an initially unliberalized Country A carrying the institutional memory of a relatively painful Great Depression output loss of 1 s.d. more than average would have retreated into protectionism, raising trade barriers by about 25 percent. But an initially unliberalized Country B carrying the institutional memory of a relatively mild Great Depression output loss of 1 s.d. less than average would have been more inclined to continue liberalization, lowering trade barriers by about 25 percent.

The net result would be a significant divergence in policy stances by the end of the decade for initially identical countries: Country A would end up with trade barriers nearly twice as large as Country B's, owing to the more severe policy persistence. If these mechanisms can be further substantiated, they will attest to a very heavy hand of history weighing on the postwar reconstruction of the global economy in the 1970s.

Previously all of this might have been intuited from the broad patterns: for example, we knew that East Asia, somewhat decoupled from the financial and output collapses in Europe and North America, suffered only a mild recession in the 1930s and liberalized more rapidly; in contrast, Latin American commodity exporters were badly hit by the West's 1930s economic disaster, and subsequently kept their trade barriers up longer.[10] To give some specific country examples from the data, there is a marked regional contrast in the measure of output loss in the Great Depression as we compare, say, the large losses of Mexico (loss of +0.43 standard deviations above the mean), Uruguay (+0.43 s.d.), Argentina (+0.50 s.d), or Chile (+1.52 s.d.) with the milder downturns in Japan (−0.60 s.d.), Taiwan (−0.83 s.d.), the Philippines (−0.99 s.d.), or Korea (−1.37 s.d.), where the deviations are cumulative lost output from a large sample of N = 51 countries. In the former group of countries, the adverse shocks were closely identified with the global economy, as in the writing of Raúl Prebisch and others, and a new reactive economic ideology replaced the old orthodoxy in the early postwar period. In the latter countries the shocks were mild to nonexistent, and comparatively little change in economic thinking ensued. The economic future envisaged by Polanyi came to pass, but it emerged in some places more strongly than in others.

It is desirable, and I argue feasible, to move beyond those broad brushstrokes and examine the links between these key transitions in economic history more closely. Clearly more analysis remains to be done to expand the sample, examine other indicators and mechanisms, and ascertain the robustness of the correlations. Nonetheless, there is suggestive evidence here that the institutional memory of the 1930s crisis was a factor that influenced policy for a long time to come, including the speed at which countries embraced the opportunities of reglobalization in the 1970s.

Lessons for Today

The Great Transformation was not an "end of history" moment, and the subsequent fifty years witnessed something of a reglobalization along classical liberal lines that Polanyi could not envisage. The new globalization differed from its laissez-faire predecessor, and its foundations were built on international and domestic institutions that supported an "embedded liberalism" with more social protection. Nonetheless, by the 1990s it could be argued that the acceleration of globalization had eroded or disembedded much of that protection.[11]

As a generality, the idea that the Great Depression was a watershed moment that echoed throughout the rest of the twentieth century is an ingrained element of conventional wisdom. It is most often viewed in this light as a story of what happened *within* countries, to explain the timing of reactions against laissez faire and in favor of more state intervention. In many scholarly as well as popular accounts these great long swings in economic ideology and policy outcomes and their similarities around the globe tend to take center stage.

These grand narratives implicitly emphasize the "common shock" of the Great Depression and the policy response worldwide. In this chapter I have sought to argue that this view is incomplete, and that we can better understand the legacy of this defining moment by using the approaches of *new comparative economic history* to see how the differences in experiences across countries led to a variety of path-dependent outcomes evolving over time. Certainly, using the depth of the slump in the 1930s is a crude indicator, and one-dimensional at that. It is a first step only, and further, deeper research will be needed to validate the argument and flesh out the linkages; but the payoffs to this scholarship could deliver important lessons for research and policymaking.

Both research and teaching in international economic history tend to treat the history of the modern world in separate phases. Major breaking points are rarely bridged by narrative, and have received much less quantitative analysis. The Great Depression is a case in point. When we discuss the origins of the postwar economic order, we tend to view Bretton Woods as a clean slate. But around the globe, countries emerged from World War II with very different experiences, ideologies, interest groups, and agendas. Outside the Communist bloc they may have signed up in some general way to a new economic order including the goal of freer trade under GATT. But how policies and economic development played out in each case over subsequent decades would reflect the countries' very different initial conditions, including the impact of the crisis of the 1930s on domestic policymaking. A more complete global economic history of the twentieth century is needed to bridge that transition with more than narrative so that we can better understand how those heterogeneous developments came about.

Research in economic growth will also benefit. Despite some skeptical resistance, one of the most widely held views in the research on postwar economic growth is that open economies have grown faster than closed economies. The divergence of economic fortunes became most apparent after 1970, when countries like the Asian NICs began their export-oriented growth, while at the other end of the spectrum, more autarkic regimes such as the import-substituters of Latin America waited much longer to liberalize. That correlation is robust, but is it causal? One way to think about the legacy of the Great Depression is that it generates some plausible exogenous variation in subsequent trade policy, and in that respect (as an instrumental variable, in econometric language) it may help us better estimate the impact of differential speeds of policy reform on growth acceleration. In a recent paper Antoni Estevadeordal and I put this idea to work, showing that even as late as the 1990s, trade reforms still carried an echo of the Great Depression, and the faster reformers saw more rapid growth acceleration than the slow reformers.[12] There is some irony here: the countries that were worst hit by the Great Depression adopted reactive policies that may have helped somewhat in the 1930s, but they fell behind economically in the long run. If that logic holds up, then one question worth investigating is whether the Great Depression was a major contributing factor to the Great Divergence, thanks to the wide range of policy responses it unleashed.

At a broader level, understanding the very-long-run persistence of policy shocks emanating from the 1930s carries lessons for policymaking. Policies are never irreversible, but they can take on a life of their own and endure for decades. Theorists have shown in various ways how policy persistence mechanisms can make this happen. Evidence isn't plentiful, but if any past episode can prove this hypothesis, it would be policy responses to the greatest slump in history, the 1930s crisis. Should the thesis be more strongly confirmed, the lesson for current times of economic turmoil would be very clear. Avoid a Great Depression, or else face a risk that policymaking could veer into a radically autarkic stance for many decades. From a historical standpoint there is good reason to put extra weight on safeguarding the world economy against a deep slump, if such a meltdown would shift the political economy equilibrium past some threshold and unleash even stronger isolationist pressures than already exist.

To sum up, in terms of global economic history the 1970s can be seen as a bookend decade matched with the decade of the 1930s. The 1930s marked an end of globalization, which, although some expected it to be a permanent shift, kept trade flows in abeyance for only a few decades. The 1970s saw a widening embrace of trade liberalization that set the world on course for reglobalization. It is a process that still continues for now, but if we want to understand better the possible risks of another reversal, we might profitably invest more attention in the historical dynamics of the last one.

CHAPTER 6

International Finance and Political Legitimacy

A Latin American View of the Global Shock

JEREMY ADELMAN

IN THE SUMMER OF 1976 the German-born writer and economist Albert
O. Hirschman traveled to some familiar cities of South America: Bogotá,
Caracas, Rio de Janeiro, São Paulo, and Buenos Aires. His trip culminated
in Santiago. These were dark times in the region: in lands for which he
had a strong affection and with which he had important intellectual ties,
Hirschman found soldiers lining the streets and university faculties shut
down. On a mission to learn more about Latin American economies, he
met with ministers and presidents (former and future) and gathered with
old friends and colleagues. As in Europe and North America, inflation and
deficits of all sorts were on the rise across Latin America, only more dramatically. In one of his reflections he scribbled, "Economic policy-making
during such a period resembles foreign policy-making of Bismarck: lots of
balls being kept in the air which can't all possibly be caught." These were
the words of a veteran observer of the complex relationship between economic performance and political liberty, who had grown up in Weimar-era
Berlin. Dictators, Hirschman noted, "thrive" in depressions and booms.
"There is an affinity with both extremes. They [the despots] alone know
how to put the economy though the wringer and how to overheat it in
turn."[1]

This chapter is about juggling under duress in the area of economic
policymaking—specifically the duress posed by the interlocking of two crises. The first involved the upheavals of the global economy as the postwar
growth model faltered, reflected in decontrol of capital markets and sharp
energy price hikes. But this crisis did not unfold uniformly across regions

113

or nations, which suggests a need for an accounting for variations in world history, what might be called regional histories of the world. Accordingly, the second crisis was more regional, associated with shifting understandings of the state, markets, and Latin America's place in the world economy. Not long after his return from Latin America, a letter arrived at Hirschman's office from Charles Maier, the Harvard-based historian, about a collaborative project called "Politics and Sociology of Global Inflation." Maier invited Hirschman to participate; he wanted "to draw if possible on your capacity for disciplined general reflection," as well as to share insights from Latin America in order "to extract 'lessons' that are illuminating for Europe and the US. My own feeling is that when one contemplates the UK or New York City the cleavages of Latin America are far more relevant than generally credited." Hirschman accepted the invitation, adding that "the inflation experience in Latin America and its analysis by social scientists from Latin America and elsewhere have something to contribute to the 'deeper' understanding of inflation."[2]

This chapter also asks what it meant to be "shocked" by the 1970s. A few clarifications are in order. First, integration into the world economy was hardly new to Latin America; the 1970s did not represent an awakening to global pressures. Indeed there had been a raging debate among policymakers and social scientists since the 1940s about the problems and possibilities posed by the world economy. By the mid 1950s there was a full-blown controversy about import substitution as a route to industrialization in Argentina, and a few years later a formative dispute over explanations for inflation in Chile, where the conflict between Marxists and monetarists anticipated the bitter showdown of the 1970s. So it was less the "global" nature of the crisis that was shocking to policymakers than the effects of the decisions they made in response to it—which is one of the reasons why this chapter accents the role of policymakers and their preferences in the shaping of crises.

The second clarification involves a term that overshadows much of the way we think about the coming of globalization: sovereignty. There is a conventional notion that the crisis of the 1970s shattered the sovereign nation-state, if not in fact at least its myth. Raymond Vernon's 1971 classic account of the "multinational" (itself a moniker to reflect the times) corporation, *Sovereignty at Bay*, captured the mood. From the 1930s, goes a conventional narrative, the nation-state enjoyed its freedom to apply Keynesian economic policies, or growth-inducing policies for the developing world, because its bounded features allowed taxes to be collected and programs to be issued without the specter of capital flight or penalties on monetary controls (whose degree has often been taken as an index of national sovereignty). The 1970s ended all that and perforated the structures of the sovereign nation-state. This takes at face value some precepts of nationalist historiography (of the Left *and* Right) about globalization: that it is an exogenous force that disrupts some cherished beliefs about the legitimate exercise of state power. But it holds little water. More and more we are coming to see that sovereignty was much more equivocal than its founders wished. Like the world economy of which it was a part, principles and practices of sovereignty have been aggregated at more than one juridical level. What the 1970s presented was less the end of national sovereignty than a transformation in the way it was assembled and linked with other levels at which legal power was expressed.[3] It was how policymakers in Latin America grappled with this reaggregation that is the concern of this chapter, fueled by a growing sense that the economy and politics were misaligned—with policymaking struggling to reengineer the relationship between capitalism and citizenship, rents and rights.

Troubles came to a head for producers, consumers, and financiers around the world in the late 1960s and early 1970s. The result was an unraveling of the basic social bargains of the postwar era and increasing stresses on the elaborate cooperative network that had sustained the Bretton Woods system. While the crisis had many sources, policymakers in the world's financial capitals faced a shared trilemma. They had to juggle the competing demands of (1) regulating foreign exchange rates; (2) preserving policy autonomy for their states (regardless of their ideological dispositions); and (3) monitoring the mobility of capital. For the most part, the ideological and policymaking preferences were to rely on the tools they were accustomed to using to keep all the balls in the air. Some balls, however, were starting to fall. Non-U.S. central banks dealt with some of the problems by absorbing dollars rather than forcing the U.S. currency's devaluation; no one wanted to rubbish the Bretton Woods system. But absorbing dollars meant adding more liquidity to local markets, which aggravated domestic inflation—especially anxiety provoking for West Germany, which gradually let the mark float upwards. Dollars began to flee the United States to various European centers until the famous summer of 1971, when Nixon suspended convertibility to gold, and industrial countries embarked on extensive efforts to patch up the system until finally, by default, regulators ceased holding and spending their reserves (and the expense of efforts to contain inflation) to defend exchange rate rigidity. The dollar plunged once more in early 1973. European central bankers let go. One by one their currencies were left to float and revalue. The exchange regime of Bretton Woods, and the complex coordination that sustained it, was history, and policymakers were free to change their juggling acts.[4]

This story is well known. But it is also often misunderstood. Whatever might be said of the origins of the crisis, it was a set of interlocking public decisions that reconstituted the rules of the global financial system in the early 1970s; it was *this* change that was shocking. This change did not emanate inevitably from some structural shift in the world economy or a compound collapse of national welfarist regimes—as if policies were merely effects of some more basic cause. Indeed the causal chain can be reversed. From 1944 there had been a debate about the rights and freedoms of possessors of short-term or portfolio capital, compared to the obligations of states to curb them in the service of other objectives (such as exchange rate stability). The Bretton Woods system offered something of an unstable compromise, leaving the decision over control of these flows to the discretion of national states, so long as they played by other multilateral rules of exchange. Indeed, as the 1960s yielded more widespread current account deficits, most industrial states relied on more, not fewer, capital controls, including the United States. It was not the increasingly freewheeling nature of capital that led to decontrol but rather a shift in preferences for policymakers. Some came from the growing sway of intellectual currents, especially influenced by Friedrich Hayek and Milton Friedman, which advocated freer markets and less tampering in all economic activities. But the immediate precipitant was a shift in policy preferences. Especially once the Nixon administration suspended gold convertibility, the balance of currency stability and policy autonomy at the expense of capital mobility gave way to capital decontrol and policy autonomy at the expense of currency stability. This occasioned the dramatic crash of the pegged exchange rate system which had ushered in the decade. What is important is that regulators did not want to forfeit sovereignty in the face of more fluid capital flows; at the time, what they wanted was to preserve autonomy over capital mobility and policymaking at the expense of exchange rate stability.[5]

It is often thought that decontrol of capital markets was the reflex to the collapse of Bretton Woods. What is frequently forgotten is how much this represented a policy choice. States began to sanction new legal ecologies for the exchange of financial assets in dollars; offshore currency trading centers took off, most notably the Eurodollar market, which required U.S. and British legal reforms governing transborder activity in the trade of assets in other currencies. Decontrol of banks and a new role for their supervisors also had to be effected. This was a more drawn-out process through the 1970s; indeed, faced with the social crises of 1978–79, regulators across the OECD were sorely tempted to reintroduce capital controls because of fear of speculation, capital flight, currency plunges, and hyperinflation. But they did not; by then the ground rules governing the circulation of capital had changed. In the midst of these policy shifts, the oil crisis plunged the world economy into its deepest recession since the 1930s. Since oil prices were denominated in dollars, the devaluation of the dollar had been a blow to its exporters, who had formed a toothless cartel in the early 1960s. OPEC overcame its internal divisions. In November 1973 oil prices quadrupled, enforcing a giant tax on oil product consumers. Output in industrialized countries slumped; unemployment rose. The combination of soaring oil prices and growing fears of price instability with the end of convertibility prompted panic that industrial societies might backslide, as they had in the 1930s, into a round of competitive devaluations, protectionism, and isolationism. The effect on policymakers was the degrading of confidence in old recipes tied to the synthesis of postwar Keynesianism. The crisis of demand-oriented economic policy fueled the beginnings of a supply-side orientation—which was hardly ascendant in the 1970s but did represent a yearning for certainties.

If the convergence of these forces tipped the intellectual scales in policy circles, it also had significant material consequences that reinforced this process. All the while, the oil-exporting countries of the Middle East—unable to absorb the massive amounts of capital suddenly produced by their oil—deposited their windfalls in offshore accounts. Oil incomes to OPEC countries rose from $33 billion in 1973 to $108 billion a year later: just as unused industrial capacity in the OECD was rising, the global stock of investible funds increased sharply; the demand for money dropped while its supply was increasing. Global inflation compounded the problem. OECD consumer price indices jumped from 4.7 percent to 12 percent between 1972 and 1980. The result: a dramatic deterioration of the returns on capital. The real (that is, adjusted for inflation) London Inter-Bank Rate (the rate charged on loans between financial institutions) dropped sharply from an average of 4.1 percent from 1960 to 1971 to −0.8 percent from 1971 to 1980; this was the shock to world financiers.[6]

What happened to the sudden surge of very cheap liquidity? Part of the answer can be found on the supply side. Decontrol coincided with and occasioned a change in the institutional makeup of world capital markets. Money was more fluid; it also flowed through new channels. A key feature of the global landscape of finance capital was the commercial bank. Until the late 1950s commercial banks had played a residual role in dispensing global capital. With the collapse of the Bretton Woods system, financial deregulation, and the emergence of the Eurodollar market in the wake of the OPEC oil price hikes of the early 1970s, banks emerged as major controllers of world liquidity. In fact a small group of very large banks with extensive overseas operations formed the nucleus of the resulting wave of international borrowing and lending. One innovation was the syndicated loan, organized around a "lead bank," which on one level was offering funds while on another was proffering a service by bundling resources and negotiating with clients on behalf of a consortium of banks that agreed to disperse the risks of default. Informal interbank activity was nothing new, but it grew, spread, and became more formal as the 1970s unfolded. More and more commercial banks, licensed by changes in local legal codes, entered the market. Especially from France, Britain, Germany, and elsewhere in Western Europe, new entrants joined the familiar big American banks; this proliferation in turn required some of them to take "leading" roles in the syndicates. For the top ten U.S. banks alone, the share of foreign earnings as a percentage of all gains rose dramatically from 1970 to 1982, on the eve of the debt crisis, from 17.5 percent to 54.7 percent. In contrast to the common view that credit markets have largely been driven by demand for money, with banks as impersonal intermediators allocating funds in accordance with expected risks and returns, their organization and behavior were important: they were active peddlers, trying to find markets for capital that was yielding dismal returns in the OECD.[7]

The combination of a perception that old Keynesian or developmentalist orthodoxies were on the ropes, steps toward greater fluidity of capital markets, and the climate of uncertainty all had effects on the mentality of policymakers. Experiments in controls and heterodox policies that might once have run counter to the policy norms of the 1950s would in the 1970s elicit sharper penalties, as Harold Wilson's Labour government learned when it came back to power in 1974, and the French socialists discovered seven years later. The result emboldened the advocates of a new kind of orthodoxy, which at the time appeared heterodox but advanced its standing as a means to restore the credibility and credentials of the policymaker who still hung on to the preference for his or her own discretion. This was especially dramatic in Latin America, where policymakers' search for certainty was reinforced by the surge of available credit from global banking syndicates, which provided the bases for a fateful convergence of recipes and resources for the region's troubles in the 1970s.

While the intellectual climate and the policy preferences were shifting in the OECD countries, there was a more dramatic, albeit uneven, lurch in Latin America. Some of the first, more audacious efforts at changing the policymaking paradigm took place not where the ideas were produced but where they were consumed. This brings us to the "demand side" of the story of international finance, the creation of a need for foreign capital out of conviction as much as necessity. It is worth reminding ourselves to start with that Latin America was not experiencing a generalized malaise in the early 1970s; growth rates from 1967 to 1973 were high. It was the political and social systems that were more in doubt. In 1968 the Mexican Institutional Revolutionary Party (PRI) initiated its own legitimation crisis after the massacre at the Tlatelolco Plaza. The same year a left-wing coup brought the military to power in Lima, and Che Guevara–inspired guerrillas appeared to be fanning out across the continent. In response, armed takeovers swept many capitals, culminating in the overthrow of Salvador Allende in Chile on September 11, 1973.

While it was politics that was in crisis, intellectuals and policymakers pointed to economic structures as the source of the trouble. By 1973 there was an impression across the board that the postwar growth model in Latin America was "exhausted" (a preferred term at the time). For those of the Right, the unrest only confirmed what they had been arguing all along: that state intrusions and growth based on the production of manufactured goods for the domestic market had steered the region into a cul-de-sac from which it could not possibly emerge. After the debacle of the episode known as the "Rodrigazo" in Argentina in June 1975, conservative critics went on the warpath arguing that no policy, especially one under a

Peronist government, could contain the disequilibrium as long as it was trying to reconcile stability with a growth model that still relied on the domestic market and native industries as its pistons. When the military seized power in March the following year, the new minister, José Alfredo Martínez de Hoz, announced that "we must go from an economy of speculation to one of production," implying that there was nothing left of the old model to salvage.[8]

The temptation to look for explanations that emphasized intractable structural problems to justify a completely different set of policies was even more pronounced in Chile, where a cadre of University of Chicago–trained economists at the Catholic University in Santiago espoused an amalgamation of Hayekian epistemology and Hispanist ontology. They were, to be sure, a much more mixed group than the term "Chicago Boys"—a Chilean coinage—implied. But a hard core of them provided the intellectual nucleus that guided economic policymaking after Augusto Pinochet took power. Only once it was clear that the military was going to stay in power, and especially after 1975, did the Chicago-trained economists begin to lend the regime a patina of coherence; Sergio de Castro, Pablo Baraona, Sergio Undurraga, and eventually Rolf Luders and many others formed the core of a new clique. Almost from top to bottom, from planning and budgeting to the central bank, these state offices were turned over to apostles determined to rid the country of entrenched dirigiste ways while relying on the levers of state power to realize the idyll of "a nation of owners."[9]

The Left, too, agreed that the model of the postwar years was "exhausted." Guillermo O'Donnell, the creative Argentine social scientist, argued that structural impediments stood in the way of "deepening" import substitution, which could not be dismantled with any consensus. As early as 1971 he was formulating causal connections between the difficulties of industrialization and the rise of dictatorships, laying the groundwork for his term "bureaucratic authoritarianism," which sought to identify economic bases for political developments. Another view argued that only a socialist demiurge could break the impasse of faltering industrialization (or, to be more accurate, see its *profundización*), a view which was especially influential on advisers to leaders such as Peru's Juan Velasco or Chile's Salvador Allende. The "exhaustion thesis" had been floating around from the mid-1960s and was closely associated with the instabilities of the populist regimes that were alleged to have sired the original strategy. But by the early 1970s it had turned into a kind of deus ex ma-china, a plot device to apply some coherence to a narrative overflowing with conflict.[10]

But the region was not of a piece. Since the 1960s Brazil's policymakers had been more eclectic, combining interventionist and market-friendly ways, amalgamating elaborate protections for national industries while ag-gressively promoting nontraditional exports. Mexico deployed its oil rents to do much the same. By contrast, the Southern Cone was more pendular, swinging from one extreme to another, as governments aimed to bury the remnants of state dirigisme and populism with principled commitments to decontrolled markets, balanced budgets, and strict monetary guidelines. But there was more than just stabilization; there was a notion that states could reset the bases of growth. A key to their policies was to alleviate what economists call (without irony) "financial repression"—freeing do-mestic capital markets from government "distortions" and reducing public borrowing from, and public ownership of, financial agencies. It was a cor-nerstone of a more general process of decontrol to release capital for private investment and to withdraw the state from the management of market relations without reducing the discretion of policymakers. It also positioned itself most clearly as a volte-face on the populist interventions of previous decades. The combination of stabilization and liberalization reinforced the impression that the new rulers were using macroeconomic policy to lay different foundations by folding policymakers' countries back into the world economy after decades of perceived isolationism. In this ba-sic respect they simply inverted their predecessors' convictions premised on a reading of recent history to create it anew. Of course, in spite of the contrasts there were also underlying continuities—an assumption about the economy's essential elasticity or nonvulnerability; it could be made to conform to the mind's eye of the policymaker.

A fundamental question arises about this démarche, noting that some-thing similar would take hold later in the OECD, especially in the Anglo-Atlantic world. Could the shift in global policy preferences have been sus-tained or permitted without changes in the functioning of global capital markets? Was the latter a condition of the former? Most approaches to globalization tend to answer in the affirmative: for conservatives the re-lease of market forces was a belated recognition of the ineluctable, as George Gilder's apostolic *Wealth and Poverty* argued in 1981; Marxists did not have to go further than the *Communist Manifesto* to argue that globalization reflected a world created in the image of the bourgeoisie, now a more fully transnationalized class. But the sequence from economics to politics is much muddier, and the causality even more so. What can be said about Latin America is that shifts in global finance created permissive conditions for new policy preferences. Financial deregulation had the effect of augmenting the circulation of capital in Latin American economies. But it was not of the domestic savings kind. By easing restrictions on capital movements and relaxing bankers' standards of operation, deregulated banking systems intensified foreign borrowing. Chile was the trendsetter, in part to separate the military regime from its socialist predecessor. Starting by auctioning state banks or repatriating socialized ones to previous owners, policymakers let interest rates float, and the monitoring of banks was pared back. For all intents and purposes the government put an end to supervision and inspection of bank portfolios. When economic policymakers fixed the Chilean peso and stripped away controls over capital movements in 1979, foreign funds flocked to Santiago. The levels of private debt rose quickly thereafter. Brazil was a counterpoint. While policymakers succumbed less to the temptations of pendularity—erasing the perceived malefactors of the past with a whole new paradigm—they still endorsed massive borrowing. The difference was that the money went less into the cost of stabilization and liberalization than to finance billowing current account deficits, especially with the rise of global oil prices; rather than absorb them, Brazilian policymakers borrowed, thereby buffering the recession of 1973–74, but created habits that would endure through the 1980s and a shift to what has been called "debt-led growth."[11]

What is important to recognize is that policymaking was more than simply coping with the exogenous shocks of the decade, as if regulators (or deregulators) were simply plugging holes and fixing leaks as global forces tossed the ship of state on ever more turbulent waters. There was much more that was *chosen* about the policies—and the politics that sustained them—than is often appreciated, especially as we tend to think of globalization as a process that happens at the expense of state sovereignty. Of course the distinction between choosing and coping can be easily overdrawn, and one is struck in retracing the steps taken in the 1970s by how much blurring went on as policymakers dressed up their emergency decrees as inspired acts and justified their audacity in the vocabulary of necessity. Still, in spite of the heterogeneity within Latin America, the 1970s recentered policymakers as the entrepreneurs of a new model of growth in which they would not—could not—forfeit their discretion precisely because turmoil required a degree of conviction and certainty to pull societies out of their crises.

Policy choices became expensive preferences. The bill, however, was only passed on to borrowers when interest rates began to spike once the same monetary doctrines took hold in world creditor countries. The result: the shock of the 1980s would make that of the 1970s seem tame. The total sum was staggering (see Table 6.1).

Hindsight biases can easily lure us into a search for underlying irrationalities or perversities. At the time, however, the borrowing habits made some sense. The flow of capital from global creditors to regional borrowers was *not* reflected in the deterioration of basic debt indicators. As Table 6.2 shows, the percentage of total debt to annual exports varied a great deal but was not so high as to set off alarm bells. And if one considers how much interest had to be earmarked from export receipts, the impression is hardly shocking, especially in comparison to the 1930s or 1980s, when annual debt service payment for many borrowers could wipe out all export revenues. In effect, as long as international interest rates were low (or especially from 1974 to 1978 when they were negative, which meant that it paid to be a borrower), the preference for debt made perfect sense. What

Table 6.1. Macroeconomic indicators for Latin America, 1973–1982

Year	Growth of real GDP (%)	Inflation (%)	External debt ($ billions)
1973	8.4	32.1	44.4
1974	6.9	37.5	58.2
1975	3.1	52.0	68.6
1976	5.5	66.1	82.0
1977	5.3	49.9	124.6
1978	4.1	41.9	154.9
1979	6.1	46.5	187.2
1980	5.3	53.7	229.4
1981	1.0	58.2	285.6
1982	−0.9	64.6	325.5

Source: United Nations Economic Commission for Latin America, *Anuario Estadístico*, various years.

is more, unlike the OECD, Latin America sustained its growth rates. To be sure, they were not as high as the 1967–1974 levels (which reached, on average, 8.4 percent in 1973), but even a tough year like 1979 recorded an average growth rate of 6.1 percent.[12]

If 1973 marked a departure, 1978 was a turning point. Until then, borrowing had risen systematically to fund current account deficits and to pay for public debts. But one of the underlying objectives, curbing inflation, did not work, in part because foreign borrowing depleted the effects of tightness on local monetary emissions. This forced central bankers to rely even more on foreign exchange rates to anchor local processes to global ones, which only led to more overvaluation. By 1978 there was a nickname for Argentine shoppers in New York and Paris: *damedós* ("gimmetwo," as the knee-jerk follow-up to the question "How much does that cost?"). By 1978, as Latin American middle classes and elites went on their buying sprees, *local* confidence in money began to wane. To compound matters, OPEC issued another round of steep oil price increases, which had to be absorbed, hitting a heavy industrializer like Brazil especially hard. And since currencies were increasingly overvalued and the constraints on capital mobility lifted as part of the deregulatory fever, there were more and more inducements and fewer and fewer constraints on shipping money out of the region, back into *global* accounts. Call this capital flight; it took off. Between 1975 and 1985 the cumulative capital flight from Latin America exceeded $100 billion—roughly $265 per capita. During the peak exodus from 1979 to 1982, Argentina sent $22.4 billion, Mexico $22.3 billion, and Venezuela $20.7 billion (Brazil began large-scale capital exports only once the debt crisis broke in 1982). The result was an utterly perverse circulation of funds from offshore commercial banks to Latin American borrowers and then back to offshore private accounts. The sum: between 1978 and 1982 the value of total debt for nineteen Latin American countries more than doubled, from $151 billion to $331 billion (see Table 6.2).[13]

Comparisons help highlight the significance of policy preferences and political choices. Consider the differences between Latin America and what were once called East Asian "tigers." The latter group, South Korea and Taiwan, for instance, also turned to banks for external funds, but the money was used to promote vigorous export diversification and growth rather than to cover current account deficits caused by the coincidence of overvalued exchange rates (meant to curb inflation) and trade opening

Table **6.2.** Principal debt ratios, 1973 and 1979, percentages of total exports

Country	Debt		Interest payments	
	1973	1979	1973	1979
Argentina	74.3	86.7	5.3	5.7
Brazil	107.0	197.3	5.5	16.2
Chile	191.7	101.4	2.5	7.5
Colombia	121.8	68.0	4.9	4.6
Mexico	115.4	182.7	7.1	17.8
Venezuela	29.2	48.9	1.9	4.0

Source: World Bank, *World Debt Tables, 1983–84* (Washington, D.C., 1984).

(meant to align domestic prices with global ones). They also kept strictures on local banking institutions, with heavy supervision of bank portfolios, requirements of substantial reserves, and tougher disclosure laws. (By contrast, on the eve of its default in 1982, Mexico was twelve to eighteen months behind on supplying the World Bank with information about basic macroeconomic balances.)[14] What Latin American policymakers had done was to assemble stabilization, financial decontrol, and trade liberalization into a single package while international bankers were "pushing" their services and loans. Although this broad-brush comparison needs qualification and nuance, it does suggest that the source of Latin America's problem was not financial dependency per se but rather the framework governing capital flows. Accordingly, while the semi-periphery absorbed a rising share of the world's billowing transborder capital flows, the big Latin American debtors were increasingly ill-prepared for any sudden change in the terms or direction of those flows.

In the summer of 1982 Mexico's finance minister, Jesús Silva Herzog, announced to the meeting of the governors of the IMF and World Bank that Mexico would have to suspend payments on its foreign debts. It simply had no reserves left in the central bank. The proclamation accelerated what was already happening—capital flight, currencies in free fall, looming hyperinflation—and it formally inaugurated Latin America's most dismal economic period. The rapid deterioration of economic fortunes contributed to the downfall of dictators. So while fledgling civilian regimes sought to break with autocratic pasts, they could not so easily distance themselves from the legacies of decisions taken since 1973 about Latin America's place in the world economy.

One might argue that Latin Americans were being asked to pay in the 1980s the costs that the OECD had borne in their adjustments to new circumstances in the 1970s. In a suggestive article about the history of the fall of communism, Charles Maier argued that the "heavy metal" regimes of the Soviet bloc were unable to adapt to the shifts ushered in by 1968: internal pressures for political reform, adaptation to new energy realities, and changes in technology and agriculture worldwide. Instead the reflex was to centralize and entrench. Was Latin America in the same position, unable to adapt to global developments initiated elsewhere? The question is valid because there is a tradition in the Anglo-American world of pointing to Hispanic lethargy and lassitude as a basic drag on modernization. This "Black Legend" has received new impetus in more recent times, as self-anointed reformers proclaim themselves the prophets of Latin America's belated entry into the freewheeling world of global capitalism. This essay has argued the opposite: if the heavy metal regimes' reflex was to deepen the model contrived in earlier decades, Latin America, and especially the Southern Cone, embarked on something very different. This was no "decade of delay." It represented a pendular swing in the region's relationship with international money as the dynamics of global capitalism severed the ties between its industrial and its financial stays.[15]

If it was the *way* Latin America adapted, and not its refusal, we can point to the role of preferences, choices, and the ideologies that shaped them as the tissue that connected regions to the world. With rising prices, slowing growth, and global imbalances, the 1970s marked a global conjuncture whose events were explained by the tenets of economic doctrines that had been in circulation for years but that, with the demise of Keynesian and development theories, acquired greater influence among policymakers. Just as Keynesian doctrine not only explained the global depression but also guided the design of national policies and institutions that would demonstrate the correctness of its principles, and developmentalism enjoyed some of the same properties in the 1950s, the 1970s appeared to be the inspired moment for neoclassical propositions about the workings of the market and perils of state control. Certain "preconditions" gave them greater credence as the coordinating system of Bretton Woods crumbled and welfare states had difficulties squaring their spending on services with the fiscal demands of the Cold War.

This confluence of circumstances gave new credence to older doctrines. But fitting doctrines to events implied policies. This chapter has explored how ideologies operated to prescribe a set of policies in Latin America that were meant to reverse the "decay" or "exhaustion" of the postwar model. The narrative is meant to challenge the propensity to explain globalization by referring to "fundamental" structural forces that drove events with no need to account for the role of states, since globalization—the story goes—was all about the waning of state sovereignty affiliated with the institutional girders of Keynesian doctrines and developmentalism. Here I have tried to invert the story, to illustrate the fate of nation-states in an era of rapidly growing economic interdependence by illustrating the ways in which policymakers clung to their autonomy in the name of universal verities about how markets work. The result was a complex and self-conscious adaptation that swung Latin America from its postwar growth model into a successor whose unstable features we are still trying to fathom.

CHAPTER 7

American Debt, Global Capital

The Policy Origins of Securitization

LOUIS HYMAN

THE FIRST SALE of mortgage-backed securities, on February 19, 1970, marked a decisive break in the history of the global economy. Beginning with American mortgages, securitization—whereby the revenue of multiple assets is channeled through a single security—became one of the defining financial innovations of the 1970s, facilitating the easy flow of investment capital around the world. While we think of the 1970s as a time of deregulation in the global economy, securitization began, as did so many earlier financial innovations, as a federal policy to solve an immediate political problem. Mortgage-backed securities originated at the intersection of turbulent global currency markets and equally turbulent urban unrest in the late 1960s.[1] American policymakers fashioned the mortgage-backed security in an attempt to harness the powers of capital markets to restore stability in the American city. As precarious global markets and domestic politics helped engender the mortgage-backed security then, so does the mortgage-backed security threaten a precarious economic and political order today.

The Credit Crunch of 1966

Abruptly, in the middle of 1966, homebuyers could no longer find mortgage money to borrow, sending the housing industries into a panic. To many policymakers and businesspeople this scarcity of mortgage capital, whose easy accessibility had underpinned the suburban expansion of the postwar period, was unimaginable and appeared to come from nowhere.

This so-called Credit Crunch of 1966, when American mortgage lenders ran out of money to lend, set the stage for the creation of the mortgage-backed security.[2]

The credit crunch arose not from the chaos of an unregulated market but from the orderly, but unintended, collision of the international Bretton Woods exchange system and domestic American financial regulation—the global dollar supply and the Federal Reserve's Regulation Q. As so many economic historians have written, the crash of the dollar in the 1960s, and the subsequent end of Bretton Woods, was like a train wreck in slow motion.[3] While Europe and East Asia were recovering after World War II, dollars remained scarce. As the global economy rebounded, however, the foreign demand for American goods slackened. A dollar scarcity became a dollar glut.[4] Inevitably, it seemed, the dollar would have to be devalued. While formally the entire system rested on a dollar pegged to gold, in practice it was the global supply and demand for the dollar, rather than gold, that provided liquidity for the worldwide economy. Gold reserves could not keep pace with the growth in the transnational economy.[5] The supply of dollars had to expand for the global economy to function, but an expanding supply of dollars threatened the stability of the dollar's value in gold. The situation was untenable.[6]

By the early 1960s American economists and policymakers began to suspect an imminent inflationary crisis born of this inevitable global oversupply of dollars. While some steps reduced the dollars held overseas, such as restrictions on corporate investment and personal travel, other expenditures, such as in Vietnam, overwhelmed the restrictions. While relative demand for American goods fell abroad, domestic expansion augured inflation. The imbalance between foreign and domestic demand for dollars threatened domestic inflation and the global stability of the Bretton Woods system.

In 1966 the Federal Reserve attempted to restore stability to the dollar by raising the interest rate and cutting banks' access to reserves. A higher interest rate, it was hoped, would simultaneously restrain domestic business demand and make investment in domestic federal securities more appealing to foreign investors, drawing dollars back into the United States and curtailing demand for foreign goods. The Federal Open Market Committee announced in February that it would be the Fed's "policy to resist the emergence of inflationary pressures and to restore reasonable equilibrium in the country's balance of payments."[7] In this regard the Fed was successful. Nineteen sixty-six saw a great influx of foreign capital and a decrease in the inflation rate.[8]

But the economic brakes affected domestic financial institutions in ways that the bankers did not fully anticipate. The Federal Reserve's Regulation Q in 1966 limited banks to paying depositors a maximum of 5.5 percent. In the past, whenever market rates had approached the Regulation Q limit, the Fed had raised the limit. Unexpectedly, this time, in an effort to stave off inflation stemming from those expanding balance of payments problems, the Fed held fast to its limit, leading to a near-panic situation for bankers.[9]

No one had expected the Fed to enforce the limit. To increase their liquidity, banks tried to sell their municipal bonds, but with so many institutions selling so many bonds in such a shallow secondary market, the prices on the bonds quickly fell. Equally important, American depositors found that the securities markets provided better returns than their savings accounts and began to withdraw their money from their local banks, accelerating a trend among American depositors toward bypassing banks entirely and moving savings directly into securities markets.[10] Constrained by their relatively low-returning mortgage portfolios, savings and loan banks could not raise interest rates to match the market, and thus could not acquire new savings funds to lend.[11] For all these reasons, banks ran out of money to lend.

While the higher interest rate restrained lending to business, it also inadvertently choked off the supply of home mortgages for consumers. The third quarter of 1966—the height of the crunch—saw an overall drop in mortgage funds of 40 percent from a year earlier. The net flow into mortgages from savings and loan banks was zero.[12] Housing starts dropped by a fifth in 1966. With the supply of mortgage capital so limited, interest rates hit heights unseen since the 1920s. The credit crunch shocked homeowners and homebuilders accustomed to easy mortgage credit, causing a slowdown in the housing industry.[13]

Despite its tough stance on Regulation Q, the Fed was not prepared for the outrage provoked by the austerity measures required to contain inflation and the balance of payments. The outcry from American business was too loud, and by the end of 1966 the Fed relented. In December it announced the end of its voluntary restriction on business loans since "the expansion of business loans has been reduced to a more moderate rate."[14] By early 1967 the Fed acted to increase the money supply, and bank credit again expanded. But such expansion came at the cost of further erosion of the value of the dollar.[15] The Bretton Woods system resumed its slow fall as the effects of the short-term austerity faded.

The memory of the credit crunch, however, did not fade so quickly. The scare of a credit crunch had been felt too intensely in the mortgage and housing industry. Oddly, most observers interpreted the crunch almost as a natural phenomenon and not the result of Fed policy intersecting with international agreements. Strangely seen as exogenous, the credit crunch, itself intentionally caused by a federal agency—the Fed—led Congress to create policies to guarantee that such a crunch, with its dire effects on mortgage lending, could never happen again. Mortgage funds had become by the end of the 1960s, for domestic political reasons, too important.

The Urban Crisis and the Credit Crunch

In the Credit Crunch of 1966 the global currency crisis collided with the American urban crisis. While IMF macroeconomists and European central bankers worried about the unraveling of the balance of payments, most American politicians and bankers were concerned far more with the perceived unraveling of the American city. More than three hundred riots broke out in over 250 cities between 1964 and 1968, primarily in African American neighborhoods. Interpretations of what caused the riots were as numerous as the riots themselves: police brutality, low wages, consumer exploitation, hopelessness, and many more. Although explanations varied, most solutions, from both Republicans and Democrats, were similar: greater black ownership in the inner city would lead to greater social stability. Policies to stop the seemingly annual riots came from all corners, from both the Left and the Right, but all centered on giving the people of the riot-torn areas more of a stake in their communities, providing capital not only for small businesses but also for mortgages for home ownership.

To solve the urban crisis would require solving the housing crisis. But to solve the housing crisis, radical financial innovation would have to occur in order to maintain the capital flows into mortgages. The Credit Crunch of 1966, with its savage interruptions to mortgage capital, could not be allowed to happen again. To these ends, in the Housing Act of 1968 disparate threads of global currency markets and domestic reforms came together. President Johnson announced that to fulfill the aims of his urban housing agenda, he would "propose legislation to strengthen the mortgage market and the financial institutions that supply mortgage credit."[16] From this act would come the first mortgage-backed security, as a means to provide new capital for America's cities. In the midst of a domestic crisis that politically outweighed any balance of payments crisis, Congress and the Johnson administration acted to create new capital channels directly connecting markets and mortgages which sidestepped the institutions that had failed to provide the needed mortgage funds.

Government studies in the aftermath of the "deplorable" credit crunch insisted, in the words of Senator John Sparkman, chairman of the Senate Committee on Banking and Currency, that action be taken to "insure an adequate flow of mortgage credit for the future."[17] One of the lessons of the credit crunch was that traditional sources of mortgage capital, like savings and loan banks and insurance companies, could not be relied on to provide the capital needed for the Great Society's ambitious program of housing growth. A congressional report found that housing "progress [had] been repeatedly interrupted by periods of tight money and budgetary pressures on the Federal Government."[18] Freeing social programs from the constraints of the federal budget and from limited mortgage capital could make housing progress possible. But, as FHA commissioner Philip Brownstein put it, "our innovations and aggressive thrusts against blight and deterioration, our massive efforts on behalf of the needy, will be lost without an adequate continuing supply of mortgage funds."[19] The solution, Sparkman asserted, lay in "correcting deficiencies in our financial structure."[20]

Disparate groups from bankers to unions demanded that Congress fashion a "new security-type mortgage instrument" to channel the money invested in the securities markets into mortgages.[21] Even the Fed, whose authority would be diminished by such an invention, encouraged Congress to consider creating debt "instruments [issued] against pools of residential mortgages" to "broaden [the] sources of funds available for residential mortgage investment" so as to "rely less on depository institutions that tend to be vulnerable to conditions accompanying general credit restraint."[22] Creating such instruments would undermine the Fed's ability to affect mortgages through its monetary policy and in turn weaken its control over the money supply, but quarantining mortgages from the rest of the economy would also put the Fed, if need be, beyond public blame. Policymakers hoped that the mortgage capital could somehow be cordoned off from other capital, but certainly the politics of the housing problem outweighed any balance of payments considerations. The U.S. mortgage industry—not as distant from cosmopolitan Eurodollar markets as it appeared—was caught in the middle. The Housing Act of 1968 would remake American financial instruments and institutions, seeking to transmute those markets into mortgages.

The Housing Act of 1968 and Mortgage-Backed Securities

International capital markets and burning cities collided to produce the Housing Act of 1968. To guarantee the flow of mortgage funds into the cities, Congress authorized the creation of the first mortgage-backed security. While in theory the security allowed borrowers to bypass financial institutions and borrow directly from capital markets, in practice a long chain of financial institutions still mediated the connection between borrower and lender. To make the mortgage-backed security work would require altering the relationships of the financial institutions that constituted the mortgage market: mortgage companies, institutional investors, and the Federal National Mortgage Association (FNMA). In the long run, the rearrangement of the mortgage finance system had far greater consequences than the urban lending which justified the rearrangement.[23]

The Federal National Mortgage Association existed before the credit crunch, but the Housing Act of 1968 remade FNMA into a new kind of institution, one even more privatized and market-oriented than before. Created during the New Deal to buy and sell government-insured mortgages across the country, FNMA had forged a national secondary market for mortgages offered through the Federal Housing Administration (FHA). During the 1960s, however, the federal government had created more specialized, socially oriented housing programs which relaxed the FHA's lending requirements, especially in the inner cities, and FNMA had resold these mortgages alongside the other mortgages but found them harder to sell to investors. Although the Housing Act privatized FNMA, it still provided for extensive federal oversight, explicitly ruling that the secretary of Housing and Urban Development, even after privatization, could still require FNMA to purchase low-income mortgages.[24] Matters internal to FNMA would be private, but larger market actions would remain partially under government control. Splitting the old FNMA into two organizations, the new FNMA and the Government National Mortgage Association (GNMA), would nonetheless cordon off the social programs

(GNMA) from the market-making programs (FNMA). Privatization of FNMA would also take the mortgage subsidies, to a large degree, out of the federal budget. Only the subsidies to the GNMA would go on the books, and not the total mortgages bought and sold by FNMA, which often remained unsold for a long time.[25] The financing of these mortgages would come from mortgage-backed securities.

Since the 1930s American mortgage financing had relied on the ability of homebuyers to borrow from mortgage companies, which acted as financial middlemen between borrowers and investors. Mortgage companies lent to homebuyers and then immediately resold these mortgages to institutional investors such as insurance companies through professional connections or, less profitably, to FNMA. In turn, FNMA would resell these excess loans to banks and institutional investors. These investors were the ultimate source of capital. The administration of such mortgages, once bought, was difficult, since the investor had to track payments, file paperwork, and perform all the other tasks associated with owning a mortgage. The mortgage-backed security offered a simpler alternative by taking the revenue of a mortgage and repackaging it to look like the coupon payments of a bond. Banks would hold the actual mortgages, collect payments, and distribute the payments to the holders of the mortgage-backed security. Policymakers hoped that the ease of administration would expand the potential pool of investors beyond the banks and insurance companies that traditionally bought individual mortgages.

The ease of administering mortgage-backed securities promised access to new sources of investment, such as pension funds, which legislators hoped would expand the pool of mortgage capital. In 1966 pension funds held $64 billion in assets, according to the Federal Home Loan Bank Board, 60 percent of which was invested in stocks and 25 percent in corporate bonds.[26] While pension funds did not have the mortgage buying departments that insurance companies had, they shared the insurance companies' interest in safe, long-term investments like bonds. With mortgage-backed securities, anyone who could pay could buy; no special staffs were need. FHA officials like Philip Brownstein, assistant secretary for mortgage credit, believed that the mortgage-backed security "may very well be the break-through we all have been seeking for many years to tap the additional sources of funds which so far have shown little interest in mortgages."[27] If mortgages could be fashioned into a form as easy to invest in as bonds, then pension funds, policymakers believed, would flock to mortgages, which promised a slightly higher return.

Mortgage-backed securities initially came in two forms: the "modified pass-through" security and the "bond-like" security. Both forms gave the investor a claim on the monthly principal and interest payments of a large, diversified portfolio of mortgages, but while the "bond-like" security offered metronomic regularity in its payments, the "pass-through" involved irregular payments, reflecting the actual irregularity of homeowners' mortgage payments. Under the FNMA regulations, the bond-like mortgage-backed securities required enormous pools of mortgages—at least $200 million—and the mortgage company had to have enough capital to guarantee the payments in case of default. Few private companies sold that many mortgages, and none had the requisite capital. Pass-through mortgage pools could be much smaller—only $2 million. Mortgage bankers, who gathered together the backing mortgage portfolios, knew they could not lend enough for a bond-like mortgage pool and worried that investors would not want the variably paying pass-through securities.[28]

In August 1969 the newly founded GNMA announced that it would be offering mortgage-backed securities for the first time.[29] After receiving suggestions from financiers, policymakers, and potential investors for the regulations surrounding the securities, GNMA, in association with FNMA, issued the first mortgage-backed securities on February 19, 1970. Three New Jersey public sector union pension funds bought $2 million worth of pass-through securities from Associated Mortgage Companies, a sprawling interstate network.[30] Soon thereafter, in May 1970, GNMA held its first sale of bond-like mortgage-backed securities, selling $400 million to investors. While at first sales of the bond-like mortgage-backed securities outweighed sales of the pass-through mortgage-backed securities, the tables quickly turned. Within a year, in 1971, GNMA and FNMA sold over $2.2 billion in pass-through mortgage-backed securities and $915 million in bonds.

The drawbacks that mortgage bankers initially feared turned out to matter little because the appeal of mortgage-backed securities was not merely in their yields. Institutional needs outweighed pure finance. Both forms of the mortgage-backed security rendered the investor's connection to the underlying assets completely anonymous and secondhand. While not a true bond, the pass-through security completely hid the hassle of mortgage ownership—the paperwork and collection—that was the most formidable obstacle to investment, while providing higher returns than government securities.[31] As Woodward Kingman, president of GNMA, noted, "this instrument eliminates all the documentation, paperwork problems, and safekeeping problems that are involved in making a comparable investment in just ordinary mortgages."[32] Institutions big and small did not need a mortgage department to track payments, check titles, or deal with any of the myriad other details involved in mortgage lending. Within a few years, in fact, GNMA stopped offering the bond-like mortgage-backed securities entirely.

Mortgage-backed securities, once proven, expanded not only the possible range of investors but the possible range of borrowers as well. While FNMA could resell federally insured mortgages, such loans grew less important each year in the 1960s. The entire mortgage banking industry had grown up around the ability to originate FHA and Veterans Administration loans, and then resell them on the secondary markets through FNMA—something that was nearly impossible to do with conventional mortgages. The challenge with all mortgages had always been that every loan was in some sense as unique as the house that the money was being lent against. The FHA and FNMA had overcome this challenge through federal guarantees and standards. All loans that were not federally insured, so-called "conventional mortgages," had no such secondary market. No single conventional mortgage could be so homogeneous as to be traded across the country. Mortgage lending, for the conventional market, required local knowledge which no distant mortgage banker could have. After World War II the use of conventional mortgages had fallen as Americans turned to FHA and VA mortgages to finance the suburban expansion. Around the late 1950s, however, the use of conventional mortgages stabilized at about half of all mortgages issued and then began to grow again. By the mid-1960s conventional mortgages accounted for two-thirds of all mortgages. In 1970, although the volume of conventional mortgages was double that of federally insured mortgages, conventional mortgages had no national secondary market. A system of finance predicated on the resale of individual mortgages could never trade conventional mortgages at a distance.

The underlying portfolio diversity behind a mortgage-backed security made possible a secondary market in conventional mortgages. To create such a secondary market, Congress, in the Emergency Home Finance Act of 1970, authorized the creation of the Federal Home Loan Mortgage Corporation (FHLMC). Like FNMA, FHLMC could trade mortgages and issue mortgage-backed securities, but it was intended to create a secondary market in conventional mortgages. Congress intended FHLMC, unlike FNMA, to buy its mortgages primarily from savings banks rather than mortgage companies. In all other respects the two corporations were largely identical. By this point mortgage experts such as FNMA executive vice president Philip Brinkerhoff recognized that finding new sources of capital could "be accomplished more efficiently through the issuance and sale of mortgage-backed securities than through direct sale of mortgages."[33]

Although FHLMC developed innovative methods for standardizing conventional mortgages, its success relied on the structure of the mortgage-backed security. Conventional mortgages could be traded because they were issued through mortgage-backed securities and not the whole mortgage system of the 1950s. A vast portfolio of conventional mortgages could mimic the safety of an FHA loan through diversification. The risk of one bad loan could be diluted across many good loans in a mortgage-backed security's underlying portfolio. For investors who would never see the property, such risk reduction was essential. At first the mortgage-backed securities offered only FHA loans, but then, beginning with FHLMC, they offered conventional mortgages as well, substituting risk-reducing portfolio diversification for risk-eliminating federal guarantees.

FHLMC learned from FNMA. In November 1970, almost immediately after its inception, it began to issue mortgage-backed securities. This first group of loans was federally insured so that FHLMC might demonstrate to skittish investors that it could, as an institution, capably buy mortgages and issue mortgage-backed securities. Thereafter FHLMC began to make the transition into conventional mortgages, developing innovative methods in standardizing conventional mortgages. By 1972 FHLMC, with established procedures for credit evaluation, loan documents, appraisals, mortgage insurance, and mortgage originators, began to issue completely conventional mortgage–backed securities, thus creating the first national conventional mortgage market. In 1973 FHLMC bought three times as many conventional as federally insured mortgages—nearly $1 billion worth.[34] The next year, in 1974, FHLMC further doubled its conventional mortgage activity to nearly $2 billion and shrank its purchases of federally insured mortgages to $261 million.[35] The federal government lent its authority to the operations of GNMA and FNMA, and in mimicking them, FHLMC acquired a patina of government insurance.

By the end of 1973 FNMA was, next to the Treasury, the largest debt-issuing institution in U.S. capital markets.[36] The mortgage-backed security had come into its own and quickly began to define how mortgage funds flowed in the United States. This connection between capital markets and mortgage funds was made just in time, not merely for American cities but for the mortgage industry in general. By 1970 withdrawals at thrift institutions exceeded deposits nearly every month, reducing available capital for traditional mortgages.[37] The president of the Mortgage Bankers of America, Robert Pease, declared at the association's annual convention that "except for FNMA, there is almost no money available for residential housing. We are in a real honest-to-goodness housing crisis!"[38] Capital markets became a reliable source of funds, as the older institutional investor and small depositor arrangements collapsed in the face of interest rate turmoil and changing saving practices, emerging from the ongoing unspooling of the Bretton Woods system. On average in 1971, each month $50 million worth of mortgages flowed from the capital markets through mortgage-backed securities into American housing.

In both the cities and suburbs, mortgage-backed securities provided new sources of mortgage funds. While direct mortgage assignment collapsed, mortgage-backed securities provided the financing to propel the new housing programs in America's cities. Federally subsidized mortgages, resold as FNMA mortgage-backed securities, propelled the American building industry in 1970, accounting for 30 percent of housing starts (433,000) and 20 percent of the mortgage debt increase.[39] In the first year of sales GNMA issued over $2.3 billion in mortgage-backed securities, funneling money backwards into federal housing programs.[40] Typifying the connection in many ways, the first company to bundle enough mortgages for resale, as discussed earlier, was Associated Mortgage Companies, whose advertisement "Ghetto ready, ghetto set, go!" illustrated the explicit connection between funds for inner city America and mortgage-backed securities.[41] Mortgage company lending surged as well, providing 90 percent of FNMA's purchases.[42] In the mid-1960s mortgage companies had originated 55 percent of federally insured loans but only 5 percent of conventional loans.[43] By January 1973 mortgage companies originated more conventional mortgages than FHA or VA loans, remaking the entire industry.[44] Moving away from a reliance on bank deposits, the mortgage finance system—consumers, businesses, and markets—had been rebuilt atop a new foundation of securities.

The mortgage-backed securities promoted the lending of mortgage dollars further down the economic ladder, even to those borrowers outside the federally subsidized programs. Although FNMA and FHLMC had been created and privatized to compete with each other and to service different kinds of financial institutions, competition drove them both to similar lending programs. By November 1972 FNMA had begun to emulate FHLMC, buying 95 percent loan-to-value mortgages, which FHLMC had offered earlier.[45] In other words, mortgages with as little as a 5 percent down payment could now be repackaged and sold as securities. FNMA actuaries calculated that the rate of default on a 95 percent mortgage was three times higher than on a 90 percent mortgage. The higher risk required a higher yield, but investors trusted the U.S. government to make good on the payments even when the borrowers could not. Still, the assurance of payment was not sufficient to draw pension funds to invest in the mortgage-backed securities in the amounts that their creators had imagined they would.

Mortgage-Backed Securities in the Global 1970s

With the creation of mortgage-backed securities, the centrality of FNMA to the American mortgage markets increased, the firm sometimes supplying by the mid-1970s as much as half of all new mortgage funds in a given quarter.[46] The mortgage-backed securities offered funds, whatever their source, to finance American homebuyers. Mortgage-backed securities by this time were selling in great numbers, but not exactly as the framers of the instrument had intended. While pensions bought over half of the bond-like mortgage-backed securities (52.72 percent), within a few years such bonds were not sold any longer, and pension funds resisted buying the far greater volume of pass-through mortgage-backed securities.[47] As Senator William Proxmire remarked in congressional hearings on the secondary mortgage markets, the increase in mortgage-backed security buying by pensions, while "commendable," still accounted for a low relative share of the market.[48] Pension funds, intended to be the primary source of investment for mortgage-backed securities, accounted for only 21 percent of FNMA mortgage-backed security ownership.[49] Although GNMA actively sought investment from pension funds, as late as 1975 such funds accounted for only 8.29 percent of annual purchases of pass-through mortgage-backed securities. At first, surprisingly, the biggest buyers of mortgage-backed securities were not pension funds but local savings and loan banks. (Thrift institutions bought 41 percent of these securities in 1975.) The savings and loans bought mortgage-backed securities because they allowed banks to evade geographic and state boundary restrictions on lending.[50] Many states forbade local banks from lending money beyond a certain distance but had no such provision against the buying and selling of bonds. Mortgage-backed securities allowed capital mobility for all financial institutions, but in allowing savings and loan banks such access, they did not increase the net available funds for mortgages nationwide, since such banks were already invested in mortgages.[51] Pension funds' share of purchases rose, but these funds did not take on the leadership role policymakers had hoped for in providing a new source of mortgage capital.

Strangely, a new and unexpected source of capital did emerge, though the records of GNMA, FNMA, and FHLMC are ambiguous about its origins. The second most frequent purchasers of GNMA securities, accounting for 22 percent of the total, were included in the mysterious residual category that the General Accounting Office referred to as "all others (i.e. Bond funds, investment firms)."[52] Similarly, of GNMA mortgage-backed securities issued by FHLMC, slightly more than two-fifths of the bonds sold went to "miscellaneous" buyers.[53] FNMA's story is similar. One-fifth of the mortgage-backed securities sold by FNMA were bought by investors in this category. While many investors came from the investment houses of Wall Street, it is also clear that many came from further afield.

These mortgage-backed securities were sold in auctions that were open to the world, and the world came to buy. Noting the relatively high yield on mortgage-backed securities, contemporary mortgage bankers remarked on the importance of the "flood of dollars from the oil exporting countries seeking an investment outlet" in U.S. capital markets.[54] Even in this early mortgage-backed debt, foreign investment seems to have played an important role. Federal flow-of-funds accounts showed a small but persistent flow of capital into the American mortgage-backed security market. In 1975, for instance, of the $25.3 billion in government-sponsored enterprise (GSE) mortgage-backed securities debt, $2.7 billion, or 11 percent, was owned abroad. Overall, as early as 1975 roughly one in twenty American mortgages was funded by foreign investors. So although mortgage-backed securities did not at first attract the intended investors, investors were nevertheless attracted (see Figure 7.1).

New sources of capital, domestic and foreign, continued to flow into American mortgages. The flow of foreign capital affected the balance of payments, perhaps very little at first, but it enabled the continued expansion of the American mortgage market. Global capital markets which had partially caused the Credit Crunch of 1966, disrupting the operations of American mortgage financing, had in turn led to the invention of the mortgage-backed security, which was then sold on those same markets, supplying needed mortgage capital. The mortgage-backed securities actually helped shore up the capital account somewhat with their flow of foreign investment. While today nearly a third of all U.S. mortgage-backed securities are owned by foreign investors, even in the early 1970s between 5 and 10 percent were owned abroad.

Though more recently mortgage-backed securities have led to frightening instability, at the outset of the 1970s this innovation promised the return of stability. Mortgage-backed securities offered institutional investors stable bond-like investments in mortgages and provided a growing source of mortgage capital for American borrowers. Low-income mortgage lending, funded through those mortgage-backed securities, contained the pos-

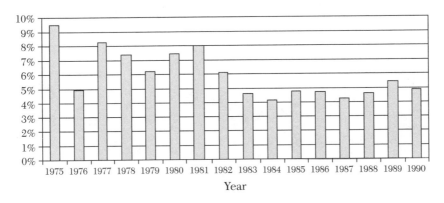

Figure 7.1. Percentage of government-sponsored enterprise (GSE) debt owned abroad, 1975–1990. *Source:* Board of Governors of the Federal Reserve System, *Flow of Funds Accounts of the United States,* June 5, 2008, Tables L.107 and L125. Calculated by author. In these years home mortgage debt accounted for 89 to 98 percent of GSE debt.

sibility of giving inner city renters a stake in their cities, thereby quelling, as legislators hoped, the urban unrest. To finance these social experiments, policymakers, in cooperation with private financial institutions, boldly re-imagined the foundations of the American mortgage system. While low-income mortgage lending quickly fizzled in scandal, not to return in great volume again until the end of the century, mortgage-backed securities equally quickly assumed a central role in the economy. At the largest level, they even held out the possibility of helping to stabilize the post–Bretton Woods capital account, bringing foreign capital into the United States. While we think of the financial changes of the 1970s as marking a time of deregulation, it was the federal government which made the mortgage-backed security possible. But the power of the state in fashioning these debt instruments, while great, was not unlimited. Some of the institutional change, like that at FNMA, could be carried out in a centralized fashion, while total reform of wealth inequality in the inner cities could not. Created by Great Society policymakers at the dawn of a newly resurgent global economy, the mortgage-backed security placed the U.S. economy on a new securitized footing, providing new sources of capital for American homeowners, who could now borrow as easily from the rest of the world as from their local savings and loan.

CHAPTER 8

The United States, Multinational Enterprises, and the Politics of Globalization

VERNIE OLIVEIRO

IN 1967 U.S. STATE DEPARTMENT OFFICIAL George Ball argued before the International Chamber of Commerce in Britain that national boundaries only "impede the fulfillment of the world corporation's full potential as the best means yet devised for using world resources according to the criterion of profit which is an objective standard of efficiency."[1] A year later Louis Banks, managing editor of *Fortune* magazine, proclaimed the existence of a "Business Internationale" that was "liberating millions of individuals in the world to work productively within a national and international framework" with the "greatest scope and opportunity imaginable."[2] Ball and Banks were just two of the many individuals in American business and government who looked optimistically upon multinational enterprises (MNEs) as symbols and agents of what we might call contemporary globalization.

Yet not everyone welcomed the rise of the multinational enterprise. The late 1960s onward saw the publication of several popular works that characterized MNEs as threats to the sovereignty of nation-states and dangers to the political and economic welfare of poorer developing nations. Jean-Jacques Servan-Schreiber asserted in *Le Défi Américain* (1967) that the growing dominance of American industry in Europe would gradually diminish the place of the latter in international affairs. Kari Levitt lamented that the high volume of American foreign investments in Canada was turning her country into a neo-colony of its southern neighbor.[3] In Mexico, Alma Chapoy Bonifaz warned of "big international corporations," mostly American, that "exercise a powerful influence on the internal economies of host countries, in world capital markets, in international commerce, and in dissemination of technology."[4] Within America, labor unionists accused MNEs of harming the country by transferring jobs, capital, and technology abroad. Nat Weinberg of the United Auto Workers union complained that American MNEs betrayed American workers by investing "where labor costs are lowest, exploitation of workers is least restrained and the degree of social responsibility required of them is in general minimal."[5] In the same vein, Howard Samuel of the Amalgamated Clothing Workers of America deplored the fact that American workers had been replaced by "the unschooled girls of Taiwan," the "untrained workers of African or Asian nations," and "the depressed inhabitants of the most squalid slums of the Far East."[6] Runaway plants, moreover, meant the loss of hard-earned seniority benefits and, worse, the dissolution of entire communities.

Leaders in American business and government realized that this rising hostility toward MNEs could not be ignored. The growing prominence of these ideas, especially in less developed countries, correlated with a general souring of the international climate for foreign direct investment. The archival records of Richard Nixon's presidential administration contain numerous letters from American businessmen seeking Washington's help in protecting their foreign investments from expropriation.[7] More broadly, the early 1970s saw a worldwide increase in the expropriation of foreign investments. There were 575 such cases in seventy-six less developed countries between 1960 and 1992; 336 of these cases, however—almost 60 percent of the total—occurred between 1970 and 1975.[8] Within the United States there were various attempts to remove incentives for American firms to invest abroad, and the Senate's Subcommittee on Multinational Corporations carried out multiple investigations into the ways in which American multinational enterprises were causing harm or contradicting U.S. foreign policy. Thus the connection between attacks on these firms and the deterioration of the international investment climate was not difficult to make, and U.S. officials indeed voiced fears that these attacks would lead to the undermining of support for capitalism more broadly. The accusations against MNEs therefore had to be answered.

How, then, did the United States government and American business engage with the "problem" of multinational enterprises during the 1970s? Additionally, what can the answer to this question tell us about America's role in the shaping of contemporary globalization? Business and political leaders in the United States adopted different strategies to cope with each issue pertaining to multinational enterprises. Nevertheless, the common theme that informed their responses was the vigorous promotion of a liberal, market-driven global economy. The positions and policies they adopted in response to attacks on MNEs committed them to reorienting states toward serving the security and, therefore, the freedom of investment capital.[9] This reorientation was facilitated by a sense of crisis that pervaded America at the time concerning the legitimacy of capitalism as well as the economic well-being of the country. At a time when the United States seemed to be losing its global economic standing, a stable and therefore predictable set of international rules for investment as well as a nondiscriminatory level playing field for multinational businesses became vital for the ability of American MNEs to compete successfully abroad.

The first thing to be done was to articulate clearly the case for globalism. The impetus for this occurred in 1971, when the appearance of America's first trade deficit since 1893 led to strong public pressures on Congress to redress the unfavorable trade balance and curb the outflow of capital. In response, Senator Vance Hartke (Democrat of Indiana) and Congressman James Burke (Democrat of Massachusetts) introduced the Foreign Trade and Investment Act, or Burke-Hartke, which sought to trim imports into the United States, stem the export of jobs and technology, and remove tax incentives for investment abroad. A *New York Times* columnist said that the bill made "the Smoot-Hawley Act of 1930 look as if it might have been written by Adam Smith."[10] To the AFL-CIO it was the "first complete legislative program" to confront the challenges to American jobs and economic well-being.[11]

American businesses, however, viewed Burke-Hartke as a serious threat to the welfare of the United States because it impeded their ability to meet the rising challenge posed by European and Japanese competitors in international commerce. They feared that the increased tax burdens promised by Burke-Hartke would severely reduce returns from investment abroad, minimizing their ability to dispatch managers and technicians to affiliates and subsidiaries overseas. Businesspeople also worried that the imposition of import quotas or the creation of presidential controls on investments abroad would encourage foreign governments to retaliate by restricting opportunities in their countries.

The danger of isolationism posed by Burke-Hartke compelled American business to get organized on issues pertaining to international commerce. Particularly notable were the efforts of the National Association of Manufacturers (NAM), which distributed an information kit on Burke-Hartke to its members. Included among the materials in the kit were a model editorial for use in local newspapers and employee publications, a sample speech against the bill, and pamphlets containing arguments in support of MNEs and foreign investment.[12] NAM further arranged a letter-writing campaign to members of Congress in February 1972.[13] By April of that year the organization had signed up over two hundred executives to serve as "legislative coordinators" in their respective firms.[14] Finally, NAM sent fifteen thousand copies of a paper titled "The U.S. Stake in World Trade: The Role of the Multinational Corporation" to its entire membership, every single member of Congress, officials in the White House, and government agencies, as well as interested academics.[15]

Multinational enterprises, independently of business associations, conducted a similar campaign of information targeted at employees and members of the public. They published pamphlets describing how their activities as MNEs directly benefited U.S. workers. 3M, for example, informed its employees through a publication titled *Your Job Is Bigger Than You Think* that one out of every eight of them owed his or her job to the company's business overseas. The company also noted that the vast majority of the world's people lived outside the United States, and that tapping this market was crucial to the firm's future. The corporation needed to be "able to operate in those countries as a *local* business employing *local* people and giving *local* service, not as a foreigner." For 3M the conclusion was not difficult to draw. It warned its employees against Burke-Hartke. "Your job is threatened. . . . Your job depends upon business abroad."[16]

Indeed for American business, the case for globalism came down to the idea that overseas investments were a *necessity* dictated by troubled times. Domestic economic challenges and unrelenting competition overseas meant that America's international standing was precarious. It was thus that Maynard Venema, chairman of the board of NAM and of Universal Oil Products Company, argued that the very "survival" of the United States was at stake. "Time is running out," he warned; "the scoreboard bears the grim portents of an unbelievable upset in the making. The United States is being beaten."[17] Disengagement from the world was not an option, so Congress had better help and not hinder American firms in international competition.

The articulation and promotion of globalism by organizations such as

NAM did much to dissuade Congress from imposing severe constraints on business abroad. Coupled with alternative legislation from the Nixon administration in the Trade Reform Act, the efforts of America's globalists succeeded in splintering what might have been a more united coalition against multinational enterprises and foreign investment. Attempts to curb investment abroad did not disappear entirely, but the momentum to restrict the readiness of American firms to engage in international business was never again as strong as it was in these early years of the decade.

Yet as American business tried to encourage support for multinational enterprises at home, it faced ominous prospects for the growth and maintenance of investment overseas. The process of decolonization had yielded a world that contained an increasing number of newly independent but poor nation-states which maintained that their political independence should have been followed by the same in the economic realm. Many, however, felt that American-led liberal capitalism had delivered nothing but continued economic dependence. By the mid-1960s this point of view had gained dominance in the United Nations, where less developed countries (LDCs), as the Group of 77 (G-77) bloc, pursued their agenda of international economic reform. This was particularly so in the UN Conference on Trade and Development, in which economic theories which posited the exploitative nature of multinational enterprises were especially popular. In 1974 the UN General Assembly adopted two resolutions: the Declaration on the Establishment of a New International Economic Order (NIEO) and the Charter of Economic Rights and Duties of States. Both resolutions adopted highly negative views of multinational enterprises and encouraged governments to take a stronger hand in regulating their affairs.[18] These developments at the UN fed the impression among many in U.S. business and government that the organization's commitment to a market-driven international economy was waning, and that it was instead increasingly amenable to dirigiste ideas.

It was in this context, and against the backdrop of accusations that the American firm International Telephone and Telegraph had interfered in Chile against President Salvador Allende Gossens, that the UN convened a "Group of Eminent Persons to Study the Impact of Multinational Corporations on Development and on International Relations." The group's hearings allowed leaders of developing countries, labor unions, and political activists to air strong criticisms of MNEs. The group's report, which counseled more governmental control of multinational enterprises, elicited strong condemnations from the State Department and U.S. business organizations. As a result of the report, the UN created the Commission on Transnational Corporations, the organization's first permanent machinery on multinational enterprises. The commission soon decided, over the objections of the United States, that its highest priority, above even the collection of information to enable research on multinational enterprises, would be the creation of a Code of Conduct on Transnational Corporations.

Washington remained skeptical about the Code of Conduct but nevertheless thought it worthwhile to participate in negotiations as a means of bettering North-South relations. Yet from the beginning, the United States and other industrialized countries on the one hand, and LDCs on the other, encountered multiple points of disagreement. While LDCs took the term "transnational corporations" to refer only to privately owned multinational enterprises from industrialized countries, American negotiators insisted that state-owned firms as well as those with mixed private and state ownership should also have to abide by the code. Indeed the United States also wanted countries to accord equal treatment to both multinational and domestic business enterprises "except under specifically defined and limited circumstances."[19] Additionally, while the G-77 saw the code as an instrument to curb the abuses of MNEs, Washington saw it as a way to establish stable and predictable rules for international business, thereby improving the global climate for foreign investment.

Perhaps the most important point of contention was the extent to which national sovereignty should be maximized or minimized in the proposed code. Hence while the United States wanted the code to comprise voluntary guidelines that would apply to both MNEs *and* governments, LDCs desired a binding code that would apply only to the former. The G-77, in other words, did not wish to encumber governments in any way but wanted to exert the fullest possible range of state authority over the activities of MNEs in any given national territory. Additionally, industrialized countries and LDCs differed on how the expropriation of investments should be managed. The United States and its allies wished for MNEs to benefit from the protection of international law. In effect this meant that while Washington recognized the right of host governments to expropriate property, host governments had to ensure in turn that compensation for the seized property would be prompt, adequate, and effective. For their part, LDCs asserted that any compensation would be decided solely by national governments. In the same vein, while the United States supported international arbitration to settle disputes between MNEs and host governments, LDCs argued that only domestic tribunals could have jurisdiction. The G-77 even argued that the principle of national sovereignty meant that MNEs should be banned from asking their home governments for help in the event of investment disputes, and that home governments in turn should refrain from intervening on behalf of firms headquartered within their borders.

For Washington, the intractability of these differences was compounded by the fact that the commission afforded a combined thirty-eight places to the G-77 and the Eastern bloc but only ten seats to the industrialized countries. U.S. negotiators realized that they would have to work more closely with their allies on the commission in order to compensate for this numerical disadvantage. Negotiations were simultaneously occurring at the Organization for Economic Cooperation and Development (OECD) on the creation of guidelines for multinational enterprises, a role originally conceded to the OECD in exchange for an instrument on national treatment for MNEs. Washington now hoped that "an agreed OECD position on a code would help to improve the developed countries' bargaining position on this issue *vis à vis* the LDCs in the UN."[20]

Negotiations at the OECD on guidelines for MNEs progressed relatively smoothly and resulted in June 1976 in the Declaration on International Investment and Multinational Enterprises. The declaration included voluntary guidelines that called upon MNEs to, among other things, protect the environment, observe human rights, and adopt high standards of corporate governance. At the same time, the declaration also contained instruments that urged governments to cooperate in order to remove conflicting requirements on MNEs, to ensure that they did not discriminate against MNEs in favor of domestic firms, and to make transparent any measures they took to encourage or discourage international investment. The pleasure with which the U.S. government greeted the declaration can be seen in the fact that Secretary of State Henry Kissinger, Treasury Secretary William Simon, and Commerce Secretary Elliot Richardson together wrote to business organizations around the country lauding the declaration's "balance of governmental and enterprise responsibilities" and praising its work in "contribut[ing] significantly to an open and stable environment for international investment." They further stated that the "maintenance of such an environment over coming years depends on strengthening mutual expectations of governments and enterprises regarding responsible policies and practices."[21]

Given America's hostility to assertions of national sovereignty over multinational enterprises, the secretaries' emphasis on cooperation between MNEs and governments in the workings of international investment might seem nothing more than platitudinous rhetoric. Yet rather than seeking the diminution of national sovereignty, Washington instead sought a transformation in governmental authority; states had to respond to the claims of capital to be secure, fairly treated, and therefore free and mobile. Hence, rather than intervening to seize value from international production, whether information on business operations, technology, profits, or indeed the entire subsidiary itself, governments were to delineate clearly the ground rules for investment in their countries, to harmonize laws on multinational enterprises, and to create and enforce rules that would encourage fair competition among all firms, no matter the number of countries in which they operated or their form of ownership. In this sense globalization was helped, not hindered, by strong, if transformed, nation-states.

Negotiations on the UN code were eventually abandoned. In contrast, the OECD declaration endures to the present day, and its signatories include nations that are not even members of the organization. In this respect the United States managed to lay the foundation for the increasing acceptance of the principle that governments should refrain from authoritative interventions against multinational businesses. This did not mean, however, that MNEs were allowed free rein in their efforts to compete with one another, especially if their activities subverted the competitive discipline of the market and harmed public confidence in the operations of the free enterprise system. A scandal that embroiled several well-known American firms as well as foreign governments would show that the interests of free enterprise and the market on the one hand, and those of MNEs on the other, were not always complementary.

The scandal in question began after a series of revelations in the first half of 1975 that several well-known U.S. companies were found to have made millions of dollars in questionable payments to government officials abroad. The affair had come to be known as the "Lockheed scandal," after the Lockheed Aircraft Company was discovered to have bribed politicians in Japan, Italy, and the Netherlands. The U.S. government unequivocally condemned corruption in international commerce; these payments distorted the competitive discipline of the market, subverted the principle of democratic accountability, and, most seriously, harmed U.S. foreign relations by tainting friendly foreign governments with the brush of corruption. Reaction elsewhere was similarly strong, with both the Permanent Council of the Organization of American States and the UN General Assembly passing resolutions against the practice.

While the scandal seemed to illustrate the deleterious impacts of MNEs on economic and political development, it also ironically revealed the limitations of conceiving of these firms as agents of globalization. Many executives, in explaining these payments, argued for the necessity of conforming to local business customs when doing business abroad even if those customs were contrary to practices at home. Bob Dorsey, chairman of the board of Gulf Oil, for example, asserted that questionable payments were often extorted, showing the vulnerability of even large American multinational enterprises to governmental pressures. Dorsey claimed that the $4 million that Gulf Oil had paid out to the Democratic Republican Party in South Korea had been wrung from the firm by "high party officials" whose demands were "accompanied by pressure which left little to the imagination as to what would occur [to Gulf's sizable investments in that country] if the company would choose to turn its back on the request."[22]

Washington recognized that since corruption in international commerce flourished in domestic environments that were conducive to the practice, the problem could be solved only through international cooperation. Yet the fact that a fair proportion of bribes probably were extorted might explain the reluctance of other governments to support the U.S. initiative for a multilateral treaty against the extortion and offering of bribes in international business. American negotiators believed that their chances of achieving an international treaty were greatest in the OECD; but OECD governments, some of whose officials publicly expressed bafflement at American "puritanism" over the practice of corporations offering "kickbacks" to local politicians, were unwilling to convene outside the United Nations. Forced to negotiate in the UN, the United States found itself stymied by reluctance and cynicism. Representation from LDCs in talks was so sparse that at times, meetings had to begin with informal discussions until a quorum of representatives was finally achieved.[23] Moreover it soon became apparent that the G-77 was intent on holding any proposed international treaty on illicit payments hostage to the ransom of concessions to be extracted for the Code of Conduct. U.S. officials, however, rejected any such linkage because of the lack of meaningful progress in negotiations on the code.

Cognizant of the difficulty of winning international cooperation against corruption and convinced of the inadvisability of unilateral measures that might handicap American businesses, President Gerald Ford nevertheless found himself under immense pressure to *do something*. Thus he convened a White House Task Force on Questionable Corporate Payments Abroad, and appointed Commerce Secretary Richardson to lead it. While several members of the Task Force were satisfied with the efficacy of existing measures against corruption, Richardson pushed for new legislation because, as his aides explained, a new law would serve as a means of "restoring public confidence and reducing cynicism with respect to business." Additionally, the president had to "take the lead in allaying concerns regarding the accountability of multinational business enterprises," especially since the "international acceptability" of multinational corporations was crucial to the maintenance of a "healthy international economic order."[24]

The desire to hold multinational enterprises to the competitive discipline of the market, assure investors of the reliability of corporate accounts, and restore public support for multinational enterprise had to be balanced with the need to avoid further embarrassing and destabilizing governments friendly to liberal capitalism but tainted by the brush of corruption. In Italy the involvement of officials at the Quirinale in the Lockheed scandal had led to Communist gains at the expense of the Christian Democrats. In the same vein, Japanese councilor Eiichi Nakao, representative of Yamashi prefecture and chairman of the conservative Seirankai faction in the Diet, warned Ford in a letter that the Liberal Democratic Party was being hurt by allegations of corruption, and that its fall might lead to the ascension of other political parties with different foreign policy agendas.[25] Bearing these sensitivities in mind, Ford chose to chart a cautious course: the deterrence of bribery through the reporting and disclosure of payments. This approach was particularly preferred over that of criminalizing bribery overseas, since investigations of criminal charges might risk offending foreign governments. In addition, criminalization would entangle the Justice Department in the difficult tasks of gathering witnesses and evidence abroad and distinguishing between legitimate and illicit payments.

Yet to many in Congress, reporting and disclosure did not go far enough. As the task force predicted, Ford's failure to support the criminalization of international commercial bribery allowed Democrats to accuse him of being lackluster in the fight against corruption. Democratic presidential candidate Jimmy Carter even asserted that Ford, through his "quiescence or reticence," was effectively condoning bribery.[26] The Georgia governor promised voters that he would be much tougher on "corporate crime" than Ford had been.[27] Once in the Oval Office, Carter duly lent his support to the Foreign Corrupt Practices Act (FCPA), which passed the House by 340 votes to none in December 1977. The act held executives criminally liable as long as they had "reason to know" of any questionable payments that might have been made by employees or agents of their firms.

The FCPA may indeed have sent the strongest possible signal of Washington's displeasure with corruption in international business, but the harsh repercussions of the FCPA combined with the lack of curbs on competitors abroad soon led to calls for the law to be reformed. Many businessmen and a growing number of members of Congress believed that the legislature had allowed itself to be carried away by moral outrage. Those in favor of reform argued that the severe penalties attached to this ambiguous bill had caused them to forgo legitimate business opportunities or lose out to foreign competitors who had no qualms about engaging in bribery. In publications and testimonies before Congress these "reformers" recounted story after story of Americans who had sacrificed business in an extra-cautious effort to comply with the FCPA. According to one account, an American firm that had done business in a particular country for more than half a century failed to gain a renewal of its concession there because it refused to make payments to certain officials. The result was the expiration of the concession, leaving the firm effectively an illegal operator in the country.[28]

Such stories persuaded more and more members of Congress to support reform of the FCPA. Those opposed cried that reform was tantamount to the support of bribery. Yet the proposed changes did not include doing away with criminalization but were instead more modest, making it clearer that "grease payments" were not considered bribes, simplifying the regulatory requirements of the law, limiting the standard for liability to knowing or intentional violations, and rationalizing enforcement of the FCPA. Many of these reforms were ultimately incorporated into the Omnibus Trade and Competitiveness Act of 1988.

The story of the reform of the FCPA may lead one to argue that the tremendous support that originally lay behind the law had been quickly eroded by the exigencies of international competition. Washington had been forced to balance its objection to certain business practices with the need to encourage and promote American participation in international commerce. Nevertheless, the central motivation behind the FCPA remained the same. That the administration of Ronald Reagan increased the criminal penalties associated with the FCPA despite raising the bar for criminal liability for corruption showed that the U.S. government still placed the utmost importance on multinational business activity adhering to the rules of the market. Additionally, while the FCPA may be viewed as an example of the kind of social regulation decried by American business during the 1970s, it played an important part in shoring up state support for the market, with government bureaucracies taking an enhanced role in ensuring that competition would not be subverted by corruption.

John Ralston Saul, writing on the "the collapse of globalism," argues that "governments no longer believe that the emergence of gigantic transnationals, free of effective state-based control, is healthy for democracy or for the market, whether it be the national or the international market."[29] I would answer Saul by pointing out that U.S.-led globalism never was about keeping multinationals "free of effective state-based control." The question in the 1970s was not whether governments would assert control but rather for what ends they would assert it. Deregulation was not the removal of governmental authority but its realignment to increasingly ensure the security and mobility of capital. Just as the claims of nationhood might commit governments to favoring domestic industries and full employment for citizens, the claims of capital meant that governments would enforce nondiscrimination on the basis of ownership and a flexible and responsive labor force. In this respect those in the 1970s who feared the powerlessness of governments against MNEs, and those who, like Louis Banks and George Ball, believed that international business had effectively transcended governmental authority, all failed to appreciate the role of domestic institutions—whether laws or bureaucracies—in facilitating and enabling the geographical spread of MNEs.

The 1970s certainly were a difficult decade for multinational enterprises. Banks may have been triumphantly confident about the new role of international business in global affairs in 1968, but the magazine he worked for had adopted a much more sober view about multinational enterprises by the mid-1970s. In August 1973 *Fortune* writer Sanford Rose lamented that American labor had "entered the hysterical phase of its long campaign against" multinational enterprises.[30] Four years later Rose proclaimed that American MNEs had "survive[d] the decline in American preeminence," but most were "showing signs of decay." They faced increasing challenge from foreign competitors. Moreover, there was the possibility that Congress could enact policies "that would make life overseas virtually unlivable for even the most redoubtable companies."[31] Banks had hubristically proclaimed to his audience in 1968 that business had won its public relations battle, and even that "the Lord is on our side."[32] The events that followed in the 1970s probably caused him a crisis of faith.

Yet developments from the late 1970s onward combined to render multinational enterprises less menacing, and therefore less appealing as a whipping boy for international economic change. Rising foreign investment in the United States chipped away at the impression that American MNEs were invincible. The "problem" of MNEs became increasingly defined as a series of diffuse challenges under the larger rubric of "trade and investment." The success of export-oriented newly industrialized countries in East Asia showed that multinational enterprises and poorer countries could work to their mutual profitability. Finally, the financial difficulties facing less developed countries during the early 1980s made them much more welcoming to MNEs than they had been in the past.

The protests in Seattle against free trade, multinational enterprises, and the Bretton Woods organizations occupy a prominent place in popular understandings of the anti-globalization movement. It was, however, the furor over multinational enterprises during the 1970s that constituted the first of several critiques of growing globalization in the late twentieth century. In the face of severe economic challenges which national governments seemed at the time incapable of solving, it was perhaps easy for many to blame highly visible, democratically unaccountable corporations whose transnational organization appeared to indicate disregard for national interests and needs. Views such as these persist to the present day, and rest on the presupposition that the welfare of globalization and that of nation-states exist in an antagonistic, inverse relationship. If anything, what I have argued in this chapter is that we should adopt a more complicated view, one that at least acknowledges the fact that the geographical spread of multinational enterprises has occurred and continues to occur in a world where the nation-state endures.

PART III

International Relations in
an Age of Upheaval

CHAPTER 9

The Vietnam Decade

The Global Shock of the War

LIEN-HANG T. NGUYEN

PERHAPS NO OTHER CRISIS contributed more to the global shock of the 1970s than the Vietnam War.[1] Even though combat remained confined to mainland Southeast Asia, between the United States and the Republic of Vietnam (RVN) on one side and the Democratic Republic of Vietnam (DRV) and the National Liberation Front–Provisional Revolutionary Government (NLF-PRG) on the other, the war unfolded on the world stage during the Cold War. By the 1970s the international character of the conflict produced unforeseen repercussions in an increasingly interdependent world system. The crisis in American power, the breakdown of unity within the Marxist-Leninist order, and the apogee of revolutionary Third World movements in the 1970s can all be traced to the Vietnam War and its aftermath. Divided into three sections, the first part of this chapter examines America's disengagement from Vietnam during the "long 1970s." Although the war ended in 1975, Americans spent the rest of the decade wrestling with the nature of U.S. involvement, coming to grips with the ignoble defeat, and rethinking the nation's role in world affairs in the aftermath of Vietnam. The second section analyzes how the Vietnam War affected relations within the Communist international society. Although the victory of the Vietnamese Communists should have represented a triumph for revolutionary internationalism, the war in Vietnam and its aftermath ushered in the deterioration of unity within the Marxist-Leninist camp, led to the rise of a genocidal regime in Cambodia, and resulted in the first declared war between Communist nations. The final section analyzes the global impact of the Vietnam War in creating transnational linkages between revolutionary political movements in the 1970s. Not only did the Vietnam War induce the breakdown of the Cold War consensus in the United States and the radicalization of social movements in the West,[2] but also the Vietnamese revolution inspired a third generation of decolonization movements and liberation struggles in Africa, the Middle East, and Latin America.

Never-Ending War: The United States and the Vietnam War

By the 1970s, to many observers, the Vietnam War seemed to augur the end of what Henry Luce deemed the "American Century," despite Henry Kissinger's assertion to the contrary in front of Time-Life executives.[3] With nearly sixty thousand lives lost, billions of dollars spent, national prestige sunk, two presidential administrations toppled, a community of veterans scorned or ignored, and a society nearly torn asunder, the Vietnam War exposed the limits of American power. The Nixon Doctrine, which represented Vietnamization writ large, sought to curtail foreign intervention through the use of regional policemen. Despite the new strategy of retrenchment, however, America's defeat in Vietnam with the fall of Saigon revealed that a militarily inferior postcolonial nation, albeit backed by strong Communist patrons, could defeat a technologically advanced superpower and its allies. As Mark Lawrence's chapter in this volume shows, the specter of Vietnam loomed over all postwar U.S. interventions in the developing world during the 1970s.

In addition to exposing the pitfalls of direct military entanglements in the Third World, America's war in Vietnam constituted a central element in the crisis of a U.S.-led liberal world economic system that had flourished since the 1940s.[4] America's economic golden age came to an end when Lyndon Johnson declared that both the war against Communist aggression in Vietnam and the war against poverty at home had broken the proverbial bank.[5] Although Richard Nixon had managed to get war expenditures under control by the time he took the dollar off the gold standard in 1971, military spending as a whole remained an important element of the country's balance of payments difficulties.

The crisis in American global power, however, manifested itself not only in terms of military trepidation abroad or the breakdown of the Bretton Woods system but also in the Vietnam War's impact on the national consciousness. Although U.S. involvement in Vietnam followed a trajectory from intervention to withdrawal, America as a nation did not receive its discharge from the war for the remainder of the decade and beyond. Nearly twenty thousand U.S. soldiers and incalculable numbers of North and South Vietnamese lives were lost as the leaders hammered out what proved to be an untenable peace. Nixon's controversial peace strategy, which embraced "madman" bombing and other escalatory military actions while seeking to exert Chinese and Soviet pressure on North Vietnam, managed to steel his adversaries and alienate his allies.[6] The January 1973 Paris Agreement on Ending the War and Restoring the Peace in Vietnam succeeded in putting an end to America's war but offered only temporary respite for the Vietnamese. With Nixon's ignominious departure amid the Watergate scandal, U.S. reentry into Vietnam became a precluded option, allowing historians to debate whether Nixon would have reintroduced U.S. military power to stave off South Vietnam's collapse had he remained president. Instead the fall of Saigon on April 30, 1975 signified America's humiliating defeat as U.S. officials carried out a hasty evacuation, leaving allies in Vietnam, Laos, and Cambodia behind to fend for themselves.

After 1975 U.S. policy toward Vietnam under Gerald Ford resembled "war by other means," and at the end of the decade under Jimmy Carter it once again became derailed by Cold War geopolitics.[7] The struggle over prisoners of war and Americans missing in action (the POW-MIA issue), which had begun under the Nixon administration, continued into the postwar period. With the United States refusing to act on its pledge of postwar economic aid, Hanoi utilized its remaining weapon: denial of the right to search for the remaining American MIAs in Vietnam. In addition to refusing aid, the United States blocked Vietnam's admission to the United Nations, first as two separate states and then as a unified country after July 1976. Under Carter, the normalization of relations with the Socialist Republic of Vietnam (SRV) appeared a distinct possibility during the first half of his presidency, but by 1978 Cold War geopolitics once again influenced Vietnam policy. While Sino-American relations improved, Sino-Vietnamese relations deteriorated, pushing Vietnam further into the Soviet orbit. Fearing a resurgent Soviet Union in the Third World, the Carter administration not only placed reconciliation with Hanoi on the back burner in order to appease Beijing but also tacitly gave China a green light to attack Vietnam in early 1979.

As America's postwar Vietnam policy was held hostage to the legacies of the war, domestic debates surrounding its meaning took place throughout the 1970s. Although the actual fighting in Vietnam became less important to Americans after 1973, for years afterwards the U.S. public was still recovering from the deep divisions created by the war. Vietnam veterans, few of whom had returned to a hero's welcome, were constant reminders of the unpopular conflict, as were the more than 100,000 South Vietnamese refugees who fled to the United States. It was no surprise, then, that a week after the fall of Saigon, Ford urged Americans to put the war behind them and look to the future. In an attempt to provide what the historian Robert McMahon has described as "premature and preemptive closure" to a war-weary public, Ford sought to suppress the painful memory of the recent conflict. By the 1976 presidential election, however, the Vietnam War resurfaced in official debates. In his campaign speeches Carter insisted on its "continuing relevance" for the United States when he warned against American military interventions abroad where U.S. security was not directly at stake. The Democratic nominee accused U.S. officials of having led the American public into war through "secrecy and deception."[8]

Presidents, however, did not possess a monopoly on public discourse surrounding the meaning of the war. By the end of the decade the Vietnam War once again entered American lives, this time through film, television, and literature. The war—while it was going on and for several years after 1973—had remained on the margins of American consciousness in popular culture, even in its immediate aftermath.[9] By the end of the decade, however, the Vietnam War arrived in full force on big and small screens, as well as in novels and memoirs. The historian Edward Martini links the proliferation of cultural reproductions of the war in the late 1970s to the formation and consolidation of America's postwar Vietnam policy, particularly with three major films of the decade: *The Deer Hunter, Coming Home,* and *Apocalypse Now.* Although these films addressed weighty issues, raised awareness of the plight of veterans, and questioned the morality of war in general, they also appeared—like postwar U.S. policy—to demonize the former enemy and to deflect blame. Given the troubled assimilation of Vietnamese in the United States, particularly after the 1978 wave of refugees settled in economically depressed areas such as the Gulf Coast, the popular depiction of the Vietnamese as an alien enemy had bloody repercussions.[10] Like high policy, popular culture continued to wage war against Vietnam.

In 1980 Ronald Reagan reified the contested terrain of Vietnam War memory when he accused the Carter administration of allowing America's "margin of safety" to disappear because it was suffering under a "Vietnam Syndrome." Rather than permit the memory of the war to paralyze American actions abroad, as he alleged the Democratic administration had done, Reagan offered an alternative lesson: "If we are forced to fight, we must have the means and the determination to prevail or we will not have what it takes to secure the peace."[11] For too long, Reagan contended, Americans had dishonored the memory of those who were killed in the war by viewing the nation's cause in Vietnam as anything but noble. Through invoking the perceived "lessons" of the war in more unequivocal terms than his predecessors, Reagan's campaign rhetoric tapped into public disquiet about America's perceived decline in the world in the aftermath of Vietnam. Even though the 1970s witnessed the country's long disengagement from the Vietnam War, it is apparent that the conflict and its aftermath continued to have a defining role in American culture, economic policy, foreign relations, and domestic politics. Contesting views of the war and its legacies, however, did not end in 1979, and in fact had only begun. If the winners generally write the history of a war, the 1970s revealed that the losers can equally debate its interpretation.

Comrades at War: The Vietnam War and the Communist World

America's defeat in the Vietnam War brought about universal celebration in the Marxist-Leninist world, but it also ushered in the end of unity within the Communist global order. At the height of the Second Indochina War, Vietnamese resistance against the United States had constituted the most important struggle for the global Marxist-Leninist community. Communist parties worldwide lent direct military and economic assistance, provided endless political and diplomatic support, and even volunteered their own troops to aid the Vietnamese resistance. In particular, China and the Soviet Union contributed massive amounts of military and economic aid and sent engineering troops and other personnel to North Vietnam. Nevertheless, the Vietnamese revolution could not mend the divisions within the Communist world. In fact the Vietnamese Communist struggle exacerbated the ideological divisions within the Marxist-Leninist international order and contributed directly to the deepening of the Sino-Soviet split.

Although the ideological rift between Moscow and Beijing predated the

Vietnam War, Chinese-Soviet competition for influence over the Vietnamese Communist revolution deepened the split. Even though Hanoi managed to maintain its independence by playing its allies off against each other, the Vietnamese Communist leadership preferred a unified Communist front during its war against the United States. Instead the Vietnamese had to endure Chinese castigation for accepting "suspect" Soviet aid and Russian pressure to denounce Chinese obstruction. During the first half of the war Hanoi was able to balance its relations with Moscow and Beijing by staying neutral in the Sino-Soviet split. Hanoi's fragile balancing act became more difficult to manage, however, when clashes broke out between Chinese and Soviet troops on the Ussuri River. At the time, North Vietnamese leaders understood that the intensification of Sino-Soviet hostilities boded ill for their war effort since it provided an opportunity for the United States to exploit the split for its own advantage in Vietnam.[12] In 1972 Hanoi's worst fears were confirmed as Nixon used Sino-American rapprochement and Soviet-American détente to force North Vietnam's hand at the negotiating table.[13]

Sino-Vietnamese relations were particularly vulnerable to Nixon's triangular offensive during the 1970s. Following the signing of the Shanghai Communiqué in 1972, Vietnamese general secretary Le Duan told Zhou Enlai that the People's Republic of China had saved a "drowning" Nixon by inviting him to visit the PRC. Although Chinese leaders vociferously denied that they had betrayed Vietnamese interests, they secretly feared a Soviet-controlled North Vietnam that would dominate all of Indochina, particularly after the anti-Sihanouk coup removed Cambodia's last vestige of neutrality in the Vietnam War. By 1973, however, Chinese leaders could rely on Pol Pot and his faction in the Communist Party of Kampuchea (CPK) to stymie any Vietnamese expansionist ambitions in greater Indochina. The Khmer Rouge, barely disguising its hatred for the Vietnamese even during the war, was able to fill the power vacuum that Nixon's expansion of the air and ground wars into Cambodia had created. Although the struggle against the United States and its allies nominally united the Asian Communist parties, with the common enemy gone, divisions between Chinese, Vietnamese, and Cambodian forces rose to the fore.

By mid-decade, then, despite the celebrations taking place over the end of the war, Indochina was a tinderbox ready to ignite. In particular Cambodia, whose postcolonial fate was tied to Vietnam's, entered its darkest period as the Khmer Rouge waged the most brutal revolution in history, exposing the limits of the emerging global human rights regime. Retreating from the international community, Pol Pot's Democratic Kampuchea (DK) set out privately to surpass all other Communist revolutions by transforming the Cambodian economy into an autarkic rice factory whose inhabitants would live in classless harmony. Going against the tide of global economic and political integration, Pol Pot and his faction displaced nearly 2 million urban residents, announced the goal of total collectivization of agriculture, and declared the abolition of private landownership as well as all currency. The Khmer Rouge practiced social engineering as it divided the Cambodian population into three workforces, separating children from their parents, the young from the old. After exterminating the enemies of the revolution, who in the Khmer Rouge's definition included not only former officials of the Lon Nol regime but also the educated and ethnic minorities, the DK leadership then forced the remaining population to labor under extreme conditions in pursuit of a chimera. By the end of the fatal revolution, approximately 1.7 million Cambodians, constituting over 20 percent of the population, had perished.

Postwar Vietnam was not nearly so bloody, although as the historian Ngo Vinh Long has shown, the Communist leadership based in Hanoi did establish political reeducation camps and undertook hasty collectivization in pursuit of premature reunification at the expense of the southern half of the country.[14] After victory, southern Vietnamese leaders envisioned a slow reunification process spread out over a dozen years in order to address the country's postwar problems, which included massive rural displacement, widespread hunger and starvation, nearly 8 million urban unemployed, and an economy in shambles. Fearing, however, that the Hanoi-led revolution was under threat in the South, particularly in the urban areas, General Secretary Le Duan pushed for speedy reunification through socialist transformation of the economy and complete political restructuring along party lines. Le Duan's model for economic development in the South was based on failed campaigns that had already been tried in the North: the land reform and political reorganization of the 1950s and collectivization from 1965 to 1975. By 1978 the exigencies of impending war with Cambodia and China were said to require the total eradication of the ancien régime's capitalist compradors in the cities and colonial and feudal landlords in the countryside as well as rapid collectivization. But just as these campaigns failed in the North during the First and Second Indochina

Wars, so too did they fail in the South during the Third Indochina War. Resistance from rich and middle peasants, who had earlier supported the revolution, ensured that socialism was for all intents and purposes dead by 1980. Even though it would take withdrawal from Cambodia to pave the way for Vietnam's 1986 shift to a market economy with Doi Moi (Economic Renovation) policies, the groundwork for Vietnam's perestroika and glasnost was laid in the 1970s.

Although Vietnam would eventually follow China's example and embrace market capitalism in the 1980s,[15] the country's economic development in the 1970s was hindered not only by its northern leaders but also by the international environment. When assistance from America proved elusive, Hanoi turned to its Communist allies to seek economic support. In the fall of 1975 Le Duan traveled to China and the Soviet Union. He drew a blank in Beijing but had more success in Moscow. As Chinese leaders castigated him for Vietnam's foreign policy, Russian leaders pledged long-term aid.

Hanoi's troubles with its Asian allies, however, did not end with Beijing: after assuming power, the Pol Pot regime forced Vietnamese residents to leave Cambodia and refused to negotiate border issues with Vietnam. In 1976, although China was friendlier with Pol Pot's DK and complained of the newly reunified SRV's tilt toward the Soviet Union, Sino-Vietnamese relations had still not completely broken down. That year Beijing urged its Cambodian allies to seek a diplomatic solution on border issues with Vietnam. Placing on the back burner its desire to reclaim all of Khmer Krom territory, the rich Mekong Delta region deemed stolen by Vietnamese settlers starting in the seventeenth century, the Khmer Rouge occupied itself instead with its domestic agenda.

By 1977, however, the Pol Pot regime began to turn its deadly gaze outwards and, in the process of doing so, changed not only the regional picture but also international relations in the late Cold War. In April, Khmer Rouge forces invaded Vietnam, attacking six out of seven border provinces. At the same time that Beijing refused to grant additional aid to Hanoi, Moscow announced long-term Soviet credits to Vietnam, reinforcing Chinese fears of a Soviet-controlled southern neighbor. Beijing finally settled on an alternative to the Sino-Soviet-Vietnamese triangle: the PRC increased military aid and political support to the Khmer Rouge. As relations between the PRC and the DK grew closer, Vietnam began to tighten its control over ethnic Chinese within its borders by encouraging the Hoa (ethnic Chinese) to adopt Vietnamese citizenship and moving them away from border areas. When Khmer Rouge forces attacked Vietnamese villages again in September, Hanoi did not adopt a conciliatory posture as it had in April but instead launched a counterattack on December 25. Six days later the DK spurned negotiations and opted instead to sever relations with the SRV.

In early 1978, however, events spun out of control. In February the Hanoi leadership resolved to sponsor a general uprising in Cambodia with the aim of overthrowing the Pol Pot regime while its troops clashed with Chinese soldiers on the northern border. By spring the Hoa problem reached crisis proportions as ethnic Chinese began to depart from major Vietnamese cities and towns. As the "boat people" fled Vietnam in 1978, Hanoi's hopes of bettering relations with Beijing went with them. On June 28 Vietnam joined the Soviet-led Council for Mutual Economic Assistance, or Comecon. At the same time, to be sure, Hanoi continued to press for improved relations with the United States. These efforts, however, were in vain. As the Soviet Union increased its activities in the Third World, the battle between National Security Adviser Zbigniew Brzezinski and Secretary of State Cyrus Vance for President Carter's ear tipped toward the former. Brzezinski, who was fiercely anti-Soviet, convinced Carter that Sino-American relations were more important than Vance's goal of normalizing U.S. relations with Vietnam.

By the fall of 1978 the die was cast for war. On November 3 Hanoi signed a mutual defense treaty with Moscow, aimed at China, and drew up plans to invade Cambodia. On December 25 Vietnamese forces, backed by the Soviet Union, crossed the western border. By early 1979 the Khmer Rouge regime was ousted from power as Vietnamese forces liberated Phnom Penh on January 7. Hanoi's bigger battles, however, were yet to come. In mid-February Beijing conspired with American and Association of Southeast Asian Nations (ASEAN) leaders to punish and isolate Hanoi for its invasion and occupation of Cambodia. Although it disavowed complicity, Washington gave Beijing its tacit blessing to attack Vietnam. On February 17 Chinese "punitive" attacks began, but they ultimately failed to compel the Vietnamese to divert their forces from Cambodia to the northern front. The Soviet Union, which along with Laos and the East European socialist countries supported Vietnam, warned the PRC that it should "stop before it was too late."[16] Beijing, however, was successful in saving the remaining Khmer Rouge forces, who were given safe haven in

Thailand, and in presenting the SRV as an aggressor state on the world stage.

Although the 1975 Communist victory in Vietnam should have ushered in a period of triumph for the Marxist-Leninist states, it actually sounded the death knell for the international Communist movement. Not only was the Vietnam War unable to mend the Sino-Soviet split, but also it further exacerbated the divisions among the Communist great powers. As Beijing increasingly viewed Hanoi as Moscow's puppet in Indochina, the Khmer Rouge lit the tinderbox and plunged the former Asian Communist allies into war. Despite their having been as close as "lips and teeth" during the previous two Indochina wars, the third conflict between China and Vietnam represented the violent severing of the Asian socialist body.

The Model Revolution: The Vietnam War and the Third World

In the early 1980s the Sandinista government invited advisers from the People's Army of Vietnam (PAVN) to Nicaragua in order to train its soldiers to put down a loose conglomerate of anti-Communist forces consisting of former National Guard troops under the deposed president Anastasio Somoza Debayle, known as the *contrarevolucionarios*. Throughout the 1970s the Sandinistas—like other revolutionary groups worldwide—believed that the triumphant Vietnamese were the leading experts in defeating the United States and its allies. For the Nicaraguans, the Vietnamese wrote the guide on how to overcome American-style counterinsurgency, a useful asset in the Sandinista war against the U.S.-trained and funded "contras." Although the SRV accepted the invitation to train the Nicaraguans and sent over two dozen personnel, it kept its Nicaraguan mission secret.[17] Though committed to passing on the torch of revolution, Hanoi did not advertise its forays into foreign terrain as the Soviets, Chinese, and Cubans had done earlier in the Cold War.[18] Even though revolutionary groups throughout the Third World appealed to Hanoi for guidance and support during and after the Vietnam War, Vietnam was in neither the economic nor the political position to assist other national liberation struggles. With international outcry over the presence of PAVN troops in Cambodia, the Vietnamese were wary of broadcasting the activities of their military in Nicaragua. Instead Vietnamese leaders contented themselves with providing the "model" for a successful liberation struggle against colonial and neoimperialist powers. Thus did the Vietnamese revolution inspire a third generation of decolonization movements in Africa, the Middle East, and Latin America.[19]

While other liberation struggles won international attention, the war in Vietnam had a global impact of unprecedented proportions. The diffusion of communications technologies and the proliferation of international media in the 1950s and 1960s created a global audience for the conflict unfolding in Southeast Asia, particularly after 1968. As Americans and Europeans watched images of the fighting in Vietnam flash across television screens during the evening news, students, political activists, and revolutionaries around the developing world read reports of the drama in newspapers and magazines. Indeed the Vietnamese Communists—like others before them—engaged in substantial efforts to win support for their cause through what they called "people's diplomacy," a powerful weapon available to small powers against greater powers during the Cold War.[20] Antiwar members of the U.S. Congress as well as activists and radicals in the West, however, were not the only audience for Vietnam's propaganda. The revolutionary Third World pored over the translated writings of Ho Chi Minh and Vo Nguyen Giap while they listened intently to the speeches of Madame Nguyen Thi Binh. As the Vietnam War haunted the American consciousness after 1975, the ghosts of Vietnam stirred the revolutionary spirits of liberation struggles worldwide.

According to Le Duan, the main architect and lead strategist in the "anti-American struggle for liberation and national salvation," the Vietnamese revolution unfolded during a historic and unprecedented moment in history. He described it as "the bridge between socialism and the revolutionary world, the spearhead for the people's movement as well as for national liberation struggles in Asia, Africa, Latin America."[21] Understanding the importance of the Vietnamese struggle not only for Vietnam but also for the socialist and revolutionary worlds, Le Duan affirmed its potential for replication and success elsewhere. Although the general secretary penned these words during the war against the U.S.-RVN coalition, they would become the official line during the post–Vietnam War period, when Hanoi could provide only its historical example as aid to revolutions worldwide.

These international efforts not only contributed to Vietnamese Communist prestige abroad but also spread the ideals and mythology of the Vietnamese revolution over a broader, global field. Revolutionary fighters around the world were inspired by the example of Vietnamese resistance against French and U.S. interventions and hoped to transplant the Vietnamese model of guerrilla warfare into their own struggles. As Odd Arne Westad has argued, the inspiration of the Vietnamese model was usually indirect and characterized by "creative misunderstandings." Nevertheless, the Vietnamese (and Cuban) examples added legitimacy to the notion of guerrilla resistance against superpower domination.[22]

One did not need to look far to find guerrilla conflicts—some brewing, some full-blown—around the Third World during the 1970s. The most obvious example of the power of the Vietnamese model could be found not far from the country's borders. Vietnam's neighbors felt the most immediate impact of DRV and NLF-PRG victories. Before the Asian Communist alliance imploded, Lao and Khmer Communists gained momentum from Vietnamese success in their struggles against the Souvanna Phouma and Lon Nol regimes respectively. Southeast Asian governments in Thailand, Indonesia, the Philippines, and Malaysia also experienced surges in left-wing activity inspired by events in Vietnam. U.S.-backed crackdowns, however, helped save many of those non-Communist governments from the same fate as Saigon, Vientiane, and Phnom Penh.[23]

Farther offshore, another guerrilla movement that was to become increasingly important in subsequent decades, the Palestine Liberation Organization (PLO), looked to the Vietnamese experience as a source of inspiration. Palestinian fighters hoped to achieve the same sorts of victories against the State of Israel that the Vietnamese resistance had won against French colonialism and American military intervention. According to the historian Paul Chamberlin, the PLO believed that "the Vietnamese revolution had demonstrated that by mobilizing the masses, studying the art of revolutionary warfare, and building international alliances, a movement could achieve victory over imperialism."[24]

Policymakers in Washington who feared a global domino effect in the wake of the Vietnam War could also point to a spate of guerrilla insurgencies in Africa and Latin America. In Ethiopia a group of military officers deposed Emperor Haile Selassie's government in 1974 and established a Marxist-Leninist regime that became a beachhead for spreading Soviet influence into neighboring countries. Meanwhile in Angola, the withdrawal of Portuguese imperial forces in 1975 sparked a civil war between the Soviet-supported MPLA (Popular Movement for the Liberation of Angola) and the U.S.- and South African–backed UNITA (National Union for the Total Independence of Angola) factions. White regimes in South Africa and Rhodesia found themselves under attack from groups such as the African National Congress, the South West Africa People's Organization, and the Zimbabwe African National Liberation Army.[25] In Nicaragua the Sandinista National Liberation Front escalated its resistance operations against the Somoza regime, using both traditional and urban guerrilla warfare against the Nicaraguan National Guard. As the 1970s drew to a close, the Sandinistas' rising power presented policymakers in Washington with the specter of a second Cuba in Latin America.[26] Although the revolutionary groups in these countries appealed to the Vietnamese for direct assistance during the 1970s, the Vietnam War and its aftermath rendered assistance impossible. Nonetheless, the leaders in Hanoi took pride in the international waves that their national liberation struggle had helped produce, content to pass along the torch of revolution.

The triumph of the Vietnamese revolution thus created a twofold problem for U.S.—and Soviet—policymakers. On the one hand, its example inspired resistance fighters around the world with the hope of replicating the Vietnamese model of guerrilla insurgency in their own nations. At the same time, the failure of Washington's counterinsurgency efforts in Southeast Asia created what Reagan and other neoconservatives would call the "Vietnam Syndrome," which sapped American will for Third World interventions. By the end of the decade the United States appeared to be on the brink of defeat in the struggle for the global South. As Henry Kissinger recalled:

> Cuban military forces had spread from Angola to Ethiopia in tandem with thousands of Soviet combat advisers. In Cambodia, Vietnamese troops backed and supplied by the Soviet Union were subjugating that tormented country. Afghanistan was occupied by over 100,000 Soviet troops. The government of the pro-Western Shah of Iran collapsed and was replaced by a radically anti-American fundamentalist regime. . . . Whatever the causes, the dominoes indeed appeared to be falling.[27]

While the United States feared the lessons that the revolutionary Third World would take from the Vietnam War, the Soviet Union disregarded the war's legacies. Even though leaders in Moscow invited Vietnamese advisers to Afghanistan in order to assist the Red Army, they ignored what those advisers had to say regarding the dangers of guerrilla warfare and the capacity of a persistent and driven enemy to expel foreign occupiers.[28]

The impact of the Vietnamese revolution on national liberation struggles in the Third World in the 1970s is perhaps the most revealing testament to the global reverberations of the Vietnam War. Unable to contribute militarily or economically to these revolutions, the Vietnamese instead provided the model for a new wave of decolonization struggles in Asia, Africa, Latin America, and the Middle East.

If Vietnam had rent asunder the international politics of the 1960s, it must follow that the 1970s constituted a postwar decade, akin to the 1920s and late 1940s, wherein the international system accommodated the deep structural changes wrought by the war. Bringing an end to the image of American omnipotence as well as to any semblance of unity in the Communist world, the Vietnam War heralded the zenith of Third World power on the global stage. It is no surprise, then, that the Cold War has been divided into pre- and post-Vietnam eras. This applies as much to the Marxist-Leninist and Third Worlds as to the United States and Vietnam themselves. Neither contemporaries nor historians would deny the global reverberations of the Vietnam War and the "shock" it delivered to the international system in the 1970s.

CHAPTER 10

Henry Kissinger and the
Geopolitics of Globalization

JEREMI SURI

"PLANS ARE USELESS," President Dwight Eisenhower once remarked, but "planning is indispensable."[1] Thinking carefully and deeply about the future does not provide a charted course for policy; the variables and the contingencies are far too numerous. The act of planning does, however, prepare the decision maker to maintain coherence and adjust effectively rather than sink in a sea of chaotic pressures.

Henry Kissinger took Eisenhower's insight to heart. More than almost any other figure in the 1960s and 1970s, he thought systematically about future challenges and opportunities. Kissinger's strategic deliberations did not always define his actions, but they guided his efforts to interpret the global transformations of the era and his reactions to policy challenges and opportunities. Although Kissinger's knowledge of economics was notoriously limited, his understanding of how systems of power among societies emerge and evolve was quite acute. Writing at the end of May 2008—four months before the financial crisis that would begin in September of that year—Kissinger predicted serious international problems surrounding the weak state regulation of global investments. "Financial institutions," he wrote, "whether investment banks or hedge funds, need oversight in a way that protects the taxpayer's interest. . . . [I]f the gap between the economic and political orders is not substantially narrowed, the two structures will wind up weakening each other." Kissinger counseled, "The parameters of the national security limits to globalization should be established on a national basis rather than left to pressure groups, lobbyists, and electoral politics."[2]

To those familiar with Kissinger's long foreign policy career, his calls for a reassertion of state power were not new. A month before making these comments, he wrote of the "three revolutions" undermining international stability: the weakening of European states, the rise of an "Islamist challenge," and the shift in power to Asia. Together these "revolutions" required what Kissinger had advocated throughout his life: strong, effective statesmanship.

For more than five decades at this writing, Kissinger has both observed the diverse forces of globalization and pushed for the energetic management of globalization by the most powerful governments, especially the United States.[3] What I call Kissinger's "geopolitics of globalization" suffers from many limitations—including a sometime excessive preference for state over non-state actors—but it embodies a consistency and a pragmatism that continue to attract attention from diverse policymakers. Kissinger's geopolitical vision also provides a foundation for understanding how he and others in government conceived of foreign policy during the 1960s and 1970s. Despite contrary assumptions, Kissinger sought to address traditional and nontraditional strategic issues, inherited political-military resources, and emerging vectors of economic and cultural change. He was, in fact, as up-to-date in this thinking as those who challenged his policies.

This essay elucidates the old and the new in Kissinger's strategy. In it I analyze his approach to the management of global change. By interrogating Kissinger's deliberations, I examine the efforts of the era's most influential policymaker to formulate diplomatic mechanisms for ensuring America's national leadership amidst a range of other important international actors. Kissinger did not master his international environment, but he understood and reshaped it in enduring ways. That is, of course, why he remains the most controversial figure from the 1970s.

Studies of globalization, and its detractors, have a tendency to emphasize the power of transnational forces that transcend traditional state controls. The world energy market and the global flow of capital, particularly in the 1970s, seriously challenged (and often undermined) established government regulation of consumption and distribution.[4] Globalization in this sense transformed state power, but it did not necessarily degrade the power of strong government actors. Quite the contrary, the disorientation (or "shock") of the international state system opened new avenues for innovative, energetic, and even charismatic statesmanship. That was the self-conscious niche for Kissinger's geopolitics. More than any of his contemporaries, he sought to turn globalization to the advantage of the American state and empower himself as the preeminent global actor. Kissinger was less a traditional realist than a political opportunist. This is what he meant when he emphasized his efforts to "rescue an element of choice from the pressure of circumstance."[5]

Kissinger's opportunism was effective, at least in the short term, because it grew out of a clear-eyed recognition of global transformations and a coherent approach to exercising power in this context. Many scholars, including this one, have given extensive attention to the successes and failures of Kissinger's particular policies in the 1970s.[6] There is little need to rehearse those arguments again here. Instead the point that is often lost in the *Sturm und Drang* of Kissinger scholarship is that he practiced a sophisticated foreign policy of globalization that rested on the reassertion of state power. As a philosopher and practitioner of geopolitics, Kissinger offered the most enduring framework for managing the post-1960s international system. Although one might legitimately criticize the self-serving and self-defeating elements of Kissinger's approach (particularly in the area of human rights), one must also acknowledge that no one in his time provided a more holistic alternative. No one else at the time stepped forward with a better system for riding the tiger of globalization. No one else at the time could integrate challenges and opportunities into workable policy with the same effectiveness. Kissinger's understanding of globalization was incomplete, but his framework for policymaking was less limited than most others. For this reason Kissinger became the foreign policy celebrity of the 1970s, the only figure who appeared to make sense of a rapidly changing world.[7]

Global Federalism

Kissinger articulated his strategic vision most clearly in a series of lectures he wrote for Nelson Rockefeller to deliver at Harvard University in February 1962. These lectures drew on the history of federalism in the United States. As James Madison and others formulated a mix of institutions and principles to address the rapid transformation in power on the North American continent almost two centuries earlier, Kissinger sought a similar mix of centralized and diffuse power sources to manage international change in the Cold War: "The Founding Fathers devised a structure of order for a nation within which free men could work and prosper in peace. We are required to help build such a framework for freedom not merely for a nation but for the free world of which we are an integral part."[8]

The "federal idea"—defined as a "balance of strengths" between different sovereign bodies "operating within a framework of laws and principles"—promised to provide opportunities for enhancing American security while recognizing limits. "It encourages," said Rockefeller, "innovation and inventiveness—governed by principle, and guided by purpose. It assures responsiveness more thoughtful than mere reflex—and liberty that does not lapse toward anarchy. In short, it seeks to hold the delicately precarious balance between freedom and order upon which depend decisively the liberty, peace, and prosperity of the individual." Federalism was an alternative to anarchy on the one hand and imperial dominion on the other. It implied a basic consensus on rules, with freedom for competition, and even conflict, within safe boundaries.[9]

On an international scale, federalism ensured basic cooperation among allies in the pursuit of peace. Adversaries could join the system if they bought into a set of "civilizing" rules of conduct, as Kissinger believed the Soviet Union and the People's Republic of China did during the era of détente. Adversaries that refused to abide by the international consensus, particularly Cuba and North Korea, would face isolation and exclusion from access to the federal system of state relations. They would also confront the combined force of internationally coordinated military, economic, and cultural pressure. In this sense federalism built order on a combination of cooperation and containment.

At the same time, federalism affirmed a diversity of cultures, ideologies, and political regimes. Instead of combating communism until it crumbled, a federalist approach integrated communism and other political organizations into a larger structure of stable relations. This was not just the American model for the Western hemisphere. It was Otto von Bismarck's late-nineteenth-century approach to security among the German states, and within Europe as a whole. The great German chancellor recognized, Kissinger wrote, that peace did not come from universal claims of authority, but emerged instead from coordination among diverse sovereigns— from managed relations between adversarial states.[10]

The United Nations or some other international body could not manage the federalist world that Kissinger imagined. Institutions of this kind provided technical and bureaucratic fixes for tasks that required deeper understanding and more imaginative leadership. Federalism, in this sense, was not about creating a world forum or a global government but instead involved nurturing a cooperative ethos through adjustments of force and inspiring direction. The enlightened statesman had to work within the system of states, crafting principles and alignments that also transformed this system.[11]

For Kissinger, a federalist foreign policy meant an acceptance of limits on unilateral power, a commitment to negotiations, and an emphasis on mutual gains rather than relative advantage. It was about balancing promises and threats, carrots and sticks. It affirmed the power and legitimacy of the largest states, but it also encouraged political activities that cut across nations. Most significantly, a federalist foreign policy hinged on the imaginative work of select leaders in the dominant countries. They would build the framework for global cooperation and shared authority. They would "create their own reality."[12]

Kissinger made these words a touchstone for his career. His federalist strategy consisted of three primary components that he outlined in his writings and implemented from the White House during the 1970s: the creation of an "Atlantic Confederacy," a world with "more centers of decision," and a set of "basic principles" to restrain international competition. These were the pillars for his alternative to traditional Communist containment. "The decade of the 1960's," Kissinger wrote, "will require heroic effort and we will not always have the solace of popular acclaim." Americans, he urged, "must be willing to face the paradox that we must be dedicated both to military strength and to arms control, to security as well as to negotiation, to assisting the new nations towards freedom and self-respect without accepting their interpretation of all issues. If we cannot do *all* these things, we will not be able to do *any* of them."[13]

Transatlantic Community

Kissinger's federalist strategy began with the assertion that the United States had to strengthen its core alliance in Western Europe. Close relations within the North Atlantic Treaty Organization would protect fundamental values and interests. This was the key area of contestation in the Cold War and the central location for possible accommodation with adversaries. In Western Europe, Washington would display its determination to prohibit Communist aggression, articulate its commitment to international peace, and showcase the possibilities of liberal-capitalist society. Security in this region was essential for broadening American efforts to build cooperation elsewhere. A strong NATO would in fact facilitate federalist overtures by coordinating the efforts of the United States and its allies. It would also provide the force to convince adversaries that their best option was negotiation rather than conflict. The transatlantic community was for a federalist global vision in the twentieth century what the eastern seaboard had been for a federalist continental vision in the nineteenth century: it was the holy land. "For more than a decade now," Kissinger wrote in 1961, "the nations bordering the North Atlantic have been living off the capital provided by the great initiative of the Marshall Plan." American aid financed reconstruction and alliance after the Second World War. It solidified a set of common purposes that, in the face of growing Communist challenges, needed renewed attention: "The leap forward required in the next decade is the creation of a political framework that will go beyond the nationalism which has dominated the past century and a half." Kissinger called for an "Atlantic Confederacy," a deeper integration of diplomatic aims and force capabilities. The "North Atlantic Community" would "increase its political cohesion so that it begins to approach a federal system." It would become a new kind of postnationalist alliance, addressing issues beyond military defense alone.[14]

Kissinger was not advocating more bureaucracy or anything approaching a super-state. That would violate the federal idea as he defined it. Instead he called for an alliance of "sovereign states" in which "the delegation of authority will clearly have to be limited." Borrowing from the proposals for a "Directorate" of transatlantic leaders put forward by French president Charles de Gaulle, Kissinger argued that a federal arrangement for diplomatic and military policy should work through an "Executive Committee" of the leaders from the largest transatlantic states. They would forge a common position for negotiations with the Soviet Union; they would formulate overtures for peace and stability in Europe; they would build programs for broader prosperity; and they would, of course, pool their resources to enhance the military pressures on Moscow to avoid conflict. Diplomacy, not international bureaucracy, provided the structure for Kissinger's federalist hopes.[15]

More organized, consensual, and effective coordination among leaders would instill confidence in citizens. It would counteract democratic tendencies toward neutrality and defeatism. It would also give NATO a positive goal beyond the reactive posture of containing communism. "A great leader," Kissinger wrote in this context, "is not so much clever as lucid and clear-sighted. Grandeur is not simply physical power but strength reinforced by moral purpose." A functioning executive committee from the largest states, in Kissinger's eyes, would provide the transatlantic community with needed direction and inspiration.[16]

Unlike most other American observers, Kissinger praised de Gaulle's understanding of this point: "His diplomacy is in the style of Bismarck, who strove ruthlessly to achieve what he considered Prussia's rightful place, but who then tried to preserve the new equilibrium through prudence, restraint, and moderation." Kissinger reminded readers that de Gaulle had "repeatedly urged the coordination of Western policies on a world-wide basis," with equal and acknowledged American, British, and French dominance.[17]

Kissinger wanted to take de Gaulle's directorate proposal and expand it in size and scope. He argued that an executive committee of the largest states—including West Germany (and perhaps Italy) as well as France, Great Britain, and the United States—was a necessary federal structure for ensuring the future dynamism of the transatlantic community. These were the natural leaders on the European continent. They were also, because of their economic and military resources, the states with the greatest leverage over Soviet policy. "European history demonstrates," observed Kissinger, "that stability in Europe is unattainable except through the cooperation of Britain, France, and Germany." In a Cold War world the United States was now a central part of this process, and it had to facilitate strategic unity in place of "old national rivalries."[18]

Despite their enormous destructive power, nuclear weapons had the potential to replace traditional markers of conflict in Western Europe with new anchors of alliance. Returning to his earlier advocacy of more diverse fighting capabilities, Kissinger argued that the most effective mechanism for ensuring transatlantic strategic coordination came through the sharing of nuclear weapons. Because of widespread criticisms of his alleged recklessness, he deemphasized (though never rescinded) his prior calls for the planned use of small nuclear weapons in conflict. Instead Kissinger argued for a controlled proliferation of nuclear capabilities to the states on the proposed executive committee. A "European nuclear force," he wrote, is preferable to the alternatives proposed for static American dominance. "It is likely," he predicted, "that nuclear autonomy is the least divisive form of European unity."[19]

Kissinger's strategic vision rested on building a stronger, more confident Atlantic community of states. The federalization of NATO would occur primarily through the federalization of nuclear weapons. Soviet thermonuclear forces posed the greatest threat to the transatlantic community, and only new methods for sharing retaliatory capabilities would preserve flexibility, cohesion, and strength. Kissinger's thinking on this point was highly revisionist; it ran against the emerging norms of nuclear nonproliferation in the 1960s and 1970s, advocated most consistently by the proponents of containment. He continued to see nuclear weapons as useful symbols and tools for leverage short of full-scale thermonuclear conflict. The spread of small nuclear capabilities would create opportunities for local defense—including limited wars—in Europe against Communist adversaries, when necessary. The spread of such capabilities would also diffuse power and limit American global responsibilities while preserving America's influence over faraway events.

Polycentrism

Kissinger's federalist approach to foreign policy focused on Europe, his primary area of expertise, but it extended over a wider landscape. The dominance of the United States and the Soviet Union after the Second World War created what most observers identified as a "bipolar" world, largely divided between allies of these two states. Nations generally turned to Washington or Moscow for aid and defense. They possessed available resources and sought to distribute them as a mechanism for building political influence. The price of assistance was alliance with the United States or the Soviet Union and conflict with its counterpart. In a bipolar world the friend of one superpower was the adversary of the other. This was a predictable but also rigid and conflict-prone environment.

For many commentators bipolarity was not just a fact of life but a source of strategic stability. It made calculations of power easy and the need for superpower restraint during moments of direct conflict obvious. It eliminated the uncertainty that could lead to a thermonuclear war no one wanted through miscalculation or blundering. Most significant, it created a set of common interests among adversaries in preserving the status quo against potentially catastrophic alternatives. This was most evident during the Cuban Missile Crisis, when both Kennedy and Khrushchev backed down from their respective aims in the Caribbean and accepted a stable basis for superpower peace rather than nuclear war.[20]

Kissinger did not accept this argument. In the aftermath of the missile crisis he wrote that bipolarity had in fact encouraged Soviet aggression. Convinced that the United States would not risk war to prevent Moscow's incursions in Cuba or other small states, Khrushchev felt that he could safely provide Fidel Castro with nuclear missiles close to U.S. territory. This move would show support for an ally, increase Soviet striking capabilities against the United States, and humiliate Washington. In a bipolar world, Kissinger explained, Khrushchev believed that the balance of power and resolve had shifted in his direction; he perceived that American fears of growing Soviet power would deter Washington from acting forcefully in response. Bipolarity encouraged risk taking by a leader who was convinced of his counterpart's aversion to such behavior. This appeared especially true in the "Third World" during the 1970s.[21]

The only practical solution to Cold War stalemate and Soviet risk taking was to transform the structure of the international system, encouraging a diffusion of power on terms favorable to the United States.[22] A world with "more centers of decision," Kissinger believed, would provide flexibility for innovative diplomacy and consensus building rather than the enforced dominance of two bullies. In a "multipolar" framework, the superpowers would feel less directly threatened by their counterpart's every move. They would have less at stake because the shifting roles of other powerful states could compensate for setbacks in "peripheral" parts of Africa, Asia, and Latin America. Instead of a duel between two heavily armed gunslingers, the Cold War would become a contest among fluid coalitions of countries working to ensure basic peace as they jockeyed for advantage.[23]

The diffusion of power "was fully compatible with our interests as well as our ideals," said Kissinger, because it encouraged states to work with the United States out of free choice rather than perceived American armtwisting. In Western Europe this would allow Washington to draw more effectively on the potential strengths of its allies, and it would ensure their firmer and more self-confident engagement with the White House. Outside Western Europe—especially within the Communist bloc and among nations emerging from colonialism—a greater American recognition of regional power centers would allow the U.S. government to formulate more appealing policies. Kissinger argued that a polycentric vision of the international system would enable Washington to escape simple slogans and find common interests with diverse states. Americans would now have a clear incentive to seek international compromise rather than impose their way of life on others.

During the 1960s Kissinger laid out a strategy for the United States to nurture a multipolar world that would serve its interests. It would replace the nuclear stalemate with a politics of movement that emphasized close working relationships with new partners. It would provide for increased American leverage, despite overstretched U.S. resources, by relying on regional actors rather than direct American dominance. Particularly in Asia, the recognition of more power centers would solve the twin dilemmas of America's long-standing conflict with Communist China and its self-defeating war in Vietnam. Kissinger's multipolar plans promised to reverse the tragic, almost paralyzing Cold War inertia in each of these areas. The "age of the superpowers is now drawing to an end," Kissinger declared. "A new concept of international order is essential."[24]

China stood at the center of Kissinger's new strategic framework. He shared with many other observers, including de Gaulle, a belief in the inner greatness of Chinese civilization. One of Kissinger's frequent interlocutors from Europe remembers, "He was fascinated by China." Despite two decades of disastrous Communist rule, this was a society with self-confidence, accumulated learning, and a sense of its historical role as a world leader. The "Middle Kingdom," like Germany, dominated its neighbors not through brute force alone but also from cultural accomplishment. Although Kissinger knew little about the substance of Chinese society, he came to believe that China could play an effective role in bringing order to the emerging nations in its region. Geopolitical and ideological antagonisms with the Soviet Union, combined with vivid memories of the brutal Japanese occupation of the mainland during the Second World War, meant that Beijing might look to the United States as a less offensive regional partner than the other available options. Despite his image as a cold-blooded analyst of *Realpolitik*, Kissinger believed that the Chinese were a natural cultural anchor for stable relations, and even cooperation, in Asia. He later commented that their society did not possess an "expansionist" disposition but was instead "inward looking," with "slow, patient resolve" and "deliberative thought, not impulsive action."[25]

These are remarkable judgments, especially in light of Chinese aggression during the Korean War and the radical violence that swept the mainland during the late 1960s as Mao Zedong encouraged a "Great Proletarian Cultural Revolution" against all vestiges of traditional society. Kissinger was not blind to the viciousness of the regime in Beijing, but he contended that "Communist China is a major fact of international life, especially in Asia." He called for "contacts without illusion," adding: "We cannot take over the responsibility for bringing Mainland China into a more normal and communicative relationship with the community of nations; she must bring herself out of the isolation which is principally self-imposed. But we can do more to advance the day when China will be able to recognize that it is in her interest to join in rational and constructive relationships with the outside world."[26]

Kissinger wrote these words in early 1968, before he went to work for Richard Nixon. Independently of his future boss, Kissinger believed that China would respond positively to American overtures that returned this civilization to its rightful place as a great power living in a stable world community. If anything, the violence and deprivation of Communist rule created a powerful urge for this reversion to geopolitical normalcy. "We must encourage Communist China," Kissinger advised, "to play a role in a peaceful and progressive order in Asia, in which her own security would not be threatened and her legitimate interests would be represented." He included this recommendation in one of presidential candidate Nelson Rockefeller's major foreign policy addresses, delivered on May 1, 1968. The speech called for nurturing international openness, limiting U.S. military commitments, and expanding consensual relations with foreign societies. It also affirmed the importance of particular regional powers, especially China. "We gain nothing, and we prove nothing," Rockefeller announced, "by aiding or encouraging the self-isolation of so great a people. Instead, we should encourage contact and communication—for the good of us both."[27]

American overtures to China were almost inevitable in the 1970s. The escalation of the Vietnam War increased the importance of China as a regional power. Mao Zedong's government offered extensive support to the North Vietnamese forces fighting American soldiers in Southeast Asia; a settlement to the conflict would benefit from an accommodation between Beijing and Washington. China had growing incentive to match American peace feelers as the Vietnam War threatened to expand throughout the region and tensions exploded along its long, disputed border with the Soviet

Union. The two Communist giants entered a period of low-level warfare during the late 1960s, with direct military clashes that threatened to include nuclear weapons. The prospect of Sino-Soviet Armageddon motivated both regimes to improve relations with the United States. Like Washington, Beijing and Moscow had strong interests in limiting their military commitments and enlisting adversaries against common enemies. Nixon and Kissinger recognized these circumstances, as did most careful observers at the time.[28]

Kissinger's thinking was distinctive for integrating China into a systematic global strategy. Improved relations with Beijing were part of a fundamental structural shift from bipolar containment to polycentric federalism. Kissinger wrote in 1968 of building "triangular relationships between Moscow, Beijing, and Washington." This vision was about more than Vietnam and the future of Southeast Asia alone. It was part of Kissinger's consistent attempt to create avenues for American global influence and flexibility by integrating calibrated force with diverse negotiations. A triangular relationship would increase Washington's regional leverage in Asia, Europe, and other continents. It would acknowledge the limits on direct U.S. intervention, but it would also create opportunities for diplomacy. The United States would retreat from its Cold War assertion of global military dominance, and it would push forward as a preponderant political influence among both Communist and non-Communist states. "The chances of peace are increased," said Kissinger, "as we are able to develop policy options toward both Communist powers." Instead of isolating adversaries through containment, continual dialogue would emphasize "accommodation" for mutual benefits.[29]

In Kissinger's federalist framework the United States would stand above its new partners as *the* central diplomatic player around the globe, *the* worldwide mediator. Leaders in Washington would become the only figures with effective networks of influence throughout the major regions and among the major powers. They would be the transcendent statesmen for the indispensable global nation. This was far more than a Cold War vision; it appreciated the power and rapidity of political transformation, particularly in East Asia. Amidst what Kissinger identified as the weakening of large authority structures and the emergence of new local allegiances, the international system needed leaders who could supply an overarching vision to organize and coordinate diverse interests. International organizations and expert bureaucracies could not substitute. This was the role for the United States, and the president in particular, ensuring that state-to-state competition remained civilized—peaceful, stable, and respectful of cultural achievements. Only the White House had the resources and the reach to act effectively on this scale. Only Washington could manage a polycentric world without falling prey to tyranny or bankruptcy.

Basic Principles

Kissinger positioned the United States as a global manager and consensus builder in a hierarchical world. He rejected the imperialist impulse for a single state's dominance over a distant landscape and, at the other extreme, the assumed equality of all nations in an institution such as the United Nations General Assembly. Empire, as he knew from the history of modern Germany, overextended the resources of society and inspired resistance. Democracy, as he witnessed in Europe after the First World War, was prone to chaos, conflict, and weakness in the face of determined evildoers.[30] Kissinger sought to use military posturing, negotiations, and persuasion to support a hierarchy where the most powerful and "advanced" countries had the greatest international influence, followed by proportional gradations for less powerful and advanced nations. By definition, this vision placed the transatlantic community—with its industrialized economies, nuclear weapons, and "civilized" traditions—at the top of the global hierarchy and the United States at the apex. China, Japan, and the Soviet Union were also near the top. The countries of Africa and Latin America, with few exceptions, ranked close to the bottom of Kissinger's hierarchy.[31]

Racial and cultural prejudices contributed to this vision, as did an inheritance of colonial attitudes from Europe. The great powers of the nineteenth century were at the "center" of Kissinger's international system; their former colonial subjects remained "peripheral" to decision making. This judgment reflected the rough allocation of military and economic power, as well as perceived civilizational sophistication. Kissinger could admit China to his pantheon of great powers because he—like many others—recognized its deep, sophisticated cultural achievements, even if his familiarity with them was superficial. Chinese society had the wisdom and maturity to act as a responsible anchor for peace in a multipolar world. To Kissinger's eyes, most "Third World" societies lacked these qualities.[32]

Kissinger advocated the recognition of "basic principles" in this context.

He did not use the phrase to promote individual or human rights. Nor did he think in terms of international legal procedures. His basic principles consisted of a set of international rules to ensure the orderly functioning of hierarchy. They set standards for acceptable behavior, the protection of particular interests, and the management of disputes. They would, once established, civilize global affairs by building consensus around practice—lending the functioning of Kissinger's system widespread legitimacy. Federalism and hierarchy would "generate willing cooperation" as the presumed method for structuring the world; other paths, including Cold War containment, would now become unthinkable.[33]

Morality and justice mattered deeply to Kissinger, but not as a universal code for right and wrong. The world was too complex for that, especially in the 1970s. The choices confronting leaders did not conform to abstract ethical standards. Kissinger had witnessed the paralysis of the self-righteous in Weimar Germany, and he had participated in the prosecution of a world war that relied on inhumane actions, including frequent attacks on civilian populations, to defeat a threat to humanity as a whole. International justice required principles that allowed tough decisions about greater and lesser evils. "A country that demands moral perfection of itself as a test of its foreign policy," he warned, "will achieve neither perfection nor security."[34]

International ethics for Kissinger turned on the application of basic principles that minimized but did not eliminate injustice. This was the true art of statesmanship, as distinguished from the work of the philosopher. It was also the place where Kissinger believed that moderation born of learning and experience, rather than the impulses of youth, should define the terms of acceptable conduct. Human rights sounded alluring to the naïve ear, but they were too universal in their popular definition. Basic principles of cultural hierarchy appeared much more useful in preventing some of the worst threats to morality, especially nuclear war. They allowed space for diversity and differential power, and yet they created order out of international chaos.[35]

Kissinger's consistent emphasis on "principles of international conduct" reflected this basic judgment about ethics in an unethical world. His perspective emerged from his experiences as a German Jewish refugee and a Cold War intellectual. It reinforced the federalist vision for the international system that he formulated as a strategist. Most significantly, it opened new avenues for American foreign policy that recognized the limits of the nation's power and ideals, especially amidst the turmoil of the Vietnam War. Consensus on the allocation of authority among unequal states ensured greater stability and created space for a "burst of creativity" that did not risk global annihilation. Basic principles were necessary for liberation from Cold War stalemate and nuclear fear.[36]

To the surprise of those who did not take his scholarly writings seriously, Kissinger applied this vision to the negotiation of an agreement on basic principles with the Soviet Union in 1972. It pledged the signatories "to behave with restraint and with a maximum of creativity in bringing about a greater degree of stability and peace." The agreement laid out a "roadmap" for governing in an "age in which a cataclysm depends on the decisions of men." Along with the major nuclear arms control treaties of 1972 (SALT I and the ABM Treaty), the agreement on basic principles moved U.S.-Soviet relations away from Cold War containment and toward a broader concept of regional and global cooperation. This was the foundation for what Kissinger and others termed "détente."[37]

Kissinger's Global Geopolitics in Retrospect

Kissinger recognized the globalization of power, and he sought more than most of his contemporaries to formulate a foreign policy that accounted for this development and enhanced the power of the American state. He authored a federalist model for governance of the international system that included a core transatlantic community, polycentric decision making, and agreements on basic principles for state behavior. This model was the foundation for his major initiatives in the 1970s—especially the opening to China, détente with the Soviet Union, peace efforts in the Middle East, and the renegotiation of the alliance in Western Europe. In all of these areas Kissinger acted with determination—and sometime pigheaded stubbornness—to limit inherited Cold War commitments while also increasing regional leverage. He tried to turn globalization into a tool for more efficient and effective American leadership.

These initiatives were not entirely successful in the 1970s, especially within the regions Kissinger knew the least about: Africa, Southeast Asia, and Latin America. He frequently neglected crucial global topics, including finance, monetary affairs, and human rights. As was true of even the most prescient of his contemporaries, Kissinger's understanding of global change was not sufficiently global.

Understanding globalization, however, does not ensure mastery. Kissinger stands out in the historical record because he recognized many of the crucial shifts in the international system, he adjusted his thinking to account for these shifts, and he made policy along precisely these lines in the 1970s. He came the closest of anyone to managing his world. He was not a Metternichean holdover from the past. He was very much a man of his globalizing times.

Kissinger's successes and failures capture the policy difficulties of a globalizing era and also the continued primacy of state power. Kissinger retains his oracular status in the early twenty-first century because his ideas still have much to offer a new generation of strategists. In the shadow of the recent military conflicts in Iraq and Afghanistan, his global geopolitics are more relevant than ever before. Although he does not offer model plans for the future, his career reinforces the need for more serious policy planning.[38]

CHAPTER 11

Wrestling with Parity

The Nuclear Revolution Revisited

FRANCIS J. GAVIN

WHAT WOULD BE THE CONSEQUENCES OF, and the appropriate response to, nuclear parity between the Cold War superpowers, the Soviet
Union and the United States? American policymakers and strategists had
anticipated and worried about this development since the Soviet Union
detonated its first nuclear device on August 29, 1949. There had been
much debate during the 1950s and 1960s about when the moment of parity would arrive, but by the 1970s its existence was accepted. The effects
and reaction to this new condition, however, were widely disputed.

Intense debate over the meaning and consequences of, and the appropriate response to, nuclear parity with the Soviet Union dominated
American strategic discourse throughout the 1970s. The answers to these
questions drove some of the most important foreign and military policies
of the decade, from arms control negotiations to alliance relations to
multibillion-dollar weapon systems deployments. The ensuing, increasingly bitter disputes over these issues helped shape and in many ways cal-
cify domestic political divisions in the United States, bringing a final end
to the remnants of the so-called Cold War consensus that had not already
been sacrificed in the quagmire of Southeast Asia.

In retrospect these disagreements seem esoteric and even bizarre. Dig
a little deeper, however, and it becomes clear that these debates had important meanings and consequences that went beyond nuclear strategy.
Arguments that appeared to focus on obscure technical terms such as
"throw weight" and "single shot kill probability" often masked divergent

views of international relations and the place of the United States in global politics during the Cold War. In other words, competing visions for America's role in the world, differing interpretations of the nature of the international system, and contested metrics for what constituted power and influence in world affairs were at stake in the fight over nuclear parity.

This essay identifies three different responses to nuclear parity that emerged during the 1970s. The best-known school of thought accepted and even embraced nuclear parity. Mutual vulnerability, it was argued, prevented war and ensured "strategic stability" by guaranteeing that a first strike by either side would be suicidal, as it risked a devastating response from the surviving forces of the adversary. While variations of this worldview existed, it made achieving arms control with the Soviet Union a priority and linked the military balance to what proponents saw as a promising "détente" between the superpowers. The second response rejected the inevitability and desirability of parity and doubted the concept of strategic stability. Critics from what might be called the "nuclear superiority" school ranged from those who believed that parity with the Soviets undermined the ability of the United States to fulfill its commitments to defend its allies, to those who thought a nuclear war could be fought and won. As a whole, this group was uncomfortable with the moral and strategic consequences of parity and détente with the Soviet Union. Proponents of these two worldviews engaged in a passionate and often bitter political struggle over the future of U.S. nuclear doctrine, military procurement, and grand strategy.

The third response—or set of responses—could not have been more different. From a variety of sources and in a variety of ways, nuclear weapons came to be seen in many circles as far less relevant to international politics than either the mutual vulnerability–strategic stability or nuclear superiority school contended. These responses ran the gamut from nuclear abolitionism to a focus on what we now call soft power, and had as many differences as similarities. All of these views, however, were connected by the belief that nuclear deterrence was not the cornerstone of international relations, and that the great shifts in world politics were driven by fundamental changes that went beyond the nuclear revolution. While this set of ideas was diffuse and had no obvious policy champion during the 1970s, these nascent ideas and forces would come to define the post–Cold War era of globalization we live in today.

A Church Divided: Mutual Vulnerability
versus Nuclear Superiority

From the first atomic detonation, strategists wrestled with the implications that nuclear weapons presented for statecraft and military competition. Among these analysts within the United States there were many disagreements, but in essence the debate revolved around a basic question: Did these fearsome weapons have any purpose other than to deter an adversary from attacking you (or your friends)? While more traditional thinkers accepted the profound implications of nuclear weapons, they did not believe it possible or wise to preclude the possibility that they might be used, and sought to develop strategies that could help the United States prevail, or at least limit the damage, should deterrence fail. Naturally this entailed having more and better weapons than the Soviet Union. A different group—one that came to be seen as more intellectually sophisticated and influential in policy circles—argued vehemently that nuclear weapons had no utility beyond deterring others from a nuclear attack, and that strategies that sought to accomplish more were foolish and often dangerous. Weapons and strategies that provided for stability, not superiority, were the goal.

These debates and discussions—which began in universities and think tanks such as RAND in the 1950s before moving to more public forums in the 1960s and 1970s—are among the best chronicled in modern strategic and political history.[1] Most accounts portray a remarkable and rare time when wise and important policymakers implemented the ideas produced by cutting-edge intellectuals. There is reason to question, however, how good these ideas were and, more important, how influential they were in the making of policy.[2] And while advocates on each side spoke from the platform of "social science," assuming their ideas were generalizable over space and time, neither the nuclear superiority–damage limitation nor the mutual vulnerability–strategic stability view found much acceptance outside the United States. Another unusual feature was that the mutual vulnerability–strategic stability school appeared to triumph in the intellectual debate—and make real headway in policy circles—at the moment of greatest American nuclear strength. Despite constant public fears during the first two decades of the atomic era that Russia would catch up with and surpass America in the number of weapons, bombers, or missiles, by the time of the greatest nuclear tension—Berlin and the Cuban Missile Crisis of 1961–62—the United States, by many measures, possessed significant nuclear superiority.

What did it actually mean to have nuclear superiority, however, and what if anything did it translate into in world politics? The question exposed the key divide within the strategy community in the United States. Many American (as opposed to Soviet) veterans of the superpower standoff concluded that U.S. nuclear superiority had little or no influence on the outcome and by itself was dangerous. Looking back on the crisis years, former national security adviser McGeorge Bundy claimed: "It is sometimes argued that in the past nuclear superiority . . . has had a decisive influence on events. I find this a very doubtful proposition."[3] One of the most important participants in the nuclear standoff, Secretary of Defense Robert McNamara, advocated a U.S. defense policy in which mutual vulnerability and strategic stability were the most important ends of American grand strategy. This led to cancellations of nuclear delivery systems and, after years of increases, a ceiling on strategic nuclear delivery vehicles. Combined with a massive surge in Soviet strategic nuclear weapons—an increase largely unforeseen by analysts and U.S. intelligence agencies—the nuclear superiority of the early 1960s gave way to parity by the end of the decade.

Oddly, this dramatic shift in the balance of military power was not lamented. In fact, within mainstream policy circles there was a strong consensus that parity was inevitable, that nuclear superiority was useless, and that mutual vulnerability should be embraced. Writing in early 1971, Paul Warnke and Leslie Gelb summed up the conventional wisdom: "The United States and the Soviet Union are now in a constellation of parity, both sides possessing a secure second strike capability. . . . As long as neither pursues an unreachable quest for 'superiority' in the form of knockout first strike capability, there will be continued strategic stability."[4] In what must have been a first in the history of great power politics, the analysts of the leading adversary welcomed the passing of its quantitative advantage, secure in the belief that both sides would see the benefits of nuclear equality.

And why would either side reach for this superiority? To the mutual vulnerability–strategic stability school, the logic of parity was less a policy choice than an inescapable fact of international political life. This attitude is borne out in the title of a chapter—"MAD Is a Fact, Not a Policy"—in

Robert Jervis's influential book on the nuclear revolution.[5] Any attempt to return to a mythical world of superiority was pointless. As William Foster, who directed the Arms Control and Disarmament Agency throughout the 1960s, asserted, "Whatever index of strategic nuclear power is used, it would seem rather fruitless for either side to claim superiority, when, no matter what it does, the other side will still have the capability to inflict unacceptable damage."[6]

This view—that mutual vulnerability was a fact of life that could not be overcome—exposed a troubling paradox. If seeking superiority was "fruitless," it would seem that there was little anyone could or should do to affect the nuclear balance. Wouldn't the best idea be to let nature—in this case the laws of international politics—take its course? This was not, however, the policy recommendation of the mutual vulnerability–strategic stability school. While the efforts to overcome mutual vulnerability were bound to fail, they were also destabilizing. As Alton Frye remarked: "One of those realities is that the attempt by either side to alter the stability of deterrence by overcoming its own vulnerabilities is bound to be dangerous. A unilateral quest for escape from the paradox of deterrence is a reckless and counterproductive gesture calculated only to jeopardize both countries' security."[7] In other words, strategic behavior that once was considered normal and expected—trying to amass more usable firepower than your enemy—was now to be avoided at all costs.

This paradox got to the heart of how proponents of the mutual vulnerability–strategic stability school understood the world. To their mind, international politics was driven by what strategists called the security dilemma. In a dangerous world, states did what they could to protect themselves. Adversaries, however, could easily misunderstand these defensive measures. A strategy or weapon system deployed to protect a country could be seen as aggressive and offense-oriented by a nervous neighbor. The threatened nation would undertake its own defensive countermeasures that could be similarly misperceived. In other words, in a world where states did not trust one another, defensive efforts could spiral into an unwanted arms race or even a conflict.[8]

This dangerous dynamic was heightened in a world of nuclear weapons, where the side that launched weapons first would have tremendous advantages, particularly if it was not vulnerable to a devastating second strike. Things could not be allowed to develop "naturally"; instead policymakers had to intervene to retard or halt the security dilemma process. Only mutually negotiated arms control that maintained each side's vulnerability could slow the arms race and reduce instability. The mutual vulnerability school's recommendations were a strange brew of realism and international law, two approaches not typically associated with each other. The world was a scary, unpredictable place, but instead of nations' seeking as much military power as possible, self-restraint and treaties could make the world safer.

This view of parity and mutual vulnerability engendered a fierce resistance from a vocal and influential minority. For them the idea of self-restraint in an uncertain world was dangerous and even bizarre. Targeting civilian populations seemed immoral. Fred Ikle charged that the "jargon of American strategic analysis works like a narcotic. . . . [I]t blinds us to the fact that our method of preventing nuclear war rests on a form of warfare universally condemned since the Dark Ages—the mass killing of hostages."[9] The notion of constructing a strategy that had no concept of victory—only deterrence—seemed beyond the pale for many who viewed nuclear weapons through a traditional political-military lens. Critics such as Paul Nitze understood the arguments about parity but were dismayed by the willingness of the mutual vulnerability crowd to embrace arms control as an end in itself, naïve to the possibility that the Soviets would exploit any advantage. "There is every prospect," declared Nitze, "that under the terms of the SALT agreements the Soviet Union will continue to pursue a nuclear superiority that is not merely quantitative but designed to produce a theoretical war-winning capability."[10] Even if the agreements were fair, could the Soviets be trusted to keep their word?

The sharpest criticism came from those who believed that the Soviet Union simply did not buy the logic behind mutual vulnerability and strategic stability. Richard Pipes argued that "there is something innately destabilizing in the very fact that we consider nuclear war unfeasible and suicidal for both [sides], and our chief adversary views it as feasible and winnable for himself."[11] Some went even further, arguing that arms control gave away the United States' greatest advantage: a powerful economy and a strong technological base that would allow it to win an arms race with the Soviets. As Colin Gray put it: "The instability arguments that are leveled against those who urge an American response (functionally) in kind are somewhat fragile. . . . [T]here is good reason to believe that the Soviet Union would be profoundly discouraged by the prospect of having to wage an arms competition against an American opponent no longer severely inhibited by its long-familiar stability theory."[12]

Did the nuclear superiority–damage limitation school offer ideas and policies that were any more logical and appealing? The ideas of the more extreme critics of mutual vulnerability—those who argued that one had to think about fighting and winning a nuclear war—seemed unsound and dangerous. And while it is easy to assume in retrospect that arms racing exposed weaknesses in the Soviet system, it was hard for anyone looking at the American economic performance during the 1970s to think that the United States had the wherewithal to excel in such a competition. The arguments that superiority was needed to "limit damage" in any nuclear exchange were hardly more convincing. Was it wise or even rational for the United States to spend hundreds of billions of dollars on complex, exotic nuclear systems to reduce, at best, American fatalities in a nuclear exchange to, say, 30 to 40 million from over 100 million?

The nuclear superiority arguments were driven, one suspects, more by political than technical arguments; namely, by a deep unease with the so-called détente that was associated with an acceptance of parity and support for arms control. Was the Soviet Union a status quo, responsible power willing to obey international law and adopt Western norms? Or was it an aggressive, authoritarian state interested in world revolution and willing to engage in nuclear diplomacy simply to dupe naïve American policy elites? And even if the Soviets were responsible and interested in maintaining the status quo, was the stability of détente, parity, and arms control worth ratifying a division of the world, and in particular Europe, between free and unfree? Did the United States—to many an exceptional nation and a beacon to the world—have a moral if not a military responsibility to expand freedom and fight tyranny? These arguments found mixed domestic support within the United States. Polls showed backing for both arms control and increases in military expenditures, support for détente and yet unease with Soviet behavior on the world stage. Members of the nuclear superiority school displayed similar inconsistency and even incoherence, as if some of the more important advocates were unsure what to believe. Policymakers such as Henry Kissinger and Paul Nitze switched sides more than once.

Was it possible that the mutual vulnerability–strategic stability crowd underestimated the political if not military utility of nuclear superiority?[13]

In the years following the showdown, American participants in the Cuban Missile Crisis argued that it was the vast conventional edge and not the nuclear superiority of the United States that determined the outcome.[14] If true, shouldn't the same logic have applied to West Berlin, where NATO and in particular the United States resisted Soviet ultimatums and pressure despite an insurmountable inferiority in conventional forces? There is at least some reason to think that nuclear superiority played some role.[15] Even if there was no *military* utility in nuclear superiority, there was certainly a *political* and even a *psychological* advantage. President Richard Nixon, for example, lamented the loss of nuclear superiority and its perceived geopolitical advantages, even as his official doctrine accepted parity and his administration pursued strategic arms control.[16] And while nuclear equality may have been enough to ensure that an adversary would not attack you, was it enough to guarantee that the same adversary would not attack your friends? In other words, could the United States "extend" deterrence to its friends and allies in an age of parity?

This pointed to a second flaw. The mutual vulnerability–strategic stability school, in its obsession with the U.S.-Soviet strategic arms rivalry, paid very little attention to nuclear dynamics outside of the superpower rivalry. Their focus was on vertical, not horizontal, arms races, and so they tended to overlook the arguably bigger long-term threat to global security, the increasing pressures of nuclear proliferation. This lack of awareness manifested itself in two ways. First, by accepting parity they risked "decoupling" the nuclear forces of the United States from the security of its nonnuclear allies, tempting them toward acquiring their own atomic weapons. In retrospect it is striking how some members of the mutual vulnerability–strategic stability school failed to appreciate the extent to which their positions—on issues ranging from arms control to no first use, specific programs such as the neutron bomb, Pershing II missiles, and even missile defense—ignored or discounted the security concerns of non-nuclear allies such as West Germany and Japan.

There was an even larger proliferation issue. Advocates of strategic stability rarely realized that their arguments endorsed the virtues of nuclear weapons. If nuclear weapons stabilized relations between the superpowers and prevented war, why wouldn't they do the same thing for other countries and regions? Is it any wonder that while the 1970s witnessed the greatest strides in vertical arms control, proliferation worries increased. Israel, India, Pakistan, South Africa, Brazil, Argentina, Taiwan, and South

Korea, among others, flirted and in some cases moved forward with nuclear weapons programs.

The third weakness in the mutual vulnerability–strategic stability school involved its understanding of what factors drove international politics. For most strategists the bipolar military competition was the ultimate example of how an uncontrolled arms race, driven by the security dilemma, could lead to instability and, without arms control, potentially to war. If the nuclear arms race could be controlled or even suspended, international politics would stabilize and the threat of global conflagration would dissipate.

Arguing that the Cold War was a product of the security dilemma, however, drained it of its political and even ideological or moral content. Would the United States and Soviet Union have avoided bitter disputes over important matters, such as the military and political status of Germany, in a world of mutual vulnerability and arms control? Would there have been no ideological competition? By focusing almost exclusively on the interaction between rival military factors, the mutual vulnerability framework tended to underplay the importance of geopolitics, ideology, and diplomacy. In fact it is difficult to find a clear-cut case of a modern war unambiguously caused by the security dilemma or an arms race.[17]

Arguably the most authoritative study on the question—a thousand-plus-page top secret scholarly study commissioned by Secretary of Defense James Schlesinger—revealed that the military competition between the superpowers was not driven by the security dilemma: "The facts will not support the proposition that either the Soviet Union or the United States developed strategic forces only in direct immediate access to each other."[18] There were other, more rational reasons for each side to increase its numbers of nuclear weapons: "Surges in strategic force deployments sprang from interaction between a scientific community producing basic technical developments and political leaders affected by immediate crisis events."[19] Furthermore, acquiring and deploying arms often acted as an effective way to signal unhappiness or aggressive intent between adversaries. By limiting this signaling device, arms control could increase the possibilities of misperception.

Looking back at the pages of the leading American academic and policy journals during the 1970s, one would think that these debates surrounding nuclear arms control and strategy were the pivot on which the future of world politics turned. In fact we now know that global order during the 1970s was driven by complex and fundamental changes in international relations that may have included but certainly went well beyond the choices of either mutual vulnerability or nuclear superiority. Were there also reactions to nuclear parity that went beyond the narrow perspective of the leading strategists?

Beyond Deterrence?

A third response to the nuclear equality between the Soviet Union and the United States emerged from diverse sources and with few champions within the strategic studies community. In fact to label it a "response" to parity, similar to mutual vulnerability and nuclear superiority, is misleading. It is perhaps better described as a sensibility, animated by the notion that that there was something not quite right about the debate within the strategy community. In other words, the rift in the strategy "church" seemed somewhat unreal and disconnected from how the world actually worked. The four strands of this sensibility—nuclear abolitionism, the rise of a nuclear taboo, the notion that major war was obsolete, and the preference for other, "softer" forms of power—shared a common trait: a skepticism that nuclear deterrence and arms control would be the cornerstone of international politics in the decades to follow. Often disregarded by contemporaries during the 1970s, these responses to the emergence of nuclear parity may, in the long run, have provided a better understanding of the profound transformation of international relations in the decades since then than the more traditional insights of the strategy community.

Nuclear Abolitionism

The nuclear age did not just produce weapons; it also produced the world's largest grassroots transnational peace movement, fostered by nongovernmental organizations. While strategies differed among the myriad groups, they shared a common belief—that eliminating nuclear weapons from the planet, not strengthening nuclear deterrence, was the key to global peace and stability.

Because their views were so much at odds with the thinking of most strategists and mainstream scholars, the influence of abolitionism on nuclear history has been understated. Worldwide pressure from nuclear abolitionists played a key role in any number of nuclear and arms control policies, from the crafting of the partial test-ban treaty to the decision not to deploy the "neutron bomb." It is important to note, however, that the view that there was something problematic about basing world peace on nuclear deterrence was not just held by so-called "peaceniks." Unlike some of their national security staff and cabinet officers, most presidents during the postwar period (with the possible exception of Nixon) felt a deep ambivalence about nuclear weapons. During the 1976 presidential campaign Jimmy Carter "proclaimed a goal of abolishing nuclear weapons, albeit one step at a time," and as early as January 26, 1977, he informed Brezhnev, "My solid objective is to liquidate nuclear weapons completely."[20] More surprisingly (and controversially), there may have been abolitionist tendencies in Carter's successor, Ronald Reagan. According to Paul Lettow, "Reagan's nuclear abolitionism, which grew out of his deeply rooted personal beliefs and religious views, resulted in some of the most significant—and least understood—aspects of his presidency." Even Reagan's call for arms increases were aimed at a belief, which he had enunciated since the early 1960s, that "the aim of his arms buildup was to attain deep cuts in nuclear weapons."[21]

Nuclear abolitionism found broader public support than many other peace movements because of a widespread abhorrence at the effects of atomic weapons and the sense that nuclear deterrence was a problematic solution at best. The absurdity of mutual vulnerability—that idea that security depended on leaving oneself open to destruction—was matched by skepticism about spending tens of billions of dollars on additional weapons systems which would only improve security at the margins, if at all. The emergence of parity highlighted long-standing fears and concerns about the nuclear age; if these weapons no longer had any conceivable political or military use, perhaps it was time to purge them from the planet.

Nuclear Taboo

A related critique of the mutual vulnerability and nuclear superiority responses to parity is that deterrence cannot by itself explain the nonuse of nuclear weapons after they were first deployed by the United States against Japan in August 1945. For one thing, the United States did not use nuclear weapons against its adversaries after the Second World War. It possessed a nuclear monopoly over the Soviets during the Berlin blockade but abstained. It enjoyed a nuclear superiority throughout the 1950s and into the early 1960s, an edge that by some estimates gave the United

States a first-strike capability. And after the attack on Japan, neither the United States nor any other nuclear power used its weapons against non-nuclear adversaries. This was not due to a lack of opportunity or support for such actions at the highest policy levels. During the bloody Korean War, talk on the American side of using nuclear weapons produced concern and even outrage at home and abroad, and the 1953 armistice was signed before such threats could be carried out. During the Vietnam War the United States at times considered but eventually turned away from using nuclear weapons, despite the military advantages it could have brought.

Nina Tannenwald has argued that moral repugnance among the wider public at the thought of using nuclear weapons restrained policymakers in ways that supplemented and even went beyond deterrence.[22] This emerging taboo against using nuclear weapons ever again arguably crystallized in the age of nuclear parity, when the taboo and the notion of mutual vulnerability came together to make nuclear use among "civilized" nations inconceivable. Parity only highlighted the absurdity of any responsible leader advocating the use of these weapons.

Obsolescence of War

War, according to the scholar John Mueller, is nothing more than an idea.[23] And like all ideas it is created in a cultural, political, and sociological context that can change over time. During the second part of the twentieth century, the idea of great power war was increasingly seen in Europe and other parts of the developed world as obsolete. Similar to dueling and slavery a century earlier, an institution or practice that was viewed as beneficial and important increasingly came to be seen as anachronistic and even repulsive. In this explanation it was not nuclear weapons that kept the peace; the peace would have been maintained even in a non-nuclear world. Furthermore, the status and prestige previously accorded to war were now granted to economic success.

According to this analysis, the endless divisive debates over the minutiae of arms control negotiations were a waste of time. Neither the United States nor the Soviet Union had the stomach for a conventional war with each other, to say nothing of a nuclear war. While these ideological rivals might trade insults and fight limited proxy wars in the developed world, by the 1970s there was almost no conceivable scenario that might lead to a nuclear exchange. There was simply nothing to be gained from great power war; the real action in international politics was now elsewhere.

The Rise of Globalization

The fourth response was the most inchoate and least noticed, and it received the least policy exposure during the 1970s. In the long run, however, it had the most significant consequences for U.S. global policy. Coinciding with the emergence of parity—a condition that rendered nuclear weapons militarily useless and politically impotent—was the rise of a new international system, with new actors, new norms, and, most important, new metrics for power. According to this view of the world, ideas, innovation, technology, and culture were more likely to shape world politics than arms control agreements or the nuclear balance between the superpowers. What happened in Wall Street, Hollywood, Silicon Valley, or even Napa Valley was as important, and sometimes even more important to America's position in the world than the decisions made in Washington, D.C. What Joseph Nye termed "soft power," in other words, was more likely than nuclear armaments to determine the outcome of the struggle with the Soviet Union.

The increasing reach of global capital markets, the spread of popular culture via Hollywood, the popularity of consumer-oriented capitalism, and in particular the influence of innovation and new technology were just some of the "soft power" phenomena that transformed the world economy after the 1970s, and with it the political landscape. These phenomena, more than nuclear weapons, were game changers for states looking to improve their global political position. Nations that had flirted with nuclear weapons in the past—such as Taiwan, South Korea, Brazil, Argentina, and Indonesia—instead focused on spurring economic growth and integrating into the world economy. Under the new metrics of power, demonstrating the economic dynamism of a "Pacific Tiger," for example, counted for a lot more than simply possessing a weapon that translated into little usable power on the world stage.

The much-anticipated arrival of nuclear parity between the United States and the Soviet Union during the 1970s unleashed a furious and often vitriolic debate over American grand strategy during the Cold War. The battlegrounds for these fights seem esoteric and strange from our current perspective, often dominated by technical debates over specific weapon systems. Should the Soviet Backfire fighter-bomber be classified as a tactical or strategic weapon? Were cruise missiles fired from airplanes qualitatively different from those fired from the sea or ground? Was the U.S. government and its command and control facilities vulnerable to a decapitating first strike? Should hundreds of billions of dollars be spent on strategic nuclear weapons, not to achieve superiority but to enhance the stability of deterrence? Would strategic defenses undermine this stability even if there were some question whether they would work? Perhaps the most fascinating aspect of this period is that so much of the time and intellectual energy of some of our most esteemed policymakers and strategists were consumed by these questions.

It is not even clear that these were the most important nuclear policy issues at the time. As nuclear parity was achieved and then institutionalized by a remarkable series of arms control treaties between the United States and the Soviet Union during the 1970s, the decade witnessed increasing pressure on the global nonproliferation regime. India detonated a "peaceful" nuclear device, and Pakistan responded with a crash program that also spawned A. Q. Khan's black market in nuclear technology. Iran and Iraq both flirted with weapons programs, as did many others, including Argentina, Brazil, South and North Korea, and Taiwan. It is not that this issue, which dominates our current policy landscape, received no policy or scholarly attention at all. It is striking, however, how much more attention was paid to strategic arms issues involving the United States and the Soviet Union.

What, then, are we to make of the reactions to nuclear parity? These debates are less interesting for their assessments of specific questions than for what they say about how leading thinkers and statesmen thought about the way the world worked and what America's role in it should be. The mutual vulnerability school argued that the nuclear revolution had fundamentally altered the laws of great power politics and statecraft. Unlike in the past, the state could no longer depend on its most powerful and innovative weapons to pursue its goals in the world. The new landscape of international relations demanded a new response: self-restraint, respect for the interests of your adversaries, and devotion to international treaties. This viewpoint sought to freeze the status quo, both militarily and politically, in order to avoid the risks of nuclear war. Most radically, the stability of the new system demanded accepting and even embracing the possibility of catastrophic destruction. This set of ideas became so enmeshed in the conventional wisdom that it is easy to forget how novel and counterintuitive this framework for understanding world politics actually was.

The superiority school did not dispute that the nuclear revolution had changed international politics in important ways. In its proponents' view, however, this did not include suspending the laws of world politics or what many saw as a moral, political, and ideological duty to challenge the Soviet Union. While many intellectuals dismissed this view, there is a strong argument to be made that policymakers on both sides of the rivalry never abandoned their search for nuclear primacy.

Who was right? This question turns upon what brought about the peaceful end of the Cold War, largely to the advantage of the United States. The mutual vulnerability school argues that the stability of deterrence allowed Gorbachev's Soviet Union to transform itself without fear that the United States could militarily exploit the situation. The nuclear superiority school argues that the arms race exposed weaknesses in the Soviet economy that eventually bankrupted the Soviet empire. Both views have some merit, but both may have missed the larger, more profound changes in international politics that have marked the decades since the 1970s.

The third set of responses—the idea that tectonic forces beyond nuclear deterrence were shaping the global order—may be the most compelling. Consider behavior in the nuclear field. First, despite the pressures on the nonproliferation regime during the 1970s, what is striking is how few eligible states developed nuclear weapons. And those that did eschewed either local nuclear superiority or even secure second-strike strategies. Several embraced minimal deterrence, believing that simply possessing a few nuclear weapons would be enough to keep their adversaries from attacking. Even China and India, which could build far larger and more sophisticated nuclear forces if they chose to, maintain relatively small capabilities and have not been drawn into either regional nuclear arms races or a nuclear arms race with the United States. Reflect upon how strategists from the 1970s would view the recent embrace by distinguished policymakers of nuclear abolitionism—an idea that was considered on the fringe in polite mutual vulnerability and nuclear superiority circles.[24]

Understanding the responses to nuclear parity within the United States during the 1970s is important for more than just academic purposes. Advocates and disciples of both the mutual vulnerability and nuclear superiority schools continue to play a large, even dominating role in recent debates over U.S. global policy. It is important to recognize the influence the debates over parity and deterrence had on their grand strategies and worldviews. It is even more important to recognize that there were other frameworks within which to analyze the emergence of parity, views that may have been more effective at explaining the great changes that began to transform global politics during the 1970s and shape our world today.

CHAPTER 12

Containing Globalism

The United States and the Developing World in the 1970s

MARK ATWOOD LAWRENCE

BY THE FALL OF 1971 Senator Frank Church had run out of patience. Just a decade earlier the Idaho Democrat and other liberals had confidently declared a new era in American foreign policy, vowing that the United States would pour energy and resources into helping the poor nations of Asia, Africa, and Latin America down the path to political and economic development. Doing so, the liberals had declared, would enable the United States to realize the moral benefits of helping people in need as well as the more tangible advantage of winning partners in the pursuit of American objectives around the world. But in practice, Church complained, good intentions and the expenditure of vast resources had yielded little. "We not only failed to accomplish what we set out to accomplish ten years ago," he asserted in a speech. "We have been thrown for losses across the board." The poor had only grown poorer throughout the developing world, he lamented, and authoritarianism, not democracy, was on the march almost everywhere.[1]

Few Americans disagreed with Church's assessment. The era of liberal ambition was decidedly over. Indeed American optimism about development and democratization in poor nations had been crumbling ever since the political coalition that sustained the reformist agenda had started to weaken in the mid-1960s. But what should replace the modernizing vision at the core of American policymaking toward Asia, Africa, and Latin America? The question proved enormously challenging for the United States during the 1970s, a decade of extraordinary tumult throughout the regions that contemporaries often lumped together, with troubling inat-

205

tention to important variations, as the "less developed," "developing," or "third" world.

Part of the difficulty of setting a new course stemmed from the bitter divisions that ran through the U.S. electorate as a consequence of the Vietnam War. For some Americans the war taught the necessity of avoiding activism of any sort in the Third World; for others the lesson was to act with redoubled boldness. Events in the international arena compounded the uncertainty. The reordering of relations among the great powers—military parity between the United States and the Soviet Union, the institutionalization of East-West détente, and the emergence of China as a participant in the international system—carried ambiguous implications. Some officials believed that these trends, which suggested a more harmonious international order, diminished the urgency of containing Communist expansion in the developing world. Others, impressed by the spread of Marxist agendas in Africa and worried by the decline of U.S. power as a consequence of the lost war in Vietnam, believed precisely the opposite.

Another problem for U.S. leaders was the declining autonomy of the United States in international affairs—a consequence of trends now loosely grouped under the heading "globalization."[2] Policymakers had only a rough understanding of the long-term process at work, but they were keenly aware of its specific manifestations. The collapse of the global monetary system and the emergence of Japan and Western Europe as major centers of economic might lessened America's power to set the international agenda and to devote resources to problems in the developing world, while the spread of multinational companies undercut the ability of nation-states to control economic interactions. Meanwhile, the United States, like other nations, faced challenges from newly assertive movements and organizations that operated outside—or, to put it differently, both above and below—the accustomed sphere of state-to-state interactions.

At the supranational level, bodies as diverse as the Organization of American States, the Organization of Petroleum Exporting Countries, and the United Nations General Assembly exerted growing influence.[3] At the subnational level, growing interconnectedness made possible by new communications technologies facilitated the flow of ideas across national borders in a manner that chipped away at American prestige and constrained choices open to U.S. leaders. The emergence of a transnational network of protest movements during the Vietnam War suggested the growing potential for nongovernmental groups to exercise influence in the geopolitical arena.[4] During the 1970s an even more potent coalition of groups gathered under the banner of human rights and achieved remarkable sway over American policymaking and the international agenda more generally. Even as the era of the Westphalian nation-state reached its apotheosis with the final flurry of decolonization during the 1970s, nongovernmental actors gained remarkable new power to set international norms and shape the diplomatic agenda. Washington's ability to act boldly was increasingly constrained at precisely the moment when its global influence seemed most threatened.

As they struggled to make sense of these transformations and cope with the consequences, U.S. policymakers crafted no fewer than three approaches to the developing world. The twelve years between Richard Nixon's and Ronald Reagan's inaugurations witnessed dramatic shifts from the cynical *Realpolitik* of Henry Kissinger to the idiosyncratic idealism of Jimmy Carter to Reagan's utopian hawkishness, a pattern that makes the 1970s perhaps the most erratic decade in the history of American foreign policy. But beneath the spectacular shifts in goals, assumptions, and style lay a basic continuity. Each of the three policy regimes that prevailed from 1969 to 1980 represented an attempt to shore up U.S. power and reassert American global leadership amid an international landscape undergoing profound transformation. In contrasting ways, leaders sought to contain—either by blunting or mastering—the trends that were eroding American influence. The first two approaches to the developing world—those crafted by Kissinger and Carter—collapsed within a short time. Only the third, conceived under Reagan's leadership, proved durable, if not exactly successful in resolving problems confronted by developing nations. The difference between the first two approaches and the third lay fundamentally in the degree of success U.S. leaders enjoyed in harmonizing the pursuit of the Cold War with the emerging imperatives of globalization.

Nixon, Kissinger, and the Quest for Stability in the Third World

As they took office in 1969, Nixon and Kissinger declared the start of a new moment in history. "The postwar period in international relations has ended," asserted an administration report to Congress. "We are in a transitional period of international politics in which the familiar structures of power are eroding."[5] In response the two men promised bold departures in relations among the great world powers. With respect to developing nations, however, they had notably limited ambitions. In part their attitude rested on the belief that liberals had badly oversold their developmental agenda during the 1960s. Too often in the past, the United States had "pursued the illusion that we alone could re-make continents," Nixon asserted in a 1969 speech. "Well," he declared, "experience has taught us better."[6] More fundamentally, Nixon and Kissinger's attitude stemmed from a conviction that the global periphery had little connection to their highest priorities, above all the establishment of a new system of consultation and balance among the mightiest nations. Nixon claimed that Latin America was at least fifty years away from mattering in international affairs, while Africa was at least five hundred.[7] Kissinger similarly wrote off the global South. "Nothing of importance can come from the South," he proclaimed in 1969. "The axis of history starts in Moscow, goes to Bonn, crosses over to Washington, and then goes to Tokyo."[8]

The developing world was significant for Nixon and Kissinger only to the extent that turmoil there might complicate the pursuit of their core geopolitical agenda. Two possibilities haunted them. First, they feared that challenges in Africa, Latin America, or South or Southeast Asia might arouse domestic opinion in ways that would limit their freedom of maneuver internationally or imperil Nixon's reelection. They had seen domestic criticism of the Vietnam War stymie the Johnson administration, and they were determined to avoid such a fate. Second, Nixon and Kissinger worried that instability on what they regarded as the periphery would weaken American credibility by inviting expansion of Soviet, Chinese, or Cuban influence. At a delicate moment when the United States was fundamentally renegotiating its place in the global order, Nixon and Kissinger believed it was crucial to avoid losses of face anywhere in the world.

Their goal, then, was to build stability where it was lacking and bolster it where it was threatened. In Southeast Asia and the Middle East—the two most troublesome parts of the developing world for the administration—Nixon and Kissinger were guided above all by a desire to guard against losses of American prestige. Numerous considerations had, of course, driven the United States to deepen its commitment in Vietnam over the years, but in the Nixon period, only anxieties about international and domestic credibility kept the United States fighting for "peace with honor." In the Middle East more tangible interests were at stake, not least American aspirations to limit proliferation of nuclear weapons and to maintain the flow of oil. More than anything else, though, Nixon and Kissinger worried that turmoil would invite Soviet meddling in a part of the world where American prestige was heavily engaged. Revealingly, the 1973 Yom Kippur War reached its most dangerous moment when the Nixon administration ordered a worldwide nuclear alert in response to Moscow's suggestion that Soviet forces might intervene to enforce a cease-fire.

Nixon and Kissinger's behavior elsewhere was even more indicative of their underlying obsession with stability. To be sure, the two men were aware of profound shifts in the global order that tended to render Cold War power politics less central to the long-term geopolitical agenda. A comprehensive statement of the administration's foreign policy objectives published in 1971 presciently acknowledged "a shrinking globe and expanding interdependence" and noted the need for a "new dimension of international cooperation."[9] Yet these observations did not guide the administration's actions. When Nixon and Kissinger acceded to the will of increasingly powerful international institutions, they did so not because of their sense of a shifting global order but because they wished to avoid counterproductive diplomatic standoffs they knew they could not win. Such was the case, for example, when the administration conceded to demands within the Organization of American States (OAS) to abolish multilateral trade sanctions against Cuba and pressure within the UN General Assembly to complete negotiations for the return of the Panama Canal to Panamanian sovereignty. More generally, and whenever possible, the Nixon administration sought to limit the impact of new participants in global affairs, whether at the international or subnational level, by bolstering the authority and legitimacy of national governments willing to cooperate closely with the United States. Nixon and Kissinger, that is, grudgingly bowed to transnational forces when they saw no other choice but generally sought to buttress a world order rooted in the primacy and inviolability of territorially bounded nation-states.

Out of this underlying predisposition emerged a characteristic pattern of American behavior during the Nixon years: the formation or intensification of close partnerships with regional powers, which in practice often meant reliance on authoritarian governments. There was, of course, nothing entirely novel in this approach. American leaders had been installing and propping up reliable nondemocratic leaders for many decades, and the flurry of U.S. support for right-wing coups during the heyday of decolonization in the 1960s and 1970s clearly began during Lyndon Johnson's presidency. In only one respect did the Nixon administration break new ground. Unburdened by the grand liberal ambitions to which the Democratic Party had committed itself during the 1960s, the Republicans were far more willing than their predecessors to acknowledge the shift away from a primary concern with democratization and development. Whereas the Johnson administration had frequently agonized over the subordination of liberal aspirations to geopolitical stability, Nixon forthrightly prioritized maintaining the status quo on what he regarded as the global periphery. Perhaps the most illuminating expression of this approach was the Nixon Doctrine, the 1969 declaration that the United States would pursue its interests around the world not by intervening with its own military forces but by sending military aid to help like-minded governments maintain order. The doctrine was unquestionably aimed at cutting costs, but viewed against the backdrop of accelerating transnational challenges, it takes on greater significance. The administration aimed to check the forces of global disorder by shoring up governmental authority and military power—key attributes of robust nation-states—around the world. The aim was to contain not just communism but also global currents eroding U.S. power.

Examples from South America and South Asia illustrate the broader pattern. The U.S.-backed coup that overthrew the socialist president of Chile, Salvador Allende Gossens, and installed military strongman General Augusto Pinochet has been thoroughly examined by historians.[10] What merits emphasis here are the reasons for U.S. anxiety about a socialist politician of questionable skill in a distant nation once famously described by Kissinger as a dagger pointed at the heart of Antarctica. Within the national security bureaucracy, officials worried about a relatively concrete risk: that Chile might become a "support base and entry point" for Soviet or Cuban activities in the hemisphere.[11] For Nixon and Kissinger, however, the dangers were more psychological. The erosion of U.S. authority around the world made it essential, in their view, to avoid further setbacks. If Allende took power, Nixon worried in late 1970, "the picture projected to the world will be his success"—and, it followed, the United States' failure. "All over the world it's too much the fashion to kick us around," the president declared.[12] Kissinger concurred. "The imitative spread of similar phenomena elsewhere would in turn significantly affect the world balance and our own position in it," he wrote Nixon.[13] In backing Pinochet, the administration resolved its anxieties through an authoritarian solution and gained an ally who promised to help bolster regional stability.

Nixon and Kissinger showed similar tendencies when India and Pakistan went to war in late 1971 over the status of East Bengal, Pakistan's easternmost province. When Nixon took office in 1969, Kissinger later recalled, the administration's aim in South Asia was "quite simply, to avoid adding another complication to our agenda."[14] But East Bengali demands for independence—and the brutal Pakistani military crackdown that followed—created an unavoidable dilemma. Should Washington join the vigorous outcry among international organizations, human rights groups, and relief agencies against Pakistani behavior and perhaps suspend aid to the Karachi government? Or should Washington recognize Pakistan's sovereign prerogatives and overlook the staggering humanitarian crisis that resulted from Pakistani repression? The administration's choice of the latter option reflected its primary concern with superpower relations. The Pakistani government's crucial role in facilitating the U.S. rapprochement with China made the Nixon administration unwilling to alienate Karachi, while India's ties to the Soviet Union rendered a pro-Indian policy distasteful. The pro-Pakistan position also reflected the administration's strategy for combating global transformations that threatened to undercut American influence. By backing the principle that national governments possessed unquestionable sovereignty within their borders, Nixon affirmed his determination to prop up the nation-state as a bulwark against non-state influences that threatened to constrain Washington's conduct of foreign policy.[15]

Backlash, Continuity, and the Carter Experiment

Evaluated in terms of its avoiding dramatic setbacks to U.S. interests, the Nixon-Kissinger approach to developing nations might be judged a success. Recent archival discoveries show, after all, that Moscow aimed to exploit Washington's problems in the early 1970s and began acting more confidently far beyond Soviet borders, especially in Africa.[16] Yet outside of Indochina few countries fell into the Communist orbit between 1969 and 1976. When viewed against the longer flow of history, however, the Nixon-Kissinger policy must be rated a momentous failure. By the mid-1970s the core tenets of the administration's foreign policy—not least its drive for stability in the developing world—lay in deep disrepute. Historians have advanced numerous explanations for Nixon and Kissinger's inability to establish a lasting new direction for U.S. policy. Some emphasize the significance of the Watergate scandal in turning Congress and the American public against the president.[17] Others blame the excessive secrecy with which Nixon and Kissinger made policy. By refusing to allow anyone else to participate in decision making, this interpretation holds, the two men lost their opportunities to build support for their ideas throughout the bureaucracy and to ensure that others would carry on once they left office.[18] Still others argue that Nixon and Kissinger, by quashing reformist change throughout the developing world, planted the seeds for their own failure by making revolutionary explosions inevitable over the long run.[19]

While these explanations hold merit, they skirt yet another cause of Nixon and Kissinger's failures. As time passed, their approach in the Third World fell increasingly out of sync with profound shifts in public opinion, both within the United States and globally. During the 1950s and early 1960s publics throughout the world had generally accepted governmental decisions to subordinate ethics to the pursuit of geopolitical advantage in foreign policy. The Cold War seemed sufficiently dire to justify the trade-off. By the early 1970s, however, the mood had changed in much of the world. The Nixon administration encouraged this trend in two ways. Its success in establishing superpower détente eased global anxieties about nuclear war, thereby creating space for the reassertion of principle in global affairs.[20] Meanwhile, its support for authoritarian governments in the developing world, along with its willingness to use power in brutal and undemocratic ways, provoked a backlash against what was widely viewed as immoral behavior. Between 1973 and 1976 the Nixon and Ford administrations found themselves increasingly on the defensive as investigative journalists and enterprising members of Congress uncovered a trail of cynicism and abuse in policymaking toward nations in Asia, Africa, and Latin America.[21]

It would be a mistake, however, to ascribe surging demands for the restoration of principle in the conduct of international affairs entirely to the Nixon administration's successes or excesses. The backlash also reflected underlying continuity across the late 1960s and 1970s in the growth of transnational movements determined to establish or extend standards of justice. This trend was already under way by the time Nixon and Kissinger took office with the intent of holding it back. As the historian Akira Iriye has written, the global antiwar movement of the late 1960s was just "part of the global forces that were producing a large number of transnational movements dedicated to humanitarian relief, developmental assistance, and the protection of human rights."[22] But increasing worldwide concern about conditions on the global periphery, Iriye observes, accelerated dramatically thereafter. Intergovernmental and nongovernmental organizations dedicated to Third World problems proliferated spectacularly in the 1970s, accounting for a substantial chunk of an overall expansion of intergovernmental organizations worldwide from 1,530 to 2,795 between 1972 and 1984 and a corresponding increase in nongovernmental organizations from 2,795 to 12,686 across the same period.[23] Just as significantly, existing organizations—not least Amnesty International, which garnered the Nobel Peace Prize in 1977—achieved unprecedented prominence, while intergovernmental organizations boldly expanded their activities into the fields of development and human rights.[24]

These trends can be explained in at least two ways. First, frustration around the world with the deadlocked Cold War and yawning gaps between grand aspirations and meager accomplishments during the 1960s diminished popular faith in governmental institutions—a trend that was only encouraged by the Watergate scandal and the worldwide economic downturn of the early 1970s.[25] As governments seemed to lose their ability to solve urgent problems, nongovernmental alternatives gained appeal. In the technological realm, meanwhile, the expansion of satellite technology and the steadily spreading availability of television made it possible for ordinary people to appreciate gaps in experience and wealth between different parts of the world as never before. Injustice and poverty became more tangible problems for many people in industrial nations at precisely the moment when the same communication technologies facilitated formation of international networks of activists.

So powerful were these trends on both the domestic and international levels that Gerald Ford and Henry Kissinger could no longer hold back the tide by their final years in office. They grudgingly acknowledged that they had no alternative but to accept the inevitable when the Conference on Security and Cooperation in Europe made human rights a central focus of the thirty-five-nation agreement reached at Helsinki in 1975, and Ford struggled during the presidential race the next year to cope with charges that the Republicans had cynically tolerated repression abroad. Only the inauguration of Jimmy Carter, however, led to a fundamental realignment of U.S. foreign policy. The new administration manifested its priorities in several ways. Carter aimed to expand U.S.-Soviet cooperation into the arenas of agriculture and population control while seeking global agreements on the use of undersea resources, which the president declared a "common heritage of Mankind" rather than the property of individual nations.[26] More famously, Carter sought to launch a new era in American foreign policy by attaching central importance to human rights as a standard for crafting U.S. decisions and weighing the performance of other nations. To facilitate this shift, Carter established the post of assistant secretary of state for human rights and humanitarian affairs, upgrading the "coordinator for human rights and humanitarian affairs" position that Ford had created under congressional pressure in 1976. Concern about humanitarian abuses ultimately led Carter to reduce or end aid programs to a range of governments, including vigorously anti-Communist regimes in Argentina, Chile, El Salvador, Guatemala, South Korea, Paraguay, the Philippines, and Uruguay.

These attitudes contrasted sharply with the U.S. approach earlier in the decade. Whereas Nixon and Kissinger had sought to contain worrying global currents by bolstering the authority and vitality of nation-states on the periphery, the new administration believed it could advance American interests by aligning U.S. policy with trends that appeared to be both profound and ineluctable. More specifically, Carter built U.S foreign policy—at least in the administration's idealistic early days—on three interlocking beliefs about the international system. First, the administration saw the internal behavior of foreign governments as a legitimate concern in crafting U.S. policy. In Kissingerian *Realpolitik,* all that counted was a nation's external behavior. The Nixon and Ford administrations were unwilling to chastise Pakistan during the Bangladesh crisis or Chile after Pinochet's rise to power since both nations' external policies served U.S. interests. Carter approached foreign policy with a more complex conception of U.S. national interests. To be sure, as Carter wrote in his memoir, he embraced human rights partly because it was "the right thing to do."[27] But he also believed that applying pressure for reform abroad would ultimately reinforce stability more effectively than the old Kissingerian approach—in other words, that national aims could be served by aligning the nation with transnational norms. Among other benefits, Carter asserted, pushing governments around the world to follow reformist paths would help "remove the reasons for revolutions that often erupt among those who suffer from persecution."[28]

Second, Carter believed that the United States had a strong interest in positioning itself alongside global public opinion. For Nixon and Kissinger, public opinion—both domestic and international—had been an unwelcome constraint and often a source of profound aggravation. Following Allende's overthrow, for example, the two men had bemoaned the fact that they could not claim public credit for engineering a coup that they believed would have earned them praise if it had it been carried out twenty years earlier.[29] During the Bangladesh crisis Nixon privately castigated the Indian government for seeking advantage by playing to "this world public opinion crap."[30] Carter's contrasting approach is best illustrated by his handling of the Panama Canal issue. Although U.S.-Panamanian negotiations had been going on for more than a decade by the time Carter assumed the presidency, U.S. opinion clearly opposed any move to hand over the waterway to Panama. Nevertheless, Carter signed a deal on September 7, 1977. The administration's determination was rooted partly in fear that saboteurs might damage the canal if there was no breakthrough. Administration policy also stemmed, however, from Carter's desire to atone for the injustice of the 1903 Hay-Bunau-Varilla treaty, which had grown into a major source of grievance against the United States throughout Latin America. Whereas Nixon and Kissinger advanced the negotiations because they saw no alternative but to yield to pressure within the OAS, Carter closed the deal out of a genuine determination to demonstrate U.S. willingness to swim with the current of global opinion. "This issue had become a litmus test throughout the world," Carter wrote later, "indicating how the United States, as a superpower, would treat a small and relatively defenseless nation that had always been a close partner and supporter."[31]

Third, Carter believed that the Cold War had ceased to be the most important—or perhaps even the only—lens through which to view global challenges. Unquestionably Carter struck a sharply critical tone about the Soviet Union from the outset of his presidency. Yet he departed from his predecessors in his openness to the idea that conflict on the global periphery might stem from causes other than Moscow's machinations. The United States, he declared in 1977, had at last rid itself of "that inordinate fear of communism which once led us to embrace any dictator who joined us in that fear." Now, he continued, it was possible to see that turmoil was often rooted in grievances spawned by poverty and oppression: "We can no longer separate the traditional issues of war and peace from the new

global questions of justice, equity, and human rights."[32] In practice, however, the administration, even in its idealistic early days, had difficulty setting aside Cold War considerations that made old decision-making patterns attractive. The presence of Cuban troops in Angola, for example,
prevented the administration from normalizing relations with the leftist
regime in Luanda. Similarly, Soviet meddling in the Horn of Africa led
Washington grudgingly to line up behind a new ally, Somalia. Yet other instances reveal an administration groping for opportunities to put new
thinking into action. Carter found his chances in southern Africa, where
he shifted U.S. support from the white supremacist regimes that Nixon
and Kissinger had backed in the name of anticommunism, and in the Middle East, where he undertook a major diplomatic initiative without explicitly invoking Cold War tensions.

A Second Backlash and the Reagan Reconciliation

In the end, Carter was unable to put his grand ideas into practice. Again
and again, as numerous historians have demonstrated, the perceived necessity of bolstering stability on the global periphery and avoiding setbacks
at the hands of Communists led the administration to compromise its
principles and to place Cold War calculation at the heart of U.S. decision
making. The potential for this sort of swing was clear from the outset of
the Carter presidency. In naming Zbigniew Brzezinski national security
adviser, Carter chose a consummate Cold Warrior. Brzezinski was aware
that instability on the periphery reflected underlying problems having little to do with East-West rivalries and counseled his boss that the United
States needed "desperately to fashion a comprehensive and long-term
North-South strategy."[33] But as problem after problem nagged at the administration in 1978 and 1979—lingering tensions in Angola, accelerating
hostilities in the Horn of Africa, revolution in Iran and Nicaragua, and
then crisis in Afghanistan—Brzezinski led the way in restoring older patterns of thinking. Under changing circumstances, concerns about human
rights took a back seat to mounting anxiety over Soviet assertiveness in
Asia, Africa, and Latin America. Carter approved dramatic increases in
military spending and endorsed development of new weapons.

These efforts were insufficient to persuade an anxious American public
that he was up to the challenge of reinvigorating U.S. foreign policy for a
new era of confrontation with the Soviet Union. Castigating Carter for

weakness, Ronald Reagan won a landslide victory in 1980 by promising to restore national strength, assertiveness, and pride. As candidate and then as president, Reagan repeatedly distanced himself from the Carter record. He attacked the Panama Canal treaty as a naïve giveaway of American sovereign rights and lambasted Carter's cherished SALT II treaty for surrendering American military supremacy to the Soviets. Less explicitly, Reagan officials disputed Carter's attempts to build U.S. foreign policy on a complex understanding of the causes of instability on the global periphery. Defense Secretary Caspar Weinberger spoke for many within the administration in 1986 when, after noting that one in four countries around the world was at war, he asserted: "In virtually every case, there is a mask on the face of war. In virtually every case, behind the mask is the Soviet Union and those who do its bidding."[34] Just as they had a decade earlier, American leaders evaluated events in the developing world overwhelmingly through their relationship to the U.S.-Soviet rivalry.

U.S. policy toward the developing world during the Reagan years was, however, no simple reversion to Nixon-Kissinger patterns. To the contrary, continuities between Carter and Reagan stand out far more than the continuities between the two Republican administrations. More specifically, Reagan, attuned to persistent moralism within the American electorate and aware of the potential to exploit transnational activist networks, retained much of Carter's tendency to speak in universalizing terms and to root U.S. policy in purported global norms. In this way the new administration did not attempt to turn back the clock so much as it tried to position the vigorous pursuit of the Cold War and the revival of U.S. nationalism as consistent with deepening global interactions and the increasing permeability of international borders. Like Carter, Reagan championed human rights as a central concern of U.S. foreign policy, though the latter broke sharply with his predecessor in practice by using human rights principally as a cudgel to beat up repressive Communist regimes rather than repressive Third World allies of the United States. Meanwhile, borrowing a concept if not the precise words from Carter, Reagan spoke of his desire not to defeat communism but to "transcend it" through the application of principle. The West, Reagan believed, was aligned with universal truths that would inevitably prevail over a rival set of principles that possessed declining legitimacy around the world. Reagan administration officials recognized that many U.S. allies in the Third World routinely abused their citizens. But through a curious rationalization expounded most eloquently by UN ambassador Jeane J. Kirkpatrick, they dodged this inconsistency by suggesting that right-wing authoritarians were more capable of evolution toward democratic decency than were their left-wing counterparts. In short, rightist regimes were ultimately consistent with the extension of global standards.[35]

Reagan also embraced another core tenet of Carter's approach to foreign policy: his flexible understanding of international borders and the acceptability of transgressing Westphalian notions of sovereignty. This attitude was manifested above all in Reagan's economic policies, which unabashedly championed free trade, the expansion of foreign investment, and restructuring the economies of developing countries in ways that would allegedly enable them to participate more fully in expanding global economic activity (structural adjustment). Reagan's agenda helped resolve an inconsistency at the heart of U.S. policy in the Nixon-Kissinger era. Even as those two men sought to bolster the administrative authority of many Third World governments, they struggled to defend the prerogatives of American investors. For Reagan, the promotion of foreign investment formed an integral part of an overall policy based in a vision of the world as an integrated whole rather than a community of distinct nation-states.

This outlook also underpinned the administration's behavior in the geostrategic realm. Reagan showed little compunction about openly meddling in the internal affairs of nations such as Nicaragua and Afghanistan by supporting anti-Communist guerrilla forces. To a degree this practice was a response to the changing nature of the Cold War in the developing world. The establishment of leftist regimes during the late 1970s created unprecedented opportunities for Washington to back antigovernment forces. But the Reagan administration's sponsorship of the Nicaraguan contras and the Afghan mujahedin—and more generally the promulgation in 1985 of the Reagan Doctrine, pledging support for anti-Communist forces around the world—represented something new in the conduct of the Cold War. The United States now signaled its intention to enlist non-state actors in the global anti-Communist struggle.

The ability of the Reagan administration to wage the Cold War in a way that meshed with mounting global consciousness made its foreign policy far more durable than the approaches pursued by its predecessors. By positioning U.S. policy as consistent with global standards of decency and justice, it avoided the charges of cynicism that had brought down the Kissingerian approach to foreign policy. By vigorously waging the Cold

War, it avoided the charges of weakness that had brought down Carter. There was no third backlash, unless one counts the relatively limited movements that attacked Reagan's policies toward South Africa, El Salvador, and other Third World countries. Indeed it is worth noting that the American electorate continued to valorize Reagan's conduct of American foreign policy even as it chastised one of his successors for veering too much toward *Realpolitik* (George H. W. Bush) and another for excessive concern for human rights abuses abroad (Bill Clinton).

Smashingly successful rhetoric and enduring popularity should not be confused, however, with admirable decision making. Reagan's legacy is besmirched by horrific bloodshed in many regions and troubling corruption in the form of the Iran-Contra scandal. Moreover, it has become increasingly clear in the twenty-first century that Reagan's approach did not position the United States well for the long term. The equating of U.S. national interests with the extension of global norms distracted attention from looming threats including resource depletion, ethnic conflict, and perhaps most consequentially for U.S. national security, inevitable rebellions against Washington's attempts to impose and maintain a global order conducive to American interests. Chinese and Russian assertiveness in the years since the Cold War offer two cases in point, but the best example may be the rise of radical Islam and the alternative universalizing vision that it embodies. The catastrophic wars that the United States waged in Iraq and Afghanistan in the first decade of the twenty-first century may one day be understood as the moment when Reagan's reconciliation of competing currents in the making of U.S. foreign policy finally fell apart, leaving policymakers to grope for a new approach to managing relations with the developing world.

PART IV

Global Challenges and International Society

CHAPTER 13

The Transformation of International Institutions

Global Shock as Cultural Shock

GLENDA SLUGA

"TRANSNATIONAL," "interdependence," "international regime," and "global" are all terms ushered into scholarly and more popular lexicons by the realities and expectations of the 1970s and the so-called expansion of international society. For some historians, the extent of these transformations marks the emergence of "a genuine world community."[1] Yet even as international institutions grew more global during the seventies—with the relative inclusiveness of the world's international institutions and the proliferation of NGOs—contemporaries concentrated on coinciding tendencies toward political fragmentation. The United States ambassador to the United Nations (1975–76), Daniel Patrick Moynihan, recorded that "it was by now common to hear the world described in images that suggested it was growing smaller: a global village, a Spaceship Earth. All manner of writers were discovering that the world had become interdependent." His own emphasis, however, was on "the opposite case," the perception "that something closer to regression has been taking place, that the world has been relapsing into the timeless mode of tribal fragmentation and strife; that in man's future lay anarchy, not dominion."[2] The symbolic focus of these seemingly paradoxical developments was the United Nations' radically expanded membership, comprising the numerous new states born of former colonial territories in Africa, Asia, the Middle East, the Caribbean, and the Pacific. UN Secretary-General Kurt Waldheim was heard to remark that "some people were shocked to see the UN reflect the 'entirely new balance of power in the world.'"[3] Typical was Moynihan's own dismissal of the UN's enlarged General Assembly as a "theatre of the absurd."[4]

This chapter tracks the cultural dimensions of the "shock" generated by the globalism of the 1970s, a time when the internationalist idealism associated with the creation of the United Nations had long expired. At the end of the Second World War, in the wake of unimaginable devastation, politicians, pamphleteers, scholars, and the public alike had come to identify supranational world-oriented politics as the most realistic alternative to the overlapping perils of racism, nationalism, and nuclear annihilation. As the UN grew in its capacity to represent a global constituency, those ambitions were regularly stifled by the Cold War politics of polarization. This imagined trend toward globalism met its most significant obstacles in the fillip granted by decolonization to social scientific theories of racial and ethnic difference, and by the state-centric bias intrinsic to the new international institutions themselves. As we will see, the institutional transformations that took place in the UN during the 1970s had a firm economic foundation. They were also profoundly entangled in coinciding perceptions of international politics as moving us, humans all, toward an ever-expanding global community, *and* as an endlessly segmenting international society of sovereign nation-states and civilizational fault lines.

The United Nations Organization, established in 1945, had fifty-one members, the majority of them European states (including the USSR), the Americas, and the so-called "White British Commonwealth." Within three decades it had accumulated an additional eighty member states (by 2009 it had a total of 192), 70 percent of which belonged to the parts of the world classified collectively and synonymously as "the have-nots," "developing," "Third World," and "the South." Postcolonial states not only were midwifed by the UN but also sought the affirmation of their national independence through its offices and protocols. In particular they mobilized the symbolic power of the UN's General Assembly and Economic and Social Council (ECOSOC), and the material resources that could be channeled by UN agencies such as UNESCO (United Nations Educational, Scientific and Cultural Organization) and the ILO (International Labor Organization). By contrast, the interests of "the North" (normatively the industrialized parts of the world) continued to dominate crucial UN organs and affiliated agencies such as the International Monetary Fund, the International Atomic Energy Agency, and the Security Council.[5]

The tag "Third World UN" was first adopted in the more celebrated decade of political and cultural change, the 1960s, and reflected radically new institutional as well as international orientations. The UN's first Third World secretary-general, U Thant from newly independent Burma, was elected by the General Assembly in 1961. During his decade-long tenure Thant prioritized the social and economic progress of colonial and decolonizing territories, and addressing global economic inequalities.[6] The sixties, proclaimed the decade of development, witnessed the creation of a new intergovernmental body, the United Nations Conference on Trade and Development (UNCTAD), devoted to integrating "developing countries" into the world economy. It was in the early 1970s, however, as OPEC's own expanding "nonwhite" membership began to exploit its control of the world's oil resources, that an increasingly self-conscious "South" generally "felt greatly encouraged" in using the UN to make the demands that would address residual economic and cultural inequalities.[7] As the Indian economist Jagdish N. Bhagwati observed, international discourse had suddenly shifted "from a bourgeois conversation during periods of undoubted Northern power and tentative Southern probing in the early postwar years, to the passionate Southern voice of solidarity and confrontation."[8]

The climax of this passion was the 1974 declaration by the Sixth Special Session of the UN General Assembly of a "New International Economic Order" (NIEO) that would "correct inequalities and redress existing injustices," as well as "eliminate the widening gap between the developed and the developing countries and ensure steadily accelerating economic and social development in peace and justice for present and future generations."[9] A Charter of Economic Rights and Duties of States adopted that same year stipulated the removal of unsatisfactory terms of trade, the affirmation of national control of natural resources, the legality of nationalization, and the right of all states to restitution and compensation for prior colonial exploitation and depletion of resources. At a time when UN expenditures on developmental activities already outstripped those on more conventional international peace and security activities by a ratio of six to one, the NIEO reinterpreted the significance of the imperial past and challenged the fundamental arrangement of the world's economy. It tackled not only the unequal economic capacities of the developed and developing world but also the continued economic domination of postcolonial Africa and Asia by the former colonial powers.

The ambitiousness of this new international order was confirmed when UNESCO announced plans for a complementary "New International Information Order" (NIIO) to redress geopolitical imbalances in control of international "public opinion."[10] Even as these demands for new international economic and information orders echoed earlier anticolonial agendas, including the stipulations of the 1955 "Afro-Asian" Bandung Conference, they were now rehearsed with the support of the Non-Aligned Movement and an interested Communist bloc, as well as a UN bureaucracy still dominated by employees from the Northern world collaborating with a burgeoning number of Northern-based international NGOs.[11] The UN had become the engine driving the reconfiguration of international institutions around older ideals of global economic, political, and cultural equality.

In 1972 Philippe de Seynes, the United Nations undersecretary-general for economic and social affairs (the administrative arm of ECOSOC, the UN body involved in the formulation of many of these demands), claimed a broad acceptance of the need for systemic change in the world economy, "relieving the rich of a sense of guilt toward the two-thirds of mankind living in poverty, disease, and ignorance."[12] UN interest in international economic and cultural transformation was also welcomed as a cure-all for the operational shortcomings of its world-ordering mission. An internal report, "A New United Nations Structure for Global Economic Cooperation" (1975), celebrated by Secretary-General Waldheim as "a historical moment in the life of the United Nations," proposed institutional reforms to strengthen the General Assembly and ECOSOC and streamline the UN Secretariat. The creation of a director-general for development and international cooperation (an office ranked beneath the secretary-general and to be occupied by an individual from a developing country) would formalize the international significance of a development-focused economic agenda. But what the plan intended to give to the South—transforming its symbolic UN power into a more potent vehicle of international agency—it also potentially took away. The existing, messy General Assembly voting process that was the basis of UN decision making was to be replaced with international governance by professionals or "experts."[13]

This was the first time since the world body was formed in 1945 that fundamental institutional change was urged from within, an impetus indebted to the renewed enthusiasm outside the UN for its unique international functions. UN bureaucrats and NGO workers alike believed enough in the core economic demands of the NIEO, if not its specific methods, to work at bolstering them by forging organizational networks across the North-South divide.[14] Even as Moynihan dismissed the NIEO as imitation British welfare statism, European economists eagerly collaborated with the UN in pursuit of systemic change. The criticism that supporters of these new international economic and cultural programs were playing out opposing European versions of liberalism—laissez-faire on the one hand and social democracy on the other—missed the point. These developments were equally informed by widely shared perceptions of the inescapably global nature of the world economy. Even the UN delegate representing a generally disapproving United Kingdom acknowledged that the NIEO would not go away since "'interdependence' is not merely one of the empty platitudes of United Nations rhetoric, it has become a fact of world trade."[15]

All the more surprisingly, then, within a few years of its introduction the NIEO program and plans for a major overhaul of the operation of the UN were all but abandoned. Those UN bureaucrats wary of the effects of change on their own administrative dominions had as much of a role to play in its demise as did skeptical Northern member states with vested political and economic interests. The NIIO suffered a similar fate as it became the unfortunate excuse for newly independent states and USSR satellites determined to curb and censor their domestic media. Finally, there were the economic realities. Again, the economist Bhagwati provides an eloquent summation, this time of the decade's anticlimactic denouement: "the early post-OPEC Northern perception of Southern strength yielded to reality," and the "passionate Southern voice of solidarity and confrontation" gave way to "a frustrated Southern monologue."[16] Intrinsic to the rise and fall of this economically induced reality were prevailing perceptions among influential social scientists of internationally induced worldwide cultural dislocation.

There is no doubt that the Cold War, particularly competition between the USSR and the United States for global influence, affected the events that took place at the United Nations in the 1970s and their reception. From a geopolitical perspective, the NIEO and the NIIO were both symptoms and casualties of a century-long ideological conflict in which the UN, like its new member states, remained a bit player. Yet for contemporary audiences, those events had as much to do with the cultural drama of decolonization as with the political antagonisms of the Cold War.

By 1969 the radical MIT China scholar Harold Isaac was among those Anglophone scholars defining "race or color" as the most visible determinant of the "wrenching rearrangement" in world affairs, "a world in which . . . white dominance no longer exists, certainly not in its old forms," and new circumstances required "the painful rearrangement of identities and relationships."[17] Given the tragic conflagrations that had spread across the United States in the late 1960s, an American would seem the most likely to bring attention to "race or color." But the point was also that the race conflicts occurring within nations had transnational implications and were crucially involved in the heated-up international scene: from the rapid and painful implementation of decolonization and the supplementary evolution of Western European immigration policies designed to thwart colored immigration and racially delimit citizenship, to the connections between the African *négritude* movement and Black Power, events in the United States, the United Kingdom, and other societies burdened by their imperial pasts, the influence of Malcolm X, and the alliance between a radical black agenda and Islam in the "internationalization of militant American Negro movements."[18] The overlapping national and international context of race politics was at the heart of a more general reconsideration by sociologists of the primordial role of color in modern society.[19] For Talcott Parsons, like Edward Shils, "the axis of color" rather than class presented the most serious provocation for a perilously polarized world.[20]

As the world's peoples gained state-based representation within the global system of international institutions, Anglophone social scientists increasingly commented on the extent to which color, usually synonymous with race, defined those same institutions. Exhibit A was the UN. The West Indian scholar Roy Preiswerk noted a color imbalance in international relations whereby "the non-Whites of the world" now held "the numerical majority in the bodies of the world organization." The problem was, however, that "the transformation of a European-Christian-White dominated world into a pluralistic world" had not been "understood or accepted in the centers of power."[21] In the wake of the UN-based demands for another new world order, the English political scientist Hugh Tinker confidently outlined his view that "the importance of race in international conflict has become startlingly clear." He described "the almost complete breakdown of a system of 'superiority' beliefs and values at the level of rational, conscious assertion and also the partial breakdown—at any rate the transformation—of the international structure of power." While "white, advanced nations" had control of international institutions representative of financial and technological interests, "the black and brown poorer nations" sought dominion over those same institutions. According to Tinker, the relative empowerment of "black and brown people" within the UN, "where racism is universally condemned, and all the states are accorded the outward signs of equal status," placed into even greater contrast the situation in countries where those same people remained vulnerable to discrimination. He went so far as to warn that "today, transcending everything (including even the nuclear threat) there is the confrontation between the races. This will spiral on, inexorably, as the twentieth century moves to its end."[22]

Scholarly commentary on the existence of an international axis of color marked a shift in the "thrust and direction" of the significance of "color in world affairs" rather than any innovation.[23] In 1903 the black American sociologist W. E. B. Du Bois had coined the term "color-line" to describe the political inequalities shaping international relations.[24] Forty years later Du Bois warned that the Dumbarton Oaks conference, at which the details for the creation of the UN were worked out, had established a framework for preserving and even extending imperial power and with it the color line that left most of the world's population without representation and rights. Only the United States, the United Kingdom, and the Soviet Union—and to a limited extent China—were privy to the conversations on world organization which concluded with no statement on racial equality, and a gesture toward the sovereign equality of all "peace loving 'states.'"[25] Equally significantly, he articulated this critique in anticipation of the UN's own antiracist mission, eventually expressed in its charter and various programs. Thus in its first years of operation, UNESCO was under instruction from the General Assembly "to study and collect scientific materials concerning questions of race; to give wide diffusion to the scientific information collected; [and] to prepare an educational campaign based on this information."[26] The program had on its side intensified postwar interest in countering racism after the fact of the Holocaust and the discovery in 1953 of DNA, a historic event that should have rendered racial categories scientifically redundant. But UNESCO's attempts to neutralize racism failed precisely because there was no scientific agreement on the view of race as less a biological fact than a social myth. From the 1960s on, UN constituents pursued a new antiracism agenda through the General Assembly, fired by the empowerment offered by decolonization and by the resistance to the more pernicious legacies of colonialism. The most notable of its numerous resolutions and programs were the International Convention on the Elimination of All Forms of Racial Discrimination and its efforts on behalf of combating apartheid in South Africa. By 1973, 12 percent of all General Assembly resolutions were devoted to attacking apartheid. The culmination of this UN-generated lobbying was the infamous 1975 resolution that linked the anti-apartheid cause with a pro-Arab policy and denounced Zionism as "a form of racism and racial discrimination."[27]

This was the setting in which contemporary social scientists returned to the theme of color in world affairs and confidently diagnosed a "trend to reverse exclusive White domination."[28] Unlike Du Bois, with his early-twentieth-century emphasis on the political nature of the international color line, however, these later-twentieth-century analysts projected a specter of ineluctable color, racial, or ethnic fault lines that haunted politics. The color counting of UN membership was crucial to their descriptions of the transformations at hand, so that, for example, the point at which, in 1961, "there were still 51 white states, but the Afro-Asians totaled 53" was historically momentous.[29]

It is salutary for understanding the historically specific basis of such analyses to remember that earlier in the century, self-consciously white social scientists would have employed a wider spectrum of colors in such analyses, with "yellow" at the fore. In the 1970s the focus was simply on black, with the occasional brown, opposed to white.[30] Nor was there any agreement or consistency in these color/race diagnoses. Some social scientists were drawn to the more malleable concept of ethnicity. Just prior to taking up the position of U.S. ambassador to the UN, and freshly returned from an ambassadorial stint in India, Moynihan began to teach a seminar on "Ethnicity in Politics" at Harvard, presenting ethnicity as "a new social category as significant for the understanding of the present-day world as that of social class itself."[31] In his UN memoir Moynihan depicted *ethnicity*, "celebrated in its most dangerous form, that of black-white confrontation," as the root of the tensions in the General Assembly.[32] Certainly, in an age when India had splintered into two and then two again, each division at the cost of hundreds of thousands of lives, and Britain's own breakup was being predicted, ethnicity was as useful a conceptual term as race or color, suggestive of different if sometimes overlapping forms of division throughout the globe.[33] Even though it was not a new concept, it gave rise to a seventies-specific language, most celebratedly in Anthony Smith's enduring "ethnosymbolism" and Walker Connor's "ethnonationalism." More important, each version rendered latent ethnicities a "primary motivating force of conflict situations" and further reified the primal political significance of differences only loosely understood as cultural.[34]

Determined as social scientists were to uncover a single cause for the ever-fragmenting kaleidoscope of political allegiance and secessionist claims worldwide,[35] even those who popularized race, color, or ethnicity were liable to concede that none of these could adequately explain the voting blocs at the UN. One had only to look at the international alliance structure of the Non-Aligned Movement; it included Yugoslavia, Argentina, Uruguay, and, at a distance, Sweden. As Ayesha Jalal's chapter in this volume reminds us, the oil-rich and oil-poor countries constituting the South hardly shared economic or political interests. At the end of the decade, J. R. P. Dumas, Trinidad and Tobago's ambassador at the UN, complained that the member states of the Third World too often hid behind generalities such as "the people." Attacking "Moynihanism at the UN"— the U.S. ambassador's allegedly "condescending" and ethnicity-obsessed posturing—Dumas also maintained that any cultural shock generated by the expansion of state membership at the international level, or by the economic demands being made by the Third World, was a matter of perspective. He argued that "the whole affair" was "largely a question of perceptions: how the US perceived itself, how it and other western countries perceived the Third World (and vice-versa), how the various elements of the Third World perceived themselves, how Mr. Moynihan perceived everybody else." By this point "there had been Cambodia; there had been Vietnam; there was the Middle East; Watergate had come and stayed; at international conferences the assaults were mounting in rhetoric, invective, and intensity as political Lilliputians, sensing a previously unsuspected vulnerability, harassed the distracted Gulliver. Things were falling apart; the centre was not holding."[36] John Wendell Holmes, a former Canadian delegate to the UN, assumed a similar "non-American" perspective when he addressed the American Academy of Political Science in 1977, reflecting that Americans had a problem with this more global United Nations because they were under the misconception that they owned the institution.[37]

Of course, singling out Americans as the obstacle to the expression of a more equitable world community and consciousness could only be a distortion of the complexity of the period and of international institutions. The 1970s belonged not only to the national solipsisms of Nixon or Ford but also to the empathetic Carter, not only to the "Fighting Irishman" Moynihan but also to his African American successor Andrew Young. There was not one United States government in the 1970s, nor only one view of America's international role. Consider Secretary of State Henry Kissinger's proposition that the "dislocations" marking contemporary world affairs also offered "an extraordinary opportunity to form for the first time in history a truly global society, carried by the principle of interdependence."[38] If anything, the American case highlighted the international and national as profoundly related and mutually reinforcing spheres of agency and experience in this history of transformative global consciousness. Take the part played by Ralph Bunche (a Nobel Prize–winning peace mediator in the Middle East), first, in 1946, as the UN's director of trusteeship, and then undersecretary-general from 1954 until his death in 1971, just as the UN was becoming the perceived theater of race, color, and ethnic conflict. A black American who despised hyphenated citizenship, Bunche had moved from the State Department to the UN at the end of the Second World War to take up the struggle against race discrimination around the world, and to bring an end to colonialism. At the turn of the 1970s, he was deeply disillusioned by the violence emanating from black ghettos in the United States, "the depths of despair experienced by the black American," and, most disorienting of all, the "common ground" of "racist approaches" arrived at by "white segregationists and black separatists . . . if for different reasons."[39] Bunche's unpublished writing indicates that he had all but abandoned hope that the United States might ever achieve meaningful integration. Although he still argued publicly that the UN had the capacity to defeat nationally entrenched racisms, he also observed that as international society was expanding, so were the essentialist and exclusive identity politics he so deplored at home.

The same year that Ralph Bunche died, the UN's Philippe de Seynes spoke confidently on "Prospects for a Future Whole World." He pictured "globalism" as the "functional expression" of the increasingly prominent notion of the "world as a whole." He went on to contrast, rather grandly perhaps, "traditional internationalism" anchored in interdependence and human solidarity with a new globalism "associated today with the ambivalence of technology, its negative effects on the degradation of the environment, the destruction of ecological balances, the limited capacity of the biosphere, the possible depletion of natural resources, the population explosion, the finiteness of the planet, and perhaps even the finiteness of knowledge."[40] This new globalism was enmeshed in an emergent international discourse on environmentalism and sustainability fostered at the UN during the 1970s and echoed in U Thant's invocation of "spaceship earth" and his call for "a new quality of planetary imagination . . . a *global* mentality that takes account of the nature of interdependence and the imperative need to change."[41] The General Assembly's adoption, in the last days of the decade, of a treaty rendering "the moon and its natural resources . . . the common heritage of mankind . . . not subject to national appropriation by any claim of sovereignty," and advocating an international regime to govern the exploitation of the moon's natural resources, manifests the seemingly unbounded character of this global mentality and its earthly limitations. The desire to protect the moon from the exclusivist forms of state sovereignty that ruled on earth put on display an unabashed UN universalist hubris which saw the organization's own international authority extended literally to the universe. Yet as de Seynes acknowledged, this globalism was itself "a relatively new approach in the United Nations," and its fate was affected by other, related, globally significant institutional and international transformations. As contributors to this volume note, between the late 1960s and early 1980s international nongovernmental actors and intergovernmental initiatives doubled in number and took on many of the global challenges on de Seynes's list. Sometimes the UN was their operational seedbed, as often the international NGOs goaded the UN into action. Nor did everyone, even on earth, share a single vision of UN-sponsored globalism. Its problematic nature was apparent in overlapping General Assembly debates during which the South contested the North's right to delimit the Third World's opportunities for industrial development in the interest of a new holistic vision of the world's environmental future.

The seventies started out with a decade-defining sense of the global as a crucial concept for considering international politics and economics. It is also true that even the most committed "globalists," such as the UN's de Seynes and U Thant, believed that global thinking did not exist and had to be cultivated. The ambivalence of this global consciousness was underscored in Stanley Hoffman's depiction of "a world community" as "fiction." But Hoffman, at the time professor of government at Harvard, also imagined that fiction as *enabling* "the organs of the United Nations to concern themselves with most of the important political and economic issues that agitate the international system and to promote that equalization of concern which is a rudimentary, first factor of homogenization in a highly diverse and uneven world."[42] Indeed, in 1974 the fiction of a world community spurred the Australian government to initiate an official inquiry into the role of the UN in its territory at home and abroad. The investigation provoked comments on the UN's bias in favor of "black" and "newly emergent nations," but it also forced an acknowledgment of the inescapable influence exerted by the UN as a global public forum.[43] More specifically, the UN's ability to act as an international agent of dissident public opinions provoked a reconsideration of Australia's regional responsibilities in the territory of the Cocos Islands, where an indigenous population under its international care still worked as indentured laborers. Of course the fiction of a world community appealed quite differently to President Gerald Ford, who that same year cautioned the General Assembly against succumbing to the "tyranny of the majority."[44] Ford's warning was an intended attack on the UN as the instrument of Soviet propaganda. But it also registered a cultural shock evocative, on a global scale, of Tocqueville's mid-nineteenth-century prediction that the promotion of a classless democracy in America would lead to the end of civilization as he knew it.

The tension between predictions of homogenization and fragmentation—between the enabling embrace of the useful fiction of a world community, on the one hand, and the trenchant exploitation of the fictions of race, color, and ethnic difference, on the other—shaped the course of international institutions in the 1970s. As the decade progressed, scholars of international thought took an increasingly cynical view of international society. In 1977 Hedley Bull, the Australian-educated Oxford don and Hoffman acolyte, posited one of the most influential and enduring theories of internationalism, which saw evidence of an actually existing expanding international society not in the "pseudo-institution" that was the UN but in the embrace by "the states of Asia and Africa" of the European ideal of state sovereignty, the rules of international law, and the procedures and conventions of diplomacy.[45] Bull's erstwhile collaborator Adam Watson later recalled that "Hedley seemed to me always somewhat uneasy about the relationship of the newly independent non-white world to Western values and standards of civilization."[46] In other words, "the anarchical society," like late-blooming theories of the overwhelming political significance of race/color/ethnic difference, was a product of its time. In a telling commentary on the mood that saw out the decade among political commentators from *all* backgrounds, the editors of the new multidisciplinary journal *Third World Quarterly* warned in 1979 that "the major western powers seem to be working towards a situation where the developing countries would be left with no forum for the resolution of their problems."[47]

Mark Mazower has emphasized the enduring stain that color and civilizational politics left on twentieth-century internationalism (if not globalism), commenting that they reduced the concept of international community to "an empty box which successive generations filled with new content—from human rights in the 1940s, [to] civil society in the 1990s," adding, "None of these, in my opinion, amounted to very much: they told one more about the latest fashion among Anglophone social scientists than they did about the world."[48] To be sure, if the fashion among Anglophone social scientists in the 1970s was to feature "common bonds," the prevalent analytical perspective, as we have seen, was equally focused on the differences that would tear the world apart. Scholars emphasized the theme of fragmentation as much as coalescence, the absurdity of a UN with parliamentary pretensions as much as the significance of an expanding international public sphere or civil society.[49] By the end of the 1970s, globalism was on a disabling, albeit temporary, course for the ghetto of peace studies, while ethnicity, an umbrella term evocative of race and color as much as culture, dominated the academy's mainstream disciplines. Despite Moynihan's contemporary claim that "in truth nothing much had happened to the true 'balance of power' since 1945,"[50] a cultural perspective on this period suggests a more contorted story of institutional transformations in the form of international political agency and representation, the changing legitimacy of different "colored" (if not yet gendered) actors on the world scene, and the political power exerted by the ideas of race, color, and ethnicity and harnessed by all sides. The paradoxes of course originated with the UN itself, an international institution that was the seeding ground for a new global fiction, even as it remained most fun-

damentally the instrument of nation-states, of a new world order that reduced democracy and egalitarianism to the "self-determination of peoples." The uneven and often contradictory developments of the global
1970s, like the trajectory of Ralph Bunche's international optimism, suggests that the history of global tendencies and opportunities is less meaningful when told as a narrative of institutional stasis, progress, or decline
than as a human story of accumulating and contingent imperatives and,
too often, tragic ironies.

CHAPTER 14

The Seventies and the Rebirth of Human Rights

MICHAEL COTEY MORGAN

NINETEEN SIXTY-EIGHT is remembered for the protest movements that swept the world. But the year also witnessed two significant episodes in the history of human rights, an idea whose ascent had a greater impact in the long run on the international system and government legitimacy than did the Latin Quarter's barricades. That year the French jurist René Cassin received the Nobel Peace Prize in recognition of his contribution to the drafting of the 1948 Universal Declaration of Human Rights. At the award ceremony in Oslo, the Nobel Committee's chairwoman preempted critics who might question whether human rights had anything to do with peace. To see the connection, she argued, one had only to look at the United Nations Charter, which affirmed that "lasting peace had to be built upon respect for the rights and worth of the individual human being." True peace was more than just the absence of war. Governments had to respect the inalienable rights of their own citizens too. "What kind of peace," she asked, "can there be in a country where the people are not free?"[1]

The connection between human rights and peace also resonated in an essay that appeared the same year in rather different circumstances. In *Progress, Coexistence, and Intellectual Freedom*, the Soviet physicist Andrei Sakharov argued that the only way to avoid "universal suicide" by nuclear war was to increase international cooperation and remove restrictions on individual rights, especially in totalitarian countries. The West was hardly a perfect model, but, he argued, his country could not afford to remain blind to the importance of personal freedom if it hoped to prosper.[2]

Both Sakharov and Cassin saw an indissoluble connection between human rights and international peace, but they had different visions for reconciling the two. Cassin's approach was legalist, Sakharov's activist. Where Cassin worked with states to establish legal norms, Sakharov worked against his own government, demanding that it live up to existing standards. Cassin followed diplomatic protocol, respected the prerogatives of sovereignty, and worked through intergovernmental organizations, especially the UN and the Council of Europe. Like many of the rights activists of the 1960s and 1970s, Sakharov operated outside government channels and in cooperation with nongovernmental organizations. The contrast between the approaches of the two men epitomizes the differences between the human rights moment of the 1940s and that of the 1970s.

Human rights were gaining new currency in international affairs by the early seventies. The attention only increased over the years that followed. This burgeoning influence was all the more remarkable when we consider that, in the two decades between the Universal Declaration and 1968, the international power of human rights had fallen far short of early postwar hopes. The revival of human rights was the result of rapid political, cultural, and technological changes that expanded the vocabulary of international ethics and transformed the moral imagination of a large segment of humanity, spawning unprecedented concern for the fate of strangers on the other side of the world. The statesmen of the 1970s had to grapple with the consequences, which took many of them by surprise.

Drawing on a flurry of scholarly work, the members of the UN Human Rights Committee called the document that they produced in 1948 a *Universal* Declaration—as opposed to an International Declaration—in order to emphasize that the rights it described applied to all people everywhere, regardless of government policy. Given that the UN relied on the consent of its member states to function, and given that the Declaration required the General Assembly's approval, the committee's attempt to circumscribe the legitimate use of state power was striking.[3]

Yet the Declaration was a statement of aspirations, not reality. In international law and practice, individuals were objects, not subjects, and human rights were subordinate to the prerogatives of state sovereignty. The Declaration was unenforceable. Even though the first article of the UN Charter declared that "promoting and encouraging respect for human rights and for fundamental freedoms" was a core goal of the organization, Article 2(7) forbade it from "interven[ing] in matters which are essentially within the domestic jurisdiction of any state." Shielded by this norm of noninterference, governments could ignore the Universal Declaration with impunity. The only possible exception was a case in which human rights abuses were so flagrant that they threatened international peace, but even this proviso only underscored that the UN's supreme commitment was to prevent interstate war, not to protect individuals.[4] Besides, in the aftermath of the Second World War, most governments were more interested in preserving international stability than in enforcing the Universal Declaration. Human rights bowed to sovereignty and the imperative of international peace.

Efforts to create enforceable international rights guarantees continued, but with mixed results. The European Convention on Human Rights, which the Western Europeans signed in 1950, was, in the words of lawyer Geoffrey Robertson, a legally binding "bulwark against the resurgence of fascism." It established a supranational court to hear individuals' complaints against their governments, but its geographic and substantive scope was limited: it protected only civil-political rights in the western half of the continent and deliberately excluded the socioeconomic rights which the Soviets emphasized.[5] Nevertheless, it offered a sharp contrast with the stalemated negotiation over the UN human rights covenants. According to the original postwar vision, the Universal Declaration required a complementary treaty. Because East-West rancor made its drafting nearly impossible, the projected single agreement split into two documents, one for civil-political and another for socioeconomic rights. Bitter ideological arguments stalled the negotiations for nearly twenty years. The signing of the covenants in 1966 only underscored the exhaustion of the UN human rights regime.[6]

Throughout this period the United States, which regarded itself as the world's leading exponent of liberty, was wary of offering anything more than rhetorical support to international human rights. This reticence had a number of sources. In the late 1940s and 1950s influential nationalists, notably American Bar Association president Frank Holman and Senator John Bricker of Ohio, warned that international human rights agreements were vehicles for Soviet influence. Holman argued that UN efforts to protect human rights would undermine the Bill of Rights and "promote state socialism, if not communism, throughout the world." Bricker's proposal to amend the Constitution to restrict the president's treaty-making power enjoyed widespread congressional support, although it ultimately failed.[7]

Second, racial segregation in the South meant that the U.S. government risked eliciting accusations of hypocrisy whenever it spoke out on international human rights questions. Indeed, American racism was a regular feature in Soviet propaganda. Third, the Cold War balance of power made it difficult for Washington to challenge Communist abuses of human rights in Eastern Europe, despite the Eisenhower administration's promises to "roll back" Soviet power. Accepting Communist rule was the price of peace. As the Cold War spread to Latin America and Africa, Washington was often willing to support unsavory leaders with questionable human rights credentials in the hope that they would hold the line against Communist expansion. Dwight Eisenhower's toleration of South Africa's apartheid government and John Kennedy's support for Joseph Mobutu in the Congo evinced the compromises that American leaders were willing to make.[8] The idealism of the Universal Declaration's drafters fell victim to the pressures of the Cold War.

How, then, did a new window of opportunity for international human rights open in the late 1960s and 1970s? Why did human rights become the common international language of the good? A confluence of factors explains this turn: European decolonization and the American civil rights movement removed the stains that had made Western statesmen reluctant to discuss human rights. A new understanding of the recent past raised public awareness of the horrors of the Second World War. The explosion of international civil society yielded new nongovernmental organizations (NGOs) devoted to promoting human rights. Technological progress made communications and travel faster and cheaper, with the result that news of humanitarian crises traveled more quickly than ever before and information moved more freely between East and West. Finally, in the Soviet bloc, rising dissent after the death of Joseph Stalin challenged the policies that were necessary to maintain domestic stability.

In the United States, Cold War pressures bolstered the civil rights movement. Institutionalized racism furnished foreign critics, especially the USSR, with potent ammunition to attack American claims of moral superiority. Although Presidents Truman and Eisenhower worried about the damage that segregation was doing to the country's international standing, it took Lyndon Johnson's civil rights legislation to remove one of the chief obstacles that had made American officials wary of discussing human rights internationally.[9] Decolonization had a similar effect on British and French attitudes. The creation of dozens of new states invigorated dis-

cussions of international justice at the UN, though many of the organization's new members repudiated universal rights as another manifestation
of Western colonialism. They preferred to emphasize collective self-
determination over individual rights.[10]

Changes in the historical imagination reflected the growing interest in
human rights and bolstered arguments about the need to protect them.
For more than a decade after the Second World War, Western historians
tended to focus on the conflict's diplomatic and military aspects, paying little attention to Germany's genocidal policies. This silence was a function
of both psychological trauma and political necessity, since the imperatives
of state-building, especially in West Germany, France, and Israel, encouraged reticence about wartime atrocities. Beginning in the 1960s, however,
the Holocaust became an increasingly important part of Western memories of the war. Owing to the prosecution of a group of former Auschwitz
officials in West Germany and of Adolf Eichmann in Israel, not to mention
the appearance of works such as historian Raul Hilberg's *Destruction of
the European Jews* (1961) and playwright Rolf Hochhuth's drama *The
Deputy* (1963), the Nazis' crimes received fresh international scrutiny. In
France, scholars and students began to challenge the Gaullist myth that
the Resistance had enjoyed widespread support during the war. There was
no better symbol of this rebellion than the documentary *The Sorrow and
the Pity* (1969), which unearthed unpleasant truths about French collaboration during the German occupation.[11]

Nongovernmental organizations, whose ranks grew during the 1960s,
played a central role in raising awareness of human rights violations. The
best known of these was Amnesty International, which a British lawyer
founded in May 1961. Its mission was to secure the release of "prisoners
of conscience," men and women in the Western, Communist, and Third
Worlds who had been jailed for questioning their governments. Sympathetic articles in influential newspapers helped the organization to expand
rapidly across Western Europe and North America. By 1970 its chapters
numbered in the hundreds, proof of a growing "global consciousness."
Amnesty's London headquarters collected information about prisoners
worldwide and distributed dossiers to its members, who would then write
to the offending governments to request the prisoners' release. The movement's core assumption was that individuals could change the policies of
foreign governments by bombarding them with mail and publicizing their
crimes. Amnesty was not the first NGO devoted to human rights, but it

was the first to act globally and to engage average citizens in a cause that had traditionally been the preserve of diplomats and lawyers.[12]

Sweeping technological advances facilitated the work of human rights NGOs and fuelled global awareness. Lynn Hunt has argued that the popularity of the epistolary novel in eighteenth-century Europe engendered humanitarian empathy and contributed to the American and French Revolutions' declarations of universal rights.[13] In the mid-twentieth century, the global spread of television and satellite technology had a similar impact. As telecommunications satellites developed in the decade following the 1962 launch of AT&T's *Telstar 1*, it became possible to transmit images around the world almost instantly, leading to an early version of what would later be dubbed the "CNN effect." Television news brought a newfound immediacy to reports of distant suffering, with significant political consequences. Satellites also slashed the cost of international telephone calls, allowing cash-strapped NGOs and activists to communicate cheaply with one another. The proliferation of air travel made it easier to establish links with like-minded activists and, as in Amnesty's case, to carry out fact-finding missions in countries suspected of rights violations.[14] An even older technology, radio, challenged state repression in Eastern Europe. Radio Free Europe and Radio Liberty served as "surrogate home radio services" for the Soviet bloc, beaming in domestic news (and Western rock music, which Communist authorities regarded as subversive) that citizens could not get from official outlets. Determined to restrict East-West flows of information, Moscow spent huge sums on jamming radio signals, but those who wanted to listen were usually able to do so.[15]

Communist leaders also had to contend with regular rebellions against their rule. In East Germany in 1953, Hungary in 1956, and Czechoslovakia in 1968, thousands of people challenged repressive policies and Soviet hegemony. The reimposition of orthodoxy required military force, carrying heavy costs in human life and eroding the popular legitimacy of communism. After 1968 many true believers who had hoped for a more humane form of communism turned their backs on Lenin and adopted confrontational attitudes toward the governments they had previously hoped to reform. Thereafter, the survival of communism in Eastern Europe depended less on public support than on the threat of force and the repression of civil liberties.[16]

The activists and intellectuals who challenged the status quo grew increasingly bold. Even after the conservative Leonid Brezhnev deposed the reform-minded Nikita Khrushchev in 1964, the price of dissent in the USSR remained lower than it had been in Stalin's day: prison or exile, not execution, had become the most common punishment for those who spoke out. As a result, a small but significant number of writers and scientists lost their fear. Aleksandr Solzhenitsyn, whose 1962 account of the gulag, *One Day in the Life of Ivan Denisovich,* had been personally approved by Khrushchev, was among the Kremlin's most persistent critics. In late 1965 the mathematician Aleksandr Esenin-Volpin organized a demonstration against the trial of writers Andrei Sinyavsky and Yuri Daniel, who had been arrested for publishing work abroad. Protesters demanded that the authorities respect the Soviet constitution, the letter of which guaranteed a host of human rights, including freedom of speech and assembly. The underground samizdat network circulated unflinching accounts of Stalinism, including Evgenia Ginzburg's *Into the Whirlwind* (1967) and Roy Medvedev's *Let History Judge* (1968). As some dissidents attracted worldwide attention, the authorities proved unwilling to bear the costs of the truly draconian measures that would be necessary to stamp out all criticism.[17]

With the growth of international concern and new avenues for action, a second human rights moment emerged in the late 1960s and early 1970s. Whereas statesmen and scholars had dominated the first human rights moment of the 1940s, this new moment enjoyed widespread popular support. Individual citizens, acting alone and through new NGOs, pressured governments to adhere to certain standards of conduct. In many cases this activism surprised the statesmen it targeted. The central question, as before, was how to reconcile territorial sovereignty with universal values. But by contrast with the 1940s, a different, more porous definition of sovereignty now began to take shape.

Global reactions to the Nigerian civil war of the late 1960s exemplified many of the trends that were shaping the new human rights moment. The war began when the federal government in Lagos besieged the secessionist region of Biafra, which had declared independence in 1967 following waves of interethnic bloodletting. With overland supply routes cut off, Biafra's besieged and overcrowded population began to starve. Insisting that the crisis was a domestic matter, Nigeria rejected all international expressions of concern. Despite the Biafrans' suffering, most of the major

powers deferred to Nigerian sovereignty and refused to intervene. The
Soviet and British governments even supplied Lagos with weapons to
crush the secessionists.[18]

International opinion was not as complacent. The International Committee of the Red Cross (ICRC) received permission from the Nigerian
government to take relief aid into Biafra, but the scale of the crisis far outstripped its capacity, and disagreements with Lagos constricted the flow of
supplies. The ICRC was reluctant to act without official consent lest it
jeopardize the relief effort or the willingness of other governments to cooperate in future crises. A number of activists rejected this legalistic approach and insisted that the delivery of aid was more important than diplomatic protocol. Daring volunteer pilots dodged Nigerian fighter planes
to deliver planeloads of food and medicine under cover of darkness.[19]

Images of suffering Biafrans struck a worldwide chord. American activists established NGOs and drew on the resurgent vocabulary of rights to
drum up popular support. In newspaper ads featuring Adolf Hitler's picture under the headline "Welcome Back," the Committee to Keep Biafra
Alive compared the crisis to the Holocaust. Having concluded that publicity was essential to alleviating the Biafrans' misery, a group of French doctors serving in Red Cross hospitals in Biafra chafed under the ICRC's
scrupulous neutrality, which forbade them to share their experiences with
journalists. One of their number, a disillusioned *soixante-huitard* named
Bernard Kouchner, declared that the rules had made the ICRC's personnel "accomplices in the systematic massacre of a population." After
Biafra's defeat, Kouchner cofounded a group dedicated to helping the
victims of war and famine—and to drawing international attention to
their plight. In 1971 it merged with another relief organization to form
Médecins Sans Frontières (MSF), whose very name encapsulated its phi-
losophy. Borders and sovereignty mattered less than human rights.[20]

The reaction to Biafra paled by comparison with the tumult surrounding the Vietnam War. The surge in violence that accompanied the 1968
Tet Offensive starkly belied reassurances from both President Johnson
and General William Westmoreland that victory was within reach. Unprecedented images of carnage and reports on the war's moral ambiguity
cast doubt on the virtue of the American cause. The Pulitzer Prize–winning photograph of a South Vietnamese police chief shooting a suspected
Viet Cong in the head raised questions about the Saigon government
on whose behalf American troops were dying. Coverage of the incident

reached 20 million viewers on NBC's news broadcast the following night. Even worse, the murder of Vietnamese civilians by U.S. soldiers at My Lai, which came to public attention in 1969, spurred allegations that Americans themselves might be responsible for war crimes.[21]

Partly in response to the horrors of Vietnam, the U.S. Congress grew increasingly activist in foreign affairs. Human rights, which promised to be both a tool for waging the Cold War and a way to bring foreign policy back in line with American ideals, appealed to both ends of the political spectrum. The members of Congress who took an interest in human rights were an eclectic group drawn from both parties. By the early 1970s, congressional pressure on human rights had become a major annoyance for the Nixon administration. In 1971, for instance, a number of legislators proposed suspending aid to Greece, a NATO ally then under military rule. The initiative implied that democracy and human rights were at least as important to American interests as the containment of communism, and that foreign policy ought not to be seen strictly through the prism of the Cold War. The proposal failed, but the Greek junta's Western European critics enjoyed greater success. Excoriated before the Council of Europe, the colonels withdrew from the organization in order to avoid the ignominy of expulsion. Citing this episode as a model to emulate, Senator Edward Kennedy of Massachusetts argued that democracy and human rights ought to be the starting point for American foreign policy, not an afterthought. Similarly, Senator Frank Church of Idaho insisted that in the era of Vietnam, support for military dictatorships, for instance in Brazil, would only further erode America's international legitimacy.[22]

In 1973 Donald Fraser, a Minnesota Democrat and chair of the House Subcommittee on International Organizations, launched a series of hearings to examine how the United States could advance human rights worldwide. A distinguished group of activists, lawyers, diplomats, and politicians testified and offered recommendations. Martin Ennals, Amnesty International's secretary-general, argued that Congress should work for "the maximum exchange of information" between NGOs and the U.S. government so as to increase the pressure on abusive regimes. In the effort to call these governments to account, information was a powerful tool. NGOs had an important role to play, but the bottom line remained that the chief responsibility for protecting human rights lay with nation-states. Fraser's landmark report, *Human Rights in the World Community,* appeared in 1974. Criticizing the Nixon administration's amoral approach to détente, it insisted that human rights ought to be a central consideration in U.S. foreign policy. Washington should not hesitate to cut off military and economic aid to foreign governments that failed to respect their citizens' rights. Over the next two years the U.S. government published detailed studies on human rights abuses in South Korea, Iran, Haiti, the Philippines, and Latin America. New legislation tied foreign aid and trade relations to human rights performance and required regular State Department reports on human rights conditions abroad.[23]

An early example of this legislation was the Jackson-Vanik Amendment, named for its sponsors, Senator Henry M. Jackson of Washington and Representative Charles Vanik of Ohio. Jackson generally supported Richard Nixon's foreign policy during the president's first term, but he soon began to question the wisdom and morality of détente. He particularly objected to Henry Kissinger's contention that the United States should not "judge other countries . . . on the basis of their domestic ideology." Not simply a critic of communism, Jackson had also spoken out against the Greek junta. In his view the United States could not abandon its core commitment to human rights for the sake of détente. Jackson's stand on human rights was not purely altruistic, since he was trying to burnish his prospects for the 1976 presidential election, nor was it entirely consistent, as his enthusiasm for strengthening Sino-American relations attested. Yet he insisted that American ideals and interests pointed in the same direction: there was no tradeoff between the two. Outraged at Soviet restrictions on Jewish emigration, he proposed that the administration use the promise of improved trade relations as leverage to force the Kremlin to grant more exit visas. This was the purpose of his amendment, which threatened to sink the 1972 Soviet-American trade deal. Nixon and Kissinger fumed that Jackson's initiative might even derail détente as a whole. Brezhnev was upset at what he saw as illegitimate interference in Soviet domestic affairs and refused to bow to the demands of the amendment, which became law in 1974. Despite Jackson's good intentions, the effects of the legislation on Soviet emigration policy were murky.[24]

In the USSR itself the loose network of activists from the mid-1960s was coalescing into a more coherent—but still tiny—movement. The dissidents' cause appealed to both conservatives and liberals in the West, though sometimes for different reasons. The same year that Sakharov's *Progress* appeared, a Moscow group began publishing the *Chronicle of Current Events*, a samizdat record of government abuses. Amnesty soon began reissuing it for Western readers. A number of human rights journals sprang up to chronicle state repression in the Soviet Union and beyond, including *Index on Censorship* in London, the *Revue des droits de l'homme* in Paris, and *Human Rights,* which the American Bar Association (having abandoned its earlier skepticism) published in Chicago. New NGOs appeared in the USSR, notably the Moscow Human Rights Committee, which pledged to work "in accordance with the laws of the land" to promote research on the meaning of human rights. Weekly telephone calls kept the committee in touch with the New York–based International League for Human Rights, which lobbied Western governments and disseminated samizdat. *Chronicle* founder Valery Chalidze and his colleagues hosted press conferences for Western journalists to publicize their findings. The Kremlin's reaction to the growing human rights movement was harsh. The authorities shut down the *Chronicle,* imprisoned some dissidents—often in psychiatric hospitals—and exiled others, including Solzhenitsyn in 1974. They refrained, however, from killing them outright.[25]

Brezhnev tried to balance internal repression and East-West détente. The centerpiece of his strategy was the Conference on Security and Cooperation in Europe (CSCE). In his vision, every European and North American state would convene at the CSCE to ratify Europe's postwar frontiers and improve East-West trade, two pillars of his grand plan to shore up Soviet legitimacy. Under Western pressure, however, the Soviets agreed to add human rights to the conference's agenda. Over the course of the negotiations, they made concessions in this area in exchange for Western consent to their own desiderata. The resulting agreement, known as the Helsinki Final Act, drew an explicit connection between human rights and international security and committed signatories to the freer movement of people and information. Although the agreement was not legally binding, it gained political force from the fanfare that surrounded its signing in 1975, including the reprinting of the full text in *Pravda.* The Communist states that had abstained from the Universal Declaration in 1948 now publicly accepted that respect for human rights was as important an international principle as respect for state sovereignty.[26]

By the decade's end, the Final Act had become a manifesto for Eastern European dissidents. In 1975, however, no one predicted this turn of events. Indeed the agreement attracted severe criticism in the very countries that would later hail it. West Germany's Christian Democrats denounced the recognition of Europe's postwar frontiers. Reflecting a wider backlash against détente, American politicians from Ronald Reagan to Jimmy Carter and lobby groups representing Polish and Baltic émigrés criticized Gerald Ford for signing an agreement that, in their view, abandoned the people of Eastern Europe to Soviet oppression. Much of the outcry was a consequence of Ford and Kissinger's failure to educate the American public about the benefits of the Final Act, especially on human rights. This failure in turn stemmed from Kissinger's strongly realist approach to international relations, which paid less attention to a country's internal character than to its international behavior. From Kissinger's perspective, making human rights a pillar of American foreign policy would only threaten the international stability that détente aimed to build. The secretary of state insisted that avoiding nuclear war—which required the superpowers to accept each other's legitimacy—was a higher goal than the defense of human rights. The result was a clash between two ethical worldviews. In the first, peace between states, regardless of their political systems, was the sole priority. In the second, true peace required governments to treat their citizens humanely, not least because regimes that violated human rights at home were also likely to cause trouble abroad.[27]

This debate reached a climax in the 1976 presidential election, in which Carter prevailed in part because of his attack on détente and his promise to hew to American ideals in foreign policy. As president, however, he found it difficult to live up to his pledge. Although he made much of creating the post of assistant secretary of state for human rights, Carter could not reconcile human rights with the pursuit of other goals, notably arms control with the USSR. There was, moreover, serious division within the government about how to deal with friendly autocracies that paid little attention to human rights. The result was inconsistency. Some countries, such as Chile, lost U.S. military and economic aid, but others, such as Guatemala and El Salvador, continued to receive assistance even as their abuses grew worse. At the same time, Washington did nothing to stop the Khmer Rouge's genocidal policies in Cambodia. Carter made human rights a central theme of his presidency, but his checkered performance pointed to the enduring challenges of reconciling ideals and interests.[28]

Meanwhile, the transnational alliances between Eastern European activists and their Western supporters grew stronger. The Moscow Helsinki Watch Group, which Yuri Orlov and other dissidents founded in May 1976 to monitor Soviet compliance with the Final Act, appealed for help to U.S.

Representative Millicent Fenwick of New Jersey, who had taken an interest in human rights in the USSR. Fenwick helped to conceive the U.S.
Helsinki Commission, a government body with a mandate to scrutinize
Soviet human rights policy. This was also the purpose of Helsinki Watch,
an NGO that Random House publisher Robert Bernstein founded in 1978
after a trip to Moscow on which he met Sakharov and witnessed the hard-
ships that dissidents faced. It began as a project of the Fund for Free Expression, which he had created three years earlier to campaign against
censorship in the USSR and beyond. After the CSCE's first follow-up conference in Belgrade in 1977–78, which gave Western diplomats a fresh opportunity to pressure the Eastern Europeans, Helsinki Watch supported
the dissidents' work and served as a clearinghouse for information on Soviet human rights policy.[29]

The Final Act also inspired dissidents in Czechoslovakia and Poland. In
protest against the arrest of a rock band, a group of Czechoslovakian writers including playwright Vaclav Havel drafted Charter 77, which exhorted
Gustav Husak's government to fulfill the promises it made in Helsinki. In
Poland the Committee for the Defense of Workers (KOR) formed in 1976
to aid those imprisoned during industrial strikes. KOR's leaders soon demanded the right to form independent labor unions. In 1980 the result was Solidarity, a new national union, which quickly won the support
of over three quarters of Polish workers. In the midst of an economic crisis—which was due in part to overreliance on Western loans, as Stephen
Kotkin shows in his chapter—Solidarity's general strikes in 1980–81 forced
the government to impose martial law in a bid to hang on to power. Yet
less than a decade later communism in Poland had collapsed, replaced by
a Solidarity-led government. The revolutions of 1989 owed an important
part of their success to the human rights revival that had taken place in the
1970s and the transnational connections between governments and civil
society that had emerged along the way.[30]

Comparing the worlds of 1970 and 1980, we find that the impact of human rights is apparent. The revival of the cause after its 1950s nadir had
been the result of technological and geopolitical change, and above all the
efforts of many individuals both within government and without. This
is not to say that the newfound attention to rights necessarily translated
into respect for them. The Soviet government, for example, finally jailed
Sakharov in 1980. Despite the growing influence of civil society, states remained the primary international actors. They regularly broke promises to

protect their citizens' rights and sometimes even used the language of rights to provide cover for hardnosed policies, as with India's 1971 "humanitarian intervention" in East Pakistan and Vietnam's 1978–79 invasion of Cambodia. Double standards endured in the West, particularly in Ronald Reagan's simultaneous demands for Soviet reform and his support for brutal Latin American leaders. Nevertheless, the ability of the human rights discourse to restrain, however modestly, the policies of the world's most powerful state testified to its power.

The universalism of human rights blurred distinctions between domestic and foreign affairs and gave rise to a more porous understanding of national frontiers. Proponents of human rights rejected absolute sovereignty and asserted an interest in the welfare of all people, regardless of what their governments might say. Much like the development of global markets, which Daniel Sargent chronicles in his chapter, the ascent of human rights lowered the barriers between countries. Intriguingly, the focus on political rights to the exclusion of socioeconomic rights coincided with a crisis of Keynesian economics and a shift toward neoliberal doctrines in the West. During the 1980s the ideal of human rights fueled challenges against governments in the Soviet bloc, China, South Africa, and beyond. The story of human rights in the second half of the twentieth century follows the model not of revolution but of erosion and integrative pressures, which, over time, shaped geopolitics in powerful but unpredictable ways.

CHAPTER 15

Smallpox Eradication and the Rise
of Global Governance

EREZ MANELA

THE YEAR 1979 was a significant one in the annals of postwar international history. Some of its familiar markers—SALT II, the Soviet invasion of Afghanistan—bring to mind the history of the Cold War, specifically the decline and fall of détente. Others, such as the Iranian Revolution or the oil shock, heralded the post–Cold War world, specifically the rise of political Islam and economic globalization. These aspects are all explored elsewhere in this volume, but they do not exhaust the significance of the year 1979 in international history. This is because that was also the year in which a commission appointed by the World Health Organization (WHO), after several years of intense work across dozens of countries, issued a report certifying that smallpox—one of humankind's oldest and deadliest diseases—had been eradicated from the face of the earth.[1] The eradication of smallpox may not be as well known as those other events, even (perhaps especially) among experts on international affairs. But consider this: in 1967, when the WHO's global Smallpox Eradication Program (SEP) effectively began, the disease was still killing some 2 million people annually.[2] And in the course of the twentieth century it caused an estimated 300 million deaths, more than twice the total death toll of all of that bloody century's wars together.[3] Smallpox is also the first and to date the only major infectious disease to be eradicated worldwide, and the campaign against it has shaped all subsequent campaigns against disease, such as those against polio and HIV/AIDS. Surely, then, the eradication of smallpox warrants a place in any international history of the 1970s.

The SEP began in the late 1960s, but all of its major signposts occurred during the 1970s. West Africa, the first regional component of the global campaign to be completed, reached "smallpox zero" in 1970, despite ongoing political turmoil and the bloody secessionist war in Nigeria during those years. Indonesia reported no cases after 1972, and Bangladesh, the last remaining endemic country in Asia, reached the target in late 1975 after suffering numerous setbacks, including the reintroduction of the disease by returning refugees who had fled to India during the country's 1971 war of independence. Finally, the last endemic region on earth, in the conflict-ridden borderland of the Ogaden Desert between Ethiopia and Somalia, experienced its last case of smallpox in late 1977 after years in which the SEP staff negotiated surveillance and vaccination activities in the midst of ongoing fighting and political upheaval. Then, at its annual session in May 1980, the World Health Assembly (WHA), the WHO's governing body, officially ratified the verdict of the certification commission. Smallpox, it announced, was no more.

So the global eradication of smallpox occurred in the 1970s. But *in* what ways was it *of* that decade, and what can it tell us about the 1970s as a pivotal period in modern international history? This essay is a preliminary attempt to broach this question. First, it briefly locates the SEP within the longer history of the emergence of international and then global health, and it asks how the story of the SEP illuminates central themes in the international history of the decade. These themes include the evolution of international society beyond bipolarity and Eurocentricity and toward global integration; the growing if ambivalent role of international organizations in the global arena; and perhaps most broadly, the emergence of patterns and mechanisms of global governance, operating on the ground and around the world. Such temporal and thematic contextualization is especially crucial because international historians have to date rarely touched on issues of public health in their study of the postwar era; at the same time, historians of medicine, even those who write about international and global health, do not usually situate their subjects within the broader history of international relations.[4]

In fact, the story of smallpox eradication and the pursuit of global health more broadly in the postwar period point toward a narrative of twentieth-century international history that moves beyond the usual emphasis on world wars and the Cold War, great power politics, and superpower conflict. Instead, this narrative highlights the gradual if fitful growth and expansion of institutions and mechanisms of global governance: the development of international norms, networks, exchanges, and organizations, both governmental and nongovernmental, whose impact permeated the boundaries and sovereignties of nations and often crossed the postwar global divides between East and West, North and South.[5] The SEP, after all, was anchored in an international body, the World Health Organization, that was part of the United Nations system, and it was carried out on the ground by experts and health workers whose sense of collective identity drew on the normative and technical discourse of their profession and who were members in a global network that straddled the political and cultural boundaries of postwar international relations.[6]

Within that narrative of postwar history, moreover, the SEP marked the advent of a new stage, and not simply because it succeeded where previous eradication campaigns—most notably the one against malaria between 1955 and 1969—had failed. The Malaria Eradication Program (MEP) had been palpably marked by Cold War tensions, supported from the mid-1950s on by the United States even as the Soviet Union and the other Eastern bloc countries persisted in their boycott of the WHO.[7] The SEP, by contrast, was from the beginning a joint U.S.-Soviet collaboration, even if U.S. officials occasionally adopted Cold War arguments to defend it domestically. Morcover, though the MEP provided individual countries with external funding and technical advice, it still operated as a collection of national programs. The SEP, too, worked through national governments and national programs, but the degree of coordination in its operations and the unity of its leadership set it apart and arguably made it the first truly global public health program. The SEP, therefore, may be seen as the public health iteration of a broader process that characterized the 1970s, namely, the beginning of the transition from an international society toward a global one and the move, however difficult and fitful, toward the institution of operational mechanisms of global governance.[8]

Smallpox, a deadly, infectious viral disease, had plagued humankind for millennia. Although the disease could take various forms, the most typical one had a 30–40 percent mortality rate. Survivors were left badly scarred, though with lifelong immunity. In many regions of the world smallpox was endemic and attacked mainly children, but at times, particularly in isolated or sparsely populated regions, it could cause devastating epidemics that swept across entire populations.[9] Evidence suggests that smallpox afflicted the ancient Egyptians—Ramses V may have been a victim—and the disease can be positively identified in Chinese and Indian medical texts from the early Middle Ages. If, as John R. McNeill has argued, disease can be considered a historical agent when it has a differential impact on groups involved in a historical encounter, then there is little doubt that smallpox played its greatest, most destructive role on history's stage as the deadliest among the horde of Old World pathogens that came across the Atlantic to decimate some 90 percent of the immunologically naïve native populations of the Americas.[10]

Techniques to induce immunity to smallpox date to ancient times, but the 1796 discovery of the smallpox vaccine by Edward Jenner, an English physician, was a crucial milestone in controlling it. Unlike the other techniques, Jenner's vaccine used a bovine virus, similar enough to the human *variola* virus to induce immunity but without the risk of contracting the disease itself.[11] The practice of vaccination spread slowly across Europe and the Americas in the ensuing decades, often in the face of stiff resistance within the medical profession and among the broader population; it also followed the pathways of imperial expansion into Asia and Africa. It was not until the mid-twentieth century, however, that vaccination had largely eradicated the disease in Europe and North America; even then it remained endemic in many parts of the global South, including South Asia, sub-Saharan Africa, Indonesia, and Brazil.[12]

The history of sustained international coordination on health begins in the middle of the nineteenth century, when successive cholera epidemics in Europe and North America prompted a series of conferences among the major powers resulting in international treaties that established and regulated international quarantine regimes.[13] It was during this period that disease control came to be viewed as an important responsibility of emerging nation-states in Europe and elsewhere, both reflecting and shaping state-building projects that sought to delineate and control the geographic and demographic boundaries of the nation and to render mass populations more legible and productive.[14] But the quarantine regimes of the nineteenth century construed disease control as primarily a *national* task even as they instituted mechanisms of *international* cooperation to achieve it. The primary purpose of the treaties, after all, was to help each government ensure that its own territory remained contagion-free rather than to control or eliminate disease on a global scale. In this context the prevalence of a certain disease elsewhere, certainly outside Europe, was important only to the extent that it could endanger European populations or colonial possessions.

By the turn of the twentieth century, the growing acceptance of the germ theory of disease introduced a range of new methods of disease control. Although it was European scientists—most famously Louis Pasteur in France and Robert Koch in Germany—who led the scientific discoveries in the field, the U.S. acquisition of overseas colonies after 1898 afforded American physicians and officials opportunities aplenty to establish disease eradication programs abroad as well as at home. Perhaps the best known among them is the campaign to control the mosquito-borne diseases yellow fever and malaria in the Panama Canal Zone, whose success made the canal project possible and established army surgeons Walter Reed and William Gorgas in the annals of public health. But the United States pursued disease control programs elsewhere, including in Cuba and the Philippines, designed both to protect the occupying forces and to help legitimize colonial rule as a civilizing mission.[15] At the same time, the Rockefeller Foundation also began to fund disease control programs abroad, largely in Latin America and China.[16] Thus the idea of disease control as a problem that was global rather than a national or even an international one began to take root, though even the Rockefellers did not yet dare to attempt anything close to a global eradication campaign.

The establishment of the League of Nation's Health Organization marked another stage in the rise of disease control as an arena of global governance, at least in theory. LNHO leaders construed their responsibilities as global, but with few resources at their disposal they could not put this notion into practice. Instead they focused largely on collecting information and developing international standards for medical practice, for example, in recording causes of death. But the professional networks of experts and activists that formed around the LNHO began to cohere into a public health "epistemic community," whose interconnections and shared outlook laid the groundwork for the postwar programs in the field.[17] And as the institutionalization of internationalism entered a new stage in the wake of World War II, the World Health Organization emerged from the ashes of the LNHO much more ambitious than its predecessor. Its designation as a *world* organization rather than an international one was not accidental and reflected the global ambitions of its founders: it would serve not nations but humanity itself.

By the time the WHO's ambitious constitution was ratified in 1948, however, the Cold War had begun. With the Soviet Union and the other Eastern bloc countries boycotting the organization, the United States remained the sole superpower backer of the WHO's first major disease control program, the one against malaria. Unsurprisingly, the program reflected U.S. strategic concerns, focusing on regions, such as Southeast Asia, where Washington wanted to increase its influence.[18]

When the Soviets returned to the WHO as part of Nikita Khrushchev's policy of "peaceful coexistence," they therefore brought with them a competing proposal for a major campaign of disease eradication. Moscow's 1958 proposal to the World Health Assembly called for a five-year plan for global smallpox eradication through a program of compulsory vaccination that would cover the entire population of endemic countries. The USSR had eradicated smallpox within its borders in the 1930s by means of a massive national campaign of compulsory vaccination, but it still experienced hundreds of cases annually owing to importations across its long borders with endemic regions to its south. And the world's growing interconnectedness meant that other smallpox-free countries were also in constant danger of importation from endemic areas and were forced to maintain costly domestic vaccination programs. A global eradication campaign, the Russians said, would cost much less than the indefinite continuation of such national vaccination programs.[19] To underline their commitment, they promised an annual donation of 25 million doses of the heat-stable freeze-dried vaccine, crucial in tropical countries where the climate was hot and refrigeration scarce.[20]

Partly as a gesture to the Soviet Union, the WHO officially established a smallpox eradication program the following year. But Washington initially remained aloof, and the program languished with only token budgets and skeleton staff.[21] By the mid-1960s, however, the U.S. position began to shift. For one thing, the malaria campaign was clearly sputtering, struggling against insurmountable logistical problems and facing growing concern about the environmental effects of one of its primary weapons, the synthetic insecticide DDT.[22] The image of the United States in the developing world, moreover, was rapidly deteriorating as the war in Vietnam escalated, and the Johnson administration was eager to shore it up by demonstrating its support for international cooperation; the United Nations, after all, had declared 1965 International Cooperation Year.[23] The United States was on a quest, the president said, to find "new techniques for making man's knowledge serve man's welfare," and smallpox eradication seemed a relatively inexpensive, uncontroversial way to showcase this commitment.[24] In May 1965 Johnson, echoing John F. Kennedy's man-on-the-moon pledge earlier that decade, announced an American commitment to wiping out smallpox within a decade.[25]

Although this effort would be carried out in close collaboration with the Russians, administration officials often justified the program domestically as a bulwark against the spread of communism in the Third World. The author of one administration document, titled "The United States and Worldwide Offensive against Disease," noted:

> Two-thirds of the human race lives on less than $100 per year, with a life span of less than 35 years, and besieged by infectious disease. . . . What does this mean for the United States? I leave aside all *soft-spoken* questions of humanity and brotherhood. I speak only of *hard-headed* self-interest. The best breeding place for Communism is disease and poverty. If we are going to lead the free world in its fight against the bondage of Communism, we have to do something about the health of these poor people.

Helping the world's millions of sick, the document continued, was "a tool which can penetrate any Iron or Bamboo curtain to reach the minds and the hearts of man." It would promote world peace, showcase the United States as "the fountainhead of medicine," and help U.S. allies combat the temptations of communism, for "what good is any man as an ally if, doubled up by disease, he is unable to rise to his full height and be counted in the militant fight against encroaching Communism?"[26] But, whether to limit the influence of Moscow or to promote cooperation with it, Washington now wanted to pursue the global eradication of smallpox.

Thus in 1967 the WHO launched an "intensified"—that is to say, an actually funded and staffed—global eradication campaign. As the SEP unfolded over the subsequent decade, it operated across dozens of countries on three continents, with the most extensive operations in sub-Saharan Africa, the Indian subcontinent, Afghanistan, and Indonesia. Progress depended on technological advances such as the jet injector and the bifurcated needle, and on epidemiological and organizational innovations such as the surveillance-containment method and the use of dedicated operations officers to facilitate the logistics on the ground. But it also required the constant management of political tensions and cultural encounters on numerous levels: delicate jockeying in international forums in Geneva, negotiation of "country agreements" with all participating governments, and the coordination of vaccination campaigns with a host of local actors, from Hausa emirs in northern Nigeria to village heads in rural Uttar Pradesh.

Operating simultaneously in numerous regions and on numerous levels, the SEP depended on close U.S.-Soviet cooperation, and the relationship occasionally required some careful handling. The Russians, for example, were initially displeased when Donald A. Henderson, an epidemiologist from the Communicable Disease Center (CDC) in Atlanta, arrived in Geneva to head the program. The SEP, after all, had been the Soviets' initiative, and they thought that a Russian should lead it. Henderson worried about the fate of Moscow's crucial vaccine donations, but when he gingerly approached the Russians about this issue, the response surprised him. "I want you to know," Henderson recalled his counterpart telling him, "that we have checked you out and are now confident that you are honest and a good scientist, that your only objective is to eradicate smallpox. You will have our full support." The Russian added that while he could not officially guarantee vaccine donations more than one year at a time, the nature of the Soviet system was such that once a certain annual production quota was decreed, it would likely remain in place in subsequent years.[27]

U.S.-Soviet collaboration also helped overcome resistance to the program at the WHA and elsewhere. Every year the U.S. and Soviet delegations worked together to ensure that smallpox was placed on the agenda for the session, which afforded the opportunity to subject endemic countries that did not report sufficient progress to a public shaming at the plenary. Henderson also enlisted the help of U.S. and Soviet diplomats in various countries to deal with health officials whom he deemed uncooperative, and he worked with the Soviets on staffing issues, traveling to Moscow to interview Russian candidates for the program personally, in English, which was the working language of the program. When problems arose with the quality of some batches of Soviet vaccine donated to the program, the Geneva staff discreetly informed the Russians, who agreed to shut down several substandard production facilities. In the final years of the program, moreover, when specimens from suspected smallpox cases required analysis in specialized laboratories, the Institute of Virus Preparations in Moscow and the CDC lab in Atlanta split the work between them.[28]

How do we account for such collaboration between avowed Cold War antagonists? For one thing, it clearly helped that elites within the two superpowers, despite their political and ideological disagreements, shared what Odd Arne Westad, following the social theorist David Harvey, has described as a "high modernist" outlook on the question of progress. Both sides subscribed to a "belief in linear progress" that would emerge from "rational planning" of the social order, and agreed on the centrality of scientific knowledge and technological expertise to achieving it.[29] When President Johnson, for example, announced his support of International Cooperation Year, he called for it to be a "year of science," one that would constitute a "turning point" in the course of world politics in which the struggle of "man against man" would be replaced by a more noble one of "man against nature." It was this shift that would allow humanity to "begin to chart a course toward the possibilities of conquest which bypass the politics of the Cold War."[30] Such a call for the conquest of nature through the power of science, a defining feature of the high modernist sensibility, was fully in tune with the approach of the Soviet elites of the time.[31]

Second, much of the global SEP operated under the radar of the top leadership on both sides and thus circumvented the currents of political tensions between the superpowers. Once the political leaders gave their initial approval for the program—the Kremlin in the context of the post-Stalin policy of "peaceful coexistence" and the White House as part of the mid-1960s push for international cooperation—they showed little sustained interest in it. The SEP, after all, did not require significant budgets, nor could it easily be used to exert pressure on Third World governments, in the way that Johnson, for example, had tried to deploy food aid to India around the same time.[32] After the initial commitment was in place and the green light was given, progress depended on the working relationships between mid-level technocrats, for whom a shared discourse of medical-scientific knowledge, technical competence, and organizational wherewithal usually trumped questions of ideological conflict or political interests. The lack of sustained attention from the top political leadership also gave mid-level officials a wide berth. Thus when the CDC's longtime director David Sencer concluded that his mandate to protect the health of Americans allowed, indeed required, him to divert staff and budgets to smallpox eradication in Bangladesh, he could do so with few questions asked.[33]

Although the international leadership of the SEP came largely from developed countries—many were Americans, though numerous other nationalities were represented—they were diverse in their backgrounds and motivations. Henderson, a native of Ohio, was an archetypical hard-charging technocrat, forceful and relentless, who did not mind occasionally highlighting his family's Canadian roots when it helped smooth relations with Third World officials who were critical of U.S. foreign policies. William Foege, an American and a leader in the West African and later in the Indian program, had been in Africa as a Lutheran medical missionary when he was recruited into the program. Yet another American, Lawrence Brilliant, who helped lead the Indian campaign, was a self-described hippie who had initially arrived in India on a spiritual quest and has credited his Indian guru with insisting that he join the SEP.[34] Then there was Nicole Grasset, a Swiss-French epidemiologist who joined the SEP after a stint with the Red Cross in Biafra, and who wrote impassioned letters to world leaders such as Indira Gandhi and the Shah of Iran asking for their support (and in the latter case also for donations of fuel for SEP vehicles). Grasset, the sole woman within the program's top tier, became something of a legend among program staff, and stories of her venturing, unruffled, into muddy fields in rural India in elegant high heels circulated widely.[35]

Bridging the global East-West and North-South divides was crucial for the success of the SEP, and here the WHO served as an indispensable forum. It provided an institutional framework for conceiving of disease control as a global problem, for coordinating a global campaign, and, no less important, for taking credit for success that neither superpower would have wanted to cede to the other. But the WHO's relationship to the SEP throughout the life of the program was more complicated and ambivalent than this summary suggests. Early on, top WHO officials, including longtime director-general Marcolino Candau of Brazil, were skeptical of the project's prospects and wary of committing to a program that might become another embarrassment for the organization. For Candau, the failure of malaria eradication had dealt a serious blow to the WHO's credibility, and he feared that another high-profile failure would cause irreparable damage. Many other top WHO officials, both in Geneva and in the regional offices, were also opposed or indifferent to the project, whether because they shared the director's views, had other priorities, or wanted to protect their turf.[36]

And while the program's apparent success by the mid-1970s rendered some of these fears moot, it gave rise to another set of concerns that were related to the contested nature of the WHO's mission. In the wake of the tumult of the 1960s—the youth revolts, decolonization, and calls for a new international economic order—in the 1970s many in the field of international health shifted away from technocratic high modernism and toward social medicine, an approach which argued that public health programs must take into account and seek to alleviate the wider social and economic determinants of illness. Advocates of this view worried that "vertical" programs such as the SEP, which targeted one specific health problem for elimination, were drawing resources away from "horizontal" programs that emphasized primary health care services and sought to transform broadly the social and economic conditions that were related to health problems in developing societies.[37] Although it may have been coincidental, it was surely significant that in 1978, just as the SEP had achieved "smallpox zero" worldwide, the WHA released the Alma-Ata Declaration, which committed the WHO to the goal of "health for all by the year 2000" and stressed the priority of promoting broad change in health conditions over the control of specific diseases.[38]

Still, even if some WHO officials were ambivalent and even hostile to the SEP, the organization remained essential to the program in all its stages. It provided a discursive space in which health officials could conceive of and articulate smallpox eradication as a problem that required a global solution and then pursue it as such, transforming the issue of disease control from a matter of defining and policing sovereign boundaries—as it was in the era of international quarantine treaties—into one of transcending them. And international organizations also played other, more concrete roles in the history of the SEP. It was after all the United Nations' declaration of 1965 as International Cooperation Year that provided internationalists in the Johnson administration with the opportunity to make global smallpox eradication an official U.S. goal, and the WHO afforded a space that allowed the two superpowers to bracket Cold War rivalries in pursuit of shared notions of progress. If the WHO as a concrete bureaucracy was more often than not an obstacle that the program had to overcome, as a symbolic and collaborative space it was indispensable.

History, of course, is rich in irony, and the story of the smallpox program is no different: even as the Russians worked with Americans to eradicate smallpox, they worked separately to weaponize the virus.[39] We should not, however, allow this irony to tempt us back into the warm embrace of the traditional Cold War narrative. First, the drive to eradicate smallpox was surely no less significant historically than the efforts to weaponize it. Second, integrating the story of the SEP into the history of the 1970s brings that decade into focus as a pivotal time in the emergence of processes of global governance. It offers a perspective on the international history of the 1970s that encourages us to look beyond nation-states and consider the impact of international organizations and other non-state actors in the global arena. It also suggests that we need to disaggregate states rather than imagine them as unitary actors in international affairs, shifting some of our attention away from the official organs of foreign policy and onto components of the U.S. government, such as the CDC, that have hitherto rarely made an appearance in traditional narratives of the international history of the decade.

Tracing the networks of historical causation and significance that neither are produced primarily by foreign policy and diplomatic establishments nor lie within the boundaries of any one state, then, permits us to explore aspects of the history of globalization and global governance—epidemic disease and public health, the dissemination of scientific and technical knowledge, and the environment in its global context, to give but a few examples—that have thus far remained on the margins of the international history of the 1970s. Given the growing salience of precisely these themes in the contemporary conversation on global affairs, it is not a moment too soon to begin writing their history.

CHAPTER 16

The Environment, Environmentalism, and International Society in the Long 1970s

J. R. McNEILL

AMONG THE UNFORESEEN DEVELOPMENTS of the 1970s was the rise of modern environmentalism around the world and the emergence of global-scale environmental anxieties and awareness. Why did this happen, and what did it matter?

Within the concept of modern environmentalism a distinction is in order. Although broadly simultaneous, there was and is a difference between environmental concern for the globe as a whole and the globalization of environmental concern. I call the first *global-scale environmentalism.* It embraces such issues as climate change, ozone depletion, population, overfishing, and so forth: matters that seem to pertain to major parts of the globe if not all of it. I call the second *globalized environmentalism,* meaning the emergence, almost everywhere around the globe, of locally focused environmental movements. The mobilizing issues discussed here varied from place to place: industrial pollution in Japan, the despoliation of natural beauty in New Zealand, dam building in India, oil spills in California, and so on. Both global-scale environmentalism and globalized environmentalism deepened and broadened in the 1970s, generating popular movements with political consequences on local, national, and international scales.

Modern environmentalism has many tangled roots. Intellectual precursors and influences are legion, from Buddha and Saint Francis to Humboldt and Thoreau. Popular indignation over specific environmental ills also has a long history. State regulation of scattered environmental matters, say, wildlife conservation efforts or antipollution measures, also extends back for centuries. Scientific concern over certain environmental issues, such as soil erosion in the 1930s, attained nearly worldwide levels. But between about 1965 and 1980 these roots somehow absorbed additional nutrients and gave flower to something new, a popular environmentalism that bloomed all around the world to become a significant factor in political life. Why? Much of the answer, I think, lies in the interactions among technology, culture, economics, and ecological change. But some of it lies within the arena of politics itself.

Technology was important in several ways. First, the ingenuity of chemical engineers combined with the availability of cheap petroleum to spawn a plethora of new organic chemicals after about 1920, and especially after 1945. Many of these, such as DDT or PCBs, proved both durable (in the sense that they do not easily break down chemically) and toxic, so that once loosed in the environment, they became persistent hazards. In general, industrial chemistry created a near infinite variety of new pollution problems that threatened the health of human beings, other species, and ecosystems.

Second, different technologies allowed detection of environmental changes and depictions of environmental conditions as never before. Photographs of the earth from space, published widely in the late 1960s, helped people to see their planet in a new way: small, alone, vulnerable. One such photo, often called "Earthrise," appeared on a U.S. postage stamp in 1969. LandSat imagery, available after 1972, showed in dramatic fashion the expansion of some deserts at the expense of pasture and farmland, encouraging the view that desertification was indeed on the march. The shrinkage of the Aral Sea became readily visible via satellite. Computers, albeit primitive by later standards, allowed oceanographers to crunch streams of data and demonstrate the global climate connections we now know as ENSO (El Niño and Southern Oscillation), a phenomenon familiar to only a few scientists until the big El Niño of 1972–73. Satellites, computers, and other new technologies allowed atmospheric scientists to hypothesize (in the 1970s) and then to prove (in the 1980s) that the earth's protective shield of stratospheric ozone was rapidly corroding under the impact of chlorofluorocarbons. In short, technological change helped to create some environmental problems but helped to reveal, measure, and study some as well.

Third, communications technology, especially television, made it easier for people to learn about environmental issues far from home. This contributed to the rise of global-scale environmentalism as, for example, TV images of starving children in the Sahel deepened worries about global overpopulation or desertification. But it also contributed to the globalization of environmentalism, as TV viewers in East Germany could see West Germans organizing marches against nuclear waste management plans, and Venezuelans could watch Californians mobilizing against oil spills. Certain environmental problems are "made for TV," such as oil spills or the decline of panda and polar bear populations; others, often more serious by most metrics, such as stratospheric ozone loss, do not measure up to the standards of TV producers. In the 1970s, it is well to remember, they were cultural gatekeepers with far greater power than they had in the 1950s, when TV was rare, or by the late 1990s, when cable and Internet diversified the media marketplace. So TV, and to a lesser extent other communications technology, assisted in the emergence of modern environmentalism while at the same time shaping its character in otherwise unlikely ways.

Fourth, a few new "greener" technologies helped focus attention on environmental problems by seeming to address them. No one likes impossible problems, but soluble ones attract people hoping to do good or add meaning to their lives (and politicians hoping to make names for themselves). Smokestack scrubbers, catalytic converters, and dozens of other new technologies carried the promise of reduced pollution and more efficient resource use. Thus technology contributed to interest in environmental problems because it seemed to provide at least a partial solution—although for a few of the most committed environmentalists the only admissible solutions involved the abandonment of modern technology altogether.

Modern popular environmentalism arose, at least in some places, in a context of countercultural critique of any and all established orthodoxies. In the late 1960s the familiar subserviences of women to men, young to old, blacks to whites (in the United States or South Africa), peasants to party cadres (in China) seemed increasingly insupportable. Authority became suspect on principle. This "counterculture" of course had different features in each setting, in some places revolving around objections to the Vietnam War, in others to racism, or merely to stifling school curricula. Broadly speaking, it was more pervasive in the prosperous lands where young people had the leisure to acquire schooling and did not worry about the source of their next meal. But cultural revolutions of one sort or another bubbled up in Mexico, Chile, South Africa, and China, as well as in Western Europe, Australia, New Zealand, and North America.

This cultural trend made it easier for popular environmentalism to succeed. At root, environmentalism was a complaint against economic orthodoxy, whether of the capitalist or Communist variety. It was a critique of the faith of economists and engineers, and their programs to improve life on earth. It was in some forms, such as what evolved into the "Deep Ecology" of the Norwegian philosopher Arne Naess, an accusation against human society of hubris and crimes against the biosphere.[1] All this fit congenially with the broader trends. In subsequent decades, parts of the counterculture became mainstream and other parts faded away, but environmentalism, despite ebbs and flows, survived as well as any component of the 1960s critique of society and authority—mainly because environmental ills remained routine and often worsened with time.

Perhaps most indispensably, popular environmentalism arose after 1965 in response to the economic and ecological trends of the postwar and decolonization era (roughly 1945–1970). This might be dubbed the Age of Exuberance. In quantitative terms, it witnessed the fastest economic growth in the history of the world. Cheap energy, postwar reconstruction, market integration, population growth, urbanization, and technological advance contributed to this boom.

In the decolonized world, newly empowered leaders generally made extravagant promises about economic growth, often sincerely imagining that once the shackles of colonialism were cast off, prosperity would lie just around the corner. Their faith in steel mills, aluminum plants, hydroelectric dams, and the like was nurtured by the World Bank and other apostles of economic development. They chose ecologically disruptive programs of economic growth as the best means to right the historical wrongs of colonialism, to bring prosperity to the masses, and in some cases to line their own pockets.

In the major Communist economies ideological commitments to proletarian society, a fervent wish to outstrip capitalism as quickly and as conspicuously as possible, and the urge to build military-industrial complexes fueled a similar investment in heavy, pollution-intensive and resource-intensive industry. Despite a flock of albatrosses around its neck, the Soviet economy grew quickly from the late 1940s to the 1970s, and so did those of Eastern Europe. China's grew too, mainly by virtue of rapid population growth.

In the industrial capitalist core, economic growth almost matched that of the Third World and the Communist economies, thanks in large part to Japan's recovery and expansion. A few lonely dissenters notwithstanding, the existing paradigm of heavy industry remained securely in place, joined by an increasingly industrialized agriculture. In quantitative terms, the world economy by 1970 was dizzy with success.

Exuberant growth, and the forms it took, quickened the metabolism of the world economy. The quantities of energy and materials required, and of wastes and pollution generated, more than tripled in a generation.[2] This unprecedented (and still unmatched) spurt of global economic growth, averaging nearly 5 percent per annum, had many cheerful effects, but it came with some unsettling ecological trends. Because of cheap energy and market integration, much of the ecological disturbance occasioned by this growth could take place in remote, lightly peopled, or politically weak regions, as the populous, prosperous, and powerful centers preferred: no French *département* would have tolerated the nickel mining and smelting that occurred in New Caledonia, nor would New York have accepted what was routine in New Mexico. But everywhere, in one form or another, economic growth made increasingly visible demands on ecological support systems.

A big part of the global economic growth spurt derived merely from global population growth. No one worried about this in the 1930s, but by the late 1940s a few voices raised doubts about the implications of further growth, and by the late 1960s many distinguished scientists and statesmen did as well. Human numbers climbed from about 2.5 billion in 1950 to nearly 4 billion in 1970. By 1968–1972 population growth reached a historic rate, just above 2 percent per annum. This provoked acute fears of famine, resource depletion, and overcrowding that would diminish the quality of life and perhaps invite epidemics and pandemics.

In low-fertility countries population growth also provoked political worries among those of a Physiocratic bent. If one believed that power accrued to countries with large populations, then the geography of the population boom held implications for the international distribution of power. The old European colonial powers, the United States, and the Soviet Union, despite their baby booms, were reproducing far more slowly than the former colonial populations in Asia, Africa, and Latin America. Europe (west of the USSR), for example, accounted for a sixth of humankind in 1945 but only a ninth by 1975. Limiting population growth in a global sense necessarily meant checking it in the "Third World" and thereby slowing the demographic eclipse of the great powers. Thus population limitation held a political appeal to some for whom environmental concerns normally did not register.

Out of genuine concern, and in response to carrots and sticks, countries around the world adopted population restriction policies, a novelty in statecraft. For most of the last five thousand years, states concerned themselves with population growth only if trying to maximize it. The most effective attempt at fertility control was China's so-called one-child policy, adopted in 1978 shortly after Mao's death. His successors, worried about the prospect of famine (they all remembered the Great Leap Forward), reversed Mao's usual position that there could never be too many Chinese. That telescoped a demographic transition into twenty years. India, building on colonial precedents, as early as 1953 adopted policies to discourage fertility, though less stringent than China's.[3] A conspicuous outlier in population policy was Ceaușescu's Romania, where after 1966 all forms of fertility control were illegal and the secret police saw to it that Romanian women did not shirk their reproductive duties.

People inclined toward a biological view (economists normally saw things differently) feared that population growth would lead to Malthusian crunches, and thereby to revolutions and wars. Hence governments took notice, and international organizations sprang up or retooled to help limit fertility, all in the interest of preserving either the environment or tranquillity among nations—or both. Population anxieties were a central part of global-scale environmentalism, and remained so until climate change seized center stage in the late 1980s.

While population growth did not in fact lead to widespread famines, other trends supported the belief that ecological stress threatened human (and biospheric) well-being. Consider, for example, the Green Revolution, urbanization, and motorization.

The Green Revolution, a technological package of high-yield crops, fertilizers, pesticides, and (in most cases) irrigation and mechanization, was the main reason why population growth did not provoke giant famines in the 1960s and 1970s. Yields per acre in wheat, rice, and maize doubled and tripled. It was the equivalent of finding a new continent with the size and soil fertility of North America. Despite the political and public relations focus on the Green Revolution in the Third World, its miracles applied in Sussex and Saskatchewan as much as in Sonora and Sindh. Only the USSR remained unaffected: Soviet commitment to Lysenkoism through 1964 prevented the necessary manipulation of crop genomes, obliging the USSR to gamble on plowups such as the ill-fated Virgin Lands scheme in place of a revolution in yields. (Trofim Lysenko, 1898–1976, Stalin's favorite biologist, maintained that acquired biological characteristics were heritable, counter to the standard view, and thus that crop breeds could be improved by manipulating their environments.) Even Mao's China, despite the disruptions of the Cultural Revolution, succeeded in developing high-yield rice strains. Everywhere, under all manner of economic systems, the technologies of the Green Revolution strongly rewarded larger scales of production: sprawling fields of single crops.

Everywhere the success of the Green Revolution required new agrochemicals. The pesticides needed to combat the vulnerability of monocropping often proved indiscriminate killers. Most of them were persistent in the environment and bio-accumulative, meaning that they worked their way up through the food web in ever larger concentrations. They killed helpful and harmful insects alike, and often birds and reptiles that ate the insects, as Rachel Carson among others pointed out.[4] Where farmworkers lacked sufficient protections, pesticides slowly killed them too, via nasty toxins absorbed through their skin and lungs. Fertilizers upset aquatic ecosystems by providing excess nitrogen and phosphorus, the key limiting elements in most plant growth, thereby leading to algal blooms, especially in stagnant and warm water. (Untreated sewage also made major contributions of excess nitrogen and phosphorus.) When they decayed, these blooms gobbled up dissolved oxygen, robbing other species of their share, creating "dead zones" without aquatic life. Huge ones developed in the Black Sea and the Gulf of Mexico, for example, and eventually in the Yellow Sea too.

Almost everywhere the Green Revolution also required a new scale of irrigation. More and bigger dams went up; the 1960s and 1970s formed the historic peak in dam construction around the world. This inevitably meant flooding out forests or populated areas, disrupting downstream aquatic ecosystems, changing the erosion and sedimentation regimes of rivers, and much more besides. People and other species had to adapt, migrate, or disappear. The irrigation water provided by the dams helped crops to grow. Most of it did not enter root systems, however, but either evaporated or lingered in the soil, leading to rising water tables and waterlogging. Where evaporation rates were high, as in Australia, Punjab, Xinjiang, or Mexico, that brought salinization. Snowy-white crusts of salt slowly appeared on farmers' fields, showing intensive irrigation to be, in places, a short-term strategy.

So the food won in the Green Revolution came at an ecological and human health cost. This accounts for part of the controversy that swirled around it from the 1970s onward (the other part derives from alleged impacts on property concentration). In Mexico and India especially, but also in California and Languedoc, the Green Revolution's chemicals earned many enemies. They seemed, to some, part of another colonial or Yankee imposition, an arrogant expression of presumed superiority on the part of technical experts at the expense of peasants.

The food surpluses of the Green Revolution helped accelerate the twentieth century's trend of urbanization. Fewer and fewer people could grow more and more food, so the villages sent their unneeded young to the cities. Whereas in 1900 about a seventh of humankind lived in cities, by 1975 more than a third did. Meanwhile (1880–1950), an unremarked turning point came in the human condition: urban death rates sank below urban birthrates for the first time in history. Formerly city life had killed people faster than others were born, but improvements in disease control after 1880 gradually revised that fundamental fact. After 1950 urban growth increasingly outpaced the capacity of municipal administrations to build infrastructure for sewage, water, or electricity. So the proportion of people living in shantytowns grew, especially in the Third World, where village birthrates remained high. Enormous—and enormously discouraging—slums soon surrounded megacities such as Manila, Karachi, Abidjan, and Lima. In the rich world, urbanization after 1950 took the form mainly of suburbanization, the auto-enabled sprawl pioneered in the United States and Canada in the 1920s.

In the proliferation of both shantytowns and suburbia it was easy to see environmental degradation. In the first case, crowded and unsanitary conditions prevailed most conspicuously, and only children born and raised among the garbage and impromptu sewers, unaware that any other human habitats existed, did not find such urban conditions a form of degradation. Ex-villagers, even if they could make a better living picking over the garbage dumps of a megacity than they could tilling a tiny plot back home, re-sented the transition they felt forced upon them. This helped fuel an urban form of what Juan Martínez-Alier calls the "environmentalism of the poor," focused on local health and quality of life issues, and informed by burning social resentments.[5] Suburbia, while it might have looked like paradise to those stuck in shantytowns, was seen by others as the loss of fertile farmland, wetland wildlife habitat, or old-growth forests, combined with the proliferation of ugly strip malls, parking lots, and soulless housing tracts. Hence the urban turn in late-twentieth-century world history, in its various forms, helped inspire notions that humans were degrading their planet and their lives.

Motorization helped support this impression too. In the nineteenth century, railroads had led to deforestation (for fuel and crossties), pollution, and the sudden ability of urban populations to escape the city and appreciate the splendors of nature. Automobiles did equivalent things, only more so. While they did not have much direct impact on forests, they led to huge expansions in road networks, pavement, and attendant changes in local ecologies; to enormous increases in urban pollution loads and changes in urban air pollution chemistry; to the proliferation of rubber plantations (for tires) in Liberia, Malaysia, and elsewhere; and to a new ability to visit nature on the weekends. Once cars became routine accoutrements of middle-class and even working-class family life (1915–1950 in the United States and Canada, 1950–1970 in Western Europe), the "demand" for nature in agreeable forms skyrocketed. After cars entered the picture, the crowded, noisy, and polluted conditions of city life, and perhaps the banality of suburbia too, drove people to seek antidotes, or at least relief, amid forest and stream. Where they did not already exist, accessible arcadias had to be created: parks and protected areas acquired political support as never before. This process obtained chiefly in those lands where cars had colonized human life, which as of the 1970s meant only North America and Western Europe, and to some extent Japan.

All these trends (and others unmentioned here) contributed to the emergence of the new environmentalism. So too did some portentous ecological and political events of the 1960s and 1970s. They might have gone unnoticed in earlier times, but in the context of the age, and with its communications media, they instead became iconic symbols of a world gone ecologically awry. Oil spills such as that of the *Torrey Canyon* off Cornwall (1967), the Union Oil platforms in the Santa Barbara Channel (1969), or the *Amoco Cadiz* off Brittany (1978) made the TV news and galvanized formerly placid populations against pollution. Plans to turn one of New Zealand's scenic wonders, Lake Manapouri, into a reservoir for a new dam turned countless Kiwis into conservationists almost overnight. A successful lawsuit against a chemical company that had lethally contaminated Minamata Bay, killing and grotesquely deforming local residents, inspired environmentalist enthusiasm in Japan. The 1973 oil crisis, while entirely unecological in character, seemed to confirm the dire predictions of resource depletion made above all in the Club of Rome's 1972 *Limits to Growth*.[6] The big El Niño of 1972–73 ruined Peru's anchovy fisheries and sent that nation's economy into a tailspin. A 1976 explosion at a chemical plant producing herbicides just north of Milan loosed a dioxin cloud on unsuspecting Italians, especially in the downwind community of Seveso. A 1979 accident at Three Mile Island (Pennsylvania) cast new doubt on the safety of civilian nuclear power.

Ten thousand more industrial accidents, mountain landslides, legal battles, and scientific revelations helped mobilize new publics in the cause of environmentalism. Sometimes, as with the oil shock or El Niño, the events had nothing to do with human mistreatment of the environment. Others, such as Three Mile Island, although it came close to a meltdown, were in fact much less serious than previous (more secret) accidents. But nonetheless, they all contributed to a general sense that things were out of whack and business as usual was responsible. Citizens, where they had liberty to do so, demanded their governments step in to protect the environment and public health.

Armed with a growing sense that the environment was under siege, and galvanized by the cultural climate in which demonstrations and marches had become commonplace, ecologically minded citizens took to the streets. Street demonstrations, long a part of politics in industrial cities, worked especially well in the TV age and proliferated in the 1960s. For American environmentalists the culmination came in 1970 with Earth Day, a demonstration and "teach-in" across the United States that by some counts involved 20 million people, or roughly a tenth of the national population. The fact that it fell on Lenin's one hundredth birthday (April 22) heightened suspicion in some quarters that its organizers, who included a senator from Wisconsin, served Communist interests.[7] Smaller demonstrations picketed notorious polluters, at least in countries where such displays carried minimal risks to life and limb: in Pinochet's Chile or Brezhnev's USSR, street demonstrations over environmental issues were few and far between.

Rural populations engaged in acts of political environmentalism too. It was much harder for them to attract attention, and more tempting for authorities to use force to disperse them. But despite the less promising ratio of risk to reward, villagers in various settings organized themselves to protest, and sometimes to try to prevent, logging or dam building or mine pollution in their vicinities. Peruvians protested the expansion of copper smelting that doused their pastures in sulfur dioxide. Ecuadorians objected to oil drilling that left pools and residues of petroleum in their forests and fields. Filipinos tried to block logging companies from harvesting timber. Hundreds of such environmental protests took place in the 1970s (and afterwards). Sometimes they involved sabotage and violence; sometimes they led to army and police massacres. Often they ended in brokered deals and financial compensation that scarcely affected the balance sheets of logging and mining companies, though they satisfied at least some of the protesting poor. Rarely did they bring about major reductions in the pace of logging or mining, but occasionally these deals lessened their environmental impacts.

Wherever the law was a suitable instrument, the environmental movement quickly became institutionalized and bureaucratized, and lost some of its spontaneous and countercultural qualities. Legislatures began to turn out environmental law, and law schools to churn out environmental lawyers. Environmental NGOs, many of which had existed as single-interest groups for decades, became lobbying and fund-raising machines, especially in the United States and Europe. This inevitably disappointed some environmentalists, for whom lawyers and lobbyists could never be on the side of the angels, and thus fragmentation followed, as a few purists preferred various forms of direct action, while the majority supported or acquiesced in the political taming of environmentalism. This rift showed most clearly in West Germany, where a Green Party formed in 1979. Electoral success in 1983 obliged it to take part in the sausage making (as Bismarck called lawmaking) of the Bundestag; its membership split into "Realos," willing to work within the system, and unwilling "Fundis." In this trajectory of growth and schism, environmentalism resembled many other social (and religious) movements that splintered under the impact of success.[8]

Even the environmentalism of the poor underwent institutionalization to some degree. In the Indian Himalaya, a landscape with a rich tradition of peasant protest, a formal organization sprang up in 1973 to contest loggers' access to montane forests (the Chipko Andalan). In 1977 the Kenyan Green Belt movement coalesced, an organization mainly of women devoted to planting trees to check erosion and desertification. These, and several hundred like movements, emerged in response to peasants' grievances over new initiatives to log, mine, or dam up parts of the environment of use to them. They did not, by and large, extol biodiversity, wilderness, or beauty in nature. They were concerned with the practical benefits of forests, soil, water, and with who had the rights to these benefits. They were, in the main, rural. Many were composed chiefly of, and some led by, women; they, after all, were the ones who collected fuel wood from the dwindling forests, carried water from stream to home, and took responsibility for the health of children. Most of the development projects intended to lift poor countries out of poverty, and much of the quickening of the globe's metabolism, carried unwelcome consequences for rural women. In many countries, India and Brazil included, it was also politically astute to have women stand athwart logging roads defying trucks and bulldozers, as it raised the political costs to the state of using violence to help the loggers and dam builders on their way. These new organizations often found allies within religious establishments dedicated to the welfare of the downtrodden, the Catholic Church (at least its liberation theology wing) in Latin America, or the Buddhist clergy in South and Southeast Asia.[9]

Meanwhile governments and state bureaucracies adapted nimbly to the political implications of popular environmentalism. Beginning in 1967 in Sweden and 1970 in the United States, ministries and agencies appeared, charged with safeguarding national environments. This was new. For centuries regulations had existed concerning specific environmental nuisances or problems such as local air pollution or regional soil erosion. A few rulers had busied themselves with forest or wildlife protection, such as Peter the Great in Russia (1672–1725). In West Germany a spate of regulations concerning air pollution had come in the late 1950s. But now the state stepped in, assuming powers to regulate the environment as a whole. Traditional conservatives who typically scorned everything associated with street demonstrations, men such as Adenauer, Pompidou, and Nixon, sought to align themselves with environmentalism and supported the new regulation. After 1970 environmental agencies and ministries pro-liferated, so that almost every country not enmeshed in civil war created one. Local and provincial governments opened their own offices for envi-ronmental protection too. Of course the impact of all this was variable. In Cuba, for example, environmental law and regulation had minimal impact. In West Germany it had a lot.[10]

On the level of international politics, modern environmentalism, espe-cially environmental globalism, made minor impacts. The exigencies (real and imagined) of the Cold War, combined with commitments to economic growth, narrowed the opportunities for environmentalism to affect world affairs. Cold War powers felt constrained to build and maintain military-industrial complexes, including nuclear weapons, and to accept the envi-ronmental costs. Indeed Cold War pressures provided convenient ways to demonize environmentalists, who in the Soviet Union were often depicted as traitorous agents of the capitalist enemy and in the West as "the Trojan horse of the Soviet cavalry."[11] Leaders of poor countries, such as Indira Gandhi, often maintained that their people wanted more pollution rather than less, because pollution meant national economic progress.[12] None-theless, the growing pressure from the grass roots, together with mounting anxieties among scientists and diplomats, brought environmental issues squarely into the arena of international politics.

There were precedents. Bilateral accords on fishing rights and seal pro-tection date back to the early twentieth century or before. Perhaps the first major instance of environmental concerns affecting international poli-tics was the nuclear test–ban treaty of 1963, intended (among other things) to limit the radioactive fallout in the atmosphere.

In the 1970s international environmental accords followed thick and fast: on dumping at sea, on Antarctica, on regional seas such as the Baltic and the Mediterranean, on acid rain. Under UN auspices nations gathered to discuss the environment (Stockholm, 1972), population (Bucharest, 1974), and food problems (Rome, 1974). The UN created its own unit for environmental preservation in 1972, the United Nations Environment Programme (UNEP), headquartered in Nairobi. The fact that the UN al-ready existed, and that preservation of the health of the earth was an easy goal for all to support, at least in the abstract, helped to turn the tide toward international cooperation and accords.

Conventional Cold War politics did not fade away: the USSR and Po-land, for example, boycotted the Stockholm gathering because East Germany was not invited. Nonetheless, almost everywhere mid-level bureaucrats, diplomats, and their masters had begun either to take environmental issues seriously or at least to calculate that they must appear to do so. No doubt many of them felt genuinely, as millions of less powerful people did, that something needed to be done, and they sought arenas where they could achieve something. Their conception of how best to protect national interests now extended into new terrain—population, food, women's reproductive rights, seafloor mining, the distribution of weather information from satellites, and so forth. In their quest to do the right thing, sometimes they negotiated accords that cost their domestic constituents.[13]

In taking this environmental turn, they received some help from détente beginning around 1969–70. As the United States began to seek a way to leave Vietnam, and the USSR grew more worried about China, the superpowers became more open to negotiation. They and their allies found that environmental issues suited their situations: little of immediate value seemed to be at stake, and something of an international community of scientists existed which could be enlisted to support negotiations, and for whom geopolitical issues were less divisive.

Thus, for example, in the late 1960s and early 1970s the states bordering the Baltic Sea came together to try to hammer out accords on pollution control. The Baltic for reasons of physical geography is especially vulnerable to pollution, and in the mid-twentieth century it got a heavy dose of urban sewage, industrial effluent, and agricultural runoff. Anyone with eyes or a nose was easily persuaded of the problem. Finland's neutrality helped to bring the parties together, but quarrels over the status of East Germany (not then recognized by West Germany) bedeviled negotiations. After much wrangling, which led to the formal recognition of East Germany in 1972, diplomats in 1974 achieved the first multilateral convention signed by members of rival Cold War alliance systems. The USSR used the Baltic environmental issue to achieve recognition of East Germany. But at the same time, the resolution of the German question and the general atmosphere of détente made environmental accords much easier to reach. It is hard to imagine diplomats negotiating the Helsinki Convention amid the chilly Cold War politics of the 1950s or the early 1980s. So in short, environmental negotiations boosted détente and détente smoothed environmental negotiations.[14]

Environmentalism also added energy to nuclear disarmament initiatives. By the 1970s the nuclear arsenals of the great powers, especially the superpowers, worried almost everyone who knew of them. Most of the anxiety concerned the possibility that nuclear weapons might be used for the purposes for which they were built. But part of it concerned the possibility of accidents and contamination. Constituencies formed, especially in Europe, for which antinuclear politics served as the unifying principle, bringing together peace activists and environmentalists. Their numbers, commitment, and influence tended to be strongest in NATO countries that hosted nuclear weapons installations, West Germany above all. People in Warsaw Pact countries often felt much the same way about nuclear weapons, and often were permitted to voice public support for peace and disarmament, but rarely for the reduction or abolition of nuclear weapons on environmental grounds.

In short, in the context of Cold War politics, while there were constraints on the degree to which states felt they could deviate from the template of heavy industrial energy- and pollution-intensive economies, these constraints loosened slightly with détente. Simultaneously, with looser constraints, the arena for environmental diplomacy widened, some agreements were reached, and some trust was built, in turn making détente a bit deeper. When détente died in 1979–80 and the Cold War entered another frosty phase, the room for political maneuver available to advocates of environmental restraint narrowed dramatically.

Détente, interestingly, had its ecological consequences too. When the United States began to ship grain to the Soviet Union, an exchange of sea creatures accompanied the cargoes. All oceangoing vessels carry ballast water from time to time, which they take in at one harbor and often deposit weeks later in another. They also take in small species of marine life, and the eggs or small fry of larger ones. In this way the Black Sea acquired a species of comb jelly *(Mnemiopsis leidyi)* via American freighters coming from East Coast harbors. In the estuaries of eastern North America it was and is an inconspicuous and inoffensive creature, sometimes called "sea walnut," easily kept in check by local predators. In the Black Sea, however, it reproduced exuberantly and ruthlessly devoured the same foods that had formerly sustained a large anchovy population on which a Soviet fishery was based. By the mid-1980s the comb jelly accounted for the majority of the biomass in the Black Sea, and the anchovy fishery vanished, adding slightly to the economic woes of the crumbling USSR. (In the late 1980s Soviet ecosystems retaliated with the zebra mussel, a major nuisance to North American aquatic life at a cost of billions of dollars a year.)

The long 1970s saw the crystallization of a new force in the culture and politics of the world: modern environmentalism. Taking shape in response to the environmental disruptions that came with pell-mell economic growth in the Age of Exuberance, in a context of counterculturalism, and with the aid of new technologies (of pollution, of detection, and of communication), environmentalism influenced political life on local, national, and international scales. A new concern emerged for global-scale issues that seemed to require international cooperation, but at the same time, local-scale environmental activism and political action proliferated around the world.

The salience and power of environmentalism have ebbed and flowed since the 1970s. Levels of concern have varied with the apparent severity of environmental problems; so, for example, the recent science and publicity concerning climate change have made global warming politically and culturally important. But the waning and waxing of environmentalism varies at least as much with the "space" available on the agendas of citizens and states after attention to the more urgent priorities of short-term security and economic growth. When security seems assured and the economic pie is growing, environmentalism flourishes in the resulting anxiety vacuum. When security is in peril and the economy shrinking, environmentalism fades into the background. That is less a reflection on the relative seriousness of the issues confronting people and politicians than on their temporal urgency: environmental issues seemingly can be put off to tomorrow at low cost. They will, most of them, grow more severe if neglected, but only slowly. Hence the 1970s added a new dimension to global politics, one which altered and complicated, but did not revolutionize, the procedures of international society. Only environmental disaster is likely to change that.

PART V

Ideological, Religious, and Intellectual Upheaval

CHAPTER 17

Globalizing Sisterhood

International Women's Year and the Politics of Representation

JOCELYN OLCOTT

ATTENDING AN OFFICIAL DINNER celebrating the 1975 International Women's Year (IWY) conference in Mexico City, U.S. feminist Betty Friedan sidled among the reflecting pools and Olmec sculptures at the National Anthropology Museum in hopes of befriending delegates from the People's Republic of China. Observing the PRC women's conspicuous indicators of oppression—they wore "blue uniforms and no make-up; the head of the delegation had square-cut black hair"—Friedan spoke to them through an interpreter, declaiming the accomplishments of the U.S. feminist movement. Suddenly the Chinese ambassador "barked out something that sounded authoritative," and the women withdrew from the conversation. Undaunted by either the obvious language barriers or the ambassador, who, as if "blocking a tackle in a football game," tried to prevent further contact, Friedan persisted: "She [the leader of the delegation] was a woman. I didn't accept the impossibility of talking to her. Maybe if I could sit next to her, some woman-to-woman things would get across."[1] In an account of the conference that tacked between outright paranoia and the style of a James Bond–esque thriller, Friedan declared:

> Despite every effort to keep the women divided—including violent disruptions played up by the media—we women united in Mexico City—women from the Third World, Latin-Americans, Africans in turbans, Indians in saris, antifascists from Greece, feminists from Japan, Australia, Mexico and women who didn't want to be called feminists from Nigeria and Ecuador,

as well as Americans, black, brown and white—to insist that women's equality couldn't wait on a "New Economic Order."[2]

Friedan echoed a concern that had haunted organizers for months before the inauguration of the conference: that "politics" would overshadow "women's issues," a formulation that assumed not only a bright line between the two but also a shared understanding of where that line lay. Friedan and others lamented the insertion of "politics" into the IWY events as the orchestration of male politicians who, like the Chinese ambassador, wanted to prevent women from expressing their sincere needs and aspirations. Remove the cynical manipulations of power-hungry male politicians, the thinking went, and authentic "woman-to-woman" solidarity would prevail.

Solidarity across geopolitical fault lines, however, seemed remote by 1975. Waves of decolonization had transformed the UN—and particularly the Economic and Social Council (ECOSOC), which organized the IWY conference—into a supranational advocate for postcolonial nations. The North Vietnamese had secured a victory earlier in the summer; Angola was on the eve of independence; and Mozambique gained independence during the conference's first week, prompting a hasty invitation to join the proceedings.[3] Puerto Rican and Panamanian representatives persistently demanded an end to U.S. sovereignty over their territories. With the UN's General Assembly rapidly growing and diversifying, the IWY, though hardly the first international women's conference, was the largest and most diverse to date in terms of regions and social sectors represented. Given such a motley cast of participants both at the intergovernmental conference and at the less decorous, more freewheeling nongovernmental organization (NGO) tribune, questions of representation became an arena of intense dispute, not only over the question of who would speak for "women" as a coherent subject but also over who would attend the IWY events and for whom they spoke, the relationship between the intergovernmental conference and the NGO tribune, and the expectations for democratic process at both venues.

Although participants concurred that women's status demanded improvement, different models for achieving social change—ranging from armed revolution to consciousness-raising sessions to state-orchestrated modernization and development schemes—competed for legitimacy. Ideological feuds between Marxists and feminists often degenerated into a

chicken-or-egg debate over the tired question of whether women's emancipation must precede or follow economic justice—the feminist imaginary
of class collaboration to wage the "battle of the sexes" versus the Marxist
paradigm of revolution through class struggle—with fervent partisans in
both camps. Amid intense disagreements about strategies and tactics,
complex webs of alliances and animosities developed over the course of
the two-week conference, and the dream of a "global sisterhood" seemed
increasingly impossible as identities and ideologies distorted communication, and parliamentary procedure clashed with expectations of direct democracy. After describing the context of the IWY events, this chapter
considers both the anticipation and the experience of identity-based representation as participants pulled at different threads of identity—based
on race, class, ethnicity, sex, sexual orientation, nationality, regionalism,
political affiliation, and ideological affinity—to insist on one being more
germane than the others.[4] In the end, the IWY efforts foundered on the
question of not only who could represent but also what they represented.[5]
As different actors pulled at these threads of identity, they collectively un-
raveled the "woman" at the center of International Women's Year.

Of course, politics had informed every aspect of the conference, from
its location to its agenda, even before its conception. In 1972 the Women's
International Democratic Federation, a Communist-dominated NGO,
persuaded the Romanian delegate to the Commission on the Status of
Women (CSW) to propose a UN Year of the Woman to assess the progress
of the CSW in improving women's status. The General Assembly designated 1975 as International Women's Year, and Warsaw Pact countries began to plan a conference in East Berlin in October 1975. Although the
U.S. State Department originally resisted holding the conference, it reversed its position when its CSW representative, Patricia Hutar, pointed
out that the only major IWY event would take place in East Berlin.[6] At the
urging of non-Communist countries, in December 1974 the UN approved
a modest budget for a conference initially planned for Bogotá and then
moved to Mexico City as civil unrest mounted in Colombia.[7] Mexican
president Luis Echeverría, who was openly jockeying to succeed Kurt
Waldheim as the UN's secretary-general, welcomed the relocation with
alacrity.

Given the UN's rapid transformation, organizers and journalists alike
seemed braced for a First World–Third World showdown. The conference's three themes of equality, peace, and development appeared to map

geopolitically, reinforcing expectations that fault lines would run between the First, Second, and Third Worlds. "These are the three main differences," Elaine Livingstone explained to her fellow members of the New York City–National Organization for Women (NOW) chapter after an IWY planning meeting:

> The developing countries feel that women cannot gain equality until their countries are more developed economically, Mexico and a few other countries feel that a *new economic* order must come first, and the USSR feels that peace is the first priority. The United States and the United Kingdom stressed that women cannot wait until these large world problems are solved, that women's problems are not a reflection of society's problems, but part of them, therefore when women's status improves so will the economy and chances for peace.

Explicitly locating herself within these debates, she went on to assure her comrades that the draft plan of action "contains many of our objectives: equality of economic and educational opportunities, equal sharing between men and women of household and child rearing duties, day care centers, etc."[8] Friedan drew the lines even more starkly, carping to *New York Times Magazine* editor Gerald Walker:

> Communists, Arabs and the Vatican are joining in a line that "women's liberation[,]" "equality" and the like are Western imperialist inventions, irrelevant to the interests of the majority of women of the world, especially the Third World women who "need to have 12 children," as the line goes, "are happily integrated into feudal economies, extended families, and tribal cultures whose ingrained values of male supremacy must be respected, etc." The proponents of this line want to turn the whole International Women's Year into a promotion of a "new economic order," or "down with western imperialism."[9]

ECOSOC organizers focused overwhelmingly on the themes of equality and development, and the theme of "peace" seemed to have dropped out entirely; as one Mexican newspaper editorialized, "development is the new name for peace."[10] Thus, before the opening session, journalists anticipated conflicts between "Third World women," who tended to focus on structural problems of economic inequality, and "Western feminists," who concentrated their energies on sex-specific issues such as reproductive freedom, wage equity, and women's educational and professional opportunities. The *New York Times* noted, "Observers agree that the major goal set out by the organizers—improving the status of women—is not going to be an easy one in light of the political arguments that are expected to erupt between delegates of the industrialized countries and the third world."[11]

As Friedan's and Livingstone's comments indicate, perhaps no "political" question absorbed U.S. observers as much as the threat of the New International Economic Order (NIEO). President Echeverría touted his advocacy of the NIEO and its UN manifestation, the Charter of the Economic Rights and Duties of States, as evidence of his international leadership, and after a Caracas planning meeting, U.S. officials reported with alarm that the Mexican delegation rallied support for a declaration endorsing the NIEO at the IWY conference.[12] State Department spokesperson Mildred Marcy acknowledged that the United States faced "public-relations challenges" related to the NIEO and disarmament but saw the IWY as an opportunity to demonstrate "a profound responsiveness to a new current which is on the side of constructive change."[13] A Ford Foundation officer explaining the need for a daily newspaper of the NGO tribune emphasized the importance of countering the "Third World political polemic" about the "world economic order."[14]

Other observers, especially those from outside the United States, cautioned organizers against assuming a universal understanding of the divide between politics and women's issues. As Waldheim's speechwriter warned, the IWY organizers "do not sufficiently appreciate the suspicion and hostility of many developing countries towards the essentially 'advanced Western' point of view which dominates their attitudes." He cautioned the secretary-general to "steer a careful course between the Scylla of vague generalities and the Charybdis of precise, and highly controversial, recommendations."[15] Challenging the idea that issues such as the NIEO constituted an unwelcome intrusion into a conference cordoned off for "women's issues," Mexico's ruling party newspaper editorialized:

> Those themes that have been dubbed political are the preoccupation of those nations that have been globalizing in the so-called Third World, and those more particular to women's conditions are raised by the rich nations. The division is fundamental, significant: each human being has the preoccupations of its moment, and if women disagree over what is most important, it is because in their personal lives and as members of a national com-

munity, they live out of sync owing to varying levels of development. It is as if there were a world conference on consumer culture or waste: the women from the Horn of Africa, India, and Latin America would immediately politicize the theme, and it would be impossible to discuss the advisability of having two cars among those who form a fourth world of hunger and desperation.[16]

Emphasizing the scale of nation and even region—positing that the non-aligned Group of 77 (G-77) countries would respond more or less as one—this formulation obscured the class disparities and social inequities within nations, communities, and of course within households.

The fault lines that developed through these debates did not always follow predictable geopolitical divisions of East-West or North-South, however. Urban liberal feminists from Mexico City and Lagos made common cause with their counterparts from New York and Sydney, while radicals tried to forge alliances across entrenched divisions of nationalism and structural differences. Delegations from France, Chile, and Nigeria shared concerns that the G-77's focus on international politics would render the IWY conference like any other—all talk and no action.[17] Two of these three countries (Nigeria and Chile) had been among the original signatories of the G-77's 1964 charter. Although conditions had changed considerably in both countries in the intervening decade, both had substantial populations struggling with hunger and desperation, along with much smaller populations debating the advisability of a second car.

Concerns about politics edging out women's issues were hardly misplaced. Given the entrance of so many new political actors, many of them doubtful of ever again having an international audience, the Mexico City conference served as a petri dish for the conflicts that roiled the global 1970s. The participation of Egyptian first lady Jihan Sadat and her Israeli counterpart Leah Rabin highlighted ongoing efforts within the UN to brand Zionism as racism, pointing Israel down the same road that had led to South Africa's expulsion from the General Assembly. Soviet cosmonaut Valentina Tereshkova, having seen the planet from space, attested that nuclear war (and, by implication, nuclear proliferation) was a bad idea.[18] Metaphors of national liberation and decolonization—in aspirations to "decolonize women's minds" or liberate the "fourth world" within industrialized nations—drew inspiration from militarized struggles. As arguments raged over the dividing line between "terrorists" and "freedom fighters," similar debates arose about the distinction between "eugenics" and "family planning."[19] Advances in contraception, the rising voices of gay and lesbian movements and prostitutes' rights campaigns, and recent victories by abortion rights activists seemed to drag issues from the most intimate corners of the bedroom into the middle of the street as participants debated where the dividing line fell between liberation and libertinage. Efforts to discipline representations of women in the exploding "mass communications media" jostled with accusations that industrialized countries monopolized the major news outlets and representations of global affairs.[20] Furthermore, a significant divide emerged over the relationship between labor and women's emancipation. Amid an emerging post-Fordist emphasis on flexible accumulation and labor systems—between the demise of Bretton Woods and what would emerge by the 1980s as a full-throated attack on Keynesianism—conflicts arose over women's labor market participation and how to value women's uncommodified labor.

These clashes reached their fullest expression at the NGO forum, which the *New York Times* described as "the scene of much shouting, scheming, plotting, and general hell-raising."[21] The NGO tribune was among the first of its kind—there had been similar events at the UN's 1972 Stockholm environment conference and 1974 Bucharest population conference and Rome food conference—and marked the beginning of the NGO-ization of activism, particularly transnational women's activism.[22] While formerly only NGOs enjoying UN consultative status could attend these thematic conferences, the introduction of parallel NGO forums created a space for smaller NGOs and unaffiliated activists to confer. Memoirs and the ephemeral feminist press are rife with accounts of activists enthusing over the possibilities offered by the NGO tribune. U.S. feminists recounted hitchhiking or borrowing semi-reliable jalopies to get themselves to Mexico City. Indeed many activists traveled to Mexico City unaware that there would be two separate gatherings, much less that the NGO tribune would have no leverage over the intergovernmental conference.[23] Nevertheless, "while earlier it was the bigger, more established NGOs that attended the international conferences," recalls one UN activist, "at Mexico City, many smaller, South-based nontraditional NGOs found a meaningful space for themselves that went beyond tokenism."[24] The more established NGOs such as the International Planned Parenthood Federation and the Young Women's Christian Association looked down their institutional noses at the upstart organizations that populated the tribune, but these smaller, more

nimble groups defined the radical democratic spirit of the tribune, transforming it from a sober conference to a "global speak-out." Although the
tribune organizers had carefully planned a formal agenda, within a few
days of its inauguration participants started planning informal sessions
and caucus meetings, fostering lively discussions about the strategies for
achieving "emancipation" or "empowerment."[25]

These elevated expectations generated conflicts over how to describe
the boundaries of feminism and who could most authentically represent
women's interests.[26] Karen DeCrow, the recently elected president of
NOW's national board, warned in preparation for the NGO tribune that
there would be "not too many feminists" there. "It is essential that the
feminists of the world get together to discuss (not foreign affairs) but ways
in which we can cooperate to assure legal rights for women, the right to
choose abortion, child care, equal opportunities in education and training,
getting feminists into politics and government, and so forth."[27] Conflicts
over representation arose before the conference started, as national delegations formed and activists made plans to attend the NGO tribune, with
U.S. participants stressing the connection between identity and representation. U.S. feminists pounced when Henry Kissinger appointed Daniel
Parker, administrator of USAID (United States Agency for International
Development), to lead the U.S. delegation, prompting the addition of Patricia Hutar, a GOP activist, as co-chair to assuage feminist concerns. Although the absence of a Y chromosome proved insufficient to secure U.S.
feminists' support—critics used the epithet "wifey-poos" to refer to the
many members and even leaders of official delegations who secured invi-
tations as spouses of elected officials—identity apparently trumped ideology.[28]

Unsurprisingly, when Echeverría exercised his prerogative as leader of
the host country and appointed Attorney General Pedro Ojeda Paullada to
preside over the intergovernmental conference, U.S. feminists balked.
Friedan, chalking up the nomination to Mexican machismo, called for a
demonstration outside the intergovernmental conference to insist on a female president.[29] The Mexican press responded with a spate of interviews with Latin American women who insisted on effective advocacy for
women's rights rather than sex as the dispositive factor in selecting a conference president. Marta Andrade del Rosal, a Mexico City politician, dismissed Friedan's "rabid feminism," and the federal deputy Aurora Navia
Millán pointed out that Ojeda Paullada (in pointed contrast to his U.S.

counterpart) had helped to usher through a constitutional amendment putting Mexican women "at the vanguard in terms of jurisprudence."[30] The Venezuelan delegate Martha Regalado averred, "I think that Friedman [sic] errs in saying that it is an insult that a man presides over the meeting, since that is how they discriminate against our problems."[31] An unnamed Latin American participant at the NGO tribune challenged Friedan during the tribune's first plenary session. "The problem is not that men are in power," she declared to an audience of five thousand women, "but rather that the great imperialist powers cling to their privileges. For you, the most important problem is to liberate yourselves while preserving your standard of living; for the underdeveloped it is to liberate ourselves to eat. . . . You ask for solidarity among all women; tell me, can the servant and the mistress unite?"[32]

U.S. women of color—widely dubbed "Third World women" within the U.S. feminist movement—disavowed the United States delegation, instead seeking alliances with women of color from other parts of the world.[33] During a rowdy demonstration, some two hundred black and Chicana women and their supporters disrupted a ceremony to dedicate a commemorative U.S. postage stamp, whistling, shouting, and stomping until Hutar and Ambassador John Jova invited them to air their grievances.[34] Seeking solidarity with the geopolitical Third World, representatives of organizations such as the Congress of Racial Equality (CORE) and Raza Unida asserted that U.S. representatives had manipulated the IWY events to exploit less developed regions. Raza Unida leader Guadalupe Anguiano insisted, "Women's liberation requires first the liberation of the people to whom they belong."[35] In a rally at the highly politicized national university, Anguiano and several other Chicana speakers distanced themselves from what they dubbed the Anglo Feminist Movement, inviting supporters to attend a session led by Angela Davis, who had become a cause célèbre of the Mexican Left during her incarceration.[36]

Although the Ford administration had not, in fact, appointed an all-white delegation, the claims of identity politics should not be dismissed as softheaded multiculturalism seeking to preserve cultural heritage and subaltern epistemologies.[37] The 1974 UN Population Conference had made population control a central tenet of development programs, but widespread evidence of forced sterilizations of poor women and women of color made the policies look more like genocide than development.[38] Discussions of controlling resource depletion on the basis of per capita consumption—targeting U.S. and European populations as well as elites in poorer nations—rarely entered the debate and never gained any traction among policymakers. Domitila Barrios de Chungara, an organizer from Bolivia's Siglo XX tin miners' union, took issue with "the women who defended prostitution, birth control, and all those things," arguing that the Bolivian government resorted to "indiscriminate birth control" to avoid addressing issues of resource distribution and starvation wages.[39] Thus, these women's identity-based demands for representation grew from explicitly material concerns about the effects of racism on their own bodies. Nonetheless, U.S. Third World women failed to establish identitarian connections with women of color from other parts of the world. Even those who tried to underscore their support for the NIEO and economic justice found their gestures of solidarity largely unreciprocated. Chicana participants recalled later that they had viewed the conference as a homecoming and anticipated sharing a "common sisterhood" with Third World women, and particularly Mexican feminists. "We thought, oh, yeah, we're Mexican Americans," recounted Chicana activist Sandra Serrano Sewell. "We're going to find all these natural connections, you know, and sort of like a romantic view that was quickly dispelled."[40]

Arguably the bitterest and most vocal dispute about representation, however, arose over the legitimacy of the official Chilean delegation appointed by Augusto Pinochet. The 1973 overthrow of the democratically elected government of Salvador Allende had galvanized protests around the world, including many by feminist activists. The U.S. feminist press included particularly lurid accounts of women political prisoners being raped and tortured. After the coup, many Chilean women lived in exile in Mexico City, and Mexican leftist women's organizations vocally protested against the Chilean regime.[41] In early June 1975 women of Mexico's Partido Popular Socialista (PPS) launched a campaign to prevent the official Chilean delegation from being seated at the intergovernmental conference, calling instead for Allende's widow, Hortensia Bussi de Allende, to head the Chilean delegation.[42] Allende's sister Laura informed Mexican reporters that clashes between exiled Chileans and Pinochetistas would inevitably arise "when we speak of the punishments and torture we have suffered at the hands of the Chilean fascists."[43] Indeed from the first day of the journalists' pre-conference workshop until the last day of the NGO tribune, confrontations over Chile drew the attention of participants and reporters. Adherents of the Chile Solidarity Movement demonstrated outside the intergovernmental conference as Waldheim, Echeverría, and IWY secretary-general Helvi Sipilä delivered their inaugural addresses.[44] Chilean officials objected that a pro-government Chilean journalist—the editor of the government daily *La Patria*—was denied a visa.[45] NGO tribune organizer Marcia Bravo, a Chilean who had resided in New York since 1960, refused to answer reporters' questions about the Chilean regime.[46] Laura and Isabel Allende as well as Hortensia Bussi all addressed the NGO tribune to denounce U.S. imperialism and the torture of political prisoners.[47] A Communist-organized "antifascist" demonstration in support of the Chilean people drew nearly a thousand people according to police reports.[48]

Alicia Romo Román, the head of the Chilean delegation, lobbed the familiar accusation that her detractors were privileging politics over women's issues. "Our delegation is concerned," she told reporters, "because the World Conference on Women digresses from its objectives, falling into the terrain of the political."[49] When Romo addressed the intergovernmental conference, the auditorium emptied out—as it had during Leah Rabin's speech—as hundreds of delegates adjourned to the vestibule in protest. U.S. ambassador John Jova remained, along with a smattering of representatives from other Latin American dictatorships, to hear Romo dismiss Pinochet's critics as the Soviets' "servants, puppets, and useful idiots" and Bussi de Allende as a false widow, having only "played the role of a wife" during the Popular Unity government. Romo derided as "inconceivable" the accusations of torture and executions of women "supposedly detained and victims of Chilean barbarism."[50] When the intergovernmental conference's second committee passed a resolution calling on the Chilean military government to "desist immediately all executions, torture, persecution and other threats to liberty," Romo lost patience entirely. "I will not participate any longer in these meetings," she fumed. "Do what you will, but as a woman I do not want to appear as an accomplice nor to be pointed to in the future as a puppet of men."[51]

Despite the IWY's complex dynamics, historiography and popular memory have distilled its tensions—between the feminist establishment and rebellious newcomers, between rich and poor, and between ideological rivals—into the synecdoche of an apocryphal confrontation between Betty Friedan and the Bolivian union activist Domitila Barrios de Chungara.[52] Most pointedly, Pacifica Radio titled its interview with Friedan "Betty Friedan versus the Third World."[53] It was not Friedan whom Barrios de

Chungara confronted, however, but rather the *Mexican* liberal feminist Esperanza Brito de Martí, the president of Mexico's Movimiento Nacional de Mujeres (MNM), who insisted on cooperation among feminists.[54] Interrupting Brito's calls for unity, Barrios de Chungara exclaimed: "How can we women be equals when we, the wives of laborers, are thrown in jail for organizing to protest their imprisonment? We cannot speak of equality between games of canasta. Women cannot be equals any more than poor and rich countries can be equals."[55] The morphing of Esperanza Brito into Betty Friedan in the scholarly and popular imaginary highlights the extent to which complicated questions of representation at the IWY events became caught up with—and occasionally even reduced to—expectations of identity.

Friedan, meanwhile, faced off against participants who challenged her authority to represent them, drawing particular ire when she coordinated a separate meeting with Helvi Sipilä to offer what she understood to be the tribune's proposed amendments to the draft World Plan of Action—a maneuver that not only arrogated considerable authority to herself but also ignored the demands of the vocal and well-organized Latin American caucus. The Argentine participant Edith Reynaldi objected: "Mrs. Friedan does not represent the Tribune. [She] arrived here with an aura of fame from her book, *The Feminine Mystique,* which she has exploited."[56] According to news reports the Chicana delegate, Raza Unida leader Guadalupe Anguiano, accused Friedan and other liberal feminists of manipulating the tribune, focusing women's liberation on issues of "little transcendence," such as the freedom to control what one does with one's body, and "distracting attention that should be focused on the regional problems of oppressed peoples."[57] According to Mexican security reports, Anguiano lumped together Mexican liberal feminists with the "Anglo Feminist Movement," insisting that they all sought equality with men rather than popular liberation.[58]

The problem, however, was not that Friedan could not represent the tribune but rather that the tribune could not be represented. Or rather the imagined political subject could not be represented; aspirations that this "global consciousness-raising session" would distill out an essential shared womanhood remained starkly disappointed. Amid carefully crafted political performances meant to communicate geopolitical alliances and ideological affinities, the shock of the global at the IWY conference emerged from the impossibility and emptiness of the categories partici-

pants carried with them. As participants and observers struggled to describe the fault lines of the many conflicts at the conference and tribune,
they found themselves grasping at air. The anticipated affinities and animosities as often as not failed to materialize and sometimes—as in the
case of the Friedan–Barrios de Chungara dispute—had to be conjured.
Although it seems comical to consider Friedan's expectation that if she sat
next to a Chinese delegate, some "woman-to-woman" things would get
across, it is really no more improbable than the expectation of affinities between Chicanas and Mexicans or across (or even within) the diverse countries of the "Third World."

CHAPTER 18

Liberation and Redemption in 1970s Rock Music

REBECCA J. SHEEHAN

IN THE 1970s ROCK MUSIC played a central role in transforming attitudes about sex and gender in the United States. Gender norms and ideas about sex were in a state of flux because of increasing sexual permissiveness, rising divorce rates, the spread of mass pornography, and the women's and gay liberation movements. A musical form with roots in black and working-class rebellion, ghosts of which lived on in its rhythms, rock music valorized the individual and promoted a message of personal liberation. Its sound and sexual spectacle transgressed taboos that relegated sex to the private domain and repressed its expression in the public sphere. Rock provided an arena for the open display of female sexual desire, modeled gender roles that were antithetical to middle-class "norms" of the nuclear family, and made androgyny and homosexuality visible.[1]

The perceived threat that the new sexual culture posed to morality and Christian values contributed to the culture wars of the 1970s.[2] In response to the state's failure to act as a moral arbiter in issues including censorship, sexual behavior, and abortion, conservatives both criticized and co-opted liberation rhetoric and popular culture. In 1966 John Lennon prefigured these clashes and scandalized Christians around the world with his claim that the Beatles were "more popular than Jesus."[3] In opposing rock to Christianity, even if facetiously, Lennon underestimated the adaptability of both. In the 1970s young Christians and older evangelicals deployed the musical form and cultural force of rock music to reinvigorate Jesus as a cultural icon and to appeal to new audiences. In so doing, they attempted to redeem their losses to an increasingly secular—and sexual—culture.

Young people, whether they sought sexual liberation or spiritual redemption, were thus connected through rock music. Rock music forged new communities of fans and listeners within the United States as well as across national borders. Although rock music originated in the United States and was launched onto the international scene through the phenomenal record sales of Elvis Presley in the 1950s, the "British Invasion" spearheaded by the Beatles in the mid-1960s established its transatlantic character. The rise of rock criticism in the United States in the late 1960s, signaled by the success of the new trade publication *Rolling Stone* magazine, helped to counter the British Invasion.[4] Rock spread American images of freedom and rebellion and contributed to a worldwide renewal of America's cultural influence. Yet this did not function purely as a new imperialism. In repressive and authoritarian regimes the very act of listening to censored or banned, sex-positive, pro-individual music was an act of rebellion, as was performing original rock music in regional styles and gathering for rock music festivals.

Young people's buying power propelled the rise of rock 'n' roll. Empowered by their new role as independent consumers, young people literally gained a voice through the music they purchased, and with it a means to subvert the older generation's authority. Music corporations expanded and grew, seeking to develop niche marketing strategies. Rock's individualism and liberated sexuality were packaged and sold by record companies and transnational corporations around the world. In fact rock's transatlantic nature, the ease with which it created a sense of shared community across national boundaries, multiplied the strategies through which it could be sold to new markets.

Thus while rock music encouraged individualism and rebellion, it also helped to build global markets. The contradiction between rock music's message and its industrial structure became increasingly apparent in the 1970s. Rock's romantic ideals of individualism and rebellion fused with the consumer culture that commodified and disseminated it. Rock music culture, then, was a realm in which a key tension of the decade played out: the extent to which an individual can be liberated when that very liberation relies on market forces.[5]

Rock's Sexual Liberation

In the late 1960s Cynthia Plaster Caster, a Catholic teenager from Chicago, began making plaster casts of the erect penises of her favorite male musicians. Her adolescent sexual desire had been turned on by British musicians who appeared on television in "tight tailored trousers."[6] Cynthia learned Cockney rhyming slang—a working-class vernacular that replaces words with rhyming counterparts—from a little-known British band. She then used it to write explicit messages to her music idols asking if she could cast them; the borrowed language enabled her to avoid the "sin" of swearing, and to distinguish herself from other American groupies.[7] Equipped with art supplies contained in a logo-bearing traveling case and business cards that read "Plaster Casters of Chicago: Lifelike Models of Hampton Wicks," Cynthia—and various assistants who provided oral sex to maintain the musicians' erections—quickly gained notoriety in the world of rock. In 1968 she cast the rock legend Jimi Hendrix. Throughout the 1970s high-profile musicians, from the Rolling Stones to Led Zeppelin, requested audiences with her. In her bold articulation of sexual desire, in her active pursuit of fulfilling it, and through exposing and literally objectifying a part of the male body—she assigned each cast a five-digit serial number—Cynthia crossed boundaries of public and private as well as norms of "decent" female behavior. Both sex and the rock 'n' roll moment were commodified and consumed in her transactions.

Although Cynthia was a unique character both within and outside rock music groupie culture, her behavior and her penis "art," as she called it, were nonetheless emblematic of the new sexual dynamics that influenced and were enabled by rock culture. In the 1950s, Cold War Americans idealized men as breadwinners and women as domestic, and sought to contain female sexuality within marriage and the home.[8] The rock 'n' roll lifestyle rejected traditional gender roles and family structure through public and promiscuous sexual behavior. Rock music helped to increase the visibility of sex: via television variety shows, rock musicians entered suburban homes. Their sexually charged performances reflected and fed relaxing censorship laws. In 1973 the Supreme Court issued a new obscenity ruling giving individual states the power to determine the meanings of obscenity and to control its dissemination. The ruling allowed representations of explicit sex and pornography to circulate more widely and publicly than ever before.[9] By the mid-1970s sex was such a booming business and had become so intrinsic to the popular vernacular that the informant for the *Washington Post*'s Watergate investigation was named after the most infamous porn film of the decade, *Deep Throat*. Anti-rock conservative and religious groups coalesced with anti-porn feminists in their concern over rock music and pornography. Conservatives feared the moral threat posed to the American family. Although pro-sex feminists argued that sexual liberation was fundamental to women's liberation, anti-porn feminists were concerned about the valorization of male sexuality and the commodification of women's bodies, which they argued came at the cost of women's liberation.[10]

Indeed for men in rock 'n' roll, the term "cock rock," popularized by rock critics in the 1970s, summarized what its culture promoted: promiscuous male sexuality focused on the satisfaction of male desire.[11] When Jimi Hendrix compared rock stars of the 1960s to generals and soldiers in wartime, he unwittingly described the transformation of the spheres in which masculine desire would circulate: "[It u]sed to be the soldiers who were the gallant ones, riding into town, drinking the wine and taking the girls. Now it's the musicians."[12] This was the liberating promise of rock masculinity: it existed outside convention. Middle-class expectations of gentlemanly behavior were smashed along with hotel rooms, television sets, and musical instruments. But the strength of these men, in contrast with warriors of the past and the men drafted to fight in Vietnam, was not in military service but in playful civic life—in the altered states produced by marijuana and hallucinogens, and in the multiple sexual partners encountered on concert tours that represented a life far removed from suburban confines.[13] Certainly the rock music business banked on the rejection of the traditional family and tailored rock stars' images in opposition to middle-class domesticity. During a publicity campaign to boost a musician's image, one executive ordered: "Get a paternity suit filed against him. . . . Get him some groupie status."[14]

Groupies, mostly female fans who sought sex with rock stars, were at the vanguard of fan culture. By the late 1960s the music industry recognized how crucial groupies were to the business: they acted as "word-of-mouth" publicists; they created success for the musicians they favored; and their presence was considered a marker of stardom.[15] Groupies lived the freedoms of an increasingly permissive sexual culture. With sex disconnected from reproduction owing to the availability of the birth control pill and the effective legalization of abortion in 1973, biology no longer necessarily determined destiny: a woman could experiment sexually without the threat of pregnancy and domestic confinement.[16]

A dominant strand in women's liberation discourse focused on women experiencing and experimenting with their long-repressed sexuality. Groupies brought rock music together with this discourse of sexual freedom. They overturned stereotypes of the passive and passionless woman in their public and active displays of sexual desire. At the same time, given the relative absence of women as stars in their own right within the rock realm, and in light of the media representations of groupies as beautiful helpmeets at best and hangers-on at worst, groupies refashioned but also fed into a traditional gender hierarchy.[17]

The sexual and gender dynamic between heterosexual men and women in rock culture reflected broader debates about women's roles. In 1973 the feminist theologian Rosemary Ruether posed a question central to the debates: "Does the encounter culture and its cult of freer sexuality offer any genuine liberation to women, or is it not a retooling of their roles as sexual pacifiers?"[18] For Cynthia Plaster Caster, the groupie experience was liberating: "The sensation of being in control or being used does not occur to me. . . . [H]opefully the two of you," groupie and rock star, "are mutually attracted to each other, each getting their rocks off. . . . Except that the groupie has the added bonus of having scored a night in the sack with the Face on the cover of her favorite album."[19] She recognized implicitly that the commodification of bodies did not apply just to women in mainstream culture and especially in pornography: male bodies were also commodified in the rock realm.

The commodification of sex and pop culture was central to the advancing consumer culture and to the globalizing music industry, but rock musicians self-consciously critiqued this commodification even while capitalizing on it. In the late 1960s "glam" or "glitter" rock emerged, captivating and horrifying audiences with its norm-confronting spectacle: male rockers in women's makeup and clothing. As the *New York Times* described it, glam rock took "standard hard rock music as a framework for kinky lyrics, bizarre costumes, garish make-up, and, most of all, flamboyant stage shows that blend homo-eroticism and sado-masochism into a goulash of degeneracy."[20] With his 1972 rock music concept album and concert tour *The Rise and Fall of Ziggy Stardust and the Spiders from Mars*, the British musician David Bowie captured the zeitgeist of glam rock. As the title character, Ziggy, Bowie played an androgynous alien rock star who comes to an environmentally degraded Earth. Ziggy Stardust, through his "otherness," communicated escape from existing gender and sex roles while at the same time commenting on rock culture's nihilism. Aware that youth was ephemeral, he offered a momentary connection through sex, drugs, and rock when he sang, "Turn on with me and you're not alone." Ultimately, though, as the lyrics described, Ziggy was a "leper messiah," destroyed by the excesses of rock's hedonism, egotism, and fan worship. Taking his cue from the news-making gay liberation movement, Bowie gave press interviews claiming to be bisexual and wore makeup and women's clothes offstage; his outré persona won him the notoriety that contributed to his rise as an international media phenomenon.[21]

Glam rock masculinities were constructed transnationally but displayed national differences. Early glam rockers in the United States performed "glamour" as violent: they conjured demonic images through monstrous makeup and bloody stage theatrics. The earliest and most visible glam rock group in the United States was Alice Cooper. The band became infamous for "shock rock" antics, which included mock executions, chopping up baby dolls, and chasing live chickens around the stage.[22] They opened up possibilities for different masculine performance styles through on-stage cross-dressing but made clear to the press that they were heterosexual offstage. Early British glam rockers like Bowie and the band T Rex, by contrast, were androgynous and sexually ambiguous both on- and offstage. They used makeup to accentuate their beauty, and suggested a "third" gender identity through the cosmic imagery of stars, glitter, and alien life forms. Using tambourines to strum electric guitars and performing rock's traditional singer and guitarist solos in an explicitly homoerotic manner, they challenged neat categorizations of gender and sexual preference.[23]

Given its mostly male stars, within the music industry glam rock conserved male power even while parodying it. But glam rock's spectacle also created a permissive arena for—and made fashionable—gender ambiguity, homosexuality, and bisexuality.[24] Fashion was, of course, another realm of consumption, but it was also a symbolic marker of rebellion and style politics that empowered identities outside the mainstream and made them recognizable to one another.[25] Through shared taste in music and fashion, individuals who had been closeted by social norms were able to form connections and communities. Gay liberation groups did not necessarily recognize or embrace glam rock as a cultural formation of their politics, in part because any implication that sexual orientation was merely a fashion could work against their cause. Nonetheless, glam rock made sex and gender play visible and audible at a time when heterosexuality was considered the universal norm and religious groups decried homosexuality as an abomination.[26]

Rock's Spiritual Redemption

For American cultural and religious conservatives, the newly permissive sexual culture threatened the existence of the normative reproductive family unit. Although many evangelical Christians believed in equal opportunity for women, evangelical women and men were concerned that female and homosexual liberation would enslave the nation to human laws instead of divine laws. They crusaded for salvation based on the Bible's sexual morality and gender order. In the 1960s, leftist social movements inspired activism among conservatives and among Christian youth across the political spectrum. Ministers proffered Christ as redemptive in a chaotic world, encouraging individualism in order to counter the impersonal and pernicious secular and materialist forces. In the 1970s, when youth culture flourished, sexual promiscuity increased, and rock music boomed, evangelical Christianity also enjoyed a resurgence.[27]

Ironically it was rock music that brought new trends in evangelical Christianity to the attention of the national media and helped the evangelical movement to reach critical mass. In 1971, just five years after one of its cover stories asked "Is God Dead?" *Time* magazine reported on the "Jesus Revolution."[28] The article connected the successful rock operas *Jesus Christ Superstar* and *Godspell* to the "God Rock" movement and the rise of the Jesus People in the United States. Also known as Jesus Freaks and Street Christians, this evangelical movement comprised young people disillusioned with the 1960s counterculture and with the New Left.[29] The movement emerged most prominently in California, where young people began turning to Jesus Christ after the various attractions of the 1960s— including Eastern religions, political groups, drug-induced psychedelic visions, and witchcraft—left them spiritually wanting. For them, Jesus, with his long hair and hippie style, offered personally identifiable redemption in the maelstrom of choice. A contemporary book commented that "the basic symbol for the Jesus movement seems to be *multiplicity*. The unconverted life is described as confused by countless options, symbols, and alluring paths."[30] Accordingly, the catchphrase of this Christian youth movement was "One Way: the Jesus Way!"

By incorporating Christian themes and inspiring a new genre of—and market for—Christian rock music, the evangelical movement harnessed rock's rhetorical forms against the notion that a body can be redeemed sexually. The movement appropriated language and style from rock culture and sexual liberation. For example, the interdenominational college group Campus Crusade for Christ organized Explo '72, an evangelical conference held in Dallas that ended with a concert that was dubbed the "Christian Woodstock." "Operation Penetration" was the code name given for the follow-up strategy in which each Explo participant was expected to recruit five others with the broader goal of converting young people around the United States and the world by 1980.[31] *Christianity Today* claimed that as the result of young people connecting with Christ through rock, record numbers of youth were entering ministries at home and overseas.[32]

Christian crusaders who used countercultural forms attracted and mobilized followers across North America and internationally whom the traditional church could not reach. As one convert said, "Straight people never could have talked to me." For them, Jesus' true message had been compromised by the Christian establishment. Although the same Christians who fought against rock as the devil's music saw Christian rock as an inherently problematic and contradictory form, other evangelicals wanted to save souls and counter moral decay more than they wanted orthodox routes to salvation. One pastor's wife reflected their viewpoint when she said that she would rather see young people "excited about God than drugs. I'm conservative but I'm for whatever reaches them for Christ."[33]

The Reverend Billy Graham exemplified the possibilities of expanding the religious flock through intergenerational connection. Graham allied himself with the Jesus Movement, became involved in Christian rock concerts, and took on an increasingly permissive tone in his public speaking. Graham spun his involvement as emblematic of his ministry in the 1960s and 1970s: it was a time when the counterculture represented generational questioning and searching, and Graham was prepared to try new avenues to appeal to young people. In 1969, as a special guest at the Miami Rock Festival, he got a feel for the crowd by circulating in disguise. He sensed in them a righteous rejection of materialism and a desire for "something of the soul." Onstage Graham promoted Jesus as the ultimate individual rebel. "Jesus was a nonconformist," he told the audience, encouraging them to avoid the ephemeral high of drugs and instead "tune in to God. . . . Turn on to His power."[34]

Secular musicians were the first to see the possibilities of marrying rock with Christian themes to draw audiences and sell records. Conceived by British composers Andrew Lloyd Webber and Tim Rice as a concept album in 1970, the rock opera *Jesus Christ Superstar* placed the biblical Jesus in the milieu of rock music stardom. It made explicit themes of idolatry, celebrity, and gender roles implicit in both narratives. *Jesus Christ Superstar* told the story of Jesus' last seven days. Its three main characters—Jesus, Judas, and Mary Magdalene—were, consciously or not, invested as the central sites of sociopolitical meaning. The rock opera portrays Jesus as a man struggling with his identity and his destiny. Once he becomes sure of his purpose, his last days are filled with doubt about the meaning of his life. Judas questions whether or not Jesus is the Messiah. Concerned that Jesus' followers will revolt against him when they realize that he is a man and not a god, Judas betrays Jesus in order, he explains, to save them all. Mary Magdalene is styled as Jesus' closest ally and as an adoring groupie—albeit one who has renounced her sexually promiscuous ways. Unlike the male characters, Magdalene does not have a rock voice: her songs are ballads. Interestingly, rock music culture and Christianity found common ground in their positioning of woman as helpmeet.

Sparking controversy among religious groups even before it was released, by 1973 *Jesus Christ Superstar* had become the biggest-selling two-disc album in recording history.[35] An example of the multiple formats and cross-marketing that came to define the entertainment industries in the 1970s, the album was turned into a Broadway stage production in 1971, and *Jesus Christ Superstar* was released as a Hollywood film in 1973. The album was an international hit, including in the Soviet Union, where young people grew their hair so as to look like Jesus, and Russian-language recordings entered the black market.[36] The rock opera's success demonstrated that global markets were open to Christian-themed music. By the end of the decade Jesus Rock had become its own industry. Contemporary Christian Music (CCM), though separate from the mainstream rock industry, paralleled it culturally and commercially by commodifying Jesus and using media networks to spread the gospel.[37] In Sri Lanka, for example, the radio program *Parables in Melody* played the recordings of Christian musicians such as Larry Norman, who came out of the Jesus Movement, and Cliff Richards, who was a Christian-identified mainstream musician. The music galvanized Christians there.[38]

Globalizing Music and Rebellion

Rock 'n' roll revolutionized the music industry. In 1970 the *Wall Street Journal* reported that rock's profits were becoming so significant that various conglomerates, including the life insurance and financial services company Transamerica Corp. and Kinney National Services (which later became Warner Communications), were rushing to buy into the music business. Rock paved the way for other popular music forms to be marketed and distributed internationally. The increasing affluence of young people drove the growth of the industry and influenced the increasing diversity of market offerings: subgenres of rock, reggae, country, R&B, folk, punk, disco, funk, soul, hip hop, and CCM. By 1973 music had become the most popular form of entertainment in the United States and indeed internationally, with $3.3 billion worldwide sales in records and tapes. By 1978 the head of Warner Communications' International Record Division claimed that "music is the most important cultural export. . . . Music's impact is tremendous. It's in every home."[39]

Disseminated through television, film, and new technologies such as the long-playing (stereophonic) record and compact audiocassette tapes, rock music and its embedded sexuality appeared at a mass level, internationally, with a global reach that film and television did not yet share.[40] FM stereo radio, newly available in the late 1960s, was static free and, because of its lower commercial airtime rates, offered airplay to songs not on the Top 40 list, including those considered too risqué for AM radio. Music's material mediums—vinyl records and cassette tapes—were widely available, and cassettes especially enabled popular music to spread through home taping, as well as bootlegging, and piracy.[41] DJs playing records in clubs and discothèques were far cheaper to hire than live bands, and the nightclub scene grew. By the end of the decade, disco was the most internationally accessible form of popular music.

Britain and America dominated popular music during the 1970s, owing to the power of rock as an Anglo-American youth-cultural formation, their resistance to foreign-language music, and the size and reach of their music corporations. Five companies (CBS, EMI, PolyGram, Warner, and RCA), each owned by larger transnational conglomerates, essentially ran the international music industry. These corporations used foreign bases around the world—from Denmark to Kenya to Chile—to manufacture and market hit records. Although countries such as Australia, France, and Canada put airtime limits on imported records, markets continued to open up: by the late 1970s Spain had lifted its censorship, and Sri Lanka had liberalized import restrictions. Following the example of the American Armed Forces Radio and Television Service (AFRTS), Radio Luxembourg spread American-style radio programming and music throughout Europe.[42] West

German television broadcast Western rock to East Germany. Bootleg recordings of Western popular music were exchanged at street fairs in Prague, and rock sold over the counter in Budapest. In 1975 Lyudmila Zhivkova, the thirty-four-year-old daughter of Bulgaria's ruler, was appointed minister of culture and opened the country to Western popular entertainment. By the end of the decade the Soviet Union was hosting international rock concerts, and even China's youth were experiencing rock and disco, once considered "the forbidden fruit of socialism."[43]

Despite the dominance of Anglo-American multinationals and the commodification of rock music's freedoms, individual listeners, music groups, and fan communities enacted rock's rebellion against oppression and authoritarianism in local contexts.[44] When students attended the 1971 Festival at Avándaro, Mexico's version of Woodstock, only months after the government massacre of protesting students in Mexico City, they marked the beginning of a new political consciousness among Mexican youth linked with rock music.[45] A 1976 New York Times article distinguished Eastern Europe from the Soviet Union by discussing the prevalence of rock music and discothèques there, arguing that "for the youth of Eastern Europe, it may represent a link with Western peers or a subtle protest against the constraints of Moscow-style Communism." That year the members of Plastic People of the Universe, a Czech rock group, were arrested for "hooliganism" simply for performing a live show: the arrest spurred the Charter 77 movement, which criticized the government for contravening the Helsinki Accords and UN human rights agreements.[46]

Rock music developed local inflections around the world during the 1970s. Original rock groups emerged throughout the Eastern bloc. Because Indonesia's first president, Sukarno, banned the Beatles in the early 1960s, rock music became there—and throughout Southeast Asia—a symbol of rebellion and populist politics. Disco and funk influenced a thriving music scene in Pakistan, and before the 1979 revolution Iranian rock and popular music flourished.[47] Bob Marley, the Jamaican son of a black woman and a white man, mixed together Caribbean and Afro-American rhythm and blues to become the Third World's first international music star. Marley sang about Rastafarianism, a religion that conceptualized God as black, acknowledged Jesus Christ as a messiah but focused on his Second Coming in the incarnation of the Ethiopian emperor Haile Selassie, advocated spiritual marijuana use, and promoted Africa as the birthplace of humankind.[48] Through reggae music and style, Marley brought black liberation politics to new audiences, including those who might not have been turned on to social issues in any other way.

In the 1970s rock as a commodity form was manipulated by the very forces that it challenged: authority, the market, and conservative sexual morality. A 1974 strategic directions report from the Pentagon discussed the crucial role that culture markets and multinational companies would play in securing and maintaining America's position in a globalizing world. The report argued that "those who will fashion tomorrow's world are those who are able to project their image (to exercise the predominant influence and long range influence)."[49] Certainly the Anglo-American popular music industry played a significant role in the competition for cultural dominance. Music conglomerates spread worldwide rock music's messages of permissive sexuality, individualism, and rebellion, and triggered cultural backlashes. The Religious Right in the United States rallied against and was invigorated by its opposition to rock music, while radical Islam surged up against Western secularization and cultural decadence.[50]

Yet rock's freedoms were undeniable. Rock music gave a measure of cultural and economic legitimacy to female sexuality and marginal gender identities. The music market facilitated individual and social rebellion and connected youth around the globe. American attitudes toward sexual permissiveness became increasingly liberal during the 1970s. In the decades that followed, more women became music stars in their own right. Androgynous styles and explicit sexuality continued to flourish in popular music, taking new forms with new generations.

CHAPTER 19

Universal Nationalism

Christian America's Response to the Years of Upheaval

ANDREW PRESTON

AMERICAN CHRISTIANS are no strangers to globalization. They were for centuries in the vanguard of the movement of people, capital, and communications around the world. Pilgrims, Puritans, Quakers, Anglicans, and Catholics spearheaded the English transplantation of North America in the seventeenth century. New England Puritans then established what was effectively America's first merchant marine and built an extensive trading network in West Africa, the Caribbean, Europe, and even China. In the nineteenth and twentieth centuries, Protestant and Catholic missionaries from the United States brought Western ways, and themselves, to Latin America, Africa, the Middle East, East Asia, and the Pacific. Throughout this entire period, moreover, the growth of international society was largely driven by the concomitant spread of the Christian faith and Western imperialism. This was no coincidence: as a monotheistic, proselytizing religion that believes itself to be the repository of humanity's past, present, and future, Christianity is at root a world religion professing a universalistic faith. And on a more secular if no less idealistic level, the same pretensions have been true of the United States and its foreign policy over the past century.[1]

But the dawn of a new era of globalization in the late 1960s and 1970s caught American Christians off balance and shook their confidence. This stemmed in part from the new humanist skepticism of the 1960s and the defensiveness with which American Protestants viewed their once sacred place in society. Also responsible was the fact that American Christianity was no longer an agent of globalism; rather than missionaries, secular

306

forces such as computerization, the spread of international communications and transportation, and the integration of markets were now driving globalization. But even more, it was the actual process of globalization itself, and the attendant "crisis of territoriality," that caused much of the soul-searching among American Christians.[2]

Globalization would have had a limited impact had it been the era's only driver of change. But crucially, the "crisis of territoriality" occurred alongside a "crisis of hegemony" in American foreign policy, a period Henry Kissinger aptly characterized as the "years of upheaval."[3] Globalization began to upset old patterns at the very moment when the United States was suffering from an unprecedentedly severe set of foreign crises. Events abroad—most notably stalemate and defeat in Vietnam, the limitation of American power codified by détente, war in the Middle East, and the Arab oil embargo—helped fuel a traumatic identity crisis within American Christianity. Reflecting on the tumultuous, ominous times, a liberal Congregationalist minister in Minneapolis told his church that the "shock of future change burst upon us as current crisis in 1973."[4] Or as a fundamentalist writer proclaimed the following year, once-confident Christians felt themselves "helpless in the face of the complexity of life" that showed no signs of relenting.[5]

Collectively these systemic shocks had a profound effect. Religious communities in the United States responded to the crises of territoriality and hegemony with a mix of defiance and accommodation that religious sociologists who study globalization call "delocalization and relocalization."[6] Occurring nearly simultaneously, the era's fundamental changes triggered the painful characteristics of *de*localization: dislocation, identity crisis, confusion, and so forth. To persevere, religious communities adapted to new developments as best they could. But they also strove to maintain their autonomy and regain their authority through *re*localization, by reasserting their core values and identity. To put it differently, religious communities responded to an increasingly interconnected and technological world by oscillating between "backlash and accommodation," by resisting what they could and accepting, on their own terms, what they could not.[7]

Although religious liberals felt more comfortable with the rapid pace of postmodern change, they joined conservatives in struggling to cope with its terms. Charles C. West, a liberal theologian at Princeton Theological Seminary, offered some "Theological Guidelines for the Future" by declaring that it "is our task, in trying to come to grips with our technological world, to be creatively ideological." West warned that "the various forces of technology which push us around in modern society—the power of mass media, the various powers of massive private enterprise, the power of computer technology and automation, and the like—are . . . rooted in human desires and decisions, but they have become powers dominating and sometimes enslaving men, while they also tempt them." West's solution—"to be creatively ideological"—was to return to the social justice precepts of Christianity by embracing "a lively sense of the reign of Christ."[8] True to form, the rhetoric of Christian conservatives was rather more direct. "We are committed to revival in our time," the fundamentalist Baptist preacher Jerry Falwell, probably the most influential religious leader of the decade, informed the White House in 1975. "We believe our nation must come back to God or else."[9]

Overall, Americans reacted to the changes of the 1970s by embracing a more individualistic ethos that rejected the liberal statism of the New Deal and the early Cold War years in favor of privatized, market-based solutions. The journalist Tom Wolfe captured the essence of the 1970s with the term "the 'Me' Decade." But Wolfe attached a different label, not as well remembered, to another of the decade's major attitudinal and social changes: "the Third Great Awakening." The most important product of this resurgence of faith in the 1970s was the rise of the Religious Right, a broad coalition of Christian conservatives, mostly but not exclusively Protestant, who sought to influence politics by pooling their strength and supporting political candidates who reflected their socially conservative views. The rise of the Religious Right, and the relative stasis of liberal Christianity, ensured that distinctly conservative visions of U.S. foreign policy and world order came to predominate. Not coincidentally, the new individualism suited traditionally anti-statist conservative Protestants just fine. Indeed they sought to apply it not only in domestic politics at home but also in foreign policy abroad.[10]

Central to this conservative worldview was an abhorrence of communism that had not dimmed during the 1960s.[11] Just as important was an exuberant, defiant patriotism. In the wake of New Left and liberal Christian critiques of American power in the 1960s, conservative Christians emphasized a renewed commitment to America as well as to Christ. After all, to evangelicals and fundamentalists the United States had long been "God's New Israel," a chosen "redeemer nation" on earth.[12] By enshrining the separation of church and state and providing a safe haven for persecuted religious minorities around the world, Christian conservatives argued, only the United States truly respected religious liberty. And when the United States ventured abroad, it did so to protect and expand that liberty. Thus, despite their anti-statist convictions, conservative Christians were among the most fervently patriotic Americans.[13] When their steadfast vision of national identity, based on power and virtue, came under threat in the 1960s and early 1970s, first from radical and liberal criticism and then from a foreign policy that had become mired in Vietnam and compromised by détente, they mounted a nationalistic counterattack. "They said the flag was just a piece of cloth," an evangelical activist in West Virginia complained of America's domestic critics. "Well, that's not what we believe. We have a lot of relatives who died under that banner. To us, it's like a sacred symbol. You don't burn the flag; you don't challenge what our Founding Fathers have done, or the Constitution."[14] It was this powerful mix of pride and resentment that helped make Falwell's annual nationwide "I Love America" tours, beginning in the bicentennial year of 1976, such a vehicle for the Religious Right's political success.[15] Foreign initiatives that appeared weak, such as arms control or the Panama Canal treaties, accordingly came under attack.[16]

As it became more broadly conservative, individualistic, and patriotic, American Christianity, particularly Protestantism, asserted itself in ways that both resisted and accepted the forces of globalization. In mounting a strong nationalist backlash, conservative Christians rejected the premise of ever deeper global integration by challenging consolidations of transnational power, such as within the United States or multinational corporations, that were thought to be undemocratic, unrepresentative, and ultimately ineffective. Yet liberal and conservative Christians also embraced the emerging global consciousness by championing the cause of universal human rights that transcended national borders and superseded national sovereignty. American Christians' response to the shock of the global, then, was characterized by a "universal nationalism" that placed the United States at the head of the family of nations and envisioned it as the arbiter of the world.

Nationalism and "Local" Autonomy

Building on their increasingly fashionable individualism and patriotism, conservative Protestants fought the institutional integration and consolidation that inevitably accompanied globalization. Leading the charge was a grassroots movement of traditionally anti-statist evangelicals and fundamentalists. Up to the 1970s, Christian conservatives had been among the most passionate defenders of the First Amendment's separation of church and state. As society's separatists and nonconformists, they feared interference from the state more than anything else. The wall of separation protected Christian conservatives from government regulation, and thus protected their identity. Long accustomed to competing in a deregulated religious marketplace, Christian conservatives embraced the decade's individualistic ethos; indeed they helped enhance and entrench it by championing the laissez-faire economic ideology of conservative Republican politicians. In between the New Deal and the Great Society, moreover, the federal government had assumed ever greater responsibilities for social welfare, usurping societal roles that the church and the family once filled.[17] Given that the church and the family have always been the staple of evangelical and fundamentalist ideology, it is unsurprising that Christian conservatives resisted this encroachment of the state into matters of social welfare.[18] Fundamentally, then, owing to a mixture of ideas and circumstances, anti-statism had to some extent become hard-wired into the Christian conservative gene.

In the 1960s and 1970s, events seemed to confirm Christian conservatives' worst fears. All around them concentrations of elite power—*secular* elite power—were totally changing the face of society as they knew it. In the first of several decisions, in 1962 the Supreme Court decided that prayer in public schools was unconstitutional; and while prayer could be banned, in 1973 the Court ruled that abortion could not. The mainstream emergence of sex and violence, and especially obscenity and pornography, infuriated Christians, but the changing attitude toward religion was perhaps best illustrated in 1966, when *Time* committed the ultimate sacrilege of asking on its front cover, in bold red letters against a stark black background, "Is God Dead?" The degradation of cultural values occurred alongside the Great Society's liberal revolution in government social policy, which extended New Deal economic provisions to ensure fairness in social and cultural matters previously untouched by the state. Perhaps most important, in the late 1970s the Internal Revenue Service, following earlier Supreme Court decisions in its favor, ruled that private religious schools which had not integrated their student body were no longer eligible for tax-exempt charitable status. Many of these Christian academies were genuine religious schools established by parents who sought refuge for their children from an increasingly secular public school system; but many others had been established in the 1960s as a way to get around the court-ordered desegregation of public schools. The Carter administration compounded conservative anger over school independence by establishing the Department of Education in 1979.[19]

Each of these developments angered and frightened conservatives because they represented a liberal, secular use of monopoly power to mandate changes to the local way of life. Thus the Supreme Court and the IRS—perhaps *the* most concentrated centers of government power—were especially loathed. Indeed local autonomy was so sacrosanct in Christian conservative circles that the Religious Right's showpiece political group, Moral Majority, was organized in 1979 in a highly decentralized fashion, in which local affiliates raised most of their own funds and had nearly total decision-making authority independent of national headquarters.[20] Little wonder, then, that in the weeks leading up to the 1976 election the editors of *Christianity Today*, America's largest evangelical magazine, asked President Gerald Ford what he planned to do about the "threat to religious liberty by big government and expanding government regulations."[21]

As evangelicals and fundamentalists consolidated their energies and built their religious communities into a political movement through the 1970s, they also began to apply their anti-statist ideology to foreign affairs. Protestant fears of concentrated power had long taken the form of a visceral anti-Catholicism. But it was just as natural for Christian conservatives to see communism—with its official atheism, its command economy, and its central planning—as the antithesis of all they held sacred in society. Communism, one fundamentalist commentator wrote, "is fundamentally a monopoly. . . . When it is complete, there is no way to counteract it, no way to escape it, and no political power left to change it. It is a total control of the life style."[22] Finding themselves in principled opposition to the Nixon, Ford, and Carter administrations' policy of détente, many Christian conservatives worked to scuttle diplomatic compromises and settlements with the Soviet Union by weakening domestic support for détente and arms control.

Yet reflexive anticommunism could not explain the entire spectrum of the Christian conservative worldview in the 1970s. Distrusting the consolidation of economic and political power within multinational corporations, nongovernmental organizations, and international agencies, conservative Protestants campaigned to weaken ties between the United States and external concentrations of power, such as the UN, the European Economic Community, and the World Council of Churches. The United States was one member nation—albeit the most powerful one—among many, and so in this sense ultra-patriotism was the Religious Right's way of preserving America's "local autonomy" against the regulatory power of a dreaded "world state." Many Christian conservatives also opposed the UN because membership and participation in its councils entailed a certain amount of dealing with the devil—that is, cooperating with atheistic Communists, anti-American leftist and nationalist regimes, and states that were inalterably hostile to Israel. While the notion of compromise is central to the diplomatic activities of the UN, it is ideologically incompatible with fundamentalism. After all, the very basis of the Religious Right is a certain ideological, theological, and cultural purity grounded in a refusal to compromise with the irreligious and immoral forces of modernism; hence the theological emphasis on biblical inerrancy.[23] Moreover, by embracing compromise, international organizations could effectively chip away at national identity and local traits—the very patriotism and localism that the Religious Right vowed to protect. For these reasons, the UN and other international organizations, along with large multinational companies, attracted so much hostility from the Religious Right's leaders, including ministers such as Jerry Falwell, Billy James Hargis, and Carl McIntire—who urged Americans not to contribute to children's UNICEF collection boxes on Halloween—and politicians such as Senator Jesse Helms.[24] "As we look at this monolithic commercial system which has controlled the world and today controls our lives, we realize that the policies of nations are formed by and for commercial interests' sake," warned Chuck Smith, pastor of the fundamentalist Calvary Chapel in southern California, one of the fastest-growing churches in America, in 1977. "More and more our lives are being manipulated. . . . We are victims, and we are helpless to do anything about it. These men play chess with the lives of the people of the world."[25]

Universal Human Rights

Many American Christians clearly had problems with the forces of integration and consolidation that globalization unleashed. But a broader range of Christians, on both the left and the right, Protestant and Catholic, accepted other aspects of the new globalist ethos. By promoting the cause of universal human rights, American Christians accepted the premise that people everywhere were bound by a common morality. Given Christianity's claims to universal applicability and its history of articulating natural rights derived straight from God rather than the state, and given America's own claims to be humanity's "last, best hope" for freedom and justice, it was natural that the cause of human rights should resonate so strongly with American Christians. Of course the idea of a set of basic human rights that was unbounded by time or space was nothing new. But human rights advocates in the 1970s, especially those who championed the cause of religious liberty, were much less respectful of national sovereignty than their predecessors had been. Up to this point, the promotion of human rights had been universal mostly in theory.

Continuing their work from the previous decade, liberal Protestants and Catholics called for an American foreign policy that would fight poverty, promote social welfare, and protect religious freedom around the world. Their crusade for human rights thus extended beyond political questions to global social problems such as food scarcity and overpopulation. The National Conference of Catholic Bishops, for example, focused its energies on the "world food crisis" as the most severe challenge to human rights and saw famine as "part of the larger pattern of global interdependence" that also included the "environment, population, economic relationships, political and military power."[26] In the 1970s liberal evangelicals, such as Sojourners founder Jim Wallis, joined their Catholic colleagues by launching themselves into the same cause of fighting racism, poverty, and hunger. Social injustices such as these were not only tragedies in themselves, Wallis and others argued, but also the ultimate causes of war.[27] Similarly, advocates of Black Power (James Cone, Cornel West) and feminism (Rosemary Radford Ruether, Mary Daly) embraced the radical tenets of Latin American "liberation theology," which viewed world tensions from an economic North-South perspective rather than the political East-West conflict of the Cold War and embraced socialism as the antidote to global injustice. Founded by Catholic priests and nuns in Colombia in 1968, liberation theology quickly spread among young liberal Christians in the United States as the preferred avenue for radical dissent.[28] And liberals agreed with conservatives that the separation of church and state, applied universally, was one of the safest ways to ensure democracy. "It is not for a

President to say who is a good priest and who is a bad priest," Robert F. Drinan, a Massachusetts congressman who also happened to be a Jesuit priest, scolded the president of El Salvador, General Carlos Humberto Romero, at a meeting in 1978. "Under the International Declaration of Human Rights, they are not under you."[29]

Liberal Christians also believed that the pursuit of justice nationally and internationally was reciprocal, that the promotion of liberty would see American democracy influenced and improved by people from abroad— even if this meant challenging the human rights record of the governments of America's allies. In other words, the United States had as much to learn from the people of the rest of the world as they could learn from the United States. Indeed, liberals charged, this was due largely to the fact that the U.S. government itself was the perpetrator of much of the world's injustice. Washington's support for the authoritarian government in Seoul was a case in point that drew sharp criticism from liberal Christians in the Protestant National Council of Churches and the Catholic Maryknoll order.[30] In drawing attention to human rights abuses in South Korea, a key U.S. ally, the Presbyterian missionary and academic Richard Shaull asked Americans to pose themselves a question: "What stand do we take vis-à-vis our own society?" The absence of democracy in Korea, Shaull argued, was not the fault of the Koreans. Instead, "our influence and power, and especially the growing penetration of multinational corporations, are the center of the whole thing."[31] South Africa provided another example. Despite its brutal record of racial apartheid, South Africa was a destination for U.S. investment and often a partner with the U.S. government in the containment of communism. In response, liberal religious leaders such as Eugene Carson Blake, a Presbyterian minister who was president of the World Council of Churches, and groups such as the Chicago-based Lutheran Coalition on Southern Africa urged the federal government to isolate South Africa and called for American companies to divest themselves of their South African holdings.[32]

President Jimmy Carter, a born-again Southern Baptist and lay Sunday school teacher, agreed with liberals that universal human rights were grounded in social justice as much as they were in political liberty. Carter's strident emphasis on pursuing a foreign policy of human rights, itself largely a product of his faith, challenged not only rivals such as the Soviet Union but also authoritarian allies such as Argentina, Brazil, and Chile. But he incurred the wrath of Christian conservatives—including many fellow Southern Baptists—by embracing liberalism at home as well as abroad, especially by rejecting the conservative view of what exactly constituted the family. Perhaps most egregiously to the Religious Right, it was Carter who had allowed the IRS to confront segregated Christian academies. Although he was an evangelical, Carter's moderately conservative theology did not translate automatically into conservative politics, and his perceived weakness on foreign affairs and liberalism in domestic policy cost him support among his fellow evangelicals.[33]

Conservatives shared the liberal belief in universal human rights, but with key differences. Their basis of the concept of human rights was instead rooted in their anti-statism and was very much grounded in the individual's freedom from interference by a government that was considered the enemy rather than the guarantor of freedom. The doctrine put forth by conservative human rights advocates promised protection from the distant, arbitrary powers of government.

Indeed conservative Christians' concern for human rights reinforced their anti-statist fears about concentrations of power. Conforming to the caricature of the United Nations as a haven for anti-American, anti-Israeli radicals, in 1975 the UN-sponsored International Women's Year conference in Mexico City condemned Zionism by equating it with apartheid. Dianne Edmondson, an antifeminist Christian activist from Oklahoma, typified the conservative response to the IWY by calling for the burgeoning ranks of her movement to show "how as Christians we must do good as the Lord commands by opposing this evil."[34] The UN General Assembly followed the example set in Mexico City by passing its own resolution, over the strenuous and nearly unanimous protests of American Christians and Jews, condemning Zionism "as a form of racism and racial discrimination."[35] The World Council of Churches, which also criticized Zionism, came in for similar criticism from conservatives. Republican congressman John Ashbrook and syndicated columnist Patrick Buchanan, both staunch Christian conservatives, castigated the international ecumenical body for its criticism of Israel, its silence on Soviet political and religion oppression, and its willingness to elect a Soviet-endorsed Russian Orthodox metropolitan to its governing council.[36]

Concerns about Zionism and fears of communism reflected the joining up of two previously unconnected viewpoints. American Christians, including many liberals such as Reinhold Niebuhr, had long been passionately anti-Communist. But they were becoming passionately pro-Israel as well, especially evangelicals and fundamentalists. Traditionally many Christian conservatives had also been anti-Semitic, for reasons of simple bigotry but also stemming from the same fears of supposed monopoly power that had animated American anti-Catholicism. But the ideological hothouses of World War II and the Cold War, pitting a newly conceived "Judeo-Christian" America against the aggressive prejudices of Nazi Germany and the "godless" communism of the Soviet Union, made the elimination of religious prejudice a matter of national security. To be sure, anti-Semitism did not disappear altogether; but it did decline dramatically to become something acceptable only to the lunatic fringe. For its part, in the late 1960s and 1970s the State of Israel was doing its best to appeal to American sensibilities. While the United States was suffering an unusual, and unusually ignominious, defeat in Vietnam, democratic Israel stood alone and routed—twice—the massed forces of the authoritarian Arab world. The rise of apocalyptic belief, which accompanied the rapid growth of evangelicalism, also contributed to a new embrace of the Holy Land. By the 1970s, then, the era of Christian Zionism had dawned in America.[37]

American proponents of religious liberty—and, more to the point, opponents of détente—combined their support for Israel and hostility to the Soviet Union by leveraging that most globalized of phenomena, trade. They did not represent the interests only of American Jews or Christian Zionists. Rather, an uncharacteristically ecumenical coalition sought the protection of Israel through the weakening of the Soviets and the death of détente. It was this coalition, which placed the freedom of religious expression at the core of an indivisible set of liberties, that pushed hardest the notion of universal human rights. The heart of the matter was the Soviet Union's treatment of its Jewish population, specifically its refusal to allow Soviet Jews to emigrate to Israel. While this issue fermented, Nixon and Kissinger were in the midst of implementing détente, a strategy to mitigate American vulnerability by influencing the Soviet Union's external behavior. The only way the United States could hope to do this was by extending Moscow a series of carrots and sticks, and the carrot that held the greatest attraction to Moscow was access to Western capital, credit, and technology. In return for open trade—which the Soviets would get by being granted most favored nation (MFN) status—Nixon and Kissinger hoped that the Soviet Union would limit its ambitions in the Third World and, above all, pressure North Vietnam into accepting a settlement to end the war in Indochina. For Nixon and Kissinger, American security was at risk. But for their domestic critics, something much higher was at stake: American values.[38]

The leading critic of détente was Senator Henry Jackson. Though an economically liberal Democrat, Jackson was also a social and foreign policy conservative who combined fierce anticommunism with the promotion of liberty to attack both the Soviet Union and détente. But he applied these principles in a new way that transcended the traditional dictates of national sovereignty. With Representative Charles Vanik, Jackson proposed an amendment to pending trade legislation that would prohibit the United States from bestowing MFN status on the Soviet Union unless Soviet Jews were allowed to emigrate freely. America's foreign economic policy, in other words, would determine Soviet domestic policy. "Without an increasing measure of individual liberty in the Communist world there can be no genuine détente," Jackson told the Tucson Jewish Community Council in 1974, and "there can be no real movement toward a more peaceful world. . . . For if new relations between East and West are to mature into long-term peaceful cooperation, there must be progress toward the freer movement of people and ideas between East and West, which is to say progress in the area of human rights and individual liberty."[39] Vanik agreed. "I think the cause of freedom is helped everywhere" by pressuring the Soviets to allow their Jewish citizens to emigrate, he argued during congressional hearings on détente. "I think that it is a service for the liberty of all mankind that this effort is being made."[40] So, too, did congressmen from both parties, including Drinan, a Massachusetts Democrat and Catholic priest, and John Buchanan Jr., an Alabama Republican, graduate of Southern Baptist Theological Seminary, and ordained Baptist minister.[41] With their promotion of national values *as* the national interest and their insistence on an abrogation of Soviet sovereignty that the Kremlin could not abide, Jackson, Vanik, and their allies helped ensure the demise of détente. Paradoxically, through their strident nationalism they also advanced a universalistic ideology that continues to underpin the process of globalization.

Faith-based conservatism continued to help shape the contours of American diplomacy as well. With the death of détente by the end of the 1970s, universal nationalism found itself providing the ideological foundations for U.S. foreign policy, a position it maintained until at least the end of the George W. Bush presidency. In 1980 Ronald Reagan completed the conservative realignment of American politics that had begun under

Nixon a decade before. Isolationism had been extinct for decades and showed no signs of returning to life. But while they were now all internationalists to some degree, both the leadership and grass roots of the new conservative order rejected the cosmopolitan, progressivist ambitions of the liberal internationalism that had dominated U.S. foreign relations since World War II. In its place, conservatives promoted American global leadership—unilaterally if necessary—that conflated America's values with universal norms and relied disproportionately on the military to solve diplomatic problems. From the humiliations and dislocations of the 1970s, then, arose a resurgent exceptionalism that propelled American globalism into the twenty-first century.

CHAPTER 20

An Uncertain Trajectory

Islam's Contemporary Globalization, 1971–1979

AYESHA JALAL

REVOLUTIONS TEND TO ELICIT teleological historical explanations. And when a heavy dose of presentism is added to that tendency, ideological and political outcomes are invested with an inexorable sense of inevitability. With the specter of Islam stalking the West in the first decade of the twenty-first century, it may be tempting to search for the origins of religious resurgence in the global 1970s. Yet at the onset of that fateful decade there was little to portend a specifically Islamic revolution or instances of state-sponsored Islamization across broad swaths of the Muslim world by decade's end. In 1970 the cafés of Kabul were vibrant hubs of cosmopolitan social and political discourse. An insightful look back at the 1970s needs to uncover the range of alternate ideological possibilities that contended with those couched in religious terms. It might then be possible to identify the combination of forces, global as well as regional, that facilitated the hoisting of the religious banner during the decades that followed.

The Significance of 1971

The first successful subversion of Westphalian concepts of the international order in the post–World War II era occurred at the start of the decade in what was then the largest Muslim state in the world. Pakistan had been created in 1947 ostensibly as the homeland for India's Muslims. The Islamic bond between its two wings separated by a thousand miles of Indian territory, however, proved to be hopelessly inadequate during the crisis of 1970–71. Alienation among the Bengali majority in the east, proud of their own language and culture, had been fueled by political denial and economic deprivation. If theirs was a devotional upheaval, it was inspired by fealty to a regional homeland rather than to a religious community. In the country's first general elections based on universal adult franchise, held in December 1970, the Awami League, campaigning on a plank of provincial autonomy, had swept nearly all the seats in the eastern wing, giving it a simple majority in the national assembly. What followed has been accurately described by Niall Ferguson as "an authentically geno-cidal campaign against the people of East Pakistan in a vain attempt to prevent their secession."[1] Even though Ferguson blames the wrong general for the brutal campaign of 1971, a closer investigation of the breakup of a nation-state that pitted Muslim against Muslim can help illuminate some broader trends of the 1970s. It foretells more numerous instances in subsequent decades of the lure of religious or ethnic majoritarianism as an illusory panacea for beleaguered, crisis-ridden nation-states.

Overall responsibility for the 1971 debacle in East Pakistan rested with Yahya Khan, who had succeeded Ayub Khan in 1969. What clinched the issue for the military high command in favor of a crackdown was the law and order situation in East Pakistan, where the Awami League, led by Sheikh Mujibur Rahman (popularly known as Mujib), was running a paral-lel government with bruising effect on the morale of the armed forces. As if the daily abuse leveled at the military presence by the Bengali press was not enough instigation, there was clear evidence that India was actively supporting the dissidents. What the military's eastern command did not gauge, thanks to a linguistically impaired intelligence network, was that its own Bengali troops strongly supported the Awami League "miscreants." A decision to use force had been taken on February 22. As early as Decem-ber 1970, East Pakistan's martial law administrator, General Yaqub Khan, had worked out the operational aspects of the plan to impose law and or-der, codenamed "Operation Blitz." Yaqub subsequently resigned, warning against taking military action in a situation that required a political resolu-tion. The alarm bells went off on March 23, when the Awami League marked Pakistan Day by hoisting Bangladeshi flags but fell short of declar-ing independence. The eastern command under General Tikka Khan was implementing the first stages of its plan, codenamed "Operation Search-light," while Yahya Khan and his aides continued their talks with Mujib and Zulfikar Ali Bhutto, leader of the Pakistan People's Party (PPP), which had won the largest number of seats in the western wing.

It is commonly held that military action followed the breakdown of negotiations. But the talks never broke down; they were unilaterally abandoned on the orders of the president, acting in unison with his inner military circle in Rawalpindi. A transfer of power acceptable to Mujib and Bhutto was still not outside the realm of possibility. The PPP leaders saw the Awami League's revised proposals on March 25. These called for a "confederation of Pakistan" and two constitutional conventions, which were to frame the constitutions for each wing. The conventions would then meet to frame a constitution for the confederation. In shifting from a vaguely federal to a clearly confederal arrangement, the Awami League addressed the PPP's main objection that the six points on which the party had campaigned said contradictory things about the future constitutional setup. Separate constitutions for the two wings, followed by one for the confederation of Pakistan, accommodated the PPP leaders' fears of being diddled out of power by the Awami League.

Bhutto's two-majority thesis for the two wings was conceded in the final version of the Awami League's constitutional proposals. The notion of a confederation, however, was wholly alien to the thinking of the military top brass in Pakistan. Having run Pakistan as a quasi-unitary state despite its federal configuration, the guardians of military privilege were not about to concede ground to traitors. In a glaring instance of strategic oversight, Yahya Khan and his aides moved to pummel the Awami League without fully considering India's, or for that matter the world's, likely reaction. Yahya left for West Pakistan a few hours before the start of the military operation. From his room in the Intercontinental Hotel, Bhutto watched the army set the horizon ablaze with breathtaking ruthlessness. While most of the top Bengali leadership fled across the border to West Bengal, Mujib was promptly arrested and transported to a West Pakistani jail.

With the international media full of harrowing tales of the army's atrocities and the plight of millions of refugees who had fled to India, Pakistan's stock had plummeted internationally. In contrast to its stance during the 1965 Indo-Pakistan war, China politely distanced itself from a regime charged with genocide. Washington was a bit more forthcoming since the Pakistan government had recently helped the secretary of state, Henry Kissinger, make contact with Beijing. American support was more symbolic than real—a morale-boosting assurance that India would not be permitted to rip through West Pakistan. It did not extend to absolving the Pakistani regime of its crimes and misdemeanors. The story of the junta's botched international diplomacy is a trifle less appalling than its abysmal failure on the military front. The army's strategic doctrine of defending East Pakistan from the western wing exploded in its face when India launched a full-scale attack on the eastern front. The surrender of 93,000 soldiers without a whimper on December 16, 1971, highlighted the magnitude of the defeat suffered by the Pakistan army at the hands of its primary rival.

Strategic bungling and political sabotage combined to create a horrific nightmare for a military high command that was mentally ill-equipped to handle the situation. Once orders had been given to put boots on the ground and enforce law and order, the pent-up frustrations shredded the last remnants of humanity still adorning the hearts of the West Pakistani troops. The ethical dilemma of killing fellow Muslims was quickly overcome, and here a resort to religious bigotry did have a role to play. Bengalis were not just black men; they were Muslims in name only and had to be purged of their infidelity. Whatever the reasoning of the perpetrators, nothing can justify the horrendous crimes committed in the name of a false sense of nationalism. As in any war, there was violence on both sides against unarmed men, women, and children. But there was a world of difference between organized state coercion against a largely unarmed populace and the targeted violence of armed dissidents against known collaborators of the military regime.

A blackout on national and international news from East Pakistan kept the majority of the people of West Pakistan in a state of blissful ignorance. Some accounts of the massacre of civilians and rape of women in East Pakistan by the national army and its hastily raised Islamist militias known as *razakars* did filter through. A handful of West Pakistanis registered their protest. But few in the western wing were listening, convinced that the armed forces were performing their duty to protect the national integrity of the country against Indian machinations. This makes the words and actions of those brave souls from the western wing who did speak out that much more significant. Every bit the people's poet, Habib Jalib bewailed the savagery that had ravished East Pakistan. "For whom should I sing my songs of love," he asked, when "the garden is a bloody mess," when there are battered flower buds and blood-drenched leaves everywhere despite an unstoppable rain of tears. Jalib had sensed that nothing could wash away the sins of the cabal of generals who had presided over the most inglorious moment in the history of a much vaunted Muslim homeland.

Alternatives to Religion as Ideology

The decade of the 1970s started in many parts of the developing world with high hopes of radical socialist reform aimed at redressing the social inequities spawned by the growth-oriented development policies of the fifties and sixties. Even after the cataclysm of 1971, both Pakistan and Bangladesh joined India and several other countries of the global South on the path of populism and socialism. There was a spate of nationalizations of key industries and financial institutions as well as land and labor reforms in the name of redistributive social justice, the populist buzzword inspired by withering left-wing critiques of capitalism. The paragons of a new and assertive "Third World" waxed eloquent against the exploitive networks of global capital at international forums and through the press and publication market. It was not as if there was no place for religion in this newfound resolve to resist more effectively the structures of Western imperialist and neo-imperialist dominance. Yet explicitly religious ideologies, certainly of the insular and orthodox varieties, had been temporarily upstaged, if not wholly buried, as politic references to "Islamic socialism" and the "true spirit of Islam" in official narratives of the time indicate.

The main impetus for the populist experiments carried out in the three main nation-states of subcontinental South Asia was the rising expectations of those freshly inducted into the arena of mass politics. By promising equal rights of citizenship to a radicalized social base with slogans like *garibi hatao* (abolish poverty) and *roti, kapra aur makan* (bread, clothing, and housing), the Congress Party led by Indira Gandhi in India and the Pakistan People's Party of Zulfikar Ali Bhutto sought to channel the frustrations of the dispossessed and downtrodden. In newly independent Bangladesh, Mujibur Rahman's Awami League used the momentum of the nationalist struggle to strike a populist note. The focus, however, remained on the charismatic personalities of these leaders rather than on providing a semblance of organizational cohesion to their emotionally charged social bases of support. Though high on prospectus and low on performance, the populist reforms of the early seventies in all three countries would long be fondly remembered. With the benefit of hindsight, supporters of the Con-

gress Party, the PPP, and the Awami League would bemoan the lost opportunities of the early seventies. Before the oil shock of 1973 knocked the
bottom out of their economies, further impoverishing the urban lower to
middle classes and politicizing the youth, parties with religiously oriented
ideological agendas in India, Pakistan, and Bangladesh had been reduced
to watching agitatedly from the margins of electoral politics.

By contrast, neighboring Afghanistan was in the throes of deadly scraps
between Marxist and Islamist students centered on the national university
in Kabul. In July 1973 a successful coup led by Mohammed Daud Khan
with the help of Soviet-trained Marxists, who had infiltrated the ranks of
the Afghan military, ended more than two hundred years of monarchy
controlled by the Durrani-led tribal confederacy. Daud soon purged the
Marxists and distanced himself from the Soviets. He instead tried consoli-
dating his regime by playing the Pakhtun nationalist card and renewing
Afghanistan's long-standing claims on the northwestern parts of Pakistan.[2]
The revival of the "Pakhtunistan" issue alarmed Bhutto, who responded by
increasing covert support for Islamist militias fighting Daud's regime. In
the political struggle that ensued, the godless Marxists prevailed in the
Saur revolution of April 1978. This set the stage for covert Pakistani and
American intelligence activity in the country. The Soviets fell into the trap
and dispatched troops to Afghanistan, dramatically altering the course of
international and regional politics for the next three decades.

The 1973 coup in Afghanistan and indications of Kabul's support for
Pakhtun dissidents in Pakistan's North-West Frontier Province (NWFP)
as well as disaffected tribes in Baluchistan occasioned closer ties between
Islamabad and Tehran. These had grown following the breakaway of Bangladesh in 1971, owing to Mohammad Reza Shah's firm belief that the stability of Iran's eastern flank depended on preserving the territorial integrity of Pakistan. Fearing the Baluch tribal insurgency would spill into
Iranian Baluchistan with or without Soviet backing, the shah gifted Pakistan with thirty helicopter gunships to help the army quash the rebellion.
This was in keeping with the shah's American-backed projection of Iran as
a regional power and an effective bastion against communism following
the withdrawal of the British from the Persian Gulf in December 1971.
Deteriorating relations between Pakistan and Afghanistan were likely to
increase their dependence on China and the Soviet Union respectively,
with large implications for the entire region. While clearly wary of the po-

tential threat posed by the Shi'a clergy, the shah in the early 1970s felt confident enough to host a celebration of 2,500 years of the monarchy's avowedly uninterrupted links with its ancient Sassanian roots. It was an extravaganza remarkable for its garish Hollywood-style opulence and shocking historical fabrications in utter disregard of the Islamic sensibilities of the vast majority of the Iranian populace. The festivities were seen to erode the Islamic basis of Iranian society and drew a sharp rebuke from Ayatollah Ruhollah Khomeini, who was then still a shadowy opposition figure living in exile in Iraq. This did not ruffle the shah, basking in the aura of unflinching American support, but was a dangerous omen for the future of his Pahlavi dynasty.

Saudi Arabia was the other pillar of President Richard Nixon's doctrine on Persian Gulf security in the early 1970s. Nevertheless, the shah's blatant display of Westernization and proactive role in the Persian Gulf irked the rabidly conservative Wahabi state of Saudi Arabia under King Faisal. The shah's relationship with Israel only added to the tensions between Tehran and Riyadh, especially in the aftermath of the ignominious Arab defeat in the Six-Day War of June 1967. Humiliation at the hands of their principal enemy plunged Arab nationalists into an emotional as well as an intellectual crisis. Conservative voices from Saudi Arabia led the chorus attributing the defeat to the loss of Islamic values among the Arabs, who had forgotten God for the sake of their countries. It was not before taking a leftist turn that Arab nationalists in Egypt, Jordan, Tunisia, Algeria, and Morocco began conceding significant ground to Islamists owing allegiance to the Saudi school of thought.[3] Moreover, when it came to relations with Iran, there was a strong element of Saudi national self-interest intermeshed with an intense dislike of the shah's promotion of an un-Islamic ethos. Often seen through the prism of sectarian differences between a predominantly Shi'a Iran and Sunni Saudi Arabia in the main, the rivalry between them for dominance in the Persian Gulf has to account for their divergent interests based on their respective territorial nationalisms.

The Waning of Secular-Socialist Alternatives

The secular-socialist alternatives in the Muslim world were scuttled by three distinct but interrelated factors: first, a global crisis of capitalism, especially the oil shock of 1973–74; second, the sterile, statist quality of the socialism advocated by populist regimes of the early 1970s; and third, continuing Cold War rivalries in the periphery during an era of supposed détente.

In October 1973 the Arab-Israeli War restored Muslim pride after the psychologically bruising aftermath of the 1967 defeat. The decisive twist to the hostilities, masterminded by Egypt and Syria, was provided by the Saudi-led oil embargo against Israel's Western allies. The quadrupling of oil prices disrupted the fragile economies of the non-oil-producing countries of the South, pushing them into an inflationary spiral and debilitating debt trap from which some have still not recovered. By the time the oil embargo ended in March 1974, the international economy was reeling. As Daniel Sargent has argued, the balance of power had shifted, and the damage to American prestige was palpable.[4] With its bulging coffers, Saudi Arabia led the spending spree of the oil-rich countries to acquire unprecedented financial clout in the international arena, which Riyadh used to offset its image as an outpost of American influence in the Middle East and, more generally, to wield influence of its own in the predominantly Sunni parts of the Muslim world. The export of Saudi Arabian Wahabi ideology was facilitated by the generous funneling of petrodollars to build mosques and all manner of ideologically driven charitable trusts from Morocco to Indonesia. For the first time in the fractured history of the faith, there was a well-funded campaign to lend doctrinal uniformity to Sunni Islam, albeit of the Saudi Wahabi ilk.

Few non-oil-producing Muslim countries within Saudi sights escaped the impact of Islam's second globalization on the strength of petrodollars. Among the common factors shaping the social horizons of these countries were pressures generated by a population boom, rapid rural-urban migration, increased overseas migration to the oil-rich Persian Gulf sheikdoms, mass education, and rapid urbanization. Governments as ideologically far afield as those in Egypt, Pakistan, and Malaysia pandered to the religious sentiments of their people in an attempt either to co-opt or to neutralize the Islamist parties. The results were dramatically different, and even the Saudis could not prevent their agenda from being hijacked by ideologically more radicalized Islamists. Although none of the Islamist groups succeeded in capturing state power in any of the countries with Sunni majorities, they did begin to make a difference in Muslim societies and politics with their brand of Saudi-inspired Islam during the decade of the 1970s.

The socialist orientation of the PPP government in Pakistan was an early casualty. Looking to revive national morale and the economy after the shattering loss of the eastern wing, Bhutto had redoubled efforts to reaffirm Pakistan's ties with Muslim oil-producing countries, especially Iran, Libya, and Saudi Arabia. His crowning achievement was Pakistan's successful hosting of the second summit of the Organization of the Islamic Conference in Lahore during late February 1974. It was a glittering occasion that was used to resolve the knotty issue of extending Pakistan's formal recognition to Bangladesh. A line of credit was opened with oil-rich Arab countries such as Saudi Arabia and Libya, but their largesse fell well below Pakistani expectations. Bhutto reacted by extending his gaze more broadly to the Third World. But the high-profile projection of Pakistan's ties with the Islamic world and the construction of a monument in Lahore to commemorate the 1974 summit conference struck a sympathetic chord with domestic public opinion. As in other parts of the Muslim world, the aftermath of the global oil shock was greeted in Pakistan with much greater enthusiasm for Islam as a panacea for all ills, whether attributable to capitalism or socialism. With the state-controlled media making a bigger play of Pakistan's Islamic credentials, Islamist parties routed in the 1970 elections were able to organize their political comeback with aplomb.

Emboldened by the regime's active cultivation of an Islamic image for Pakistan, the Jamaat-i-Islami strengthened ties with Saudi Arabia, in return for which it became the recipient of largesse, both in cash and in kind. Projecting their Wahabi ideology with a newfound confidence, the Saudis called for the excommunication of the heterodox Ahmadi sect and began denying its members hajj visas.[5] Delighted with the turn of events, the Jamaat-i-Islami and like-minded Islamist parties reopened their long-standing demand to declare the Ahmadis non-Muslims. A secular politician contemptuous of self-styled guardians of the faith, Bhutto buckled under pressure and became a party to declaring Ahmadis a minority. (It was a defining moment for Pakistan. Acquiescing in an exclusionary idea of citizenship undermined the very basis of the nation-state.) Emboldened by their success, the Islamists demanded the immediate institution of Nizam-i-Mustapha, the golden age of the Prophet Muhammad. As Bhutto realized, this was just a ruse by the Islamist parties to orchestrate a movement to oust him from office. What he underestimated was the capacity of these parties to use the transformations on the global scene to their domestic political advantage.

More than the distortions in the capitalist world economy caused by the oil shock, statist socialism undermined the South Asian experiments with leftist populism during the seventies. The blunt instrument of an overcentralized state, an inheritance from colonial times, proved useless in one country after another in fulfilling populist promises, especially in a context of soaring prices and steeply rising oil import bills. In Pakistan the Islamists exploited the failure of the PPP to use the populist reforms to consolidate its bases of support. Radical left elements were purged, and bigger landlords, otherwise lambasted for their tyrannical hold over the peasantry, were inducted into the upper echelons of the party. The reversal of popular commitments dampened the spirit of loyal party workers just when the land and labor reforms were creating some momentum for the PPP. Like Indira Gandhi in India, Bhutto feared the consequences of leading a truly democratic political party. Relying on their personal charisma, they chose not to organize their parties at the grass-roots level. All semblance of intraparty democracy was dispensed with as a threat to their preeminent power at the national level. Both relied on the powers of the centralized state to project themselves as the main repository of political patronage. This was a riskier option for Bhutto than for Mrs. Gandhi since the Pakistani army, despite being humbled by India, remained the most powerful institution of the state.

In Bangladesh, Mujibur Rahman did try building the Awami League organizational machinery. The radicalization of the party's support base during a bloody liberation struggle, however, forced Mujib to rely increasingly on his personal stature. Confronted with the monumental task of repairing a war-torn economy that was subjected to a series of natural and manmade disasters—drought, flash floods, and the hike in oil prices—the Awami League government abandoned its socialist pretenses. In a carbon copy of his counterparts in India and Pakistan, Mujib took recourse to authoritarian measures once socialist populism had lost its shine. As would happen in Pakistan a few years later, this paved the way for a military takeover in 1975 and, most tragically, the assassination and execution of two of the three paragons of socialism in South Asia by decade's end. Indira Gandhi survived in India until her assassination in 1984 but was forced to spend a couple of years in the political wilderness between 1977 and 1979. As the ideological pillars of socialism and secularism began to crumble, would-be defenders of the centralized postcolonial Indian state were increasingly attracted by the lure of Hindu majoritarianism.

The Irrelevance of Détente

Populist leaders tended to be paranoid about the machinations of the United States, but there were some solid grounds for their paranoia. The fate of Salvador Allende in Chile is simply the best remembered instance of covert action by the United States to force a regime change in the pursuit of its national interest. Less well known is the role of the CIA in dislodging governments in parts of the world not considered to be in the United States' own backyard like Latin America. Bangladesh and Pakistan are two suspected if not fully proven cases in point, while the well-documented and overt American meddling in Iran makes for an interesting contrast with the recently disclosed furtive methods deployed to oust the pro-Soviet Communist regime in Afghanistan. All carried out in furtherance of Cold War purposes, these instances of American intervention underline the limitations, indeed the irrelevance, of the famed doctrine of détente that is supposed to have underwritten the superpower equation in the wake of the U.S. withdrawal from Vietnam.

On a short trip to the country after its independence from Pakistan, Secretary of State Henry Kissinger responded to an assertion about Bangladesh being a "basket case" by quipping that it would "not necessarily be our basket case."[6] This perception changed once Mujib, at the prodding of the left wing of the Awami League, began to flirt with the idea of forging a closer relationship with Moscow and New Delhi. Although the incriminating evidence is scanty, the predawn military coup on August 15, 1975, that led to the murder of Mujib and forty members of his family is widely believed to have had the tacit support of the Americans.[7] On being briefed about the coup, Kissinger remarked that Mujib, "one of the world's prize fools," had refused to take the American forewarning of the threat to his life seriously. Upon hearing that the coup plotters were pro-American and anti-Indian, the secretary of state noted that he always knew India would "rue the day that they made Bangladesh independent."[8]

The United States had more pressing reasons for wanting to see the back of Zulfikar Ali Bhutto once he publicly vowed to press ahead with Pakistan's nuclear program in response to India's testing of a nuclear device in the summer of 1974. Making no secret of its disapproval, the new American administration under Jimmy Carter was strongly opposed to Pakistan's proceeding with the purchase of a nuclear processing plant from France. The friendly advice of the outgoing U.S. ambassador in Pakistan was that if Bhutto wanted to remain in office, he should back down on his nuclear ambitions. This was impossible for a politician for whom the nuclear issue was not a secret plan to achieve parity with India but a rhetorical device to win all-around popular acclaim. When Bhutto decided to renew his mandate in early 1977, the opportunity was seized upon by the Americans to surreptitiously encourage his political enemies to engineer his downfall. Once the opposition launched street protests against Bhutto's alleged rigging of the elections, it was Pakistan's army chief who had the last laugh. After dislodging his boss in a bloodless coup, General Zia-ul-Haq proceeded to hang him on spurious charges of plotting the murder of a political opponent. It was a Pyrrhic victory for the former prime minister's detractors. The end of Bhutto brought eleven years of military rule and state-sponsored Islamization in Pakistan, a period during which the nuclear program came to full fruition, paradoxically enough, with Washington's tacit support.

The year 1979 was calamitous for American foreign policy. It started ominously with the collapse of the shah's regime in Iran, the bedrock of U.S. policy in the Persian Gulf, and the unexpected emergence of Shi'a clerics harboring a visceral hatred for America, the great Satan in the words of Ayatollah Khomeini. If the future of Iran and the entire region was a source of consternation for Washington, the global unraveling of the Nixon-Kissinger policy of détente was nothing short of catastrophic. It was now apparent that the Soviets had used détente to work on closing the military gap through huge expenditures on defense. The results were manifestly evident in various corners of the globe where there was much greater assertion of Soviet power—from Angola and Ethiopia to Southwest Asia, Central America, and the Caribbean, culminating in the invasion of Afghanistan on Christmas Day.

How had the little-known ayatollahs ripped apart the Iranian script the United States had taken over a quarter of a century to write? American involvement in bolstering the shah's regime in Iran since the 1953 coup against Mohammad Mossadeq was an open secret. The surprise lay in the sheer fragility of a monarchical regime that had substituted the uncertain politics of conflict with those of closely monitored social engineering. Despite uneven development, egregious levels of corruption in the royal family, and modernization policies undertaken in indecent haste, the Pahlavi regime in the mid-1970s wore the look of invincibility following a fivefold increase in Iran's oil revenues. The shah enjoyed the solid support of an army equipped to the teeth with the latest American weaponry; a bur-geoning and penetrative bureaucracy assisted by a notoriously effective in-telligence agency (SAVAK), and a state-sponsored political party entirely at his beck and call. There were few signs of coherent political opposition until, in a typical case of overreaching, the regime decided to extend state control to the urban shopkeepers, the *bazaaris*, who had close social and ideological ties with the Shi'a clergy. These attempts to expand the state's field of patronage and manipulation incurred the wrath of the more tradi-tional commercial middle classes, who had mostly desisted from actively opposing the shah. The ultimate triumph of the bazaar and the clerical al-liance, however, was by no means a foregone conclusion.

Seen against the backdrop of Iranian political history, the success of the religious elements in mobilizing the masses was a departure from earlier protests against established structures of power before 1953. Previously the urban intelligentsia tended to be in the vanguard of revolts fanned by the discontentment of the salaried middle classes and urban wage earners. The slogans that were chanted then were about socialism and secular na-tionalism rather than Islam. A simple catalogue of the events leading up to the overthrow of the Pahlavi state in early 1979 shows that things were ac-tually not very different in the period from late 1977 to the end of 1978. The urban intelligentsia lighted the first fires of the revolution in the streets of Tehran. University students, who initiated street demonstra-tions, and white-collar workers, who brought the economy to a standstill, joined them. Armed guerrilla fighters, college students in the main, cover-ing the entire political spectrum from the extreme left to the far right, dealt the coup de grâce to the tottering regime. Once his prized weapon, the Iranian army, refused to fire on unarmed protesters, the game was up for the shah. What served to tilt the balance in favor of the clergy was the quarter-of-a-century-long systematic decimation of the organizational ba-sis of secular political parties. Lacking a nationwide network capable of mobilizing and sustaining mass support, the urban intelligentsia and the working classes gravitated toward Khomeini, both on account of his per-sonal charisma and also because he had come to symbolize the highest common denominator of Iranian political differences.[9]

The Iranian Revolution was more than an intelligence fiasco for the Americans. Relying on a tyrannical monarchy utterly out of touch with the Islamic sensitivities of its own people to do their bidding in a volatile geostrategic region represented a complete failure of political and strategic imagination in Washington. Nothing else can explain why the United States could do so little to succor a high-value client in a time of acute crisis, thereby conceding vital strategic advantage to the Soviets. Looking to compensate for their sins of omission and commission in Iran, the Americans mercifully found their opening in Afghanistan. Iran's woefully poor Muslim neighbor was on the brink of disintegration with the pro-Soviet Communist regime trying forcibly to impose Marxist reforms in an insular and fiercely traditional tribal setting. Stung by the loss of Iran, American intelligence sounded the alarm bell on growing Soviet involvement in Afghanistan as early as March 1979. The majority of the CIA's analysts doubted whether the Kremlin was prepared to go so far as to commit ground troops to keep its proxy government afloat in Afghanistan. But there were also those who could see the strategic gains for the United States in supporting the Iranian- and Pakistani-backed Afghan rebels. It would "turn the tables on the Soviets for their actions in Africa and Southeast Asia . . . [and] encourage a polarization of Muslim and Arab sentiment against the USSR," thereby "offer[ing] an opportunity to establish relations with the Iranian government."[10]

Toward that end, President Carter on July 3, 1979, is said to have granted approval for secret aid to Afghan militants opposing the pro-Soviet regime in Kabul. The funds were also to be used more generally for the spread of Islamic "fundamentalism" in Central Asia with the explicit intention of destabilizing the Soviet Union.[11] This as Andrew Preston has shown was consistent with the rise of the religious right in the United States and its increasing efforts to influence foreign policy even though the geostrategic motivation was more salient than the religious one.[12] American covert aid to the rebels, who were already receiving assistance from Pakistan and Iran, was a red flag for the Soviets, who made the catastrophic error of invading Afghanistan. Washington was determined to make sure that Afghanistan turned out to be Moscow's Vietnam. Communist bashers like the flamboyant Texas congressman Charlie Wilson had found the moment to deal the fatal blow to America's archenemy. In a breathtaking demonstration of the potential excesses of power based on personalized networks in Washington, Congressman Wilson metamorphosed the CIA's engagement with Afghanistan into the largest covert operation in U.S. history.[13] There is a profound irony in the United States' bemoaning the loss of an important ally to a clutch of obscurantist Shi'a clerics, only to bend over backwards to facilitate an Islamic jihad against the Soviet Union in a country that had barely ever found a place on the American radar screen.

The Correct Chronology of an "Islamic" Resurgence

The U.S.-backed jihad unfolded in the rugged terrain of Afghanistan during the 1980s, well beyond the decade that is the focus of our interest. The spotlight on the 1970s nevertheless enables an understanding of the contingent nature of ideological upheavals and placing these in their global economic and strategic contexts.

One regime that straddled the two decades was the military dictatorship of General Zia-ul-Haq, owing its longevity to the frontline status of Pakistan in the war against the Soviets in Afghanistan. A veritable international pariah following Bhutto's judicial murder in April 1979, Zia faced an uncertain political future until the Soviet invasion turned things around. Looking to perpetuate his regime, Zia used the opening to drive a hard bargain with Washington. His price for supporting U.S. strategic goals in Afghanistan was the funneling of all assistance to the mujahidin, financial and military, through the Pakistani army's intelligence apparatus, especially the ISI (Inter-Services Intelligence). Billions of dollars of American and Saudi money earmarked for Afghanistan found its way into the hands of senior generals, several of whom made handsome fortunes in the process. Awash in unaccounted dollars, the ISI in time became a state within a state, causing severe headaches to recalcitrant domestic politicians and hostile regional neighbors alike.[14] Both Iran and Pakistan ended up housing millions of Afghan men, women, and children. But the pressures on Pakistan's delicate social weave were far more pronounced since support for the resistance movement also gave rise to a parallel arms and drugs economy, aided and abetted by the ISI.

After Pakistan became the staging ground for the American-supported Afghan jihad, religious extremism in what was still a largely moderate country assumed menacing proportions. The formal aspects of the Zia regime's state-sponsored Islamization found expression in laws that were wildly discriminatory toward women. Another dimension of religion as state ideology was the general's decision to give the army the motto "Islam, Piety, and Jihad." Informal state support was extended to Sunni militias, loosely labeled mujahidin, with a view to waging jihad in Afghanistan and snuffing out any signs of Shi'a resurgence or a Marxist implosion in Pakistan. The policy of arming Sunni surrogate militias was to destabilize not only the tribal areas but also the rest of the country. A portion of the windfall in greenbacks was used to recruit civilian militias that could act as surrogates for the Pakistani army. In the predominantly Pakhtun federally administered tribal areas of Pakistan (FATA) that border Afghanistan, Sunni clerics linked to the Deobandi school of Islamic thought were encouraged to give the call of jihad to their madrasa students in return for generous sums of money. Many of the future leaders of the Afghan Taliban, notably Mullah Omar, were educated at religious seminaries run by the Jamiat-i-Ulema-i-Islam (JUI) in the North-West Frontier Province. While the JUI leadership went from rags to riches, the flow of easy money into FATA shifted the balance of power from the tribal chiefs to the suddenly enriched and well-armed radical clerics who had typically depended on the former for their wherewithal and personal security.

The fires lit by the Soviet invasion of 1979 served to destroy the social and political equilibrium of Pakistan's northwestern tribal lands, gradually encircling the rest of the country with menacing implications for the region as well as the world. The Afghan jihad morphed into the dreaded Taliban regime, increasingly linked to al-Qaeda, and was redirected to Kashmir by its agile handlers in the ISI. Long after the Soviets had dismantled their empire, disaffected Pakistani youth armed with Kalashnikovs and distorted interpretations of Islam persisted in waging total war against rival linguistic communities and sects. The Cold War may have been over in the rest of the world. Yet its legacies rooted in critical policy shifts in the late seventies never ceased taking a deadly toll in Pakistan, a nuclear-armed state that has earned the unenviable distinction of being regarded as the global epicenter of Islamic terror.

Fissures within a Globalized Islam

While a crisis of authority in several modern nation-states paved the way for transnational religious connections, the economic and strategic contexts of ideological shifts in the global 1970s ensured the fissured nature of globalized Islam in the contemporary world. This is hardly surprising since the ideological upheavals had little to do with religion as faith, but rather flowed from contestations over religion as a demarcator of identity.

The distinction is an important one. Religion, loosely defined and inadequately contextualized, is used all too easily as an undifferentiated category to characterize a range of social anxieties that plague the contemporary world. Upon closer examination, many of these are more aptly seen as a product of temporal or worldly concerns than of specifically religious ones. It may be that there is a difference in attitudes toward religion in the United States and much of the rest of the world. In America there may well be a genuine disaffection felt by people of faith toward the condescending attitude they detect among upholders of the secular dogma in the public sphere. In South Asia and the Middle East, however, religious ideologies have been deeply enmeshed in the politics of identity, whether as a means for state legitimacy or resistance to overcentralized and unresponsive authoritarian regimes.

This political feature of religion as identity gave rise from the late 1970s to a novel kind of sectarian conflict as well as wars between countries in an era of acute crisis for the nation-state. The most dramatic example of a conventional territorial war stemming from these contradictions was the eight-year Armageddon between Iran and Iraq, the latter supported during the 1980s by the United States. The proxy war between Iran and Saudi Arabia was fought in the same period on the battlefields of Afghanistan and a multitude of urban and rural neighborhoods in Pakistan. Neither faith nor doctrine contributed to the noxious brand of Sunni-Shi'a sectarian strife that appeared to tear apart the social fabric of the Islamic world. In some instances what was at stake was regional dominance, as in the case of Iranian, Iraqi, and Saudi nationalisms. In others the tussle was over the exercise of political power within nation-states that had failed to deliver on their much-touted promises of modernization, democracy, and development, as in the cases of Pakistan, Egypt, Algeria, Turkey, and Indonesia or even in the microcosm of Palestine. The Islamists in their various guises from North Africa to Southeast Asia exploited the widespread social disenchantments to offer their alternative, if ultimately illusory, models of salvation.

What got misdiagnosed in certain circles as the "clash of civilizations" was in reality a set of conflicts triggered by unfulfilled expectations, growing disparities, and humiliating indignities. The ideological upheavals of the 1970s may not have been disparate phenomena. But they were hardly monolithic. The structural transformations that attended the onset of the contemporary phase of globalization drew a new set of frontiers, external and internal, even while forging connections across them. The Cold War's geopolitical stasis lasted much longer in the peripheries than it did in defining relations between the two superpowers. Stretching into the era of a crisis in global capitalism and the collapse of the socialist alternative, the Cold War's most poisoned legacy was not the division between religions but the splintering of the religious community itself.

CHAPTER 21

Future Shock

The End of the World as They Knew It

MATTHEW CONNELLY

SINCE THE END OF THE COLD WAR, historians have come to understand that a preoccupation with the U.S.-Soviet confrontation distorted our understanding of the rest of the world. A more global and transnational perspective reveals that long before the end of the East-West struggle, interdependent capital markets, population growth and movement, environmental challenges, new media, and international and nongovernmental organizations were combining to cause radical change of a recognizably new kind. This broader vision, less centered on interstate relations, can show the roots of the contemporary phenomenon called globalization.

Of course historians differ on when and where to begin. There are different ways to define globalization, and it has proceeded in episodic fashion. Whether any particular development really had worldwide impact is usually debatable, and one can often find precursors from earlier periods, such as in the rise and fall of world migration and commodity flows. The problems are particularly acute when we try to analyze changing perceptions of space—"the shock of the global"—with a unit of analysis defined by time. The most important historical developments do not usually organize themselves by decade. What seems distinctive about a period as it was experienced or remembered may not help explain an ongoing geopolitical process.

This essay explores this space-time relationship by focusing on how contemporaries understood their times. As it happens, long before historians began studying the 1970s, even before the decade began, people expected it to bring rapid and dramatic changes that would be global in scope. History seemed to be accelerating, and over the course of the decade people became extraordinarily focused on the future.[1] These changing perceptions of time help explain how people began to see the world as becoming more interconnected. New transportation and communications technologies promised to collapse space and make the world one. But global crises also annihilated distance while at the same time making differences between people all the more palpable. What made the global seem local, and shocking, was that people in the 1970s believed that the world—all of it—was rapidly changing, but with radically different effects for rich and poor, the "developed" and the "underdeveloped." While some were stuck in gas lines—or breadlines—and seemed to be living in the past, others were booking advance tickets on supersonic transports and speeding into the future.[2]

In the 1970s "futurology" itself became a site of political conflict. Forecasts, projections, and future scenarios became common tools of governance in the public, corporate, and philanthropic sectors. Some of these exercises had a real-world impact, such as the "Team B" assessment of a growing Soviet advantage in waging nuclear war, which became a keynote of Ronald Reagan's presidential run in 1980. The Club of Rome report "The Limits to Growth" inspired scientists in China to use similar forms of systems analysis to calculate the need for a one-child policy.[3] Beyond government forecasting and projections, the 1970s also witnessed the revival of millenarian fervor among evangelical Christians and the increasing popularity of paranormal beliefs and practices, especially astrology. These too could have a real-world impact, such as in the growing support for Israel, which evangelicals believed was the fulfillment of prophecy. In time, government agencies began to offer fanciful and frightening visions of the future to marshal public support, especially for building up U.S. military capabilities against the Soviets. Some of the most important political struggles would therefore turn not just on contending visions of the future—such as different scenarios for World War III—but on whether it was even possible to plan and prepare for it.

How do we explain why people became more preoccupied with the future in the 1970s, to the point where even intelligence agencies began to employ psychics and "futurology" became a lucrative field for business consultants? Can we generalize about larger trends—such as the public's disenchantment with earlier, more optimistic visions of technological progress and a new taste for more dystopian visions that were also more global in nature? Considering the very limited utility or reliability of most forecasts, projections, and scenarios—which usually failed to anticipate the most important events and trends of the era—could they be seen as serving other, unacknowledged purposes? As we shall see, what historians now call the shock of the global was experienced by contemporaries as the shock of the future, shocking because—for all their efforts to forecast and plan for it—the future arrived suddenly and without warning.

In 1970 Alvin Toffler published what would become one of the best-sellers of the decade, a foundational work in the fast-growing new field of futurology. A former editor at *Fortune,* Toffler focused on emerging trends that indicated new business opportunities, such as increasing labor mobility, lifestyle drugs, divorce, and gay marriage. But Toffler made a larger argument about how the pace of historical change was overtaking society's capacity to cope, coining the term "information overload." He predicted that some people would suffer "future shock" and become increasingly disoriented and irrational, a phenomenon he thought was already evident in the emergence of anarchist and terrorist groups. People needed help in adapting to the pace of change, including "enclaves of the future" in which they could learn how to interact with new technologies, "enclaves of the past" where they could find refuge, and ombudsmen who would challenge technocrats and delay disruptive innovations.[4]

By the late 1960s there were already popular movements afoot aiming at historical and environmental preservation, each in its own way reflecting a protest against the nature and pace of change. The National Historic Preservation Act was passed in 1966, and the following decade witnessed rapid growth in degree programs, grass-roots campaigns, and historic districts across America. Concern about environmental conservation also grew apace during the same period with the creation of the Environmental Protection Agency in 1970 and the Endangered Species Act three years later. In 1972 UNESCO combined the two agendas with its Convention Concerning the Protection of the World Cultural and Natural Heritage, or Heritage Convention, which provided funding, expert advice, and international recognition for similar efforts around the world.[5]

Historians now recognize this impulse to preserve and commemorate the past as resulting from a perception that the pace of change is accelerating.[6] But Toffler was not the only one to foresee how it would also lead people to be more preoccupied with the future. The idea of "future shock" was first introduced by the prominent defense intellectual Herman Kahn in 1967 in a more optimistic Hudson Institute study, *The Year 2000,* a book that forecast undersea colonies and weather control. That same year the American Academy of Arts and Sciences published a special issue of *Daedalus* presenting the work of some three dozen luminaries charged with considering the long-range consequences of contemporary policy decisions. They included Zbigniew Brzezinski, Karl Deutsch, Theodosius Dobzhansky, Samuel Huntington, Daniel Patrick Moynihan, and Roger Revelle. The chairman of the Year 2000 Commission, Daniel Bell, used the opportunity to introduce his concept of a "post-industrial society," another idea that Toffler would appropriate and popularize.[7]

Whether known as futurology or futurism, the field grew to become an international phenomenon. The First World Future Research Conference was held in Oslo in 1967, and by 1980 the World Future Society claimed fifty thousand members.[8] Hudson had its European counterpart in France, where Bertrand de Jouvenel directed the Association Internationale Futuribles. He, like Bell, described his work as exploring alternative futures in a way meant to illuminate the scope of human agency.[9] Like the American Academy, the English Social Science Research Council created a Committee on the Next Thirty Years. The rise of futurology also transcended Cold War divisions. A Czechoslovak Futurological Society was founded in 1968, and the Soviet independent Scientific Forecasting Association grew to more than 1,500 members before authorities shut it down in 1970. The party leadership insisted that this work be done through proper channels, but also gave ten- and even fifteen-year forecasts increasing weight in research and capital investment decisions.[10]

Different forms of futurology also made deep inroads in the private sector in the 1970s. Shell Oil began to use future scenarios for long-range strategic planning, now considered a model of prescient corporate leadership. Many more corporations created long-range planning departments or hired "strategy boutiques" like the Boston Consulting Group. This was also the heyday of economic forecasting, which would grow to become a $100 million industry by the early 1980s. In annual gatherings of the World Future Society, reporters described the emergence of a new profession as a host of consultants jetted about the world offering their services as trend-spotters.[11]

In the United States the increasing interest in forecasting was both bipartisan and competitive. In the 1970s a series of presidential commissions and reports examined issues such as "Population and the American

Future" and "Critical Choices," culminating with the Carter administration's Global 2000 Report. Nixon created an Office of Net Assessment under Andrew Marshall in 1971 to forecast technological developments and the shifting correlation of forces with the USSR. A concern that the executive branch had developed an edge in evaluating prospects for technological change prompted Congress to create the Office of Technology Assessment in 1972. In 1976 the House of Representatives implemented a rule that required committees and subcommittees to undertake futures research and forecasting.[12] Toffler went on to become an adviser to another self-described futurist, Congressman Newt Gingrich. Gingrich and Senator Al Gore would later cosponsor legislation to create an office in the executive branch charged with determining whether laws and regulations adequately took account of "critical trends and alternative futures."[13]

The professional success and political influence of futurology was only part of a broader public fascination with prevision. Toffler's book sold more than 6 million copies, but it was not actually the best-selling work of nonfiction in the 1970s. That was a work of prophecy: Hal Lindsey's *Late Great Planet Earth*. The book was an extended commentary on how current events were portents of the impending Apocalypse. Most important among them was the creation of the State of Israel. Lindsey also used scripture to describe how the battle of Armageddon would unfold, drawing sweeping arrows across the Middle East to indicate the coming Soviet assault on Israel. And he translated scripture into modern weapons systems, such that fire and brimstone were said to signify nuclear weapons. Starting with a religious publishing house in 1970, Lindsey continued issuing new editions for the trade, revising the predictions that did not pan out—such as the notion that, once it had ten members, the leader of the European Community would be the Antichrist. He inspired a legion of imitators as well as documentaries, popular films, and radio talk shows.[14] Here again, the renewed interest in millenarianism was not only an American phenomenon. The 1979 seizure of the Grand Mosque at Mecca was intended as preparation for the Apocalypse, and eschatological writings would flood the Islamic world over the following decades.[15]

The Late Great Planet Earth began by noting that many were turning away from religion in their search for insight about the future. For Lindsey and other evangelicals, the contemporary boom in astrology constituted one of the signs of the last days.[16] Beginning in 1968, astrology books also began to appear on best-seller lists, and by 1975, 1,250 of

1,500 newspapers offered regular columns on the subject.[17] Whereas the preachers warned of a new period of unprecedented violence and destruction, for astrologers like Linda Goodman, humanity was entering the "Age of Aquarius," marked by "higher love, every man is my brother."[18] The term is usually associated with the 1960s and the musical *Hair*. But for believers the "New Age" was supposed to last over two thousand years. What seemed remarkable to social scientists in the 1970s was that, far from being a fringe phenomenon, belief in astrology and other paranormal phenomena was becoming mainstream. In a 1978 Gallup poll, 39 percent of respondents reported that they believed in precognition, or the ability to foretell the future.[19]

Futurologists like Toffler insisted that their work had nothing to do with astrology and prophecy (one reason he preferred the term "futurism"). "Today's futurists, for the most part," he maintained, "lay no claim to the ability to predict." Accordingly, they used a range of methods, and those who offered projections and scenarios were usually careful to specify that they were not intended as forecasts. Population projections, for instance, could never be wrong if they were properly understood as calculations based on specified assumptions about fertility, mortality, and migration. Similarly, future scenarios were usually described as thought exercises meant to provoke people to question their assumptions and think harder about how their decisions would open up or foreclose opportunities.[20]

Yet it is doubtful that so much demand would have developed for this kind of work were it not for expectations that it offered a privileged vantage point on the future. And those expectations shaped both how the work was performed and how it was sold. Given the infinite number of possibilities for projecting a population, "high" and "low" projections were inevitably taken as confidence intervals, with the medium projection interpreted as the one that seemed most likely. The confidence people had— and continue to have—in population projections helps to explain why they are so often the starting point for speculation about the future.[21] In addition, the scenarios that are described as the most successful are not the ones that persuaded policymakers to change course, with the result that the scenario itself diverges from events as they unfolded. Instead the success stories invariably refer to the rare instances in which scenarios actually anticipated reality, such as Shell Oil's early consideration of a price shock in the 1970s.[22]

Moreover, many futurists did offer explicit predictions, and claimed credit for those that came true. In the 1970s the U.S. intelligence community in particular began to adopt new methods of forecasting that promised to overcome the groupthink and "defensive writing" that had rendered national intelligence estimates (NIEs) virtually useless for policy-making. The Delphi method anonymously polled experts and shared peer reviews in order to produce an unbiased consensus on a given question. Previously used by the RAND corporation for technological forecasting, in the 1970s it began to be applied to political problems and policymaking. In the same period, Bayesian exercises had CIA analysts assessing the probability of specific events and the predictive weight of individual indicators. After a series of these exercises, in which they estimated from zero to 100 percent the probability of Sino-Soviet hostilities or the likelihood of a new Middle East war, analysts themselves could be assessed for their success in predicting the future.[23]

For their part, astrologers and interpreters of biblical prophecy were usually more guarded in their predictions, instead indicating possibilities and probabilities without associating specific events with specific dates (though 1982 was a tough year for Pat Robertson). Astrologers, like futurologists, offered vague advice more often than actual forecasts. And like scenario writing, the prophetic tradition was dedicated to warning people about the possible consequences of their actions. All of these fields claimed to be evidence-based, even if the rules of evidence differed. "Astral analysis" and biblical exegesis could actually be quite sophisticated, in their own way, with recognized gradations between levels of expertise. And astrologers and biblical interpreters, no less than economic forecasters and Bayesian analysts, seized on the use of computers, claiming that it would make revolutionary advances in accuracy possible.[24]

An increasing interest in prevision was therefore both an elite and a popular phenomenon in the 1970s. The different forms it assumed cannot easily be disaggregated. Thus in the same period in which the CIA adopted new methods of expert forecasting and the Defense Department conducted elaborate war games based on future scenarios, both the CIA and the Defense Intelligence Agency also hired psychics. Beginning in 1970 these programs in "remote viewing" were assigned a range of intelligence problems, from the location of kidnapped servicemen to the launch date of Soviet submarines. Subjects were asked not merely to see places where they had never been but to peer into the future.[25]

The same people—and some very important people—sometimes displayed a fascination with both prophecy and astrology, with no apparent sense of inconsistency. Ronald Reagan's 1967 inauguration as governor of California took place at 12:16 AM, the moment when Jupiter was highest in the night sky.[26] Reagan's chief of staff, Donald Regan, would write that astrologers were consulted about "virtually every major move and decision Reagan made," from the invasion of Grenada to disarmament negotiations with Mikhail Gorbachev.[27] But Reagan was also someone who believed, as he said in 1971, that "everything is in place for the battle of Armageddon and the Second Coming of Christ."[28] The same 1978 Gallup poll that found high levels of belief in the paranormal also indicated that Christians and atheists were equally likely to believe in astrology.[29]

There was also overlap and cross-fertilization between futurologists and eschatologists. The movie version of *The Late Great Planet Earth*, for instance, cited respected futurologists who shared Lindsey's pessimism, albeit for different reasons. They included Nobel Prize winner Norman Borlaug; Paul Ehrlich, author of *The Population Bomb;* and Aurelio Peccei, president of the Club of Rome, who predicted that "we are a few minutes before possible disaster." Whereas preachers increasingly pointed to political developments as portents, such as Communist coups or EC enlargement, Ehrlich and Peccei—like latter-day millenarians—invoked famines, freaks of nature, and natural disasters as signs that humanity was beginning to pay for its sins and faced inevitable doom.[30]

There are several reasons why so many both in the United States and abroad, both at the popular level and among intellectuals and policy-makers, seemed preoccupied with the future in this period. An insightful early commentator, Michael Barkun, began by noting the obvious: the late 1960s and 1970s were a turbulent period. The events of 1968, 1973, and 1979, in particular, reverberated around the world. But he also pointed out how the different strains in apocalyptic thought appeared to be developing in parallel, in conscious or unconscious imitation, and could be mutually reinforcing. Even Barkun could not resist the temptation to end with the dark premonition that panic created by the combined efforts of secular and religious Jeremiahs might produce a self-fulfilling prophecy.[31]

One reason why people were prepared to listen to them was that more mainstream experts repeatedly failed to predict the most important crises of the decade. In the field of economic forecasting, the failures were overwhelming and impossible to deny. U.S. government agencies and the leading private firms were all surprised by the 1974 recession and also failed to anticipate the severity of the 1980 downturn. Government agencies, whether the Federal Reserve, the Council of Economic Advisers, or the Congressional Budget Office, were particularly poor at forecasting inflation. Over the course of the decade, the U.S. consumer price index more than doubled.[32]

Of all economic phenomena, inflation is particularly pernicious in stoking anxiety about the future. It forces people to readjust their expectations continuously, since their wages are worth less every day, while the goods they need cost more all the time. In the 1970s many opted to hedge risk in new futures markets—another consequence of the free-floating dollar and commodity inflation—or simply hoarded gold and silver bullion. Uncertainty itself began to sell in the form of stock options. With the founding of the Chicago Board Options Exchange in 1973, speculators could gain and lose fortunes betting on volatility. Communist societies officially had no inflation or commodity markets, but these were hidden: consumers lined up to pay the same price for increasingly shoddy goods, or simply bartered for basic necessities.[33]

Another trend that would have accentuated personal insecurity was the rise in divorce rates in virtually all the industrialized nations. At the same time, more people were delaying marriage. And those who did marry tended to plan smaller families. Fertility rates were falling in almost every region of the world in the 1970s. Many parents were made to feel guilty about the few children they did choose to raise. Ehrlich called the birth of each new American a "disaster for the world." Family planning campaigns in dozens of different countries depicted large, unplanned families as hungry and violent. In the 1970s the most common contraceptive method worldwide was not the pill but sterilization.[34]

The 1970s were also a period when more wars and revolutions were breaking out all across the world. There was a discernible trend from interstate to intrastate and transnational conflict. Civil wars were particularly unsettling, and not just for those directly involved. Many created refugee flows that brought these events home to people in distant regions, including Bangladesh, Vietnam, Lebanon, Afghanistan, Iran, Nicaragua, Guatemala, and El Salvador. So too did satellite television broadcasting. For international terrorists, the media outlets constituted the main target. From 1968 to 1978 the number of groups engaged in terrorism that crossed or challenged state borders increased from eleven to fifty-five. In a period when the number of international air passengers carried and miles traveled doubled, the international hijacker became an emblematic figure. In 1970, the same year Toffler published *Future Shock,* there were sixty-four international hijackings, an all-time high, and an apt metaphor for the anxiety of the age.[35]

Finally, this was a period when no one appeared capable of restoring order. U.S. power was discredited and appeared to be in decline, a trend personified in the office of the president. Before he was driven from power, Richard Nixon reneged on a long-standing commitment to back the dollar with gold and signed a Strategic Arms Limitation Treaty that seemed to concede Soviet nuclear superiority. Gerald Ford could not stop Communist advances in Southeast Asia and Africa, even if he preferred to blame Congress. And Jimmy Carter appeared powerless even to protect American diplomats.

In the most famous speech of his administration, Carter argued that the true crisis facing the country at the end of the decade was a "crisis of confidence," a loss of faith in institutions and the very idea of progress. "The erosion of our confidence in the future," he warned, "is threatening to destroy the social and the political fabric of America." Sympathetic to Carter's predicament, some asked whether the presidency itself had become too big a job for anyone to perform effectively. After three decades during which presidents had free rein in setting foreign policy and the United States exercised hegemonic power in the world, even critics were unsettled by the sense that the center could no longer hold.[36]

There were thus many reasons why people in the 1970s would have been more than usually apprehensive about their future and proceeded to act on these anxieties in ways that changed history. Some of the key struggles of the era reflected contending ways of coping with an uncertain future. This would include efforts to impose wage and price controls in the industrialized countries, but also successful demands for automatic cost-of-living adjustments, more generous pensions, and health insurance. Developing countries troubled by population projections tried to orchestrate "incentives" and "disincentives" to pressure couples to have fewer children, but many subverted these schemes, and fertility rates largely reflected couples' own preferences for large or small families. And while the superpowers collaborated in controlling the pace of nuclear weapons development, many people began to take to the streets to demand an end to the arms race, culminating in calls for a nuclear "freeze." While all political struggles relate to the future, each of these struggles centered on specific forecasts, projections, and scenarios.

No struggle seemed more fateful than that surrounding nuclear weapons, in which people were asked to choose between equally frightening visions of the future. Since the 1960s, when Robert McNamara tamed the Pentagon through cost-benefit analyses and long-term programming, the U.S. nuclear arsenal was meant to match the projected Soviet threat five years out. CIA analysts, having been so wrong about the bomber gap and the missile gap, tended to be conservative in their estimates. By the early 1970s, senior military officers and defense intellectuals were increasingly determined to challenge these estimates and demand a more rapid U.S. buildup. Soviet technological advances were said to be creating a "window of vulnerability," a period in the near future when a first strike could eliminate land-based U.S. strategic forces and Moscow would hold American cities hostage.[37]

In May 1976 CIA director George H. W. Bush agreed to bring in an outside team, including Richard Pipes, Paul Wolfowitz, and Paul Nitze, to offer an alternative assessment of Soviet intentions and capabilities. "Team B," as they were called, argued that the Soviets, unlike the Americans, did not believe in nuclear "sufficiency," but instead were seeking to develop the means to win a nuclear war. These means included more accurate nuclear warheads, large numbers of strategic bombers, and a new means of locating ballistic missile submarines that—amazingly—would not depend on sound and would therefore be undetectable.[38]

At the same time Team B was at work, Ronald Reagan was gaining ground in his campaign for the Republican presidential nomination by warning that the United States was losing ground to the Soviet Union. Although President Ford defeated him in a close vote at the convention, Reagan was invited to deliver impromptu remarks to close the proceedings. He noted how he had recently been asked to deposit a letter in a time capsule to be opened on America's tercentennial. He wondered aloud whether, in 2076, there would be anyone left to read it, or whether —if some survived nuclear war but lived under communism—anyone would have permission. The speech brought delegates to their feet, and many regretted that they had not chosen Reagan as their candidate.[39]

After Carter won the 1976 election, Team B members decided to leak their findings to the press. Several went on to found the Committee on the

Present Danger and continued lobbying to increase U.S. defense spending.[40] Meanwhile a new wave of fictional accounts of a future Soviet attack began to appear, starting in 1978 with *The Third World War: August 1985* by General Sir John Hackett. It depicted a blitzkrieg attack which, upon faltering, leads to a nuclear strike on Birmingham. After NATO retaliates against Minsk, the Warsaw Pact finally falls to pieces. The book concludes with a warning that a less happy result was becoming increasingly likely, and that those who were reducing defense spending "live in a land of total make-believe."[41]

In the late 1970s preachers like Jerry Falwell and Pat Robertson continued to predict that a Soviet attack on Israel would be followed by nuclear war. During his 1980 presidential campaign, Reagan reiterated that "we may be the generation that sees Armageddon" in an interview for Jim Bakker and the PTL network. The Republican Party Platform of 1980 was filled with references to "signs" and "signposts" portending American decline, and evangelical Christians would become a key component of Reagan's winning coalition.[42]

But conservatives did not have the field all to themselves. Antinuclear activists fought back with their own vision of the future: a post-apocalyptic landscape, or what Jonathan Schell called "A Republic of Insects and Grass." The *New Yorker* journalist explained that "since we cannot afford under any circumstances to let a holocaust occur, we are forced in this one case to become the historians of the future." But unlike Hackett, Schell spent only a few pages speculating about how a nuclear war might begin, instead devoting his book to describing its aftermath. What mattered to him and his readers was not who would start a nuclear war but how it would end. It would not merely kill hundreds of millions of people and wreck the planet; it would also—by extinguishing generations to come—constitute a "murder of the future."[43]

The global movement to "freeze" the arms race grew to become one of the greatest challenges to confront the Reagan administration. In a March 1983 address to the National Association of Evangelicals he was defiant, relating a story about a young father he had heard speaking about the threat of nuclear war:

I heard him saying, "I love my little girls more than anything—" And I said to myself, "Oh, no, don't. You can't—don't say that." But I had underestimated him. He went on: "I would rather see my little girls die now, still believing in God, than have them grow up under communism and one day die no longer believing in God." There were thousands of young people in that audience. They came to their feet with shouts of joy.

In the most memorable words of the speech, Reagan concluded by declaring that, as long as the Soviets "preach the supremacy of the State, declare its omnipotence over individual man, and predict its eventual domination of all peoples on the earth, they are the focus of evil in the modern world."[44]

Two weeks later the president offered a different, more appealing perspective in a nationally televised address, one that looked not to heaven but to space. He vowed "to break out of a future that relies solely on offensive retaliation for our security." The United States would instead create a shield to defend itself against nuclear attack. Glossy magazines such as *Popular Science* responded with cover stories showing how fleets of space-based "battle stations," electromagnetic railguns, "nuclear-pumped x-ray lasers," and "giant mirrors" would engage and destroy Soviet intercontinental ballistic missiles. Defense contractors such as TRW provided full-color illustrations of what these space weapons would look like, while scientists on staff projected the funding required to make them work. But a legion of critics rose up and derided the whole idea as "Star Wars." Nuclear activists depicted it as not merely science fiction but dangerous fantasy. The *Bulletin of the Atomic Scientists* moved the doomsday clock to three minutes to midnight, closer than at any other time since the Korean War.[45]

Any effort to trace the origins of the post–Cold War era to the 1970s must acknowledge the many ways in which this period was quite unlike the present. After all, the Cold War did not end during this decade but instead entered a dangerous new phase. But the renewal of the Cold War was at least in part a struggle over contending visions of the future that began in the 1970s. For Reagan and his supporters, there was no negotiating with the Soviets as long as they planned to take over the world, even if that meant bringing on Armageddon. His opponents warned that continued confrontation endangered not just life on earth but future generations too. And what neither side realized was that, even when the Soviet Union self-destructed, their conflict would continue. For religious nationalists—Muslim as well as Christian—the demise of communism did not end the danger of godless hedonism, while environmentalists warned that other-worldly thinking served as a distraction from the continuing threat to life on earth.

In tracing these different strains of eschatology, especially among evangelicals and environmentalists, we can discern what truly distinguished the 1970s from what came before and after, while at the same time discovering some of the roots of our own time. Forecasters have proved no better in predicting the recent period of turbulence than they were in foreseeing the economic shocks of the 1970s, a decade that was supposed to bring unprecedented prosperity. And yet they continue to offer their forecasts, revising as necessary, and the public still listens with rapt attention. We expect, even need, our leaders to see the future better than we can, never so much as during the most uncertain times. If history provides any guide, the years to come will be boom times for forecasters, astrologers, and prophets. Looking back to the 1970s, the shock of the global, and the shock of the future, may also bring a shock of recognition.[46]

The Shock of the Global

THOMAS BORSTELMANN

FOR AMERICANS, the 1970s are an era of ill repute. "A kidney stone of a decade," one "Doonesbury" character called it. The aesthetics were grim, from polyester pantsuits to Pet Rocks. Writer Joe Queenan recalled it as a time of "bad hair, bad clothes, bad music, bad design, bad books, bad economics, bad carpeting, bad fabrics, and a lot of bad ideas." President Ford agreed. "I must say to you that the state of our Union is not good," he announced in 1975. The use of addictive drugs, both legal and illegal, was widespread. Indeed one nonpartisan critic observed wryly that having had Ford and Jimmy Carter actually living in the White House was "a possible explanation for the rampant substance abuse at the time." Pulitzer Prize–winning historian David Kennedy lamented what he called "the odd blend of political disillusionment and pop-culture daffiness that gave the 1970s their distinctive flavor." Two of the best historians of these years, Beth Bailey and David Farber, have found them to be perhaps "our strangest decade," a period of "incoherent impulses, contradictory desires, and even a fair amount of self-flagellation." Self-flagellation, of course, used to be an admired sign of monastic spiritual devotion and discipline, but by the era of hot tubs, "self-flagellation" was now code for failing to absorb the message of one of the decade's best-selling books, *I'm OK—You're OK*.[1]

The neighbors, chronologically speaking, are part of the problem for Americans. Both the 1960s and the 1980s have clear storylines of strong reforming forces and exciting social and political conflicts, and each of those decades has developed a substantial literature of memoir and historical analysis. For the 1970s, this is somewhat akin to the old problem faced

351

by historically minded residents of North Carolina who liked to refer to their state, situated between South Carolina and Virginia, as "a valley of humility between two mountains of conceit." The 1970s have a similar status, falling between two "real" decades, when important movements and great events took place, for better or worse.[2]

In fact the 1970s turned out to be a crucial period of change and adjustment that has shaped the contours of U.S. history and global history ever since. The decade began and ended with trauma for Americans, a series of jolts like a line of thunderstorms rolling across the prairie: defeat in Southeast Asia, "stagflation," the OPEC oil crisis, and Watergate to start, and the near disaster at Three Mile Island, the hostage crisis in Tehran, the second oil crisis, and the Soviet invasion of Afghanistan to finish.[3] If the United States did not win all its wars, if its leaders could not be trusted, if its oil wells did not provide enough fuel for its drivers, and if its jobs no longer paid rising real wages, what was the nation's future? The answer came in the form of two powerful undercurrents that flowed just beneath the more readily visible surface waves of economic, political, and cultural turmoil. These undercurrents turned out to be global currents, as the United States was neither unique nor exceptional, moving instead in the same direction as most of the rest of the world.

The first undercurrent was formal equality for all U.S. citizens. While homosexuals and the disabled gained new status by dismantling old restrictions, and even animals won legal standing with the Endangered Species Act of 1973, women made the most important gains of all in the 1970s. Women surged past long-standing barriers that had constrained them in education, work, public life, and personal relationships. They challenged people to reconsider assumptions and behaviors regarding precisely what it meant to be a male human being or a female human being. The intimate involvement of women and men, of girls and boys, in each other's lives meant that few American families were unmarked by this reconsideration of one of the most fundamental touchstones of human identity.[4]

As Americans moved to eliminate the remnants of discrimination from public life, so too did the world make a major turn in the 1970s away from formal inequality, colonialism, and empire. In the European sphere, the last great overseas empire, the Portuguese, caved in with the liberation of Angola and Mozambique. Rhodesia became Zimbabwe, and in South Africa the final wave of liberation began to build among the students of Soweto. In the less formal U.S. sphere of empire, Vietnam fought its way free of American occupation, Panama negotiated a return of control over the Canal Zone, Nicaragua overthrew the Somoza regime, and Iran drove the last shah into exile. In the Soviet sphere, empire entered its terminal stage when Red Army troops marched into Afghanistan and eventual disaster. Dissident movements in Russia and Eastern Europe gained traction, leading to the creation in Poland of Solidarity and the beginning of the end for Communist rule. Across the globe, human rights organizations such as Amnesty International became an important force in world affairs in the 1970s, and old hierarchies of race and sex lost much of their power to be understood as natural and right. Indeed the flourishing of postmodernism in this era challenged all forms of received truth and deference to traditions.[5]

Replacing race and sex was a new hierarchy considered more truly natural: the sorting out of people into what were seen as their natural socioeconomic levels by the operation of the free market. With artificial barriers based on irrelevant group identities eliminated now from public life, free market enthusiasts could more readily claim that the inequalities remaining were the just and reasonable result of letting the natural laws of supply and demand operate, and allowing people to rise and fall on the basis of their abilities and how hard they worked. What was understood to be "natural" in social relations had changed. The historian George Frederickson has called this "a global capitalism that draws no color line, because it seeks customers and collaborators from every race."[6]

This turn to the market was the second major undercurrent, along with formal equality, that was reshaping American society in the 1970s. The new volunteer military after 1973 meant that the nation's very security was now provided for by the logic of the market—through competitive recruiting rather than a draft.[7] In education, with the decisions in *San Antonio v. Rodriguez* (1973) and *Milliken v. Bradley* (1974), the Supreme Court sharply limited the means for desegregating and equally funding public schools, allowing the real estate market instead to be the prime determinant of educational quality. In *Buckley v. Valeo* (1976), the Court also ruled that campaign finance laws could not limit the freedom of individuals to spend as much as they wished on their own campaigns—the same logic of letting the market decide. Abortion became legal, but the Hyde Amendment of 1976 prevented the government from funding it; if you could pay for it, it was yours. The tax revolt that began with Proposition 13 in California in 1978 cut public revenues and expenditures, limiting social provision by the government in favor of letting individuals rise and fall increasingly on their own. Congress deregulated major industries, beginning with airlines, trucking, and telecommunications. In an era of letting markets provide what consumers wanted, pornography and gambling both exploded into major industries in the 1970s. And economic inequality began to climb steadily by the end of the decade.[8]

A parallel turn to market solutions took hold around the globe. China led the way with Deng Xiaoping's market-oriented reforms and the start of a process of industrialization that has since altered world economic history. Margaret Thatcher brought privatization to the United Kingdom. In Latin America, the military regime in Chile enshrined the free market gospel of economist Milton Friedman, who won the Nobel Prize in economics in 1976, while Argentina's military rulers moved in a similar direction. Dissident movements in Eastern Europe built on the increasingly obvious gap in material well-being between the affluent West and the decaying Soviet bloc.[9] Even those new socialist governments that took power in this decade, such as Vietnam south of the seventeenth parallel and Nicaragua, would keep to the left for only a decade before also turning onto the alluring capitalist road.

Together these two central developments that gathered force in the 1970s—greater egalitarianism and inclusion, and deregulation and free market economics—have shaped an America and a world that have granted greater formal recognition of the dignity and value of all persons, on the one hand, while permitting increasingly sovereign market forces, on the other hand, to further widen distinctions of wealth and class. A fiercely competitive, if more inclusive, individualism has been the result, a nation and a world simultaneously more equal and less equal.[10]

Notes

Contributors

Index

Notes

Introduction

1. The entire press conference can be viewed at http://news.bbc.co.uk/onthisday/hi/dates/stories/january/10/newsid_2518000/2518957.stm.
2. Bruce J. Schulman, *The Seventies: The Great Shift in American Culture, Society, and Politics* (New York, 2001), p. 1.
3. Tom Wolfe, "The 'Me' Decade and the Third Great Awakening," *New York*, August 23, 1976, pp. 26–40.
4. See http://www.tkb.org/IncidentDateModule.jsp.
5. George Modelski and Gardner Perry III, "'Democratization in Long Perspective' Revisited," *Technological Forecasting and Social Change* 69 (2002): 359–376.
6. Available at http://www.systemicpeace.org/inscr/inscr.htm.
7. All figures calculated from the consumer price inflation rates in the World Bank's World Development Indicators online database.
8. Wolfe, "'Me' Decade."
9. See http://www.nber.org/cycles.html.
10. Real gross domestic product data are from *Economic Report of the President* (2008), table B-2, http://www.gpoaccess.gov/eop/.
11. Data from http://www.statistics.gov.uk/.
12. Robert J. Barro and José F. Ursúa, "Macroeconomic Crises since 1870," *Brookings Papers on Economic Activity* (March 2008).
13. See Carmen M. Reinhart and Kenneth S. Rogoff, "This Time Is Different: A Panoramic View of Eight Centuries of Financial Crises," NBER Working Paper no. 12882 (March 2008); "Banking Crises: An Equal Opportunity

Menace," NBER Working Paper no. 14587 (December 2008); and "The Aftermath of Financial Crises," draft paper (December 19, 2008).

14. A. J. P. Taylor, *An Old Man's Diary* (London: Hamish Hamilton, 1984).

15. Kathleen Burk, *The Troublemaker: The Life and History of A. J. P. Taylor* (New Haven, 2000), p. 407.

16. A. J. P. Taylor, *Letters to Eva, 1969–83* (London, 1991), p. 156. Indeed Taylor estimated that the value of his share portfolio had been reduced from £100,000 to £20,000. Ibid., pp. 198, 211.

17. Ibid., p. 184.

18. Ibid., p. 191.

19. Jeremi Suri, *Power and Protest: Global Revolution and the Rise of Détente* (Cambridge, Mass., 2003).

20. Calculated from United Nations, "World Population Prospects: The 2006 Revision," http://esa.un.org/unpp/index.asp?panel=1.

21. Malcolm Bradbury, *The History Man* (New York, 1975).

22. Germaine Greer, *The Female Eunuch* (1970; reprint, New York, 2001), pp. 13–21, 353–371.

23. Daniel Bell, *The Coming of Post-Industrial Society: A Venture in Social Forecasting* (New York, 1973).

24. Alvin Toffler, *Future Shock* (New York, 1970).

25. Niall Ferguson, "Siegmund Warburg, the City of London and the Financial Roots of European Integration," *Business History* 51, no. 3 (2009): 362–380.

26. See Nicholas Nassim Taleb, "The Fourth Quadrant: A Map of the Limits of Statistics," *Edge,* September 15, 2008, http://www.edge.org.

27. Michael Crozier, Samuel Huntington, and Joji Watanuki, *The Crisis of Democracy: Report on the Governability of Democracies to the Trilateral Commission* (New York, 1975).

1. "Malaise"

1. The "Malaise Speech" of 1979, available at www2.Volstate.edu/geades/FinalDocs/1970s&beyond/malaise.htm. Circumstances recounted in www.pbs.org/wgbh/amex/carter/peopleevents/e_malaise.html.

2. Spencer R. Weart, *Nuclear Fear: A History of Images* (Cambridge, Mass., 1988), pp. 375–388. The strategic issues were arcane: multiple reentry vehicle technology or "Mirvs" and new Soviet intermediate range missiles (SS-9s) targeted on Europe threatened to undermine the balance of terror that the USSR and the United States had groped toward through the sixties and enshrined in Salt I. Helmut Schmidt led the way in calling for a NATO

response after 1976, while in the United States, conservative Democrats and Republicans pressed for a "Team B" intelligence estimate that would effectively paralyze lingering détente efforts. See Jan M. Lodal, "Salt II and American Security," *Foreign Affairs* 57, no. 2 (Winter 1978–79): 245–268; Raymond Garthoff, *Détente and Confrontation: American-Soviet Relations from Nixon to Reagan* (Washington, D.C., 1994).

3. Daniel Yankelovich, "The Noneconomic Side of Inflation," in *Inflation and National Survival,* ed. Clarence C. Walton (New York, 1979), p. 20, cited in Robert J. Samuelson, *The Great Inflation and Its Aftermath: The Past and Future of American Affluence* (New York, 2008), pp. 19–20.

4. Growth rates continued to rise through the late 1960s until the oil crisis— see Jean Fourastié, *Les trente glorieuses, ou, la révolution invisible de 1946 à 1975* (Paris, 1979)—but monetary stability was clearly breaking down earlier; see Fred L. Block, *The Origins of International Economic Disorder: A Study of United States International Monetary Policy from World War II to the Present* (Berkeley, 1977); and Samuelson, *The Great Inflation and Its Aftermath.*

5. See Charles S. Maier, "The Two Postwar Eras and the Conditions for Stability in Twentieth-Century Western Europe," *American Historical Review* 86, no. 2 (April 1981): 327–352; and Maier, "The Politics of Productivity: Foundations of American International Economic Policy after World War II," in *Between Power and Plenty: Foreign Economic Policy of Advanced Industrial States,* ed. Peter Katzenstein (Madison, 1978), pp. 23–50, reprinting *International Organization* (Autumn 1977): 607–633, both essays now included in Maier, *In Search of Stability: Explorations in Historical Political Economy* (Cambridge, 1987), pp. 121–184.

6. Daniel Bell, *The End of Ideology: On the Exhaustion of Political Ideas in the 1950s* (Boston, 1959); Otto Kirchheimer, "The Waning of Opposition in Parliamentary Regimes" (1957), in *Politics, Law, and Social Change* (New York, 1969); Robert A. Dahl, ed., *Political Oppositions in Western Democracies* (New Haven, 1966).

7. See Stephen Graubard, ed., *The New Europe* (Boston, 1964); Michele Salvati, "May 1968 and the Hot Autumn of 1969: The Responses of Two Ruling Classes," in *Organizing Interests in Western Europe,* ed. Suzanne Berger (Cambridge, 1981), pp. 331–363.

8. See Block, *Origins of International Economic Disorder;* the McCracken report issued by the Organization for Economic Cooperation and Development, *Toward Full Employment and Price* Stability (Paris, 1977); Arthur N. Okun, *Prices and Quantities: A Macroeconomic Analysis* (Washington, D.C., 1981); Lawrence B. Krause and Walter S. Salant, eds., *Worldwide Inflation: Theory and Recent Experience* (Washington, D.C., 1977); James

O'Connor, *The Fiscal Crisis of the State* (New York, 1973); and Francis J. Gavin, *Gold, Dollars, and Power: The Politics of International Monetary Relations, 1958–1971* (Chapel Hill, 2004).

9. This chapter asks why the growth trends of the 1950s and early 1960s broke down. Economists have asked why the growth trends since the 1970s have become less volatile—which leads to different answers. See Stephen G. Cecchetti, Alfonso Flores-Lagunes, and Stephen Krause, "Assessing the Sources of Changes in the Volatility of Real Growth," NBER Working Paper no. 11946 (January 2006); and Olivier Blanchard and John Simon, "The Long and Large Decline in U.S. Output Volatility," *Brookings Papers on Economic Activity*, no. 1 (2001): 135–164. Needless to say the events beginning in 2008 have interrupted this decline in volatility.

10. See Charles P. Kindleberger, *Europe's Postwar Economic Growth: The Role of Labor Supply* (Cambridge, Mass., 1967); also Ingvar Svennilson, *Growth and Stagnation in the European Economy* (Geneva, 1954); Alan S. Milward, *The European Rescue of the Nation-State* (London, 1992); Nicholas Crafts and Gianni Toniolo, *Economic Growth in Europe since 1945* (Cambridge, 1996); and Andrea Boltho, ed., *The European Economy: Growth and Crisis* (Oxford, 1982). On oil, see David S. Painter, *Oil and the American Century: The Political Economy of U.S. Foreign Oil Policy* (Baltimore, 1986).

11. OECD, *Toward Full Employment and Price Stability*, p. 14.

12. Arthur M. Okun, *Prices and Quantities: A Macroeconomic Analysis* (Washington, D.C., 1981), p. 3.

13. For a thorough review of the Phillips curve controversies, see Anthony M. Santomero and John J. Seater, "The Inflation-Unemployment Trade-Off: A Critique of the Literature," *Journal of Economic Literature* 16 (June 1978): 499–544.

14. See David R. Cameron, "Does Government Cause Inflation? Taxes, Spending, and Deficits," in *The Politics of Inflation and Economic Stagnation: Theoretical Approaches and International Case Studies*, ed. Leon N. Lindberg and Charles S. Maier (Washington, D.C., 1985), pp. 224–279. On the role of unions, see Robert J. Flanagan, "Macroeconomic Performance and Collective Bargaining: An International Perspective," *Journal of Economic Literature* 37, no. 2 (September 1999): 1150–76.

15. Robert Mundell, Mario Baldassari, and Massimo di Matteo, eds., *International Problems of Economic Interdependence* (Houndsmill, Basingstoke, 1994).

16. Arthur Okun, "Political Economy: The Lessons of the Seventies," in *Current Issues in Political Economy*, ed. Arthur Okun and Robert Solomon, Ontario Economic Council Discussion Paper Series (Toronto, 1979),

p. 1, cited by Leon N. Lindberg, "Models of the Inflation Disinflation Process," in Lindberg and Maier, *Politics of Inflation and Economic Stagnation,* p. 26.

17. See discussions in Philip Armstrong, Andrew Glyn, and John Harrison, *Capitalism since 1945* (Oxford, 1991); and essays in Lindberg and Maier, *Politics of Inflation and Economic Stagnation.* This was a doctrine associated with the New Cambridge school, represented by Joan Robinson, the unorthodox Michal Kalecki, and thereafter, in part, Wynne Godley. For Kalecki, see George R. Feiwel, *The Intellectual Capital of Michal Kalecki: A Study in Economic Theory and Policy* (Knoxville, 1975). For conservative interpretations, see Brian Barry, "Does Democracy Cause Inflation? Political Ideas of Some Economists," in Lindberg and Maier, *Politics of Inflation and Economic Stagnation,* pp. 280–317; also Fred Hirsch and John Goldthorpe, eds., *The Political Economy of Inflation* (Cambridge, Mass., 1978).

18. Robert Boyer and Yves Saillard, *Regulation Theory: The State of the Art,* trans. Caroline Shread (London, 2002).

19. O'Connor, *The Fiscal Crisis of the State.* The earlier landmark works were Rudolf Goldscheid, "A Sociological Approach to the Problem of Public Finance," in *Classics in the Theory of Public Finance,* ed. Richard Musgrave and Alan T. Peacock (New York, 1958), pp. 202–213; and Josef Schumpeter, "Die Krise des Steuerstaates," in *Aufsätze zur Soziologie* (Tübingen, 1953), pp. 1–71.

20. Edward F. Denison, *Accounting for Slower Economic Growth: The United States in the 1970s* (Washington, D.C., 1979).

21. Philippe Schmitter and Gerhard Lehmbruch, eds., *Trends toward Corporatist Intermediation* (Los Angeles, 1980); John H. Goldthorpe, ed., *Order and Conflict in Contemporary Capitalism* (Oxford, 1984).

22. See Douglas A. Hibbs Jr., "Inflation, Political Support, and Macroeconomic Policy," in Lindberg and Maier, *Politics of Inflation and Economic Stagnation,* pp. 195–223; also Brian Barry, "Political Ideas of Some Economists," ibid., pp. 303–307.

23. Alfred E. Kahn, "Market Power Inflation: A Conceptual Overview," in Gardiner C. Means et al., *The Roots of Inflation: The International Crisis* (New York, 1975), p. 239.

24. Barry, "Political Ideas of Some Economists," p. 317.

25. Thomas J. Sargent, "The End of Four Big Inflations," in *Inflation: Causes and Effects,* ed. Robert Hall (Chicago, 1982), pp. 41–98; also Sargent, *Rational Expectations and Inflation* (New York, 1986).

26. See Thomas J. Sargent, *The Conquest of American Inflation* (Princeton, 1999); and the useful review of this book by Ramon Marimon in the *Journal of Economic Literature* 38 (June 2000): 405–411.

27. Quoted by Theodore H. White, *America in Search of Itself: The Making of the President, 1956–1980* (New York, 1982), p. 149; and by Samuelson, *The Great Inflation and Its Aftermath*, p. 24.

28. For an encompassing comparative study, see the essays in Ingrid Gilcher-Holtey, ed., *1968: Vom Ereignis zum Gegenstand der Geschichtswissenschaft* (Göttingen, 1998), with bibliographic references. Some of these essays and others are included in *Novecento: Rassegna di Storia Contemporanea*, no. 1 (July–December 1999). See also Carole Fink, Philipp Gassert, and Detlef Junker, *1968: The World Transformed* (Cambridge and Washington, D.C., 1998).

29. Clark Kerr, *The Uses of the University* (Cambridge, Mass., 1963); Paul Goodman, *Growing Up Absurd: Problems of Youth in the Organized System* (New York, 1960).

30. See Samuel Huntington in Michel Crozier, Samuel Huntington, and Joji Watanki, *The Crisis of Democracy* (New York, 1975), esp. pp. 59–63, 102.

31. My argument runs parallel to that of Jeremi Suri in *Power and Protest: Global Revolution and the Rise of Détente* (Cambridge, Mass., 2003), but I would underline two differences: first, the concern of conservatives was as much about an economic entitlements policy they believed had escaped control as it was about protesters' agitation in the streets; and second, I find unconvincing the argument that *Ostpolitik* and détente were policy reactions to the disorder of the late 1960s. For another related argument, see Francis Fukuyama, *The Great Disruption: Human Nature and the Reconstitution of Social Order* (New York, 1999).

32. Jürgen Habermas, *The Theory of Communicative Action*, 2 vols. (Cambridge, 1986–1989), and *Legitimationsprobleme im Spätkapitalismus* (Frankfurt am Main, 1973); Claus Offe, "The Attribution of Public Status to Interest Groups: On the West German Case," in *Organizing Interests in Western Europe: Pluralism, Corporatism, and the Transformation of Politics*, ed. Suzanne D. Berger (Cambridge, 1981), pp. 123–158.

33. Richard Cooper, *The Economics of Interdependence: Economic Policy in the Atlantic Community* (New York, 1968). An early discussion is in Albert O. Hirschman, *National Power and the Structure of Foreign Trade* (Berkeley, 1945); and also in Robert Gilpin, *The Political Economy of International Relations* (Princeton, 1987).

34. John Maynard Keynes, *The Economic Consequences of the Peace*, vol. 2 of *The Collected Works* (Cambridge, 1984), pp. 11–13.

35. See Charles S. Maier, "Two Sorts of Crisis? The 'Long' 1970s in the West and the East," in *Koordinaten deutscher Geschichte in der Epoche des Ost-West-Konflikts*, ed. Hans Günter Hockerts (Munich, 2004), pp. 49–62.

36. For the crisis of representation, see Charles S. Maier, "Political Crisis and

Partial Modernization," in *Revolutionary Situations in Europe, 1917–1923*, ed. Charles L. Bertrand (Montreal, 1977).

37. For a persuasive argument about its causes as well as an authoritative history, see Barry Eichengreen, *Golden Fetters: The Gold Standard and the Great Depression, 1919–1939* (Oxford, 1992); international aspects in Dietmar Rothermund, *The Global Impact of the Great Depression, 1929–1939* (London, 1996); Keynesian responses in Peter A. Hall, ed., *The Political Power of Economic Ideas: Keynesianism across Nations* (Princeton, 1989). I have provided only a skeletal citation of recent scholarly sources; many of the works cited offer detailed bibliographical guidance.

38. Daniel Bell, *The Coming of Post-Industrial Society: A Venture in Social Forecasting* (New York, 1973).

2. The United States and Globalization in the 1970s

1. Jidda Embassy to State Department, October 23, 1973, Digital National Security Archive, http://nsarchive.chadwyck.com.

2. Daniel Yergin, *The Prize* (New York, 1993), pp. 619–632.

3. Transcript of Kissinger Staff Meeting, January 7, 1974, National Archives and Records Administration (hereafter NARA), RG–59, Office of the Secretary of State, Transcripts of Staff Meetings, Box 2.

4. James Akins, "The Oil Crisis," *Foreign Affairs* 51 (1973): 462–490; and Walter Levy, "Oil Power," *Foreign Affairs* 49 (1971): 652–668.

5. Transcript of Washington Special Action Group Meeting, October 17, 1973, Nixon Presidential Materials Project (hereafter NPMP), National Archives, NSC Institutional Files, Box H-92.

6. Statement by Henry Kissinger, *Department of State Bulletin* (hereafter *DOS Bulletin*), no. 70, February 11, 1974, pp. 201–206.

7. Kissinger Staff Meeting, January 8, 1974, NARA, RG–59, Office of the Secretary of State, Transcripts of Staff Meetings, Box 2; Kissinger to Nixon, "Meeting with Shultz, and Simon," February 9, 1974, NPMP, NSC Files, Box 321.

8. Henry Kissinger, "A New National Partnership," *DOS Bulletin*, no. 72, January 24, 1974, pp. 197–204; and Memorandum of Conversation between Kissinger and Ford, May 24, 1975, Gerald Ford Presidential Library (hereafter GFPL), Ann Arbor, NSA Files, Memoranda of Conversations, Box 12.

9. Robert Keohane and Joseph Nye, *Power and Interdependence* (Boston, 1977), pp. 8–9.

10. Zbigniew Brzezinski, "The Trilateral Policy Program," August 29, 1973, Jimmy Carter Presidential Library (hereafter JCPL), Atlanta, Brzezinski Collection, Trilateral Commission File, Box 1.

11. Anthony G. Hopkins, ed., *Globalization in World History* (London, 2002).
12. Theodore Levitt, "The Globalization of Markets," *Harvard Business Review* 61 (1983): 92–102.
13. David Held et al., *Global Transformations* (Stanford, 1999), pp. 169, 204.
14. Union of International Associations, *Yearbook of International Associations* 3 (1995–96): 1733.
15. Richard Barnet and Ronald Müller, *Global Reach* (New York, 1974), p. 19.
16. Saskia Sassen, *Territory, Authority, Rights* (Princeton, 2006), p. 3.
17. Philip Bobbitt, *The Shield of Achilles* (New York, 2002); Richard Rosecrance, *The Rise of the Virtual State* (New York, 1999).
18. Nixon to H. R. Haldeman, May 13, 1970, NPMP, President's Personal File, Memoranda from the President, Box 2.
19. John Ruggie, "International Regimes, Transactions, and Change," *International Organization* 36 (1982): 379–415; and Jeffrey Frieden, *Global Capitalism* (New York, 2006), pp. 297–300.
20. Burns to Nixon, January 22, 1970, NPMP, White House Special Files, President's Office Files, Handwriting File, Box 1.
21. Peter Peterson, *The United States in the Changing World Economy* (Washington, D.C., 1971).
22. "Remarks to News Media Executives," July 6, 1971, *Public Papers of the Presidents* (hereafter *PPP*), *Richard Nixon: 1971* (Washington, D.C., 1971), p. 812.
23. U.S. Congress, Committee on Finance, Report, "Implications of Multinational Firms for World Trade and Investment," 93rd Cong., 1st sess. (Washington, D.C., 1973), p. 45.
24. "Meeting on Proposed Trilateral Commission," July 23–24, 1972, JCPL, Brzezinski Files, Trilateral File, Box 1.
25. "The Trilateral Commission," Grant Proposal, October 16, 1973, JCPL, Brzezinski Files, Trilateral File, Box 1.
26. Michael Crozier et al., *The Crisis of Democracy*, Trilateral Report no. 8 (New York, 1975).
27. Karl Kaiser, "Transnational Relations as a Threat to the Democratic Process," *International Organization* 25, no. 3 (1971): 706–720.
28. Raymond Vernon, *Sovereignty at Bay* (New York, 1971), p. 5.
29. National Security Study Memorandum 200, "Implications of Worldwide Population Growth," August 7, 1974, NPMP, NSC Files, Institutional Files, Box H–268.
30. "The Global Challenge and International Cooperation," *DOS Bulletin*, no. 72, August 4, 1975, pp. 149–160.
31. June 29, 1976, GFPL, NSA Files, Memoranda of Conversations, Box 20.
32. Giovanni Arrighi, *The Long Twentieth Century: Money, Power, and the Or-*

igins of Our Times (New York, 1994), pp. 300–301; and David Harvey, *The New Imperialism* (New York, 2003), p. 129.

33. Robert Osgood, "Overview of World Situation," NPMP, NSC, Subject Files, Strategic Overview, Box 397.

34. Kissinger, Transcript of Conversation with James Reston, May 1, 1969, NPMP, Kissinger Telephone Conversations, Chronological, Box 1; and Kissinger, Memorandum of Conversation with James Schlesinger, February 8, 1975, GFPL, NSA Files, Memoranda of Conversations, Box 9.

35. Zbigniew Brzezinski, *Between Two Ages* (New York, 1970), pp. 18, 52, 274.

36. Richard Gardner, "To Make the World Safe for Interdependence," JCPL, Pre-Presidential Papers, 1976 Campaign, Issues Office, Foreign Policy, Box 17.

37. Memorandum of Conversation, "Economic Summit at Puerto Rico," June 14, 1976, GFPL, NSA Files, International Economic Affairs Staff, Puerto Rico, Box 3.

38. OECD Working Party Three, "Financing the Oil Deficits," April 6, 1974, United Kingdom National Archives (hereafter UKNA), FCO 59/1173.

39. "Note for the Record," April 10, 1974, UKNA, FCO 59/1168.

40. Talking Points, February 7, 1978, JCPL, Anthony Solomon Materials, Chronological File, Box 3.

41. Kissinger, Transcript of Press Conference, November 17, 1975, GFPL, NSA Files, International Economic Affairs Staff, Rambouillet, Box 4.

42. Paris Embassy to [State] Department, Evening Report, December 8, 1976, GFPL, NSA Files, International Economic Affairs Staff, Puerto Rico, Box 4.

43. Charles Maier, *Among Empires* (Cambridge, Mass., 2006).

44. Transcript of Schmidt conversation with Kissinger and Ford, May 29, 1975, GFPL, NSA Files, Memoranda of Conversations, Box 12.

45. Michael Webb, *The Political Economy of Policy Coordination* (Ithaca, N.Y., 1995), chap. 6.

46. Charles Schultze to Blumenthal, "Macroeconomic Assessment," May 15, 1978, JCPL, CEA, Subject File, Box 6.

47. Schultze to Carter, "Conversation with Count Lambsdorff on the Bonn Summit," June 27, 1978, JCPL, Staff Secretary, Handwriting File, Box 93; and Henry Owen to Carter, July 19, 1978, JCPL, WHCF, Foreign Policy FO 6–5, Box 44.

48. Blumenthal, "Remarks at the National Press Club," June 30, 1978, JCPL, WHCF, FO 6–5, Box 44.

49. Nixon to Burns, November 4, 1971, GFPL, Arthur Burns Papers, Box N1.

50. W. Carl Biven, *Jimmy Carter's Economy* (Chapel Hill, 2002); Paul Volcker and Toyoo Gyohten, *Changing Fortunes* (New York, 1992), chap. 6.

51. Paul Volcker, "The Political Economy of the Dollar," *Federal Reserve Bank of New York Quarterly Review* 3 (Winter 1978–79): 1–12.

52. Brent Scowcroft to Ford, "Call from Prime Minister Callaghan," September 29, 1976, GFPL, NSA Files, International Economic Affairs Staff, Box 3, United Kingdom; "Note of Meeting Held at 11 Downing St.," December 6, 1976, http://www.bankofengland.co.uk/publications/foi/disc060519.htm/.

53. Brzezinski and Frank Moore to Carter, "Administration Strategy on Human Rights Amendments," April 16, 1977, JCPL, Staff Secretary, Handwriting File, Box 18; and Brzezinski to Carter, "State Department Report Concerning Human Rights Policy and the IFIs," March 27, 1978, JCPL, WHCF, HU [Human Rights], Box 1.

54. Susan Strange, "The Persistent Myth of Lost Hegemony," *International Organization* 41 (1987): 551–574.

55. Paul Kennedy, *The Rise and Fall of the Great Powers* (New York, 1987). Also Michael Cox, "Whatever Happened to American Decline? International Relations and the New United States Hegemony," *New Political Economy* 6 (2001): 311–340.

56. Maier, *Among Empires.*

3. The Great Transformation

1. There is, of course, already a *Nixon in China* opera and at least one recent account (by Margaret Macmillan) of the event that presents it in the grand opera style.

2. I have been working with Chen Jian of Cornell University on a project provisionally titled "The Great Transformation: China's Road from Revolution to Reform." This chapter is a think piece that has been fed by long conversations between the two of us; while I am grateful to Chen Jian for his insights, he is of course not responsible for the preliminary conclusions I draw here.

3. This overview is based on interviews with former political leaders in the South and with former factory managers, military officers, and local CCP cadres. Some of the more general conclusions are supported by the recent scholarly literature in Chinese; see for instance Chen Yongjun, *Cong jihua dao shichang: Zhogguo jingji tizhi gaige de xuanze* [From Plan to Market: Choices in the Reform of China's Economic System] (Fuzhou, 1999); Han Guangfu and Hu Yongxiang, *Gaige niandai: Deng Xiaoping de gaige suiyue* [The Reform Decade: Deng Xiaoping's Reform Period] (Shenyang, 2004); and Zhonggong zhongyang dangshi yanjiushi disan yanjiubu, comp., *Deng Xiaoping yu gaige kaifang de qibu* [Deng Xiaoping and the Rise of the Reform and Open Door Policy] (Beijing, 2005). For valuable reminiscences of

early reform in the South, see Li Junxiao, *Bi lu lan lu xian xing yi bu: Guangdong gaige kaifang chuqi lishi janjiu* [Arduous First Steps: Historical Research on the Initial Period of Reform and Opening in Guangdong] (Guangzhou, 2008).

4. Two good recent overviews of party politics in this crucial period are Shi Yun and Li Danhui, "Nanyi jixu de 'jixu geming'—cong pi Lin dao pi Deng 1972–1976" [Difficult Continuation of the "Continuous Revolution"—from Criticizing Lin to Criticizing Deng, 1972–1976]; and Xiao Donglian, "Lishi de liangui: Cong boluan fanzheng dao gaige kaifang" [The Changing Paths of History: From Bringing Order Out of Chaos to Reform and Open Door], both 2008 working papers from the Chinese University of Hong Kong's Contemporary China Research Center. In English, see Frederick C. Teiwes and Warren Sun, *The End of the Maoist Era* (Armonk, N.Y., 2007), esp. pp. 110–186.

4. The Kiss of Debt

1. This chapter is adapted from *Uncivil Society: 1989 and the Implosion of the Communist Establishment* (New York, 2009), by Stephen Kotkin, with a contribution by Jan T. Gross.

2. As cited in Jeffrey Kopstein, *The Politics of Economic Decline in East Germany, 1945–1989* (Chapel Hill, 1997), pp. 43–44. Between 1949 and 1990 approximately 2.7 million people permanently crossed from East Germany to West Germany, almost all of them before 1961; about 200,000 people crossed in the other direction.

3. In 1963, on a visit to Moscow, Ulbricht remarked that "even after the closing of the state borders, the high living standards [in West Germany] strongly affect the population of the GDR and its political attitudes." Kopstein, *Politics of Economic Decline*, p. 48.

4. Ibid., pp. 68–69.

5. Ibid., p. 80.

6. André Steiner, *Von Plan zu Plan: Eine Wirtschaftsgeschichte der DDR* (Munich, 2004), p. 190.

7. Kopstein, *Politics of Economic Decline*, pp. 93–94.

8. Schürer blamed the Eighth Party Congress of 1971, when Honecker had taken over, for deciding that the GDR must underwrite a consumer society and welfare state. Charles S. Maier, *Dissolution: The Crisis of Communism and the End of East Germany* (Princeton, 1997), p. 60.

9. Kazimierz Z. Poznański, *Poland's Protracted Transition: Institutional Change and Economic Growth, 1970–1994* (New York, 1996), pp. 3–4. See also Włodzimierz Brus, "Economics and Politics: The Fatal Link," in *Po-*

land: Genesis of a Revolution, ed. Abraham Brumberg (New York, 1983), pp. 26–41; and Alex Pravda, "Poland 1980: From 'Premature Consumerism' to Labour Solidarity," *Soviet Studies* 34, no. 3 (1982): 167–199.

10. Quoted in Zdeněk Mlynář, *Nightfrost in Prague: The End of Humane Socialism* (New York, 1980), p. 143.

11. Much of the scholarly literature blames the relative "backwardness" of East Europe on Soviet backwardness. By contrast, Iván Berend has argued that in the twentieth century, the Eastern European countries mounted two revolts against the West out of humiliation: an antiliberal right-wing rebellion in the interwar years and an antiliberal left-wing rebellion in the postwar years, both motivated by "economic backwardness and the increasing gap which separated them from the advanced Western core." Iván T. Berend, *Central and Eastern Europe, 1944–1993: Detour from the Periphery to the Periphery* (New York, 1996), p. x.

12. Charles Gati, *The Bloc That Failed: Soviet–East European Relations in Transition* (Bloomington, Ind., 1990), p. 119. When it came to higher oil prices, the Soviets felt that they could not stick the satellites with the entire bill because of possible political fallout, so Moscow tried to adjust prices moderately, absorbing some of the economic costs, but enduring the fallout anyway. Paul Marer, "Has Eastern Europe Become a Liability to the Soviet Union: (III) The Economic Aspect," in *The International Politics of Eastern Europe,* ed. Charles Gati (New York, 1976), pp. 59–81 (quotation p. 70). Romania imported oil from the USSR but not at subsidized prices.

13. Hajna Istvanffy Lorinc, "Foreign Debt, Debt Management Policy, and Implications for Hungary's Development," *Soviet Studies* 44, no. 6 (1992): 997–1013; Jan Vaňous, "East European Economic Slowdown," *Problems of Communism* 31, no. 4 (1982): 1–19; Gati, *Bloc,* pp. 108–9; Katherine Verdery, "What Was Socialism, and Why Did It Fail?" in *The Revolutions of 1989,* ed. Vladimir Tismăneanu (New York, 1999), pp. 63–85 (quotation p. 81).

14. Derek H. Aldcroft and Steven Morewood, *Economic Change in Eastern Europe since 1918* (Aldershot, 1995), p. 170; Valerie Bunce, "The Empire Strikes Back: The Evolution of the Eastern Bloc from a Soviet Asset to a Soviet Liability," *International Organization* 39, no. 1 (1985): 1–46 (quotation p. 39).

15. Aldcroft and Morewood, *Economic Change in Eastern Europe,* p. 137. For a high-end estimate ($87 billion) of Soviet trade subsidies to Eastern Europe between 1960 and 1980, see Michael Marrese and Jan Vaňous, *Soviet Subsidization of Trade with Eastern Europe* (Berkeley, 1983).

16. Retrospectively, Valerie Bunce has suggested that the choice had narrowed to two unpalatable options: liberalize and thereby destroy the system, or put off reforms and purchase short-term stability but long-term doom.

Jeffrey Kopstein has written that "leaders throughout the bloc faced two alternatives, either retreat to a conservative immobilism or proceed down the road of gradual capitalist restoration." Valerie Bunce, *Subversive Institutions: The Design and Destruction of Socialism and the State* (New York, 1999), p. 37; Kopstein, *The Politics of Economic Decline,* p. 46.

17. In 1966 a pro-Chinese "Polish Communist Party" in exile was proclaimed by Kazimierz Mijal in Albania, advocating for a return to orthodoxy (Stalinism) at home and a more revolutionary policy abroad, against Gomułka's "revisionism" and alleged "renunciation of socialist conquests." See http://files.osa.ceu.hu/holdings/300/8/3/text/44–5–8.shtml.

18. Bruce J. Dickson, *Democratization in China and Taiwan: The Adaptability of Leninist Parties* (Oxford, 1998).

19. Jason McDonald, "Transition to Utopia: A Reinterpretation of Economics, Ideas, and Politics in Hungary, 1984 to 1990," *East European Politics and Societies* 7, no. 2 (1993): 203–239 (Kádár quoted p. 214).

20. Elemér Hankiss, *East European Alternatives* (Oxford, 1990), p. 203; McDonald, "Transition to Utopia," pp. 217–228; Rudolf L. Tőkés, *Hungary's Negotiated Revolution: Economic Reform, Social Change, and Political Succession, 1957–1990* (New York, 1996), pp. 297–298; Paul Lendvai, "The Many Faces of Károly Grósz," in *Hungary: The Art of Survival* (London, 1988), pp. 127–155.

5. The Global 1970s and the Echo of the Great Depression

1. Karl Polanyi, *The Great Transformation* (New York, 1944).

2. Hyman P. Minsky, "The Financial Instability Hypothesis," Jerome Levy Economics Institute Working Paper no. 74 (May 1992).

3. On trends in financial globalization, see Maurice Obstfeld and Alan M. Taylor, *Global Capital Markets: Integration, Crisis, and Growth* (New York, 2004). On the evolution of international financial policies, see Rawi Abdelal, *Capital Rules: The Construction of Global Finance* (Cambridge, Mass., 2007).

4. On various interpretations of the limited role of developing countries in GATT prior to the Uruguay Round, see Rorden Wilkinson and James Scott, "Developing Country Participation in the GATT: A Reassessment," *World Trade Review* 7, no. 3 (June 2008): 473–510.

5. Carlos Díaz-Alejandro, "Latin America in the 1930s," in *Latin America in the 1930s: The Role of the Periphery in World Crisis,* ed. Rosemary Thorp (London, 1984), pp. 17–49; Deepak Lal, *The Poverty of "Development Economics"* (Cambridge, Mass., 1986); Peter Temin, *Lessons from the Great Depression* (Cambridge, Mass., 1989).

6. Theoretical treatments of policy persistence include, inter alia, Gordon

Tullock, "The Transitional Gains Trap," *Bell Journal of Economics* 6, no. 2 (Autumn 1975): 671–678; Raquel Fernandez and Dani Rodrik, "Resistance to Reform: Status Quo Bias in the Presence of Individual-Specific Uncertainty," *American Economic Review* 81, no. 5 (December 1991): 1146–55; Alberto Alesina and Allan Drazen, "Why Are Stabilizations Delayed?" *American Economic Review* 81, no. 5 (December 1991): 1170–88; and Stephen Coate and Stephen Morris, "Policy Persistence," *American Economic Review* 89, no. 5 (December 1999): 1327–36. A recent empirical work which uses this idea to explain growth outcomes is Antoni Estevadeordal and Alan M. Taylor, "Is the Washington Consensus Dead? Growth, Openness, and the Great Liberalization, 1970s–2000s," NBER Working Papers 14264 (August 2008). A recent theoretical paper argues that openness spread slowly after 1950 because policymakers were subject to learning and policy frictions; see Francisco J. Buera, Alexander Monge-Naranjo, and Giorgio E. Primiceri, "Learning the Wealth of Nations," UCLA (May 2008).

7. Computations of GDP loss are based on data from Angus Maddison, *The World Economy: Historical Statistics* (Paris, 2001).

8. Jeffrey D. Sachs and Andrew Warner, "Economic Reform and the Process of Global Integration," *Brookings Papers on Economic Activity* 26, no. 1 (1995): 1–118; Romain Wacziarg and Karen Horn Welch, "Trade Liberalization and Growth: New Evidence," *World Bank Economic Review*, 22, no. 2 (June 2008): 187–231.

9. Data from the Economic Freedom in the World Annual Report for 2005 and previous issues; see http://www.freetheworld.com/.

10. Angus Maddison, *Two Crises: Latin America and Asia, 1920–1938 and 1973–1983* (Paris, 1985).

11. John Gerard Ruggie, "International Regimes, Transactions, and Change: Embedded Liberalism in the Postwar Economic Order," *International Organization* 36, no. 2 (Spring 1982): 379–415; Dani Rodrik, "How Far Will International Economic Integration Go?" *Journal of Economic Perspectives* 14, no. 1 (Winter 2000): 177–186.

12. See note 6.

6. International Finance and Political Legitimacy

1. Albert O. Hirschman, "Notes on Latin American Trip, Summer 1976," ms., p. 15, Hirschman Papers, Seeley Mudd Library, Princeton University Archives.

2. Maier to Hirschman, July 26, 1977, "Inflation file," ibid.

3. James J. Sheehan, "The Problem of Sovereignty in European History," *American Historical Review* 111 (2006): 1–15.

4. Harold James, *International Monetary Cooperation since Bretton Woods* (Washington, D.C., 1996), pp. 205–227.

5. Louis W. Pauly, "Capital Mobility, State Autonomy and Political Legitimacy," *Journal of International Affairs* 48 (1995): 369–388; Eric Helleiner, *States and the Reemergence of Global Finance* (Ithaca, N.Y., 1994).

6. William R. Cline, *International Debt, Systemic Risk, and Policy Response* (Cambridge, Mass., 1983), p. 11.

7. Robert Devlin, *Debt Crisis in Latin America* (Princeton, 1989). See also Carlos F. Díaz-Alejandro, "The Post 1971 International Financial System and the Less Developed Countries," in *A World Divided,* ed. G. K. Helleiner (Cambridge, 1976), pp. 177–205.

8. Guillermo Calvo, "Fractured Liberalism: Argentina under Martínez de Hoz," *Economic Development and Cultural Change* 34 (1986): 511–514.

9. Juan Gabriel Valdés, *Pinochet's Economists* (Cambridge, 1995).

10. Guillermo O'Donnell, *Modernización y autoritarismo* (Buenos Aires, 1972).

11. Carlos F. Díaz-Alejandro, "Good-bye Financial Repression, Hello Financial Crash," *Journal of Development Economics* 19 (1985): 1–24; Albert Fishlow, "Coping with the Creeping Crisis of Debt," in *Politics and Economics of External Debt Crisis,* ed. M. S. Wionczek (Boulder, Colo., 1985), pp. 100–111.

12. Albert Fishlow, "Lessons from the Past: Capital Markets during the Nineteenth Century and the Interwar Period," *International Organization* 39 (1985): 383–439.

13. United Nations Economic Commission for Latin America and the Caribbean, *Statistical Yearbook for Latin America and the Caribbean* (New York, 1986), pp. 514–515; Robert Cumby and Richard Levich, "Definitions and Magnitudes: On the Definition and Magnitude of Recent Capital Flight," in *Capital Flight and Third World Debt,* ed. Donald Lessard and John Williamson (Washington, D.C., 1987), pp. 27–67.

14. Stephan Haggart, *Pathways from the Periphery* (Ithaca, N.Y., 1990).

15. Charles S. Maier, "The Collapse of Communism: Approaches for a Future History," *History Workshop Journal* 31 (1991): 34–59.

7. American Debt, Global Capital

Portions of this chapter are adapted from Louis Hyman, *Debtor Nation* (Princeton, 2010).

1. While the precipitating events that caused the creation of the first mortgage-backed securities occurred in the 1960s, these events are better thought of as part of the "long" 1970s. If the collapse of the Bretton Woods system and the reemergence of global financial capitalism define the 1970s, these events are better thought of as part of that decade than the 1960s.

2. A similar financial instrument, called the participation certificate, was common in the 1920s but was regulated out of existence during the 1930s by the Federal Reserve.

3. The best introduction to this vast literature is Barry Eichengreen, *Globalizing Capital: A History of the International Monetary System* (Princeton, 1996).

4. *Economic Report of the President: Transmitted to the Congress January 1968* (Washington, D.C., 1968), p. 166.

5. *Economic Report of the President: Transmitted to the Congress January 1967* (Washington, D.C., 1967), pp. 195–196. World reserves grew 2.7 percent annually through the 1960s, while trade grew faster, at 7.9 percent annually (*Economic Report, 1968*, p. 179).

6. This contradiction, of course, was famously first recognized by Robert Triffin in 1960 and is therefore called the Triffin Dilemma.

7. Board of Governors of the Federal Reserve System, *Annual Report Covering Operations for the Year 1966* (Washington, D.C., 1967), p. 130.

8. Albert Burger, "A Historical Analysis of the Credit Crunch of 1966," Federal Reserve Bank of St. Louis, *Review* (September 1969): 27; Federal Reserve, *Annual Report, 1966*, p. 55.

9. Burger, "A Historical Analysis of the Credit Crunch," p. 22; "The Fabled CD's in a Test of Fire," *New York Times*, October 23, 1966, p. F1.

10. Federal Reserve, *Annual Report, 1966*, pp. 52–53; "Borrowers Find New Credit Lines," *Wall Street Journal*, July 7, 1966, p. 65. It was at this moment that American bankers began to become obsessed with the idea of "disintermediation," or depositors skipping the bank middleman and going directly to the stock market.

11. *Economic Report, 1968*, p. 56.

12. *Economic Report, 1967*, p. 57.

13. U.S. Congress, Senate, Committee on Banking and Currency, "A Study of Mortgage Credit," 90th Cong., 1st sess. May 22, 1967, p. v.

14. "Federal Reserve Ends Its Request That Banks Curb Loans to Business," *Wall Street Journal*, December 28, 1966, p. 3.

15. The GNP deflator grew to 4.2 percent in 1967. Burger, "A Historical Analysis of the Credit Crunch," p. 28.

16. *Economic Report, 1968*, p. 22.

17. U.S. Congress, "A Study of Mortgage Credit," p. v.

18. U.S. Congress, House, "Housing and Urban Development Act of 1968," 90th Cong., 2nd sess., p. 1.

19. Philip Brownstein, "The 1968 Housing Bill," *Mortgage Banker* (May 1968): 21.

20. U.S. Congress, "A Study of Mortgage Credit," p. v.

21. U.S. Congress, Senate, "Mortgage Credit," 90th Cong., 1st sess., June 12, 26, 27, and 28, 1967, pp. 274–275.

22. U.S. Congress, "A Study of Mortgage Credit," p. 18.

23. For more on the urban lending program, see Louis Hyman, "The First Subprime Crisis: The Section 235 Loan Program, 1968–1971," *Business History Review* (Autumn 2010).

24. Ibid., p. 70.

25. FNMA and GNMA are hard-to-pronounce acronyms, so both have folksy artificial names: Fannie Mae (FNMA) and Ginnie Mae (GNMA). Later, FHLMC would be called Freddie Mac.

26. FHLBB testimony in U.S. Congress, "A Study of Mortgage Credit," p. 33.

27. Brownstein, "The 1968 Housing Bill," p. 23.

28. Editorial, "Much Ado About Very Little," *Mortgage Banker* (May 1970): 4.

29. GNMA Annual Report, 1970, p. 5.

30. Ibid.

31. Philip Greenawalt, "Title VIII—and 'Ginnie Mae,'" *Mortgage Banker* (September 1968): 14.

32. Woodward Kingman, "The Mortgage-Backed Security," *Mortgage Banker* (April 1970): 66.

33. U.S. Congress, Senate, Committee on Banking, Housing and Urban Affairs, "Housing Goals and Mortgage Credit: 1975–80," 94th Cong., 1st sess., September 22, 23, and 25, 1975, p. 250.

34. Ibid., p. 241.

35. Ibid., p. 242.

36. "FNMA Explains Debt Financing Structure," *Mortgage Banker* (August 1973): 45.

37. Robert Pease, "The Mortgage Market: A Crisis That Seeks and Demands a Remedy," *Mortgage Banker* (April 1970): 51.

38. Ibid., p. 51.

39. Everett Spelman, "Federalization and Housing: At Point of No Return?" *Mortgage Banker* (June 1971): 54; Eugene Cower, "The Nixon Program for Housing," *Mortgage Banker* (July 1971): 10.

40. Woodward Kingman, "We Round Out Our First Year with Sales Over $2 Billion," *Mortgage Banker* (May 1971): 14–23.

41. Advertisement, *Mortgage Banker* (May 1969): 30.

42. Pease, "The Mortgage Market," p. 64.

43. Oliver Jones, "Pursuing the Elusive Conventional Mortgage," *Mortgage Banker* (November 1966): 38.

44. See "The Washington Scene," *Los Angeles Times,* July 15, 1973, p. K23.

45. Russell Clifton, "FNMA Conventional Mortgage Program Shows Dramatic Growth," *Mortgage Banker* (July 1973): 52.

46. Ibid., p. 36.
47. U.S. General Accounting Office (hereafter GAO), "Government National Mortgage Association's Secondary Mortgage Market Activities," March 8, 1977, p. 46.
48. U.S. Senate, "Housing Goals and Mortgage Credit," p. 254.
49. Ibid., p. 233.
50. Philip Kidd, "One Year Old and Going Strong," *Mortgage Banker* (May 1971): 27.
51. John Wetmore, "FHA Operation Now Vital to Secondary Mortgage Market," *Mortgage Banker* (December 1973): 24, 27.
52. GAO, "Government National Mortgage Association's Secondary Mortgage Market Activities," p. 47.
53. GAO, "Information on the Secondary Mortgage Market Activities of the Federal National Mortgage Association and the Federal Home Loan Mortgage Corporation," May 1975, p. 33.
54. Editorial, "Mortgage Market Trends," *Mortgage Banker* (July 1974): 57.

8. The United States, Multinational Enterprises, and the Politics of Globalization

1. George Ball, Remarks, Annual Dinner of the British National Committee of the International Chamber of Commerce, London, October 18, 1967, pp. 2, 11, Walter Reuther Library and Archives of Labor and Urban Affairs (hereafter ALUA), Nat Weinberg Papers, Part 2 (hereafter NWP2), Box 31, Folder 1.
2. Louis Banks, Public Relations Seminar speech, Phoenix, May 3, 1968, pp. 2–3, Hagley Museum and Library (hereafter HML), National Foreign Trade Council Records (hereafter NFTC), Record Group (hereafter RG) D, Ser. 22, Box 142, Folder 1.
3. Kari Levitt, *Silent Surrender* (New York, 1970).
4. Alma Chapoy Bonifaz, *Empresas Multinacionales: Instrumento del Imperialismo* (Mexico City, 1975), p. 7.
5. Nat Weinberg, Speech to International Executive Board, June 10, 1971, 1, ALUA, NWP2, Box 56, Folder 2.
6. Howard D. Samuel, "A New Perspective on World Trade," *AFL-CIO American Federationist* (June 1971): 1, George Meany Memorial Archives (hereafter GMMA), AFL-CIO Records (hereafter AFL-CIO), RG 34–002, Ser. 1, Box 15, Folder 15.
7. See National Archives and Records Administration (hereafter NARA), Richard Nixon Presidential Library and Museum, Yorba Linda, Calif. (hereafter RNPL), FO 4–3, Boxes 47–50.

8. Data from Michael S. Minor, "The Demise of Expropriation as an Instrument of LDC Policy, 1980–1992," *Journal of International Business Studies* 25, no. 1 (1994): 180, 182.

9. See Saskia Sassen, intro. and chap. 10 in *Globalization and Its Discontents* (New York, 1998), and *A Sociology of Globalization* (New York, 2007), pp. 30–47.

10. Leonard Silk, "Protectionists Mobilize," *New York Times,* January 12, 1972, p. 55.

11. "Foreign Trade and U.S. Jobs," AFL-CIO Legislative Department, Fact Sheet 4 (1972), GMMA, AFL-CIO, RG 34–002, Ser. 1, Box 15, Folder 35.

12. "Can Any U.S. Business Find Happiness with the Burke-Hartke Bill?" Pamphlet in NAM, *Information Kit on the Multinational Corporation and the Burke-Hartke Bill* (1972), HML, National Association of Manufacturers Records (hereafter NAM), Ser. 16, Box 217.

13. See HML, NAM, Ser. 4, Box 21.

14. NAM to Legislative Coordinators, March 9, 1972, HML, NAM, Ser. 4, Box 22.

15. "Progress Report on Implementation of Multinational Corporation Legislative Strategy," in *Update, Progress Report on MNC Strategy, February 1–April 19* (April 1972), HML, NAM, Ser. 4, Box 22.

16. 3M, *Your Job Is Bigger Than You Think* (1972), pp. 3, 9, HML, NFTC, RG D, Ser. 12, Box 140, Folder 3.

17. M. P. Venema, Speech, Institute on Industrial Relations, March 19, 1972, HML, NAM, Ser. 4, Box 22.

18. See UN General Assembly Resolution 3281 (29), December 12, 1974, UN Doc. A/RES/2/3281; and Resolution 3202 (S-6), May 1, 1974, UN Doc. A/RES/S-6/3202.

19. U.S. Government (hereafter USG), Position Paper, "UN Commission on Transnational Corporations, Intergovernmental Working Group, New York, January 10–14, 1977," December 17, 1976, NARA, RG 56, Subject Files Related to United Nations Economic Organizations, 1969–1985, Box 1, Folder: United Nations, 1976.

20. USG Strategy Paper, "Investment and Transnational Corporations," April 25, 1975, p. 3, NARA, RG 56, United Nations Economic Organizations, 1969–1985, Box 1, Folder: United Nations, 1975.

21. Henry Kissinger, William Simon, and Elliot Richardson to Robert Norris, August 19, 1976, HML, NFTC, RG F, Ser. 1, Box 169, Folder 2.

22. Bob Dorsey, Statement in Hearings before the Senate Subcommittee on Multinational Corporations, 94th Cong., 1st Sess., on Political Contributions to Foreign Governments, May 16, 1975, p. 9.

23. Cable, U.S. Mission to the UN in New York to the Secretary of State, April

13, 1978, Subject: ECOSOC Working Group on Corrupt Practices, NARA, RG 56, Subject Files Relating to International Economic Development Organizations, 1969–1981, Box 20, Folder: UN 941 Working Group on Corrupt Payments.

24. Memo, Richard G. Darman and J. T. Smith to Members of the Task Force on Questionable Corporate Payments Abroad, May 16, 1976, pp. 6–8, Gerald R. Ford Presidential Library, Ann Arbor (hereafter GRFPL), Lazarus Files, Box 51, Folder 5.

25. Eiichi Nakao to President Gerald Ford, February 24, 1976, GRFPL, CO 75, Box 31, Folder: Executive—2/1/76–3/31/76.

26. Carter Presidential Campaign, "White Collar Crime," 1976, pp. 1–2, Jimmy Carter Presidential Library, Atlanta (hereafter JCPL), Records of the 1976 Campaign Committee to Elect Jimmy Carter, 1976, Box 37, Folder: White Collar Crime.

27. Carter-Mondale on the Issues, Transcript of Foreign Economic Policy Press Briefing, August 18, 1976, pp. 2, 5, JCPL, Records of the Domestic Policy Staff, Box 207, Folder: Foreign Affairs—Corporate Bribery.

28. Howard L. Weisberg and Eric Reichenberg, *The Price of Ambiguity* (Washington, D.C., 1981), pp. 19–20.

29. John Ralston Saul, *The Collapse of Globalism and the Reinvention of the World* (London, 2005), p. xiii.

30. Sanford Rose, "Multinational Corporations in a Tough New World," *Fortune* (August 1973): 52–53.

31. Sanford Rose, "Why the Multinational Tide Is Ebbing," *Fortune* (August 1977): 111.

32. Banks, Public Relations Seminar speech, p. 3.

9. The Vietnam Decade

1. For the purposes of this essay I use the terms Vietnam War and Second Indochina War interchangeably to refer to the fighting that took place from roughly 1959 to 1975 in order to distinguish it from the First Indochina War, also referred to as the French-Indochina War, from 1945 to 1954, and the Third Indochina War between China, Vietnam, and Cambodia, which began in the late 1970s.

2. According to Richard Melanson, the Vietnam War severely damaged U.S. foreign policy by contributing to the breakdown of its three main components: policy, cultural, and procedural. Richard A. Melanson, *American Foreign Policy since the Vietnam War: The Search for Consensus from Nixon to Clinton* (Armonk, N.Y., 1996), pp. 3–40.

3. Memorandum of conversation, July 29, 1971, at Time-Life Washington office, August 13, 1971, quoted in *The Kissinger Transcripts: A Verbatim Record of U.S. Diplomacy, 1969–1977,* ed. William Burr (Washington, D.C., 2005), p. 17.

4. See the essays by Daniel Sargent and Charles Maier in this volume for a fuller discussion of the crisis of the United States and other capitalist democracies in the 1970s.

5. Robert M. Collins, "The Economic Crisis and the Waning of the 'American Century,'" *American Historical Review* 101, no. 2 (April 1996): 396–422.

6. Lien-Hang T. Nguyen, "Cold War Contradictions," in *Making Sense of the Vietnam Wars: Local, National, and Transnational Perspectives.* ed. Marilyn Young and Mark Bradley (New York, 2008), pp. 219–249.

7. See Robert Schulzinger, *A Time for Peace: The Legacy of the Vietnam War* (New York, 2006).

8. Robert J. McMahon, "Contested Memory: The Vietnam War and American Society, 1975–2001," *Diplomatic History* 26, no. 2 (Spring 2002): 159–184.

9. Edward Martini, *Invisible Enemies: The American War on Vietnam, 1975–2000* (Amherst, 2007), pp. 46–47.

10. Paul D. Starr, "Troubled Waters: Vietnamese Fisherfolk on America's Gulf Coast," *International Migration Review* 15, no. 1–2, *Refugees Today* (Spring–Summer 1981): 226–238.

11. "Ronald Reagan's Speech at the VFW Convention, August 18, 1980," Public Papers of Ronald W. Reagan, www.Reagan.utexas.edu/archives/reference/8.18.80html (accesed February 15, 2009).

12. See Luu Van Loi and Nguyen Anh Vu, *Cac cuoc thuong luong Le Duc Tho–Kissinger tai Paris* (The Le Duc Tho–Kissinger Negotiations in Paris), 1st ed. (Hanoi, 1996), p. 55.

13. For an example of Vietnamese consternation over Nixon's visit to Moscow, see "Anh Trinh + Xuan Thuy gui anh Tho" (Telegram from Nguyen Duy Trinh and Xuan Thuy to Le Duc Tho), Dien di Q. 185, LT-BNG, June 13, 1972, in *Dai su chuyen de: Dau tranh ngoai giao va van dong quoc te trong nhung chien chong My cuu nuoc* (The Diplomatic Struggle and International Activities of the Anti-American Resistance and National Salvation), 5 vols., comp. Bo Ngoai Giao (Ministry of Foreign Affairs) (Hanoi, 1987), 4:326.

14. Ngo Vinh Long, "The Socialization of South Vietnam," in *The Third Indochina War: Conflict between China, Vietnam, and Cambodia, 1972–79,* ed. Odd Arne Westad and Sophie Quinn-Judge (New York, 2006), pp. 126–151.

15. See Odd Arne Westad's essay in this volume, discussing China's economic development during the 1970s.
16. Luu Van Loi, *Fifty Years of Vietnamese Diplomacy, 1945–1995* (Hanoi, 2006), p. 380; *Ngoai giao Viet Nam, 1945–2000* (Hanoi, 2002), p. 306.
17. Colonel Pham Xuan Truong, ed., *So tay tu lieu dac cong* (Sapper Handbook) (Hanoi, 1992), p. 130. I thank Merle Pribbenow for this reference.
18. Interview with Colonel Nguyen Manh Ha, associate director of the Vietnam Institute of Military History, Hanoi, November 24, 2008.
19. Much of my thinking for this section comes from the doctoral thesis of Paul Chamberlin, "Preparing for Dawn: The United States and the Global Politics of Palestinian Resistance, 1967–75" (Ohio State University, 2009).
20. Interview with Nguyen Thi Ngoc Dung, delegate-member of the Provisional Revolutionary Government of South Vietnam to the Paris peace talks, Ho Chi Minh City, December 13, 2008. Nguyen Thi Ngoc Dung directly worked on people's diplomacy involving outreach to antiwar groups in North America. For the Vietnam Workers' Party's definition of "people's diplomacy," see "8. Ve cong tac quoc te" (8. International Work), in "Nghi quyet cua Bo Chinh Tri ve chuyen huong va day manh moi mat cong tac o mien Bac de tiep tuc dang thang giac My xam luoc" (Politburo Resolution Regarding the Direction and Acceleration of All Aspects of Work Regarding the North in Order to Defeat the Invading Americans), June 1, 1972, reprinted in *Van kien dang toan tap* (Complete Collection of Party Records), comp. Dang Cong San, 39 vols. (Hanoi, 1994), 33:317–318.
21. Le Duan, *Thu vao nam* (Letters to the South) (Hanoi, 1986), pp. 252–253.
22. See Odd Arne Westad, *The Global Cold War* (New York, 2007), p. 158.
23. Ibid., pp. 189–190.
24. Chamberlin, "Preparing for Dawn," p. 48.
25. See Piero Gleijeses, *Conflicting Missions: Havana, Washington, and Africa, 1959–1976* (Chapel Hill, 2002).
26. See Walter Lafeber, *Inevitable Revolutions: The United States in Central America* (New York, 1993).
27. Henry Kissinger, *Diplomacy* (New York, 1994), pp. 698, 763.
28. Edgar O'Ballance, *Afghan Wars, 1839–1992* (New York, 1993), p. 101. I thank Daniel Headrik for this reference.

10. Henry Kissinger and the Geopolitics of Globalization

1. Quoted in Richard Nixon, *Six Crises* (Garden City, N.Y., 1962), p. 235.
2. Henry Kissinger, "Globalization and Its Discontents," *International Herald Tribune*, May 30, 2008.

3. Henry Kissinger, "The Three Revolutions," *Washington Post,* April 7, 2008. See also Jeremi Suri, *Henry Kissinger and the American Century* (Cambridge, Mass., 2007), chap. 4.

4. For an excellent analysis of globalization that gives attention to both state and non-state actors, see Jeffry A. Frieden, *Global Capitalism: Its Fall and Rise in the Twentieth Century* (New York, 2006).

5. Henry Kissinger, *White House Years* (Boston, 1979), pp. 54, 70. See also John Lewis Gaddis, "Rescuing Choice from Circumstance: The Statecraft of Henry Kissinger," in *The Diplomats, 1939–1979,* ed. Gordon A. Craig and Francis L. Loewenheim (Princeton, 1994), pp. 564–592.

6. See, among others, Robert D. Schulzinger, *Henry Kissinger: Doctor of Diplomacy* (New York, 1989); Walter Isaacson, *Kissinger: A Biography* (New York, 1992); Jussi Hanhimäki, *The Flawed Architect: Henry Kissinger and American Foreign Policy* (New York, 2004); Margaret Macmillan, *Nixon and Mao: The Week That Changed the World* (New York, 2007); Robert Dallek, *Nixon and Kissinger: Partners in Power* (New York, 2007); Jeremi Suri, *Power and Protest: Global Revolution and the Rise of Détente* (Cambridge, Mass., 2003), esp. chap. 6; Suri, *Henry Kissinger and the American Century.*

7. See Suri, *Henry Kissinger and the American Century,* chap. 6.

8. Nelson A. Rockefeller, *The Future of Federalism* (Cambridge, Mass., 1962), pp. 3–4. Rockefeller delivered his three Godkin lectures at Harvard, February 7–9, 1962. For a reference to Kissinger's work on the Godkin lectures, see Kissinger to Rockefeller, February 24, 1961, Folder 184, Box 31, Ser. J.2, Record Group (hereafter RG) 4, Nelson A. Rockefeller Papers (hereafter NAR), Personal, Rockefeller Archive Center, Pocantico Hills, N.Y. (hereafter RAC).

9. Rockefeller, *The Future of Federalism,* pp. 4, 6–7.

10. Henry Kissinger, "Coalition Diplomacy in a Nuclear Age," *Foreign Affairs* 42 (July 1964): 542; Kissinger, "The White Revolutionary: Reflections on Bismarck," *Daedalus* 97 (Summer 1968): 909–918. Kissinger's understanding of federalism drew on the pioneering work of one of his mentors at Harvard, Carl J. Friedrich. See Friedrich's seminal 1937 book *Constitutional Government and Democracy: Theory and Practice in Europe and America,* rev. ed. (Boston, 1950), esp. pp. 73–88, 173–221.

11. Kissinger to Rockefeller, November 18, 1960, Folder 184, Box 31, Ser. J.2, RG 4, NAR, Personal, RAC.

12. Henry Kissinger, *The Troubled Partnership: A Re-appraisal of the Atlantic Alliance* (New York, 1965), p. 251.

13. Henry Kissinger, *The Necessity for Choice: Prospects of American Foreign Policy* (New York, 1961), pp. 4, 7–9.

14. Henry Kissinger, "For an Atlantic Confederacy," *The Reporter,* February 2, 1961, p. 20; Kissinger, *The Necessity for Choice,* p. 121.
15. Kissinger, *The Troubled Partnership,* p. 246.
16. Ibid., p. 47.
17. Ibid., pp. 47, 54–55.
18. Ibid., p. 244. See also Kissinger, "Coalition Diplomacy in a Nuclear Age," pp. 544–545.
19. Henry Kissinger, "For a New Atlantic Alliance," *The Reporter,* July 14, 1966, p. 27.
20. See John Lewis Gaddis, *The Long Peace: Inquiries into the History of the Cold War* (New York, 1987), pp. 215–245.
21. Henry Kissinger, "Reflections on Cuba," *The Reporter,* November 22, 1962, pp. 21–24. Evidence from Russian archives indicates that Khrushchev did not act according to the logic that Kissinger assumed. See Aleksandr Fursenko and Timothy Naftali, *Khrushchev's Cold War: The Inside Story of an American Adversary* (New York, 2006); Odd Arne Westad, *The Global Cold War: Third World Interventions and the Making of Our Time* (Cambridge, 2005), chaps. 6–7.
22. Kissinger was, of course, not the only policymaker to contemplate a global diffusion of power. Walt Rostow, President Lyndon Johnson's special assistant for national security affairs and Kissinger's predecessor in that position, thought in similar terms. Kissinger, however, implemented policies that were much more multipolar, especially with regard to China, than those of any of his predecessors. See Walt Rostow, *The Diffusion of Power* (New York, 1972).
23. See Henry Kissinger, "Coalition Diplomacy in a Nuclear Age," *Foreign Affairs* 42 (July 1964): 529–530; Kissinger, "Central Issues of American Foreign Policy," in *Agenda for the Nation,* ed. Kermit Gordon (Washington, D.C., 1968), pp. 585–614.
24. Kissinger, "Central Issues of American Foreign Policy," p. 588.
25. Ernst Hans Van der Beugel oral history, chap. 7, Archive Location 2.21.183.08, Inventory 60–65, National Archive, The Netherlands; author's interview with Henry Kissinger, June 11, 2005. I thank Floris Kunert for helping me use the Van der Beugel materials and Danielle Kleijwegt for her translation of the Van der Beugel oral history.
26. "Recommended Position: Communist China," prepared by Kissinger for Nelson Rockefeller's briefing book, May 15, 1968, Folder 89, Box 5, Ser. 35, RG 15, NAR, Gubernatorial, RAC. The same text is included in another section of the same briefing book; see Folder 88.
27. "Recommended Position: Communist China"; Excerpts of Remarks by

Governor Nelson A. Rockefeller, World Affairs Council of Philadelphia, May 1, 1968, Folder: 5/1/68—World Affairs Council, Box 59, Ser. 33, RG 15, NAR, Gubernatorial, RAC.

28. "Recommended Position: Communist China."

29. "Recommended Positions: United States' Relations with the USSR," prepared by Kissinger for Nelson Rockefeller's briefing book, May 15, 1968, Folder 89, Box 5, Ser. 35, RG 15, NAR, Gubernatorial, RAC; "Recommended Position: Communist China."

30. See Suri, *Henry Kissinger and the American Century*, chap. 1.

31. For Kissinger's reflections on "advanced" and "new" countries, see "Central Issues of American Foreign Policy," pp. 603–606.

32. Ibid., p. 603.

33. Ibid., p. 612.

34. Henry Kissinger, *Diplomacy* (New York, 1994), p. 471.

35. Henry Kissinger, *A World Restored: Metternich, Castlereagh, and the Problems of Peace, 1812–1822* (1957; reprint, London, 2000), pp. 316–317; Kissinger, "The Policymaker and the Intellectual," *The Reporter,* March 5, 1959, pp. 30–35.

36. "Recommended Position: U.S.-U.S.S.R.," prepared by Kissinger for Nelson Rockefeller's briefing book, May 15, 1968, Folder 8, Box 5, Ser. 35, RG 15, NAR, Gubernatorial, RAC; Kissinger, "Central Issues of American Foreign Policy," pp. 585–589, 610–614.

37. "Basic Principles of Relations between the United States of America and the Union of Soviet Socialist Republics," May 29, 1972, in *U.S. Department of State Bulletin* 66 (June 26, 1972): 898–899; Kissinger's News Conference, Kiev, May 29, 1972, ibid., pp. 890–897. See also Suri, *Power and Protest,* pp. 256–258.

38. On this last point, see Robert Kagan, *The Return of History and the End of Dreams* (New York, 2008); Melvyn P. Leffler and Jeffrey W. Legro, eds., *To Lead the World: American Strategy after the Bush Doctrine* (New York, 2008).

11. Wrestling with Parity

1. For popular accounts, in addition to Gregg Herken, *The Winning Weapon: The Atomic Bomb in the Cold War* (New York, 1980), see Fred Kaplan, *The Wizards of Armageddon* (Stanford, 1991); and John Newhouse, *War and Peace in the Nuclear Age* (New York, 1990).

2. For a trenchant analysis of these debates, see Bruce Kuklick, *Blind Oracles: Intellectuals and War from Kennan to Kissinger* (Princeton, 2006).

3. McGeorge Bundy, "To Cap the Volcano," *Foreign Affairs* 48, no. 1 (October 1969): 11.

4. Paul C. Warnke and Leslie H. Gelb, "Security or Confrontation," *Foreign Policy*, no. 1 (Winter 1970–71): 23.

5. Robert Jervis, *The Meaning of the Nuclear Revolution: Statecraft and the Prospects of Armageddon* (Ithaca, 1989), pp. 74–106. MAD, in the language of nuclear strategists, stood for Mutually Assured Destruction.

6. William C. Foster, "Prospects for Arms Control," *Foreign Affairs* 47, no. 3 (April 1969): 416.

7. Alton Frye, "The Vindication of Robert McNamara," *Washington Post*, July 6, 1972.

8. Robert Jervis, "Cooperation under the Security Dilemma," *World Politics* 30 (1978): 167–214.

9. Lawrence Freedman, *The Evolution of Nuclear Strategy*, 2nd ed. (New York, 1997), p. 349.

10. Paul H. Nitze, "Assuring Strategic Stability in an Era of Détente," *Foreign Affairs* 54, no. 2 (January 1976): 207.

11. Richard Pipes, "Why the Soviet Union Thinks It Could Fight and Win a Nuclear War," *Commentary* 64, no. 1 (July 1977): 34.

12. Colin S. Gray, "Nuclear Strategy: The Case for a Theory of Victory," *International Security* 4, no. 1 (Summer 1979): 87.

13. For contrasting views, see Richard Betts, *Nuclear Blackmail and Nuclear Balance* (Washington, D.C., 1987); and Gareth Porter, *Perils of Dominance: Imbalance of Power and the Road to War in Vietnam* (Berkeley, 2005).

14. See Marc Trachtenberg, "The Cuban Missile Crisis," in *History and Strategy* (Princeton, 1991), pp. 235–260.

15. See Marc Trachtenberg, "The Berlin Crisis," ibid., pp. 192–193, 218–221.

16. Francis J. Gavin, "Nuclear Nixon: Ironies, Puzzles, and the Triumph of Realpolitik," in *Nixon in the World: American Foreign Relations, 1969–1977*, ed. Fredrik Logevall and Andrew Preston (New York, 2008), p. 133.

17. For an excellent assessment of this question, see Marc Trachtenberg, "The Past and Future of Arms Control," *Daedalus* 120, no. 1 (Winter 1991): 203–216.

18. Ernest May, John Steinbruner, and Thomas Wolfe, "History of the Strategic Arms Competition, 1945–1972," pt. 2, p. 810, Office of the Secretary of Defense, Historical Office, March 1981, Department of Defense.

19. Ibid., p. 828.

20. Lawrence Wittner, *Toward Nuclear Abolition: A History of the World Disarmament Movement, 1971 to the Present* (Stanford, 2003), pp. 41–42.

21. Paul Lettow, *Ronald Reagan and His Quest to Abolish Nuclear Weapons* (New York, 2005), p. iv.

22. Nina Tannenwald, *The Nuclear Taboo: The United States and the Non-Use of Nuclear Weapons since 1945* (Cambridge, 2007).

23. John Mueller, *Retreat from Doomsday: The Obsolescence of Major War* (New York, 1989).

24. George P. Shultz, William J. Perry, Henry A. Kissinger, and Sam Nunn, "Toward a Nuclear-Free World," *Wall Street Journal Online*, January 15, 2008.

12. Containing Globalism

1. Frank Church speech, "Farewell to Foreign Aid: A Liberal Takes Leave," October 29, 1971, Stuart Symington Papers, Ellis Library, University of Missouri, Columbia.

2. Works that emphasize the 1960s as a takeoff point for globalizing trends include Akira Iriye, *Global Community: The Role of International Organizations in the Making of the Contemporary World* (Berkeley, 2002), chap. 4; Alfred E. Eckes Jr. and Thomas W. Zeiler, *Globalization and the American Century* (New York, 2003), chap. 7; A. G. Hopkins, "The History of Globalization—And the Globalization of History?" in *Globalization in World History*, ed. Hopkins (New York, 2002), 12–44; and Jürgen Osterhammel and Niels Petersson, *Globalization* (Princeton, 2003), pp. 132–139.

3. Iriye, *Global Community*, pp. 103–104.

4. Jeremi Suri, *Power and Protest* (Cambridge, Mass., 2003).

5. Quoted in Daniel Jonathan Sargent, "From Internationalism to Globalism: The United States and the Transformation of International Politics in the 1970s" (Ph.D. diss., Harvard University, June 2008), p. 124.

6. Nixon speech, October 31, 1969, White House Central File, Subject Categories: Speeches, Box 113, Nixon Presidential Materials, National Archives and Records Administration, College Park, Md. (hereafter NARA).

7. Recording of Nixon's meeting with Donald Rumsfeld, March 8, 1971, Nixon tapes, conversation 463–466, www.whitehousetapes.org/pages/listen_tapes_rmn.htm.

8. Quoted in Seymour M. Hersh, *The Price of Power* (New York, 1983), p. 263.

9. Richard M. Nixon, *United States Foreign Policy for the 1970s* (New York, 1971), p. xi.

10. For example, Jonathan Haslam, *The Nixon Administration and the Death of Allende's Chile* (New York, 2005).

11. Ibid., p. 56.

12. Memorandum of conversation, "NSC Meeting—Chile," November 6, 1970, in *The Pinochet File*, ed. Peter Kornbluh (New York, 2003), Document 1, pp. 116–120.

13. Quoted in Haslam, *The Nixon Administration and the Death of Allende's Chile,* p. 56.

14. Henry Kissinger, *White House Years* (Boston, 1979), p. 848.

15. Sargent, "From Internationalism to Globalism," pp. 291–324.

16. See Odd Arne Westad, *The Global Cold War* (New York, 2005), pp. 206, 241–242.

17. For example, Robert Dallek, *Nixon and Kissinger* (New York, 2007), esp. chaps. 15–17.

18. For example, David Reynolds, *Summits* (New York, 2007), chap. 5.

19. For example, Walter LaFeber, *Inevitable Revolutions,* 2nd ed. (New York, 1993).

20. See Jeremi Suri, "Détente and Its Discontents," in *Rightward Bound,* ed. Bruce J. Schulman and Julian E. Zelizer (Cambridge, Mass., 2008), esp. pp. 237–245.

21. On this backlash, see especially Kathryn Sikkink, *Mixed Signals* (Ithaca, N.Y., 2004), chap. 3.

22. Iriye, *Global Community,* p. 115.

23. Ibid., p. 129.

24. Ibid., pp. 128–142.

25. See Suri, *Power and Protest.*

26. Quoted in Gaddis Smith, *Morality, Reason, and Power* (New York, 1986), p. 59.

27. Jimmy Carter, *Keeping Faith* (New York, 1982), p. 143.

28. Ibid.

29. Transcript of conversation between Nixon and Kissinger, September 16, 1973, Kissinger telcons, Box 22, Nixon Presidential Materials Project, NARA.

30. Memorandum of conversation, Nixon, Kissinger, and Alexander Haig, December 12, 1971, in U.S. Department of State, *Foreign Relations of the United States, 1969–1976,* vol. E-7, http://www.state.gov/r/pa/ho/frus/nixon/e7/48544.htm.

31. Carter, *Keeping Faith,* p. 156.

32. Carter commencement speech at Notre Dame University, May 22, 1977, in *Public Papers of the Presidents of the United States: James E. Carter, 1977,* vol. 1 (Washington, D.C., 1977), pp. 954–962.

33. Quoted in Melvyn P. Leffler, *For the Soul of Mankind* (New York, 2007), p. 265.

34. Quoted in Keith L. Shimko, *Images and Arms Control* (Ann Arbor, 1992), p. 63.

35. Jeane J. Kirkpatrick, *Dictatorships and Double Standards* (New York, 1982).

13. The Transformation of International Institutions

1. Akira Iriye, *Global Community: The Role of International Organizations in the Making of the Contemporary World* (Berkeley, 2002), p. 129.

2. Daniel P. Moynihan, *A Dangerous Place* (London, 1979), p. 82.

3. Cited ibid., p. 114. Waldheim's personal links to the race crimes of the Nazi period were exposed only belatedly.

4. See "Moynihan Attacks Colonialism Report of U.N. Assembly," *New York Times*, December 12, 1975, p. 9.

5. David Armstrong, Lorna Lloyd, and John Redmond, *From Versailles to Maastricht* (London, 1996), pp. 88, 103; Hugh Tinker, *Race, Conflict and the International Order* (London, 1977), p. 112.

6. U Thant, *View from the UN* (New York, 1968), p. 36.

7. Armstrong, Lloyd, and Redmond, *From Versailles*, p. 95.

8. Jagdish N. Bhagwati, intro. to *Power, Passions, and Purpose*, ed. J. N. Bhagwati and John Gerard Ruggie (Cambridge, Mass., 1984), p. 1.

9. General Assembly, Sixth Special Session, Supplement no. 1 (A/9559), United Nations, 1974, 3201 (S-VI), Declaration on the Establishment of a New International Economic Order, May 1, 1974.

10. Jan Pronk, "Some Remarks on the Relation between the New International Information Order and the New International Economic Order," International Commission for the Study of Communication Problems, UNESCO, 1978.

11. See Thomas G. Weiss et al., *UN Voices* (Bloomington, 2005).

12. Philippe de Seynes, "Prospects for a Future Whole World," *International Organization* 26 (1972): 1–17, esp. p. 5. De Seynes was a former French bureaucrat.

13. Ronald I. Meltzer, "Restructuring the United Nations System: Institutional Reform Efforts in the Context of North-South Relations," *International Organization* 32 (1978): 993–1018, esp. p. 998.

14. Richard Jolly, "Society for International Development, the North-South Roundtable and the Power of Ideas," *Development* 50 (2007): 47–58, esp. p. 55.

15. Ivor Richards, "The United Nations and the New International Economic Order," *Millennium* 4 (1975): 68.

16. Bhagwati, intro. to *Power, Passions, and Purpose*, p. 1.

17. Harold R. Isaac, "Color in World Affairs," *Foreign Affairs* 47 (1969): 235.

18. Tinker, *Race*, pp. 77–132.

19. Edward Shils, "Colour and the Afro-Asian Intellectual," in *Colour and Race*, ed. John Hope Franklin (Boston, 1968), p. 5.

20. Talcott Parsons, "The Problem of Polarization on the Axis of Color," ibid.

21. A. R. Preiswerk, "Race and Colour in International Relations," in *The Year Book of World Affairs, 1970* (London, 1970), pp. 60, 87.
22. Tinker, *Race,* pp. 3, 129, 130, 135.
23. Isaac, "Color in World Affairs," p. 235.
24. W. E. B. Du Bois, *The Souls of Black Folk* (Chicago, 1903).
25. W. E. B. Du Bois, preface to *Color and Democracy* (1945), ed. Henry Louis Gates Jr. (Oxford, 2007), chap. 1, esp. p. 252.
26. "The Programme of UNESCO in 1950," Resolution 4.2, in *Records of the General Conference of the United Nations Educational, Scientific and Cultural Organisation, Fourth Session, Paris, 1949: Resolutions* (Paris, 1949), p. 22.
27. See Armstrong, Lloyd, and Redmond, *From Versailles,* p. 117.
28. Preiswerk, "Race and Colour," p. 58.
29. Tinker, *Race,* pp. 100, 132.
30. By contrast, the paltry representation of women in those same institutions—fewer than 20 percent of the bureaucracy, let alone delegations—failed to draw the attention of concerned observers or UN member states, despite the persistent urgings of feminists working with sectors of the UN bureaucracy. See Jocelyn Olcott's essay in this volume.
31. See Nathan Glazer and Daniel Moynihan, *Ethnicity* (Cambridge, Mass., 1975), p. 3.
32. Moynihan, *A Dangerous Place,* p. 65.
33. See Ayesha Jalal's essay in this volume; and Tom Nairn, *The Break-up of Britain* (London, 1977).
34. Preiswerk, "Race and Colour," pp. 54–55.
35. See Jeremy Adelman's essay in this volume.
36. J. P. Dumas, "Moynihanism at the UN," *Third World Quarterly* 2 (1980): 518.
37. John W. Holmes, "A Non-American Perspective," *Proceedings of the Academy of Political Science* 32 (1977): 30–43. See also Mark Lawrence and Daniel Sargent's analyses of U.S. foreign policy in this volume.
38. Henry Kissinger, interview, 1975, www.youtube.com/watch?v=EBhExOoX _P0 (accessed August 20, 2008). For further discussion of the complex dimensions of Kissinger's role in this decade, see Daniel Sargent's essay in this volume.
39. Ralph Bunche, "Race and Alienation," in *Ralph J. Bunche,* ed. Charles P. Henry (Ann Arbor, 1995), p. 314.
40. De Seynes, "Prospects," p. 1.
41. Thant, *View from the UN,* p. 441. See the essays on environmentalism and human rights in this volume.
42. Stanley Hoffman, "International Organization and the International System," *International Organization* 3 (1970): 389–413, esp. p. 392.

43. Australia, Parliament, Senate, Standing Committee on Foreign Affairs and Defence, *The Role and Involvement of Australia and the United Nations in the Affairs of Sovereign Australian Territories: Official Hansard Report* (Canberra, 1979), pp. 849–850.

44. President Gerald R. Ford, *Address to the Twenty-ninth Session of the General Assembly of the United Nations,* September 18, 1974, available on-line in John T. Woolley and Gerhard Peters, *The American Presidency Project,* www. presidency.ucsb.edu/ws/?pid=4718.

45. Hedley Bull, *The Anarchical Society* (London, 1977), p. xiv. See also Hedley Bull and Adam Watson, *The Expansion of International Society* (Oxford, 1984).

46. Adam Watson, "Recollection of My Discussions with Hedley Bull about the Place in the History of International Relations of the Idea of the Anarchical Society," Paris, July 2002, www.polis.leeds.ac.uk/assets/files/research/English-school/Watson-bull02.pdf (accessed September 10, 2008).

47. Editorial, *Third World Quarterly* 1 (1979): vi. The editors were Altaf Gauhar and Khalid Hasan, Pakistani nationals with broad experience in the civil service and journalism newly based in London.

48. Mark Mazower, "An International Civilization? Empire, Internationalism, and the Crisis of the Mid-Twentieth Century," *International Affairs* 82 (2006): 566.

49. Tinker, *Race,* p. 175.

50. Moynihan, *A Dangerous Place,* p. 114.

14. The Seventies and the Rebirth of Human Rights

1. Aase Lionaes, Nobel Prize Presentation Speech, 1968, nobelprize.org (accessed September 2, 2008). On Cassin's work, see Jay Winter, *Dreams of Peace and Freedom* (New Haven, 2006), chap. 4.

2. Andrei D. Sakharov, *Progress, Coexistence, and Intellectual Freedom* (New York, 1968).

3. See Mary Ann Glendon, *A World Made New* (New York, 2001), chap. 10. See also H. G. Wells, *Rights of Man* (Harmondsworth, 1940); Jacques Maritain, *Les Droits de l'homme et la loi naturelle* (New York, 1942); and Hersch Lauterpacht, *An International Bill of the Rights of Man* (New York, 1945).

4. Amos Yoder, *The Evolution of the United Nations System,* 2nd ed. (London, 1993), p. 129.

5. Geoffrey Robertson, *Crimes against Humanity* (London, 1999), pp. 51–53. See also Brian Simpson, *Human Rights and the End of Empire* (Oxford, 2001).

6. Roger Normand and Sarah Zaidi, *Human Rights at the UN* (Bloomington, 2008).

7. Natalie Hevener Kaufman, *Human Rights Treaties and the Senate* (Chapel Hill, 1990), p. 69.

8. David S. Fogelsong, *The American Mission and the "Evil Empire"* (Cambridge, 2007), chaps. 5 and 6; and Odd Arne Westad, *The Global Cold War* (Cambridge, 2007), chap. 4.

9. Mary L. Dudziak, *Cold War Civil Rights* (Princeton, 2000).

10. Raymond F. Betts, *Decolonization* (London, 1998), chap. 4.

11. David S. Wyman, ed., *The World Reacts to the Holocaust* (Baltimore, 1996); Dan Stone, *Constructing the Holocaust* (London, 2003); Peter Novick, *The Holocaust in American Life* (Boston, 1999); Henry Rousso, *The Vichy Syndrome,* trans. Arthur Goldhammer (Cambridge, Mass., 1991); and Robert Paxton, *Vichy France* (New York, 1972).

12. Egon Larsen, *A Flame in Barbed Wire* (London, 1978), chaps. 1 and 2; Jonathan Power, *Like Water on Stone* (London, 2001), chap. 4; and Akira Iriye, *Global Community: The Role of International Organizations in the Making of the Contemporary World* (Berkeley, 2002), chap. 4. See also Ann Marie Clark, *Diplomacy of Conscience* (Princeton, 2001).

13. Lynn Hunt, *Inventing Human Rights* (New York, 2007), chaps. 1–3.

14. David Reynolds, *One World Divisible* (London, 2000), chap. 14.

15. Arch Puddington, *Broadcasting Freedom* (Lexington, Ky., 2000), p. ix and chaps. 8 and 13.

16. Christian F. Ostermann, ed., *Uprising in East Germany, 1953* (Budapest, 2001); Charles Gati, *Failed Illusions* (Stanford, 2006); Jaromir Navratil, ed., *The Prague Spring, 1968* (Budapest, 1998); and Zdenek Mlynar, *Nightfrost in Prague* (New York, 1980).

17. Joshua Rubenstein, *Soviet Dissidents,* 2nd ed. (Boston, 1985); and Michael Scammell, *Solzhenitsyn* (New York, 1984).

18. John J. Stremlau, *The International Politics of the Nigerian Civil War, 1967–1970* (Princeton, 1977).

19. Dan Jacobs, *The Brutality of Nations* (New York, 1987).

20. On the Committee to Keep Biafra Alive, see Daniel Sargent, "From Internationalism to Globalism: The United States and the Transformation of International Politics in the 1970s" (Ph.D. diss., Harvard University, 2008), chap. 4. On Bernard Kouchner and the creation of MSF, see Alain Guillemoles, *Bernard Kouchner* (Paris, 2002), chaps. 4 and 5; and Tim Allen and David Styan, "A Right to Interfere? Bernard Kouchner and the New Humanitarianism," *Journal of International Development* 12, no. 6 (2000): 825–842. Kouchner quoted in David Chandler, "The Road to Military Humanitarianism: How the Human Rights NGOs Shaped a New Humanitarian Agenda," *Human Rights Quarterly* 23 (2001): 684.

21. Don Oberdorfer, *Tet!* (Baltimore, 2001); David D. Perlmutter, "Photojournalism and Foreign Affairs," *Orbis* 49, no. 1 (Winter 2005): 109–122; William M. Hammond, *Reporting Vietnam* (Lawrence, Kans., 1998); and Michal R. Belknap, *Vietnam War on Trial* (Lawrence, Kans., 2002).

22. Kathryn Sikkink, *Mixed Signals* (Ithaca, 2004), chaps. 3 and 5.

23. Kenneth Cmiel, "The Emergence of Human Rights Politics in the United States," *Journal of American History* 86, no. 3 (December 1999): 1235–36.

24. Robert G. Kaufman, *Henry M. Jackson* (Seattle, 2000), chaps. 13–14; Noam Kochavi, "Insights Abandoned, Flexibility Lost: Kissinger, Soviet Jewish Emigration, and the Demise of Détente," *Diplomatic History* 29, no. 3 (June 2005): 503–530; and Jussi M. Hanhimäki, *The Flawed Architect* (Oxford, 2004), pp. 340–344.

25. Andrei Sakharov, *Memoirs,* trans. Richard Lourie (London, 1990), chap. 20; Richard Lourie, *Sakharov* (Hanover, N.H., 2002), chap. 9; Peter Reddaway, ed., *Uncensored Russia* (New York, 1972); Laurie S. Wiseberg and Harry M. Scoble, "The International League for Human Rights: The Strategy of a Human Rights NGO," *Georgia Journal of International and Comparative Law* 7 (1977): 289–313; and Michael Scammell, "How *Index on Censorship* Started," in *They Shoot Writers, Don't They?* ed. George Theiner (London, 1984), pp. 19–28.

26. John J. Maresca, *To Helsinki* (Durham, 1987).

27. Michael Cotey Morgan, "The United States and the Making of the Helsinki Final Act," in *Nixon in the World,* ed. Fredrik Logevall and Andrew Preston (New York, 2008), pp. 164–182.

28. Gaddis Smith, *Morality, Reason, and Power* (New York, 1986); Sikkink *Mixed Signals,* chap. 6; and Samantha Power, "*A Problem from Hell*" (New York, 2002), chap. 6.

29. Paul Goldberg, *The Final Act* (New York, 1998); and Sarah Baldwin Snyder, "The Helsinki Process, American Foreign Policy, and the End of the Cold War" (Ph.D. diss., Georgetown University, 2006).

30. Daniel C. Thomas, *The Helsinki Effect* (Princeton, 2001); Michael Simmons, *The Reluctant President* (London, 1991); Timothy Garton Ash, *The Polish Revolution* (New Haven, 2002).

15. Smallpox Eradication and the Rise of Global Governance

1. *The Global Eradication of Smallpox: Final Report of the Global Commission for the Certification of Smallpox, Geneva, December 1979* (Geneva, 1980).

2. This is approximately equivalent to the number of annual global deaths currently attributed to HIV/AIDS and twice the number currently attributed to malaria. See www.globalhealthfacts.org.

3. The figure of 300 million smallpox deaths in the twentieth century is cited,

inter alia, in Michael B. A. Oldstone, *Viruses, Plagues, and History* (New York, 1998), p. 27. Given the state of the worldwide data, this is necessarily a broad estimate. The death toll of the twentieth century's wars is tallied in Niall Ferguson, *The War of the World: Twentieth-Century Conflict and the Descent of the West* (New York, 2006).

4. The few exceptions include Akira Iriye, *Global Community: The Role of International Organizations in the Making of the Contemporary World* (Berkeley, 2002), which discusses the role of the Red Cross in the construction of international norms and practices; Amy L. S. Staples, *The Birth of Development: How the World Bank, Food and Agriculture Organization, and World Health Organization Have Changed the World, 1945–1965* (Kent, Ohio, 2006); and Marcos Cueto, *Cold War, Deadly Fevers: Malaria Eradication in Mexico, 1955–1975* (Baltimore, 2007).

5. See esp. Iriye, *Global Community,* and idem, *Cultural Internationalism and World Order* (Baltimore, 1997). I prefer the term "society" to Iriye's "community," since the latter term suggests a degree of intimacy and homogeneity, while the former can be diverse, even fractious.

6. On the identity of international technocrats, see Staples, *Birth of Development,* esp. pp. 1–7.

7. On the MEP, see ibid., chap. 10; Randall M. Packard, "'No Other Logical Choice': Global Malaria Eradication and the Politics of International Health," *Parassitologia* 40 (June 1998): 217–230; Packard, "Malaria Dreams: Postwar Visions of Health and Development in the Third World," *Medical Anthropology* 17 (1997): 279–296. A popular, heroic account is Malcolm Gladwell, "The Mosquito Killer," *New Yorker,* July 2, 2001, pp. 42–51.

8. On this transition in the field of public health, see Theodore M. Brown, Marcos Cueto, and Elizabeth Fee, "The World Health Organization and the Transition from 'International' to 'Global' Public Health," *American Journal of Public Health* 96, no. 1 (2006): 62–72. For a broader theoretical discussion, see Barry Buzan, *From International to World Society: English School Theory and the Social Structure of Globalisation* (Cambridge, 2004).

9. Cyril William Dixon, *Smallpox* (London, 1962), chap. 10.

10. Alfred W. Crosby, *The Columbian Exchange: Biological and Cultural Consequences of 1492* (Westport, Conn., 1972), pp. 42–62; John R. McNeill, *Mosquito Empires: Ecology, Epidemics, War, and Revolution in the Greater Caribbean, 1640–1900* (New York, 2010). I thank the author for sharing his manuscript prior to publication.

11. Dixon, *Smallpox,* chap. 12. The term "vaccine," derived from the Latin *vacca,* or "cow," was coined to honor Jenner's discovery.

12. Frank Fenner, Donald A. Henderson, Isao Arita, Zdenek Jezek, and Ivan D. Ladnyi, *Smallpox and Its Eradication* (Geneva, 1988), chap. 8.

13. Norman Howard-Jones, "Origins of International Health Work," *British Medical Journal* 1 (May 1950): 1032–46; idem, *The Scientific Background of the International Sanitary Conferences, 1851–1938* (Geneva, 1975).

14. On disease control and the formation of modern European states, see Peter Baldwin, *Contagion and the State in Europe, 1830–1930* (New York, 1999).

15. Warwick Anderson, *Colonial Pathologies: American Tropical Medicine, Race, and Hygiene in the Philippines* (Durham, 2006).

16. John Farley, *To Cast Out Disease: A History of the International Health Division of the Rockefeller Foundation, 1913–1951* (New York, 2004); Anne-Emanuelle Birn, *Marriage of Convenience: Rockefeller International Health and Revolutionary Mexico* (Rochester, N.Y., 2006); Marcos Cueto, *Missionaries of Science: The Rockefeller Foundation and Latin America* (Bloomington, 1994).

17. Neville M. Goodman, *International Health Organizations and Their Work* (London, 1952); Norman Howard-Jones, *International Public Health between the Two World Wars: The Organizational Problems* (Geneva, 1978).

18. The WHO, however, argued that its constitution contained no provision for withdrawal and continued to count the Soviet bloc countries among its members. Javed Siddiqi, *World Health and World Politics: The World Health Organization and the UN System* (London, 1995), pp. 104–109, 141–145.

19. "Eradication of Smallpox: Report Submitted by the Government of the Union of Soviet Socialist Republics," in *Official Records of the World Health Organization* (hereafter *ORWHO*), no. 87 (1958), Annex 19, pp. 508–512; Fenner et al., *Smallpox and Its Eradication,* pp. 366–371.

20. Resolution EB22.R12, "Gifts of Smallpox Vaccine," WHO Executive Board, 22nd Session, Minneapolis, June 16–17, 1958, *ORWHO,* no. 88, p. 7.

21. Donald Henderson, "Smallpox Eradication: A Cold War Victory," *World Health Forum* 19 (1998): 114.

22. Staples, *Birth of Development,* pp. 177–179.

23. White House Press Release, November 24, 1964, United States National Archives (hereafter USNA), RG 90, Box 42, Folder: "International Cooperation Year (Committee)."

24. "President Johnson on International Cooperation Year," in Department of State, *Foreign Affairs Outline, 1965: International Cooperation Year;* and James Watt, "International Cooperation for Health: A Modern Imperative," both in USNA, RG 90, Box 42, Folder: "International Cooperation Year."

25. White House press release, May 18, 1965, Lyndon Baines Johnson Library and Museum, Austin (hereafter LBJ Library), White House Central Files, Ex HE/MC, Box 6.

26. Undated memo, LBJ Library, Office Files of Joseph A. Califano, Box 29 (1737), Folder: "Health."

27. From 1958 to 1979 Moscow donated 1.4 billion doses bilaterally to endemic countries, in comparison to Washington's 190 million doses. In addition, from 1967 to 1984 the USSR accounted for 298 million of the 465 million doses given directly to WHO, while the United States gave only 2.4 million doses. Fenner et al., *Smallpox and Its Eradication*, pp. 469, 564; Henderson, "Smallpox Eradication," pp. 115–116.

28. Henderson, "Smallpox Eradication," pp. 116–117.

29. Odd Arne Westad, *The Global Cold War: Third World Interventions and the Making of Our Times* (Cambridge, 2005), p. 397.

30. "President Johnson on International Cooperation Year."

31. Work that explores the origins, contours, and consequences of high modernist policies includes James C. Scott, *Seeing Like a State: How Certain Schemes to Improve the Human Condition Have Failed* (New Haven, 1998); and Timothy Mitchell, *Rule of Experts: Egypt, Techno-politics, Modernity* (Berkeley, 2002). But the story of the SEP serves to remind us that, on occasion, some schemes to improve the human condition have in fact succeeded.

32. Kristin L. Ahlberg, "'Machiavelli with a Heart': The Johnson Administration's Food for Peace Program in India, 1965–1966," *Diplomatic History* 31, no. 4 (2007): 665–701.

33. Sencer was CDC head from 1966 to 1977. On his and the CDC's role in the SEP, see Elizabeth W. Etheridge, *Sentinel for Health: A History of the Centers for Disease Control* (Berkeley, 1992), chap. 14; also Lawrence Brilliant to Califano, February 26, 1977, copy in possession of author.

34. Foege was later CDC director and then a senior adviser on global health to the Bill and Melinda Gates Foundation. Brilliant has served as head of the Google Foundation and other philanthropic organizations.

35. Jonathan Tucker, *Scourge: The Once and Future Threat of Smallpox* (New York, 2001), pp. 94–104.

36. Mani to WHO DG, March 16, 1967, World Health Organization Archive, Geneva, Box 193, Folder 416. Also Fenner et al., *Smallpox and Its Eradication,* pp. 417–418; Henderson, "Smallpox Eradication," pp. 114–115.

37. Socrates Litsios, "The Christian Medical Commission and the Development of the World Health Organization's Primary Health Care Approach," *American Journal of Public Health* 94, no. 11 (2004): 1884–93; Sung Lee, "WHO and the Developing World: The Contest for Ideology," in *Western Medicine as Contested Knowledge,* ed. Andrew Cunningham and Bridie Andrews (Manchester, 1997), pp. 24–45. The "horizontal" versus "vertical" debate is sometimes described as one between "holistic" and "reductionist" approaches.

38. David A. Tejada de Rivero, "Alma-Ata Revisited," *Perspectives in Health: The Magazine of the Pan American Health Organization* 8, no. 2 (2003), www.paho.org; Socrates Litsios, "The Long and Difficult Road to Alma-Ata: A Personal Reflection," *International Journal of Health Services* 32, no. 4 (2002): 709–732. The full text of the declaration is available at http://www.who.int/hpr/NPH/docs/declaration_almaata.pdf.

39. Tucker, *Scourge*, esp. chaps. 8–10.

16. The Environment, Environmentalism, and International Society in the Long 1970s

1. Arne Naess (1912–2009) was an academic philosopher who began writing about truth, language, and other such matters in the late 1930s, then in the 1950s about Gandhi's political ethics, and by 1969 about mountains and ecology. He developed the position that humankind is but one among many species and is ethically constrained from harming others except in instances of vital need.

2. Relevant figures from J. R. McNeill, *Something New under the Sun* (New York, 2000); HYDE database of the Dutch Environmental Assessment Agency, http://www.mnp.nl/en/themasites/hyde/index.html.

3. Sanjam Ahluwalia, *Reproductive Restraints: Birth Control in India, 1877–1947* (Urbana, 2008).

4. Rachel Carson, *Silent Spring* (New York, 1962).

5. Juan Martínez-Alier, *The Environmentalism of the Poor: A Study in Ecological Conflicts and Valuation* (Cheltenham, 2002).

6. Donnella H. Meadows et al., *The Limits to Growth: A Report for the Club of Rome's Project on the Predicament of Mankind* (New York, 1972). The book sold 30 million copies and was translated into at least thirty languages. Its particular novelty was the use of computer-based projections, which its sponsors insisted upon in the belief that this would enhance its prestige and impact.

7. It was also the birthday of Saint Francis, and by some accounts the organizers thought it was John Muir's too. According to the *New York Times*, April 15, 1971, p. 1, the FBI "spied" on Earth Day activities.

8. This also resulted from aging. People eager to engage in mass action in the streets at age twenty-five normally showed less enthusiasm by age forty. The problem with socialism, said Oscar Wilde, is that it takes up too many evenings; the problem afflicts grass-roots activism of all sorts unless new young people keep joining up.

9. See Ramachandra Guha, *Environmentalism: A Global History* (New York, 2000). In Burma and Thailand "ecology monks" spearheaded resistance to development projects that seemed to undermine the interests of the ru-

ral poor. In India and elsewhere, Gandhian ideology also made a contribution.

10. Sergio Díaz-Briquets and Jorge Pérez-López, *Conquering Nature: The Environmental Legacy of Socialism in Cuba* (Pittsburgh, 2000). Of the dozens of studies of German environmental regulation, a recent example is Sandra Chaney, *Nature of the Miracle Years: Conservation in West Germany, 1945–1975* (New York, 2008).

11. The Bavarian conservative politician Franz-Josef Strauss's epithet for German Greens. Guha, *Environmentalism,* p. 97.

12. Ibid., p. 112; Shawn Miller, *The Environmental History of Latin America* (New York, 2007), p. 206.

13. For example, U.S. farmers would have enjoyed advantages if U.S. satellite weather data had been kept from farmers elsewhere; U.S. oil companies would have profited from unrestricted seafloor mining; Soviet and Japanese fishing fleets would have benefited from unrestricted fishing and whaling.

14. The Baltic case is illuminated by Finnish archival material used in Tuomas Räsänen and Simo Laakkonen, "Cold War and the Environment: The Role of Finland in International Politics in the Baltic Sea Region," *Ambio* 36 (2007): 229–236.

17. Globalizing Sisterhood

1. Betty Friedan, "Scary Doings in Mexico City," in *"It Changed My Life"* (Cambridge, Mass., 1998), p. 454.

2. Ibid., p. 440.

3. *El Nacional,* June 26, 1975, p. 9.

4. I draw here on Rogers Brubaker and Frederick Cooper's specification of identity as a self-understanding or situated subjectivity that serves as the basis for social or political action—what Gayatri Spivak dubbed "strategic essentialism"—rather than a fixed ontological essence. Rogers Brubaker and Frederick Cooper, "Beyond 'Identity,'" *Theory and Society* 29 (2000): 1–47; and Elizabeth Grosz, "Criticism, Feminism, and the Institution," in *The Post-Colonial Critic,* ed. Sarah Harasym (New York, 1990), pp. 11–12.

5. Judith Butler, "Contingent Foundations," in *Feminists Theorize the Political,* ed. Judith Butler and Joan Scott (New York, 1992), pp. 3–21.

6. Virginia R. Allan, Margaret E. Galey, and Mildred E. Persinger, "World Conference of International Women's Year," in *Women, Politics, and the United Nations,* ed. Anne Winslowe (Westport, Conn., 1995), p. 30. For examples of continued liberal-socialist conflicts, see correspondence in the International Women's Tribune Centre, Accession No. 89S-27, Box 1, Sophia Smith Collection, Smith College (hereafter IWTC Collection).

7. Aurelio Caicedo (Colombian Ambassador to the UN) to Kurt Waldheim, October 17, 1974, UN Archives, S-0971–0012–05.

8. Elaine Livingstone to Arlie [Scott], Betty [Friedan], Karen [DeCrow], and Jackie [Ceballos], March 22, 1975, Betty Friedan Papers, Arthur and Elizabeth Schlesinger Library on the History of Women, Radcliffe Institute for Advanced Study, Betty Friedan Papers (hereafter Friedan Papers), Accession No. 71–62, 77-M105, Carton 37, File 1247.

9. Friedan to Walker, May 19, 1975, Friedan Papers, Accession No. 71–62, 77-M105, Carton 37, File 1248.

10. [Margaret K. Bruce], "Report of the Economic and Social Council," October 23, 1974, NOW-NYC Records, Box 23, Folder 11, National Organization for Women–New York City Records, Tamiment Library, New York University Libraries (hereafter NYC-NOW Collection); *Excélsior,* June 19, 1975, p. 7A.

11. *New York Times,* June 19, 1975, p. 41.

12. Telegram, Curtis H. Taylor to Secretary of State, May 9, 1975, National Archives and Records Administration, Record Group 220, Records Relating to the U.N. IWY World Conference, Mexico City, June–July 1974, Subject File A–G, Box 22.

13. Marcy to Ingersoll, June 9, 1975, ibid.

14. Adrienne Germain memo, March 17, 1975, IWTC Collection, Accession No. 89S-27, Box 3.

15. Robert Rhodes James to Waldheim, June 13, 1975, UN Archives, S-0273–0012–03.

16. Vicente Lascuráin, "Las dos Conferencias del Año Internacional de la Mujer," *El Nacional,* June 27, 1975, p. 5.

17. *El Nacional,* June 25, 1975, p. 7.

18. *El Universal,* July 2, 1975, p. 1.

19. Matthew Connelly, *Fatal Misconception* (Cambridge, Mass., 2008), esp. chaps. 7 and 8.

20. Thomas L. McPhail, *Electronic Colonialism,* 2nd ed. (London, 1987), esp. chaps. 1 and 3.

21. *New York Times,* June 29, 1975, p. 2.

22. Akira Iriye sees the 1970s as a turning point in the expansion of numbers and influence of international NGOs. See Akira Iriye, *Global Community: The Role of International Organization in the Making of the Contemporary World* (Berkeley, 2002), pp. 128–131. For a history of the emergence of NGOs in transnational activism, see chapter 2 of Margaret E. Keck and Kathryn Sikkink, *Activists beyond Borders* (Ithaca, 1998). On the growing role of feminist NGOs in international governance, see Elisabeth J. Friedman, Kathryn Hochstetler, and Ann Marie Clark, *Sovereignty, Democracy,*

and Global Civil Society (Albany, 2005); Elisabeth Jay Friedman, "Gendering the Agenda: The Impact of the Transnational Women's Rights Movement at the UN Conferences of the 1990s," *Women's Studies International Forum* 26, no. 4 (2003): 313–331 . At the IWY conference some observers also suspected NGOs of acting on behalf of their home governments, despite explicit UN proscriptions. See Laura Bolaños, "La tribuna de Organizaciones ¿'No Gubernamentales'?" *El Universal,* June 25, 1975, p. 5.

23. Marisela R. Chávez, "Pilgrimage to the Homeland," in *Memories and Migrations,* ed. Vicki Ruíz and John R. Chávez (Urbana, 2008), p. 178.

24. Devaki Jain, *Women, Development, and the UN* (Bloomington, 2005), p. 68.

25. Although it is tempting to romanticize this atmosphere, feminist political theorists have long observed that these trappings of radical democratic practice often mask the ways in which unequal resources—financial, educational, political, and cultural—make such forums less accessible to non-elite actors than more formal political structures. See in particular Anne Phillips, *Engendering Democracy* (University Park, Pa., 1991).

26. To avoid conflicts among activists, the tribune did not take minutes, issue a final report, or make any formal recommendations to the intergovernmental conference, further limiting its capacity to represent participants.

27. "Report to the National Board," March 29, 1975, NYC-NOW Collection, Box 25, Folder 2.

28. *New York Times,* June 19, 1975, p. 41.

29. Pacifica Radio Archives, *Betty Friedan vs. the Third World,* sound recording (North Hollywood, Calif., 1975).

30. *El Nacional,* June 22, 1975, pp. 6 and 9. In late December 1974 Echeverría had pushed through an amendment to Article 4 of the Mexican constitution declaring men and women equals before the law—a development that highlighted the continued floundering of the Equal Rights Amendment in the United States.

31. *El Universal,* June 22, 1975, p. 9. The *El Universal* article insisted that in a "survey" (of unspecified size and method) of Latin American women, 99 percent responded similarly. The Mexican press consistently misspelled Friedan's surname, instead using a dizzying array of similar-sounding Semitic names.

32. *El Universal,* June 21, 1975, p. 10.

33. In her discussion of the interchangeability of "women of color" and "Third World women," Chandra Talpade Mohanty explains that these terms refer not to a biological or sociological designation but rather to a "viable political alliance" formed through a *"common context of struggle* rather than color or racial identifications." Chandra Talpade Mohanty, Ann Russo, and

Lourdes Torres, eds., *Third World Women and the Politics of Feminism* (Bloomington, 1991), p. 7.

34. *El Nacional,* June 22, 1975, pp. 6; *El Universal,* June 22, 1975, p. 1; *Washington Post,* June 25, 1975, p. A27.

35. *Excélsior,* July 2, 1975, p. 20A.

36. Archivo General de la Nación, Mexico City (hereafter AGN), Investigaciones Políticas y Sociales, Caja 1163-A, Vol. 1, Hoja 511–512. On Mexican leftist women's support for Angela Davis, see the secret police reports on the Communist Party–organized Unión Nacional de Mujeres Mexicanas, AGN, Dirección Federal de Seguridad, Exp. 9–116–71, Leg. 2, Hojas 59 and 61.

37. For this characterization, see Iriye, *Global Community,* pp. 148–153.

38. On international population control efforts, see Connelly, *Fatal Misconception;* Laura Briggs, *Reproducing Empire* (Berkeley, 2002).

39. Domitila Barrios de Chungara and Moema Viezzer, *Let Me Speak!* trans. Victoria Ortiz (New York, 1978), pp. 199–200.

40. Quoted in Chávez, "Pilgrimage to the Homeland," p. 176.

41. The NGO tribune organizers identified most of the registered Chilean participants as living in Mexico City. "Organizing Cttee IWY Tribune list of Int'l participants," IWTC Collection.

42. Reports from June 12, 1975, AGN, Dirección Federal de Seguridad (DFS), Exp. 11–2–75, Leg. 25, Hoja 140; AGN, IPS, Caja 1162-B, Vol. 4, Hojas 373–374. The PPS was closely allied with Mexico's ruling party.

43. *El Universal,* June 17, 1975, p. 21.

44. Report from June 19, 1975, AGN, DFS, Exp. 9–342–75, Leg. 5, Hoja 66–68.

45. *El Universal,* June 20, 1975, p. 9.

46. Ibid., p. 10.

47. Report from June 23, 1975, AGN, IPS, Caja 1163-A, Vol. 1, Hojas 306–308. Other tribune participants called for the expulsion of the Chilean delegation and boycotts of Chile. *El Nacional,* June 24, 1975, p. 7.

48. Report from June 29, 1975, AGN, IPS, Caja 1163-A, Vol. 1, Hojas 579–586.

49. *El Nacional,* June 25, 1975, p. 7.

50. *Excélsior,* June 29, 1975, p. 1A. The characterization of Bussi de Allende as a false widow apparently points to Allende's notorious womanizing; by 1970 he was living with his personal secretary, although Bussi de Allende continued to act as first lady. Personal correspondence with Peter Winn, October 2, 2008, based on his 1972 interviews with both Salvador Allende and Hortensia Bussi de Allende.

51. *Excélsior,* July 2, 1975, pp. 20A.

52. See, for examples, Francesca Miller, *Latin American Women and the Search for Social Justice* (Hanover, 1991), p. 200; Göran Therborn, *Between Sex and Power* (London, 2004), p. 103; Bina Agarwal, "From Mexico 1975 to Beijing 1995," *Indian Journal of Gender Studies* 3, no. 1 (1996): 88.
53. "Betty Friedan versus The Third World," Pacifica Radio Archives.
54. Barrios de Chungara describes this confrontation in Barrios de Chungara and Viezzer, *Let Me Speak!* pp. 202–203. On the MNM, see Ana Lau Jaiven, *La nueva ola del feminismo en México* (Mexico City, 1987), p. 18.
55. *El Universal,* July 1, 1975, p. 1; *El Nacional,* July 1, 1975, p. 1.
56. *El Nacional,* July 1, 1975, p. 8.
57. *Excélsior,* July 2, 1975, p. 20A.
58. AGN, Investigaciones Políticas y Sociales, Caja 1163-A, Vol. 1, Hoja 511–512.

18. Liberation and Redemption in 1970s Rock Music

1. On rock music's roots, see George Lipsitz, *Time Passages* (Minneapolis, 1990), pp. 133–160. Eli Zaretsky discusses the impact that youth culture, liberation movements, and market forces had on the new emphasis placed on individual expression in *Secrets of the Soul* (Westminster, Md., 2004).
2. For a discussion of culture as a terrain of struggle, see Robin Kelley, *Yo' Mama's Disfunktional! Fighting the Culture Wars in Urban America* (Boston, 1997), pp. 8–9.
3. "According to John," *Time,* August 12, 1966; Linda Martin and Kerry Segrave, *Anti-Rock* (Hamden, Conn., 1988).
4. "Gathering No Moss," *Time,* July 16, 1973; Robert Christgau, "U.S. and Them," in *This Is Pop,* ed. Eric Weisbard (Cambridge, Mass., 2004), pp. 26–38.
5. Stuart Hall examines the contradictions of popular music and commodification in "Notes on Deconstructing 'the Popular,'" in *People's History and Socialist Theory,* ed. Raphael Samuel (London, 1981), pp. 227–240; see also Lawrence Grossberg, "Another Boring Day in Paradise," *Popular Music* 4 (1984): 225–258. On the relationship between individualism and the free market, see Thomas Borstelmann's epilogue to this volume.
6. Quoted in Lisa L. Rhodes, *Electric Ladyland* (Philadelphia, 2005), pp. 143–144.
7. Cynthia Plaster Caster, personal interview, November 17, 2007; letters reprinted in Ellen Sander, "The Case of the Cock-Sure Groupies," *The Realist,* no. 84 (November 1968): 15.
8. Elaine Tyler May argues that the domestic containment of the 1950s was a

response to Cold War fears: the family home became a site of control. See Elaine Tyler May, *Homeward Bound,* rev. and updated 20th anniversary ed. (New York, 2008). On sexuality in the 1950s, see Miriam G. Reumann, *American Sexual Character* (Berkeley, 2005). On sexuality in the 1960s and 1970s, see Beth Bailey, "Sexual Revolution(s)," in *The Sixties,* ed. David Farber (Chapel Hill, 1994), pp. 235–262; Bailey, *Sex in the Heartland* (Cambridge, Mass., 1999); David Allyn, *Make Love, Not War* (Boston, 2000).

9. Ralph Blumenthal, "Porno Chic," *New York Times,* January 21, 1973.

10. On the pornography debates, and for a critique of the "cultural feminists" who saw feminism and sexual liberation as opposed, see Alice Echols, "Cultural Feminism," *Social Text,* no. 7 (Spring–Summer 1983): 34–53.

11. "Cock Rock," *Rat,* October 15–November 18, 1970; Jay Ehler, "Cock Rock," *Los Angeles Free Press,* March 1, 1974; Simon Frith and Angela McRobbie, "On the Expression of Sexuality," *Screen Education* 29 (1979): 5–8, 12–15.

12. John Burks, Jerry Hopkins, and Paul Nelson, "The Groupie Issue," *Rolling Stone,* February 15, 1969.

13. Barbara Ehrenreich, *The Hearts of Men* (New York, 1983).

14. Earl C. Gottschalk, "The Sound of Money," *Wall Street Journal,* January 13, 1970. Peter Biskind discusses the impact of this culture on the New Hollywood in *Easy Riders, Raging Bulls* (New York, 1999).

15. Gottschalk, "The Sound of Money"; "The Groupie Issue"; "The Groupies," *Time,* February 28, 1969.

16. John D'Emilio and Estelle Freedman, *Intimate Matters* (New York, 1988); Beth Bailey and David Farber, eds., *America in the Seventies* (Lawrence, Kans., 2004).

17. Germaine Greer, *The Female Eunuch* (London, 1970); Barbara Ehrenreich, Elizabeth Hess, and Gloria Jacobs, "Beatlemania," in *Re-making Love* (New York, 1986), pp. 10–38; Pamela Des Barres, *I'm with the Band* (New York, 1987).

18. Rosemary Radford Ruether, "The Cult of True Womanhood," *Commonweal,* November 9, 1973, p. 132. Alice Echols traces the deepening division between feminists in *Daring to Be Bad* (Minneapolis, 1989).

19. Cynthia Plaster Caster, personal correspondence, April 20, 2005.

20. Grace Lichtenstein, "Alice Cooper? David Bowie? Ugh! And Ugh Again!" *New York Times,* September 24, 1972.

21. "Oh You Pretty Thing!" *Melody Maker,* January 22, 1972; Peter Holmes, "Gay Rock," *Gay News,* July 1972; Robert Hilburn, "David Bowie Arrives with a Burst of Stardust," *Los Angeles Times,* November 5, 1972; Cameron Crowe, "Candid Conversation," *Playboy,* September 1976.

22. Don Heckman, "Alice Cooper Plays Rock to Sink Your Fangs Into," *New York Times,* August 12, 1972.

23. Philip Auslander, *Performing Glam Rock* (Ann Arbor, 2006); Shelton Waldrep, ed., *The Seventies* (New York, 2000).

24. Jim Farber, "The Androgynous Mirror," in *Rolling Stone,* ed. Ashlye Kahn, Holly George-Warren, and Shawn Dahl (Boston, 1998), pp. 142–145; John D'Emilio, *Sexual Politics, Sexual Communities* (Chicago, 1983).

25. On style as a form of cultural commentary or resistance, see Dick Hebdige, *Subculture* (London and New York, 1979).

26. Joan Scherer Brewer, "A Guide to Sex Education Books," *Interracial Books for Children Bulletin* 6, nos. 3 and 4 (1975): 1, 12–17.

27. On the fears for the American family and the conservative backlash, see Natasha Zaretsky, *No Direction Home* (Chapel Hill, 2007); Lisa McGirr, *Suburban Warriors* (Princeton, 2001). On evangelical Christianity during the 1970s, see Andrew Preston's chapter in this volume.

28. "The New Rebel Cry: Jesus Is Coming!" *Time,* June 21, 1971. On Jesus in American culture, see Richard Wightman Fox, *Jesus in America* (New York, 2004); Stephen Prothero, *American Jesus* (New York, 2003).

29. On the failure of New Left politics in the counterculture and the role of Christian liberalism in the search for an authentic existence, see Doug Rossinow, *The Politics of Authenticity* (New York, 1998); James Farrell, *The Spirit of the Sixties* (New York, 1997); Peter Braunstein and Michael William Doyle, *Imagine Nation* (New York, 2002).

30. Robert S. Ellwood Jr., *One Way* (Englewood Cliffs, N.J., 1973), p. 54.

31. Steven M. Tipton, *Getting Saved from the Sixties* (Berkeley, 1982); Larry Eskridge, "'One Way': Billy Graham, the Jesus Generation, and the Idea of an Evangelical Youth Culture," *Church History* 67, no. 1 (March 1998): 83–106.

32. "Discovering Jesus, 1973," *Christianity Today,* August 31, 1973.

33. David Fortney, "The Jesus People," *Chicago Tribune,* July 4, 1971.

34. Billy Graham, *Just As I Am* (New York, 1997), p. 420.

35. R. Serge Denisoff, *Risky Business* (New Brunswick, N.J., 1991); Ellis Nassour and Richard Broderick, *Rock Opera* (New York, 1973).

36. Sergei I. Zhuk, "'Westernization,' and Youth in the 'Closed City' of Soviet Ukraine, 1964–84," *Russian Review* 67, no. 4 (2008): 661–679; Timothy Ryback, *Rock Around the Bloc* (New York, 1990).

37. Jay R. Howard and John M. Streck, *Apostles of Rock* (Lexington, Ky., 1999), p. 30. On the impact of *Jesus Christ Superstar* on the rise of CCM, see William David Romanowski, "Rock 'n' religion" (Ph.D. diss., Bowling Green State University, 1990).

38. See http://parables-in-melody.tripod.com/index.html (accessed December 10, 2008).

39. John Joyce, "The Globalization of Music," in *Conceptualizing Global History*, ed. Bruce Mazlish and Ralph Buultjens (Boulder, 1993), pp. 205–224; Gottschalk, "The Sound of Money"; John J. O'Connor, "Pop Music Explosion," *New York Times*, April 9, 1969; "Pop Records," *Time*, February 12, 1973; Steve Ditlea, "Rock Sings an International Tune," *New York Times*, June 11, 1978.

40. "The Big Beat of Bread," *After Dark* 10, no. 6 (October 1968): 26.

41. See Roger Wallis and Krister Malm, *Big Sounds from Small Peoples* (Hillsdale, N.Y., 1984); Ryback, *Rock Around the Bloc*.

42. Pekka Gronow and Iipo Saunio, *An International History of the Recording Industry* (London, 1998).

43. David K. Willis, "Soviet Cities Throb to Live American Rock," *Christian Science Monitor*, June 1, 1977; Timothy McNulty, "Disco in China," *Evening Independent*, August 7, 1980.

44. George Lipsitz, "Foreword," in *My Music*, ed. Susan D. Crafts, Daniel Cavicchi, Charles Keil, and the Music in Daily Life Project (Hanover, N.H., 1993), p. xvi.

45. Héctor Castillo Berthier, "My Generation," in *Rockin' Las Américas*, ed. Deborah Pacini Hernandez, Héctor Fernández L'Hoeste, and Eric Zolov (Pittsburgh, 2004), pp. 241–260.

46. Christopher S. Wren, "Rock Music, Loud and Public, Is Barometer of Relaxation in Parts of Eastern Europe," *New York Times*, December 29, 1976; and see Michael Cotey Morgan's chapter in this volume.

47. Thomas Cushman, *Notes from Underground* (Albany, N.Y., 1995); Krishna Sen and David T. Hill, "Global Industry, National Politics," in *Refashioning Popular Music in Asia*, ed. Allen Chun, Ned Rossiter, and Brian Shoesmith (London, 2004), pp. 75–88; Craig A. Lockard, *Dance of Life* (Honolulu, 1998); Debra Baer, "Culture Clash," www.iranproject.org (accessed October 30, 2008).

48. Grant Farred, *What's My Name? Black Vernacular Intellectuals* (Minneapolis, 2003).

49. Quoted in Wallis and Malm, *Big Sounds from Small Peoples*, pp. 7–8; Ian Tyrrell, *Transnational Nation* (Basingstoke, 2007).

50. Annabelle Sreberny-Mohammadi, *Small Media, Big Revolution* (Minneapolis, 1994).

19. Universal Nationalism

1. On the influence of religion on historical globalization, see Robert Wuthnow, "World Order and Religious Movements," in *Studies of the Modern World-System*, ed. Albert Bergesen (New York, 1980), pp. 57–75; Hedley Bull, "The Emergence of a Universal International Society," in *The*

Expansion of International Society, ed. Hedley Bull and Adam Watson (Oxford, 1984), pp. 117–126; and John L. Esposito, Darrell J. Fasching, and Todd Lewis, *Religion and Globalization* (New York, 2008).

2. For the "crisis of territoriality," see Charles S. Maier, "Consigning the Twentieth Century to History: Alternative Narratives for the Modern Era," *American Historical Review* 105 (June 2000): 807–831.

3. Henry Kissinger, *Years of Upheaval* (Boston, 1982). For the "crisis of hegemony," see Fredrik Logevall and Andrew Preston, eds., *Nixon in the World* (New York, 2008).

4. Howard Conn, "Future Shock—Now," sermon, December 30, 1973, Plymouth Congregational Church, Minneapolis, Record Group 30, Conn papers, Box 299, Special Collections, Yale Divinity School, New Haven. Conn's sermon played upon the themes of one of the era's best-selling books, Alvin Toffler's *Future Shock* (New York, 1970).

5. Gary North, "Backward, Christian Soldiers?" *Applied Christianity,* June 1974, p. 5.

6. Manuel A. Vásquez and Marie Friedmann Marquardt, *Globalizing the Sacred* (New Brunswick, N.J., 2003), pp. 35, 49–64. More generally, see James H. Mittelman, *The Globalization Syndrome* (Princeton, 2000).

7. James Davison Hunter, *Evangelicalism* (Chicago, 1987), pp. 195–196; Lisa McGirr, *Suburban Warriors* (Princeton, 2001), pp. 94–95, 256–257, 261.

8. Charles C. West, "Theological Guidelines for the Future," *Theology Today* 27 (1970): 286, 288–289.

9. Jerry Falwell to Ted Marrs, July 10, 1975, Marrs papers, Box 25, Gerald R. Ford Library, Ann Arbor (hereafter GRFL).

10. Tom Wolfe, "The 'Me' Decade and the Third Great Awakening," *New York,* August 23, 1976, pp. 26–40. On the new individualism of the 1970s, see Bruce J. Schulman, *The Seventies* (New York, 2001); and Edward D. Berkowitz, *Something Happened* (New York, 2006). On American religion's general embrace of individualism in the decade, see Wade Clark Roof, *Spiritual Marketplace* (Princeton, 1999). Much has been written on the emergence of the Religious Right, but see especially William Martin, *With God on Our Side* (New York, 1996); and Paul Boyer, "The Evangelical Resurgence in 1970s American Protestantism," in *Rightward Bound,* ed. Bruce J. Schulman and Julian E. Zelizer (Cambridge, Mass., 2008), pp. 29–51.

11. McGirr, *Suburban Warriors,* pp. 102–109, 168–176.

12. Conrad Cherry, ed., *God's New Israel,* rev. ed. (Chapel Hill, 1998); Ernest Lee Tuveson, *Redeemer Nation* (Chicago, 1968). See also Anatol Lieven, *America Right or Wrong* (New York, 2004); and George McKenna, *The Puritan Origins of American Patriotism* (New Haven, 2007).

13. Michael Lienesch, *Redeeming America* (Chapel Hill, 1993), pp. 154–157.

14. Quoted in Martin, *With God on Our Side,* p. 123.

15. Mark Silk, *Spiritual Politics* (New York, 1988), pp. 163–164.

16. James L. Guth, "The New Christian Right," in *The New Christian Right*, ed. Robert C. Liebman and Robert Wuthnow (New York, 1983), pp. 34–35; Lienesch, *Redeeming America,* pp. 162–163.

17. Robert Wuthnow, *The Restructuring of American Religion* (Princeton, 1988), pp. 318–319.

18. Hunter, *Evangelicalism,* pp. 76–115; James M. Ault Jr., *Spirit and Flesh* (New York, 2004).

19. *Time,* April 8, 1966. On school prayer, see Joseph P. Viteritti, *The Last Freedom* (Princeton, 2007), pp. 100–113. On abortion, see Donald T. Critchlow, *Intended Consequences* (New York, 1999). On moral values, see James Davison Hunter, *American Evangelicalism* (New Brunswick, N.J., 1983), pp. 103–107. On the IRS controversy, see Joseph Crespino, "Civil Rights and the Religious Right," in Schulman and Zelizer, *Rightward Bound,* pp. 90–105.

20. Robert C. Liebman, "Mobilizing the Moral Majority," in Liebman and Wuthnow, *New Christian Right,* p. 69.

21. David Gergen to Bill Rhatican and Dick Brannon and attached questions from *Christianity Today* to President Ford, September 23, 1976, David Gergen Files, Box 8, Religion Folder, GRFL.

22. Ralph Michaels, "What Is Communism?" *Applied Christianity,* November 1973, p. 6.

23. Nancy T. Ammerman, "North American Protestant Fundamentalism," in *Fundamentalisms Observed,* ed. Martin E. Marty and R. Scott Appleby (Chicago, 1991), pp. 14–16; George Marsden, *Understanding Fundamentalism and Evangelicalism* (Grand Rapids, 1991), pp. 67–68.

24. For McIntire, see Lester Kinsolving, "Witness," *Abilene Reporter-News,* February 9, 1969, p. 12C.

25. Quoted in Paul Boyer, *When Time Shall Be No More* (Cambridge, Mass., 1992), p. 263.

26. Most Rev. James S. Rausch to Ford, December 9, 1974, Marrs papers, Box 50, GRFL; "Fast Days Urged to Aid Starving," *New York Times* (hereafter *NYT*), November 22, 1974.

27. Jason C. Bivins, *The Fracture of Good Order* (Chapel Hill, 2003), pp. 35–78.

28. J. Philip Wogaman, *Christian Perspectives on Politics,* rev. ed. (Louisville, Ky., 2000), pp. 79–101; Patrick Allitt, *Religion in America since 1945* (New York, 2003), pp. 113–114, 127–128, 174–175.

29. Memo of conversation, January 10, 1978, in Robert F. Drinan et al., *Human*

Rights in El Salvador—1978: Report of Findings of an Investigatory Mission (Boston, 1978), pp. 67–69.

30. "Carter Urged to Intervene in Seoul," *NYT,* April 20, 1977.

31. Richard Shaull, "American Christians and the Human Rights Struggle in Korea: An Opportunity for a New Venture in Ecumenical Solidarity," October 1978, Shaull papers, Box 2, Special Collections, Henry Luce III Library, Princeton Theological Seminary, Princeton (hereafter PTS).

32. "Church Unit Acts on South Africa," *NYT,* August 23, 1972; Lutheran Coalition on Southern Africa, "We Extend to You a Call into Coalition," May 1, 1979, E. Theodore Bachmann papers, Box 2, PTS.

33. On Carter's faith, see Leo P. Ribuffo, *Right, Center, Left* (New Brunswick, N.J., 1992), pp. 214–248. On Carter and the family, see Martin, *With God on Our Side,* pp. 154–156, 173–180; and Natasha Zaretsky, *No Direction Home* (Chapel Hill, 2007), pp. 214–221.

34. Quoted in Donald T. Critchlow, *Phyllis Schlafly and Grassroots American Conservatism* (Princeton, 2001), p. 245.

35. UN General Assembly Resolution 3379, November 10, 1975, http://www.un.org/documents/resga.htm; "Resolution in U.N. on Zionism Scored," *NYT,* November 9, 1975.

36. "World Council of Churches: A Case of Pinkeye," *Congressional Record: House,* December 18, 1975; "Will WCC Come Back to Reality?" *Washington Star,* January 3, 1976; Patrick Buchanan, "The Clerics Wore Black in Nairobi," *Chicago Tribune,* December 11, 1975.

37. On the emergence of a national "Judeo-Christian" civil religion, see Silk, *Spiritual Politics,* pp. 40–53; David A. Hollinger, *Science, Jews, and Secular Culture* (Princeton, 1996), p. 23; Jeremi Suri, *Henry Kissinger and the American Century* (Cambridge, Mass., 2007), pp. 59–65; and William Inboden, *Religion and American Foreign Policy, 1945–1960* (Cambridge, 2008). On the decline of anti-Semitism, see Wuthnow, *Restructuring of American Religion,* pp. 95–96; and Ribuffo, *Right, Center, Left,* pp. 59–66. On the cultural appeal of Israeli military strength, see Melani McAlister, *Epic Encounters,* rev. ed. (Berkeley, 2005), pp. 155–197. On the importance of Israel to Christian biblical prophecy, see Boyer, *When Time Shall Be No More,* pp. 152–224.

38. On the premises of the Nixon-Kissinger grand strategy, see Raymond L. Garthoff, *Détente and Confrontation,* rev. ed. (Washington, D.C., 1994), esp. pp. 28–39.

39. Jackson statement to the Jewish Community Council Dinner, Tucson, February 9, 1974, Jackson papers, Series 6, Box 10, Folder 104, Special Collections, Allen Library South, University of Washington, Seattle.

40. U.S. Congress, House Committee on Foreign Affairs, Subcommittee on

Europe, *Soviet Jewry: Hearings, Ninety-second Congress, First Session. November 9 and 10, 1971* (Washington, D.C., 1972), p. 92.

41. For Drinan, see "Nixon Asked to Plead for Soviet Jews," *NYT,* March 21, 1972. For Buchanan, see the joint resolution on religious liberty in the Soviet Union he cosponsored with Jackson in *Congressional Record: Senate,* October 1, 1976.

20. An Uncertain Trajectory

1. Niall Ferguson, *The War of the World* (London, 2006), p. 625.
2. Afghanistan never accepted the Durand Line drawn by the British in 1893 to demarcate its frontier with British India and which served as the de facto border with Pakistan after 1947.
3. See Giles Keppel, *Jihad: The Trail of Political Islam* (Cambridge, Mass., 2002), pp. 62–65.
4. See Daniel Sargent's chapter, "The United States and Globalization," in this volume.
5. The Ahmadis are seen to undermine the finality of the Prophet Muhammad by conferring on their founder, Mirza Ghulam Ahmad (1835–1908), the status of prophethood.
6. Cited in *Independent Bangladesh,* January 27, 2008, http://www.independent-bangladesh.com/about-us.html.
7. An allegation made by Lawrence Lifschultz in a number of newspaper articles. His main source was the U.S. ambassador in Bangladesh, Eugene Booster, an opponent of the coup, but who was overruled by the CIA's station chief in Dhaka. See Lawrence Lifschultz, *Bangladesh: An Unfinished Revolution* (London, 1979); and http://nandigramunited.blogspot.com/2008/08/hasina-takes-award-from-henry-kissinger.html.
8. Minutes of the secretary of state's regional staff meeting in Washington, D.C., August 15, 1975, in *Foreign Relations of the United States, 1969–1976,* vol. E-8, *Documents on South Asia, 1973–1976,* no. 42, http://www.state.gov/r/pa/ho/frus/nixon/e8/97038.htm.
9. Ervand Abrahamian, *Iran between Two Revolutions* (Princeton, 1982), pp. 435–446, chap. 11, and conclusion; Said Amir Arjomand, *The Turban for the Crown* (New York, 1988), pp. 91–128.
10. See Robert M. Gates, *From the Shadows* (New York, 1996), pp. 131–132.
11. Interview with Carter's national security adviser Zbigniew Brzezinski, *Le Nouvel Observateur,* Paris, January 15–21, 1998, http://www.globalresearch.ca/articles/BRZ110A.html.
12. See Andrew Preston's chapter, "Universal Nationalism," in this volume.
13. George Crile, *Charlie Wilson's War* (New York, 2004).

14. For a detailed account of the ISI's activities and the CIA's role in them, see Steve Coll, *Ghost Wars* (New York, 2004), passim.

21. Future Shock

1. Counting articles containing the search terms "1940s" or "1950s" in Proquest Historical Newspapers provides a rough measure of how it became increasingly common to speculate about approaching decades (though one that has to be corrected for the overall increase in the volume of coverage). For examples of how contemporaries expected the pace of change to pick up in the 1970s, see Anthony Lewis, "The Necessary Choice: Technology or Contentment," *New York Times,* November 15, 1969; Karl W. Deutsch, "Political Science Seeks New Solutions," *New York Times,* January 12, 1970; and Heidi Sinick, "If Tempus Must Fugit, Then Let It Do So Fashionably," *Washington Post,* January 25, 1970.

2. On the sometimes paradoxical relationship between spatial and temporal perceptions, see Stephen Kern, *The Culture of Time and Space: 1880–1918* (1983), rev. ed. (Cambridge, Mass., 2003), a book that was originally inspired by the energy crises of the 1970s (see p. xii).

3. Susan Greenhalgh, "Missile Science, Population Science: The Origins of China's One-Child Policy," *China Quarterly* 182 (June 2005): 258–259. On Team B, see my discussion later in this chapter.

4. Alvin Toffler, *Future Shock* (New York, 1970).

5. William J. Murtagh, *Keeping Time: The History and Theory of Preservation in America,* 3rd ed. (Hoboken, N.J., 2005), pp. 31–32, 147–148.

6. Pierre Nora, "Between Memory and History: Les Lieux de Memoire," *Representations* 26 (Spring 1989): 8.

7. Herman Kahn and Anthony J. Wiener, *The Year 2000: A Framework for Speculation on the Next Thirty-three Years* (New York, 1967); Daniel Bell and Stephen R. Graubard, *Toward the Year 2000: Work in Progress* (1967; reprint, Cambridge, Mass., 1997); Bell, *The Coming of Post-Industrial Society: A Venture in Social Forecasting* (New York, 1973); Alvin Toffler, *The Third Wave* (New York, 1980).

8. Frank Feather, *Through the '80s: Thinking Globally, Acting Locally* (Bethesda, Md., 1980), p. 421.

9. Bertrand de Jouvenel, *The Art of Conjecture,* trans. Nikita Lary (New York, 1967).

10. Bell and Graubard, *Toward the Year 2000,* p. 1; Gordon L. Rocca, "'A Second Party in Our Midst': The History of the Soviet Scientific Forecasting Association," *Social Studies of Science* 11 (May 1981): 204–205; Directorate

of Intelligence, CIA, "USSR: Forecasting and Planning Weapons Acquisition," 1988, www.foia.cia.gov (accessed September 20, 2009).

11. On Shell, see Peter Schwartz, *The Art of the Long View: Planning for the Future in an Uncertain World* (New York, 1991), pp. 7–9. On corporate planning and forecasting, see William A. Sherden, *The Fortune Sellers: The Big Business of Buying and Selling Predictions* (New York, 1998), pp. 58, 229–232

12. "Congressional Clearinghouse on the Future," http://www.wilsoncenter.org/index.cfm (accessed December 23, 2008).

13. Gingrich made Isaac Asimov's *Foundation* trilogy required reading for his congressional aides. John J. Pitney, "The Many Faces of Newt Gingrich: A House Speaker Divided," *Reason*, February 1997.

14. Hal Lindsey, *The Late Great Planet Earth* (Grand Rapids, 1970). For an especially insightful reading of Lindsey and his imitators, see Paul Boyer, *When Time Shall Be No More: Prophecy Belief in Modern American Culture* (Cambridge, Mass., 1992), pp. 126–130.

15. Jean-Pierre Filiu, *L'Apocalypse dans l'Islam* (Paris, 2008).

16. Lindsey, *The Late Great Planet Earth*, pp. 11–14, 116–118.

17. "Astrology: Fad and Phenomenon," *Time*, March 28, 1969; "Gallup Poll Indicates 32 Million Believe in Astrology," *New York Times*, October 19, 1975.

18. Marcia Seligson, "Publishing Enters the Age of Aquarius," *New York Times*, September 28, 1969.

19. Charles F. Emmons and Jeff Sobal, "Paranormal Beliefs: Functional Alternatives to Mainstream Religion?" *Review of Religious Beliefs* 22 (June 1981): 304; Frederick R. Lynch, "'Occult Establishment' or 'Deviant Religion'? The Rise and Fall of a Modern Church of Magic," *Journal for the Scientific Study of Religion* 18 (1979): 281–282.

20. Alvin Toffler, ed. *The Futurists* (New York, 1972), p. 4.

21. See, for instance, the National Intelligence Council's "Global Trends" reports for 2010, 2015, 2020, and 2025, http://www.dni.gov/nic/NIC_2020_project.html (accessed December 23, 2008).

22. Dennis A. Ahlburg and Wolfgang Lutz, "Introduction: The Need to Rethink Approaches to Population Forecasts," *Population and Development Review* 24, Supplement (1998): 1–2; Schwartz, *Art of the Long View*, pp. 7–9.

23. On problems with the NIEs and the move toward quantitative forecasting, see Andrew Marshall to Henry Kissinger, May 1, 1970, and June 4, 1970, National Archives and Records Administration, College Park, Md. (hereafter NARA), Nixon Papers, National Security Council Files, Name Files,

Box 825, "Andrew Marshall." For examples, see CIA Planning and Research Staff, "Report of an Experimental Use of the Delphi Technique," February 1972, CIA-RDP82M00531R0004000200002–1, CIA Records Search Tool (hereafter CREST), NARA; Office of Political Research, "Handbook of Bayesian Analysis for Intelligence," June 1975, CIA-RDP86T00608R000600180019–8, CREST, NARA.

24. James Herschel Holden, *A History of Horoscopic Astrology: From the Babylonian Period to the Modern Age* (Tempe, Ariz., 1996), pp. 185–186.

25. "INSCOM Grill Flame Program: Session Report," December 1981, CIA-RDP96–00788R000700070001–8, CREST, NARA. For the history of U.S. intelligence community funding for "parapsychology," see Federation of American Scientists, "STAR GATE [Controlled Remote Viewing]," December 2005, http://www.fas.org/irp/program/collect/stargate.htm.

26. Benson Bobrick, *The Fated Sky: Astrology in History* (New York, 2005), p. 290.

27. Donald Regan, *For the Record: From Wall Street to Washington* (New York, 1988), p. 3.

28. Lou Cannon, *President Reagan: The Role of a Lifetime* (New York, 2000), p. 248.

29. Emmons and Sobal, "Paranormal Beliefs," p. 304.

30. *The Late Great Planet Earth,* directed by Robert Amram and Rolf Forsberg, 1979. On environmentalists' rhetorical use of portents, see Michael Barkun, "Divided Apocalypse: Thinking About the End in Contemporary America," *Soundings* 66 (1983): 268–270.

31. Barkun, "Divided Apocalypse," pp. 275–278.

32. Sherden, *Fortune Sellers,* pp. 61–62.

33. On inflation, see Claudio Lomnitz, "Times of Crisis: Historicity, Sacrifice, and the Spectacle of Debacle in Mexico City," *Public Culture* 15 (2003): 132–134. On futures and options, see Peter L. Bernstein, *Against the Gods: The Remarkable Story of Risk* (New York, 1996), pp. 312–316.

34. W. Parker Mauldin, "Patterns of Fertility Decline in Developing Countries, 1950–1975," *Studies in Family Planning* 9 (1978): 75–84; Matthew Connelly, *Fatal Misconception: The Struggle to Control World Population* (Cambridge, Mass., 2008).

35. Bruce Hoffman, *Inside Terrorism* (New York, 1988), p. 75.

36. Jimmy Carter, "Address to the Nation," July 15, 1979, American Presidency Project, http://www.presidency.ucsb.edu/ws/ (accessed July 17, 2009).

37. On McNamara and the Pentagon, see Joint Chiefs of Staff to McNamara, August 31, 1962, NARA, RG 200, Records of Robert S. McNamara, Defense Programs and Operations, Box 28; and McNamara to Kennedy,

November 21, 1962, NARA, RG 200, Records of Robert S. McNamara, Defense Programs and Operations, Box 25. On the Soviet threat in the 1970s, see William Kaufmann, "A Summary of U.S. Defense Posture for the 1970s," December 11, 1970; and untitled memorandum by Charlie Herzfeld, November 30, 1970, both in Declassified Documents Reference System, Document no. CK3100519442.

38. Tim Weiner, *Legacy of Ashes: The History of the CIA* (New York, 2007), pp. 407–408; "Intelligence Community Experiment in Competitive Analysis, Soviet Strategic Objectives: An Alternative View," www.gwu.edu/~nsarchiv/NSAEBB/NSAEBB139 (accessed July 18, 2009).

39. Reagan remarks at the Republican National Convention, August 19, 1976, www.nationalcenter.org/ReaganConvention1976.html (accessed July 18, 2009).

40. Weiner, *Legacy of Ashes,* p. 408.

41. John Hackett, *The Third World War: August 1985* (New York, 1978), p. 472; I. F. Clarke, *Voices Prophesying War: Future Wars, 1763–3749,* 2nd ed. (New York, 1992), p. 201.

42. Cannon, *President Reagan,* p. 248; Boyer, *When Time Shall Be No More,* pp. 137–138; Republican Party Platform, July 15, 1980, http://www.presidency.ucsb.edu/showplatforms.php?platindex=R1980.

43. Jonathan Schell, *The Fate of the Earth* (New York, 1982), pp. 21, 167–168.

44. Ronald Reagan, "Remarks at the Annual Convention of the National Association of Evangelicals," March 8, 1983, www.americanrhetoric.com/speeches/ronaldreaganevilempire.htm (accessed July 18, 2009).

45. Edward Edelson, "Space Weapons: The Science behind the Big Debate," *Popular Science,* July 1984, pp. 53–59; "Three Minutes to Midnight," *Bulletin of the Atomic Scientists,* January 1984, p. A2.

46. Participants in the conference that inspired this volume may recall the remarks given by Lawrence Summers on the economic crisis. He cited forecasts on unemployment levels and argued that, even if worse than predicted, they would not approach the worst crises of the past century. When the author asked whether recent events should make us skeptical about economists' ability to predict, Summers readily admitted that it was impossible to make accurate economic forecasts.

Epilogue

1. Joe Queenan, "The Decade That Won't Die," *New York Times Book Review,* December 2, 2007, pp. 50–51; Gerald Ford, "State of the Union" address to Congress, January 15, 1975, *Public Papers of the Presidents, 1975,*

*Book   1,   http://www.presidency.ucsb.edu/ws/index.php?pid=4938&st=
&st1=* (accessed January 25, 2009); David Kennedy, "Editor's Introduction" to James T. Patterson, *Restless Giant: The United States from Watergate to Bush v. Gore* (New York, 2005), p. xii; Beth L. Bailey and David
Farber, intro. to *America in the Seventies* (Lawrence, Kans., 2004), p. 1;
Thomas A. Harris, *I'm OK—You're OK* (New York, 1969).

2. Two strong recent overviews are Maurice Isserman and Michael Kazin,
America Divided: The Civil War of the 1960s, 3rd ed. (New York, 2007);
and Robert M. Collins, *Transforming America: Politics and Culture in the
Reagan Years* (New York, 2007).

3. Bruce J. Schulman, *The Seventies: The Great Shift in American Culture,
Society, and Politics* (New York, 2001); Edward D. Berkowitz, *Something
Happened: A Political and Cultural Overview of the Seventies* (New York,
2006); Peter N. Carroll, *It Seemed Like Nothing Happened: America in the
1970s* (1982; reprinted with new preface, New Brunswick, N.J., 1990);
Andreas Killen, *1973 Nervous Breakdown: Watergate, Warhol, and the
Birth of Post-Sixties America* (New York, 2006); Philip Jenkins, *Decade of
Nightmares: The End of the Sixties and the Making of Eighties America*
(New York, 2006).

4. Sara Evans, *Tidal Wave: How Women Changed America at Century's End*
(New York, 2003); Ruth Rosen, *The World Split Open: How the Modern
Women's Movement Changed America* (New York, 2000); Winifred D.
Wandersee, *On The Move: American Women in the 1970s* (Boston, 1988).

5. Akira Iriye, *Global Community: The Role of International Organizations
in the Making of the Contemporary World* (Berkeley, 2002); David J.
Hoeveler, *The Postmodernist Turn: American Thought and Culture in the
1970s* (Boston, 1996).

6. Brian Doherty, *Radicals for Capitalism: A Freewheeling History of the
Modern American Libertarian Movement* (New York, 2007); George
Frederickson, *Racism: A Short History* (Princeton, 2002), p. 143.

7. Beth Bailey, "The Army in the Marketplace: Recruiting an All-Volunteer
Force," *Journal of American History* 94 (June 2007): 47–74.

8. Jacob S. Hacker, Suzanne Mettler, and Joe Soss, "The New Politics of Inequality: A Policy-Centered Perspective," in *Remaking America: Democracy and Public Policy in an Age of Inequality* (New York, 2007), pp. 3–24.

9. Stephen Kotkin and Jan Gross, *Uncivil Society: The Communist Establishments' Implosion in 1989* (New York, 2009).

10. Thomas Borstelmann, *More Equal, Less Equal: How the 1970s Reshaped
America and the World* (Princeton, forthcoming).

Contributors

Jeremy Adelman is Walter Samuel Carpenter III Professor in Spanish Civilization and Culture, Princeton University.

Thomas Borstelmann is Elwood N. and Katherine Thompson Distinguished Professor of Modern World History, University of Nebraska.

Matthew Connelly is Professor of History, Columbia University.

Niall Ferguson is Laurence A. Tisch Professor of History, Harvard University, and William Ziegler Professor, Harvard Business School.

Francis J. Gavin is Tom Slick Professor of International Affairs, LBJ School of Public Affairs, University of Texas at Austin.

Louis Hyman is an Associate at McKinsey & Company.

Ayesha Jalal is Mary Richardson Professor of History, Tufts University.

Stephen Kotkin is Rosengarten Professor of Modern and Contemporary History, Princeton University.

Mark Atwood Lawrence is Associate Professor of History, University of Texas at Austin.

Charles S. Maier is Leverett Saltonstall Professor of History, Harvard University.

Erez Manela is Professor of History, Harvard University.

411

J. R. McNeill is University Professor, Department of History and School of Foreign Service, Georgetown University.

Michael Cotey Morgan is Assistant Professor, Strategy and Policy Department, Naval War College.

Lien-Hang T. Nguyen is Assistant Professor of History, University of Kentucky.

Jocelyn Olcott is Associate Professor of History, Duke University.

Vernie Oliveiro is a Ph.D. candidate, Department of History, Harvard University.

Andrew Preston is Senior Lecturer in History and Fellow of Clare College, Cambridge University.

Daniel J. Sargent is Assistant Professor of History, University of California, Berkeley.

Rebecca J. Sheehan is a Post-Doctoral Fellow, United States Studies Center, University of Sydney.

Glenda Sluga is Professor of International History, University of Sydney.

Jeremi Suri is E. Gordon Fox Professor of History, University of Wisconsin, Madison.

Alan M. Taylor is Professor of Economics, University of California, Davis.

Odd Arne Westad is Professor of International History, London School of Economics and Political Science.

Index